EUROCOMMUNISM
AND DÉTENTE

COUNCIL ON FOREIGN RELATIONS BOOKS

EUROCOMMUNISM AND DÉTENTE

Edited by
RUDOLF L. TŐKÉS

A Council on Foreign Relations Book
Published by
New York University Press · New York · 1978

Copyright © 1978 by Council on Foreign Relations, Inc.

Library of Congress Cataloging in Publication Data
Main entry under title:

Eurocommunism and détente.

"A Council on Foreign Relations book."
Includes bibliographical references and index.
1. Communism—Europe—Addresses, essays,
lectures. 2. Communism—1945-   —Addresses,
essays, lectures. 3. Communist parties—
Addresses, essays, lectures. 4. Detente—
Addresses, essays, lectures. I. Tőkés, Rudolf L., 1935-
HX238.5.E76   335.43'094   77-92750
ISBN 0-8147-8161-6
ISBN 0-8147-8162-4 pbk.

Manufactured in the United States of America

For my mother and father
R.L.T.

The Contributors

John C. Campbell. Formerly Senior Fellow and Director of Studies, Council on Foreign Relations; author of *American Policy Toward Communist Eastern Europe*, and *Tito's Separate Road: America and Yugoslavia in World Politics*, and other works.

William E. Griffith. Ford Professor of Political Science, Massachusetts Institute of Technology; author of *Sino-Soviet Relations* and *The World and the Great Power Triangles* among other works.

Pierre Hassner. Senior Research Associate, Centre d'Etudes des Relations Internationales, Paris, and Professor of Politics, Johns Hopkins University European Center, Bologna; author of *Europe in the Age of Negotiation*, and other works.

Norman Kogan. Professor of Political Science, University of Connecticut; author of *The Politics of Italian Foreign Policy* and *A Political History of Postwar Italy* and other works.

Robert Legvold. Senior Fellow, Council on Foreign Relations; author of *Soviet Policy in West Africa* and other works.

Eusebio Mujal-León. Doctoral candidate in political science at M.I.T.; author of articles on the Iberian Left and *The PCE and the Post-Franco Era* (forthcoming).

Ronald S. Tiersky. Associate Professor of Political Science, Amherst College; author of *French Communism, 1920-1972*.

Rudolf L. Tőkés. Professor of Political Science, University of Connecticut; author of *Béla Kun and the Hungarian Soviet Republic*, and *Dissent in the U.S.S.R.: Politics, Ideologies and People*, among other works.

Contents

[vii]

Preface

This book had its genesis in the deliberations of a Council on Foreign Relations discussion group on relations among Communist states and parties, initiated in the fall of 1974 under the chairmanship of Marshall D. Shulman. In what was essentially an exploratory exercise, a number of experienced individuals from government, business, and the universities came together for a series of meetings. The essential conclusion of the inquiry was that the role of the Communist parties of Western Europe, both in the local political context and in relation to Soviet policy, was extraordinarily complex and imperfectly understood both inside and outside of government. It was then decided, in view of the growing importance of this question for the Atlantic Alliance and for East-West relations, to undertake a much more intensive study concentrated on European developments and aimed at the production of an authoritative book. Because of the nature of the subject, this aim could best be achieved by a collaborative effort of qualified scholars rather than by the work of a single author. To this end, I was appointed to direct the project and to edit the published volume.

The first authors' conference was held in April 1976, and a second, for discussion of draft chapters, in February 1977. The group's deliberations substantially benefited from written and verbal comments from several prominent experts: David Bell (University of Sussex), Archie Brown (St. Antony's College, Oxford University), Georges Lavau (Fondation Nationale des Sciences Politiques), Gianfranco Pasquino (University of Bologna and *Rivista Italiana di Scienza Politica),* Heinz Timmerman (Bundesinstitut für Ostwissenschaftliche und Internationale Studien), Suzanne Berger (M.I.T.), Donald L. M. Blackmer (M.I.T.), Alexander Dallin (Stanford University), Anton DePorte (Department of State), Kenneth Maxwell (Columbia University), Zygmunt Nagorski (Council on Foreign Relations), Armando de Miguel (then Visiting Professor, Yale University) and Eric Willenz (Department of State).

As the editor of this volume, I would like to acknowledge my indebtedness and sincere appreciation to several individuals and organizations that have materially contributed to the successful completion of this study: to John C. Campbell for his wise counsel and generous support in every phase of this project; to the authors of this collaborative study for their prompt and cheerful compliance with numerous and occasionally onerous editorial requests; to the Rockefeller Foundation and the German Marshall Fund for financial assistance; to Richard H. Ullman and Abraham F. Lowenthal, former Directors of Studies, Council on Foreign Relations, for their encouragement and support; to Grace Darling and Robert Valkenier for their help in the process of transition from manuscript to published book, and to Lynne Salinger and Karen A. Greenleaf for their administrative assistance in all stages of this undertaking.

Rudolf L. Tőkés

Storrs, Connecticut
March 1978

Introduction

Rudolf L. Tőkés

The purpose of this book is to analyze the development and dynamics of a significant new political reality of European politics and East-West relations in the late 1970s. Eurocommunism in the limited sense is a combination of ideological and political tendencies displayed be several non-ruling Communist parties in Western Europe. In a broader sense it extends geographically to parties beyond Europe (most specifically the Japanese), and politically to ruling parties which have questioned or opposed the "general line" of the international Communist movement as defined by Moscow.

In its negative aspect Eurocommunism implies the repudiation of the Soviet Communist party's leading role over the whole, or any component unit, of the community of ruling and non-ruling Communist parties; the rejection of Marxist-Leninist (and indeed, Maoist) orthodoxy in ideology, politics, economics and cultures; the denial of the universal applicability of the revolutionary experience, or "model" represented by countries of "scientific socialism" or "socialism-in-being" for the tasks facing Communist and workers' parties in other, and

[1]

particularly in highly developed industrial societies; and the refusal to subordinate national interests to those of the U.S.S.R. or to that of the "international revolutionary movement," however defined.

In a positive sense Eurocommunism involves the assertion of each Communist party's autonomous right to pursue its political destiny without interference from Moscow; the affirmation of each party's right to interpret freely, to update and, if necessary, to revise the teachings of Marx, Engels and Lenin with respect to all key elements of Communist strategy and tactics such as revolution, dictatorship, alliances, economic and cultural policies; the advocacy of indigenous models and political programs that are consonant with a country's history, traditional beliefs and levels of socio-economic development; and unconditional insistence on the shared interest of humanity, regardless of class status, political persuasion or religious belief, in the prevention of a nuclear war to assure survival in the nuclear age. Moreover, several Western European Communist parties are on record as supporting the principles of civil and political liberty and constitutional guarantees of liberal democracy. Freedom of speech, assembly, religion, and political choice are now components of the Eurocommunist platform.

The list of these tendencies is incomplete and so is our understanding of the dynamics of the still unfolding phenomenon of Eurocommunism. For this reason one is inclined to agree with the Spanish Communist leader, Santiago Carrillo, who calls Eurocommunism "one of the current communist trends" and "an autonomous strategic conception, in the process of formation" [1] among Western European and other, ruling and non-ruling, Communist parties.

However, neither the eroding influence of Moscow over foreign Communist parties, nor the declining appeal of the

Soviet model for the Communists of Western Europe and Japan necessarily represents a net gain for the United States and for the cause of liberal democracy in Western Europe and in the "trilateral" community. Santiago Carrillo, Enrico Berlinguer, and Georges Marchais and the parties they lead are still staunch opponents of the capitalist economic system and are unrelenting critics of America's role in world affairs and its leadership of the Western world. Therefore, as recent and hesitant converts to the ground rules of liberal democratic politics, they must be viewed as highly unreliable participants in Spanish, Italian, and French politics, let alone the NATO alliance. And these are additional reasons for launching an inquiry into the origins and development of this new political reality that we and these Communist leaders call Euro-communism.

The postwar evolution of Western European political institutions and the ability of the governments to satisfy popular expectations with respect to public services and improved quality of life have failed to keep pace with citizen demands for effective participation in the political process. Between 1955 and 1975 the composition of the labor force in five major industrial nations (France, the Federal Republic of Germany, Italy, Sweden, and the United Kingdom) has shifted in the agricultural and service sectors from 23.4 percent to 9.1 percent and from 35.6 percent to 50.4 percent, respectively.[2] The major beneficiaries of these changes and frustrated expectations have been the Social Democrats, the liberals and, at least in Italy, the Communists.

When comparing the combined results of parliamentary elections held in 15 democracies of Europe between 1971 and 1975 with elections held in these countries in the early 1950s, we find that of the approximately 160 to 127 million votes cast, the conservatives received 36.9 percent (down from 38

[3]

percent), the Social Democrats 31.2 percent (up from 29.5 percent), the liberals 10.7 percent (up from 7.9 percent), the Communists 10.2 percent (down from 10.5 percent), and 'others' 11 percent (down from 14.1 percent).[3] Surely, Europe is not about to go Communist, but it might, as the late Anthony Crosland predicted in 1975, embrace democratic socialism in one form or another.[4]

Therefore, it is not the extremely unlikely event of Communist takeover of Western Europe through free elections, but the present and the future of Latin Europe—Portugal, Spain, Italy, and France—that is the central concern of this book. Specifically, the following studies seek to provide a comprehensive overview of most, though not all, foreign policy dilemmas posed by the recent emergence of Communist parties as major contenders for governing power and political influence in those four Western European states. Our purpose is to offer informed up-to-date analyses of the political situation in key European countries where the Communists are a significant factor; evaluation of trends in the international Communist movement, especially the issue of independence versus central direction from Moscow; and prudent speculation regarding Soviet aims and strategy, and policy alternatives for the West in the age of détente.

Pierre Hassner's study seeks to relate the rise of Eurocommunism to the evolution of Western Europe since the Second World War. He distinguishes among three separate Western Europes: the more developed, predominantly Protestant north where Communist parties have no strength; the less developed south, dominated until recently by right-wing dictatorships, where Communist parties have emerged as a significant but by no means predominant force; and standing somewhere in between, France and Italy, where mass Communist parties exist and are likely to participate in power. These trends are

[4]

interpreted both as manifestations of success of the Western economic, social and political model and as a failure of its elite and institutions to maintain law and order and to solve social and economic problems that have created formidable pressures for change. Caught in the vortex of conflicting, and to a considerable extent irreconcilable, demands advanced by the economic and psychological victims and beneficiaries of Europe's postwar development, both governments and their left- and right-wing opponents are attempting to cope with and, if possible, benefit politically from the current crisis. The out-come is still uncertain. European integration and democratic socialism versus "authoritarian and nationalistic communism" are the "best case-worst case" alternatives; and the choices, according to Hassner, are being determined largely by forces of international economics and "Leninist authoritarianism" over which the European governments have insufficient control.

Hassner's chapter is followed by four studies by Norman Kogan, Ronald S. Tiersky and Eusebio Mujal-León, describ-ing the politics of Italy, France, Spain and Portugal and the role of Communist and left-wing forces in each. Each country study tells its own story, but in combination, it should be possible to establish what is comparable and what is unique both in the nature of national politics and in the respective Communist parties. Each study takes account of the Commu-nist party's historical background, ideological traditions, politi-cal style, leadership, organization, popular base, and plans for the future. Questions of electoral strategy, propaganda tactics, coalition with other parties of the left, or of the center and right, as means of gaining political influence and governmental power are discussed in these studies. The authors have also considered the links between the Communist parties and have sought to determine how they influence each other and whether such influence may move them toward closer ties with, or greater independence from the U.S.S.R. The studies pay particular attention to Communist views on European unity, regional economic problems, détente, and NATO.

Portugal, Spain, France, and Italy were chosen for intensive examination because of the actual and potential political importance of their Communist parties. In Italy the rapidly growing signs of economic and social crisis and the threatened erosion of government authority by political extremists of various kinds have made the question of *de jure* (rather than *de facto*) Communist participation in the government the single most important concern of Italian and international politics. In France much will depend on the political fallout of the March 1978 elections and on whether the Communists' alliance with the Socialists will survive the March debacle or break down completely. In Spain, following the elections of June 1977, a new political structure has been taking shape, and the Communist role, despite the party's modest electoral gains, may be crucial, especially in the coming period of resurgent regionalism and possible devolution of Madrid's central authority. In Portugal the Communists are in the process of regrouping and retrenchment to slow down or to reverse their fading from political prominence under the Soares government, but their part in the events of the two years following the revolution of April 1974 has been instructive not only for Portugal but for the rest of Europe as well.

Communist parties in Western European countries other than these four are less significant, but the policies of *all* the major governments on the "Communist question" must be taken into account in the assessment of Europe's future. For this reason the sixth chapter by Robert Legvold shifts the focus to Moscow, in order to reconstruct the strategy and tactics of Soviet policy in Europe in recent years, looking particularly at the ways in which the Soviets have attempted to use Communist parties in the service of their own ends. In Legvold's analysis the issue of Eurocommunism as an object of Soviet foreign policy concern is posed in three aspects: the dimension of inter-party relations between the Western European Communists and the ruling Communist parties; the intra-party dimension within each European nation; and the international dimension, focusing on the role that Western European Communist parties play in East-West state relations.

The "inter-party dimension" is fully discussed in William Griffith's chapter on "The Diplomacy of Eurocommunism," which considers how the trends in Western European communism affect, and are influenced by, the developments in the so-called international Communist movement. Central to the analysis is the question of how the factors of unity and of conflict in ideology and policy evident in the different courses taken by Communist parties in the U.S.S.R., China, Yugoslavia, Western Europe and elsewhere bear on the future of European communism. Griffith also reconstructs the European Communist parties' "road to East Berlin" and discusses the ripple effects of the (perhaps last?) East-West Communist summit regarding future Eurocommunist policies toward Asian communism, European socialism, NATO, EEC, and the Third World.

The impact of Eurocommunism and détente on the Communist states and parties of Eastern Europe is the subject of Rudolf Tőkés' chapter. Following an appreciation of the Communist regimes' postwar record, the discussion shifts to the aftermath of the Helsinki Conference on Security and Cooperation in Europe and takes stock of the reaction of peoples and regimes to the Helsinki Final Act, especially its "Basket Three" component on human rights. The concluding part is addressed to an areawide and a country-by-country analysis with particular attention to the potential of Eurocommunist influences to generate changes in the domestic and international political conduct of the states of Communist Eastern Europe. Close scrutiny is given to Yugoslavia, Romania, and to the newly evolving foreign policy postures of Hungary and Poland as still open-ended and inconclusive first results of the effects of Eurocommunism and détente in this part of Europe.

John Campbell's concluding chapter endeavors to spell out the policy implications of Eurocommunism for the West. He submits at the outset that judgments about the national, regional, and global implications of Eurocommunism are, of necessity, informed by incomplete data about policies, personalities and motivations of the main protagonists of European and world politics with a stake in the outcome; but that judgments and policy decisions must nevertheless be made. Although no drastic and immediate changes in the European balance of power can be expected to materialize because of Communist advances in Latin Europe, these are viewed as signs of the current malaise that, unless checked, may bring Western Europe and, with it, the NATO alliance and the cause of European integration, to a point of acute crisis. The West, however, is not without resources and, without minimizing the problem, should not react in panic to exaggerate dangers. In so far as Eurocommunism represents a challange, the task of free societies in the West is to strengthen their own democratic institutions so that the Communists must either adapt to them or be reduced to a negligible role. With skill and foresight American and European leadership may influence the present still fluid situation in ways that could both strengthen European stability and enhance and reward autonomist tendencies in East Europe without generating undue Soviet apprehensions about Western threats to its legitimate security interest. As Campbell suggests, "while the 'Communist' part of our title word is cause for vigilance, the 'Euro' part of it is cause for hope."

From the foregoing summary of the volume's general objectives and thematic outline it should be apparent that by design, we have not considered certain matters that a more comprehensive study of Eurocommunism might have addressed in a systematic fashion. We chose not to discuss in any depth the general issue of European political and economic integration although we allude to the positions the individual Communist parties have taken toward it; and this matter, however important, does not have a direct bearing on two of the four Latin European countries under the purview of this work. In order to focus our analysis on Eurocommunism mainly as a political question, we did not take up, except peripherally, European military and defense policies, economic development and international trade, and the extremely complex issues of political, cultural and linquistic nationalism, regionalism, and north-south ideological and political cleavages of today's Europe.

Finally—and this may be a more significant omission—we chose not to address the postwar political record, both as government and opposition forces, of the Social Democratic parties of Western Europe, although we have dealt in some detail with Communist-Socialist relations in each country. Because recently published material on European socialism has given a thorough airing to this subject, we felt that this effort need not be duplicated here.[5] On the other hand, in view of the Italian Communist party's recent overtures to establish consultative relationships with Scandinavian Social Democratic parties, this volume may perhaps be faulted for not going more deeply into the recent interaction between the forces of Eurocommunism and Eurosocialism. Thus far there is remarkably little hard evidence on the specifics of interparty discussions and negotiations on a broader than national basis between the Socialists and Communists of Europe. It was not until October 1976 that former Chancellor Willy Brandt, speaking in Locarno as President of the Socialist International, publicly entertained the possibility of initiating discussions with Eurocommunist parties about matters of mutual concern. As far as it can be established, these tentative expressions of Socialist interest in a dialogue have not yet matured into a formal relationship. There is no doubt, however, that the outcome of Socialist-Communist dialogues, both on the national and on the regional level, will be crucial to the future of Europe and indeed may become a critical factor in East-West relations in the 1980s.

With these caveats in mind it seems appropriate to summarize, in a tentative fashion, the essential conclusions of this study as the editor sees them.

Eurocommunism is a latter-day variant of an international political movement that owes its origin to the Russian Revolution, to the Communist International, and to early Soviet efforts to promote social revolutions in Europe and elsewhere in the world. In the 1930s partly in self-defense against the threat of fascism and Nazism, and partly in support of Soviet foreign policy objectives, the Communist parties of Western Europe joined with the Social Democrats in Popular Front electoral alliances. These alliances, though they did not survive the Stalin-Hitler Pact of 1939, can be regarded as precedent-setting for current Eurocommunist coalition tactics. Following the war, similar socialist-communist political blocs were formed in Eastern and Western Europe. Because of the Soviet-backed Communist takeover in the former and because of Stalin's orders for the termination of Communist participation in the latter, both of these experiments came to an end with the onset of the cold war. An important exception to this was

Italy, where the Unity of Action Pact between the PCI and the PSI was not dissolved until 1957-59, and then by action of the PSI rather than on Soviet orders.

In the years following Khrushchev's secret speech and his criticism of the Stalinist pattern of inter-party relations, Western European Communists, especially Palmiro Togliatti and the PCI, felt compelled to re-examine their entire approach to the tasks facing the party under conditions of economic prosperity at home and peaceful coexistence in East-West relations. This process of policy re-evaluation led to an increasingly revisionist and autonomist stance and to a gradual acceptance of the liberal democratic ground rules of the political game. The Soviet crushing of the Czechoslovak reform experiment in 1968 and the new international climate of U.S.-Soviet détente further reinforced these latent political tendencies, which finally surfaced at the East Berlin Conference of European Communist Parties in June 1976 as full-fledged Italian, French, and Spanish ideologies of Eurocommunism.

This sketch of the political genealogy of Eurocommunism suggests that certain Communist parties, under the leadership of astute and bold politicians have shown the ability to learn from past mistakes and to adapt to changed circumstances even at the cost of what the Soviets regard as ideological heresy and the "opportunism of conciliation" with new political realities. On the other hand, common to both Popular Front and present day Eurocommunist tactics of alliances has been the effort to benefit from unsettled economic conditions, political instability, and the crisis of popular confidence in the established liberal democratic governments. On the whole, the available evidence is reasonably clear and indicates that Eurocommunism is more of an *aggiornamento* than a "Reformation." In any case, Eurocommunism as we know it is certainly not an unconditional and irreversible break with the past with respect to traditional Western European Communist strategy and tactics.

In the fundamental sense, a Marxist-Leninist Communist party, and even one that chooses to drop the name "Leninist," is a well-organized revolutionary protest movement against existing conditions in politics, economics, and society. As an organization, the sole reason of its being is the attainment of political power in order to bring about a revolutionary transformation of the existing socio-economic order. In the pursuit of these objectives the Communists—whether liberal or orthodox, revisionist or conservative—have historically adhered to an operational code and a set of organizational principles that have remained fundamentally unaltered since 1920 when Lenin issued the "Twenty-One Conditions of Admission into the Communist International." As Neil McInnes in his perceptive study, *Euro-Communism,* points out, it is the spirit rather than the letter (say, by way of revisionist manifestos of independence from Moscow) of adherence that matters in the present context.[6] Carrillo's abandonment of the concept of proletarian dictatorship and its replacement with "the hegemony of the bloc of forces of labor and culture in society" does not tell us anything about the "new political formation" with which the Eurocommunists seek to replace the classic authoritarian Communist party of the "vanguard" type. By defining the party as "at one and the same time a party of the masses and of cadres, of members and militants," [7] the question of "democratic centralism," or the absolute authority of the leaders over party members in the "execution of collective political tasks" (outside of which "each member" is said to be "master of his fate"), remains unresolved, though in the same passage Carrillo "clarifies" matters by adding, "The party as such does not pass judgment except on questions of revolutionary strategy and political tactics." [8] For a revolutionary party can there be anything *not* falling under the rubric of "revolutionary strategy and tactics"?

The Eurocommunist party is not a debating society but, as Carrillo submits, a "vanguard," whose task is to "strictly carry out a concrete analysis of concrete reality, which at times means not only going with the stream, but swimming against it." The similarity between Carrillo's homilies and Lenin's instructions to the embattled Bolsheviks in *Two Tactics of Social-Democracy in the Democratic Revolution* is compelling and so is the Communist habit of "swimming against the stream" of the established rules of the liberal democratic political process.[9] The following quote from *"Eurocommunism" and the State* helps support this proposition:

> . . . the mass of people and the political forces should fully retain other rights (i.e., "universal suffrage . . . the criterion by which . . . the role of the masses of the people . . . [is reduced to] . . . simply voting for their representatives at intervals of x number of years") to intervene in political life, over and above the classical freedoms of the press, of assembly, of association, etc. For instance, demonstrations and political strikes are a democratic right which cannot be given up in a truly democratic society.[10]

While Eurocommunist strategy and tactics vary from country to country, certain common features do stand out. The Communists, as the prominent PCI spokesman, Giorgio Napolitano put it, are seeking to transform themselves from a "fighting party to a government party." [11] This involves not merely opposition to government policies, but the development of alternative programs with which to enlist the support of specific social groups and members of certain occupational

[13]

entities, including those of the government bureaucracy. For example, the trade unions are promised "total autonomy"; [12] the military, the mission to become "a participant in a teaching body devoted to imparting certain specific information to the citizens so they can defend the country's territorial integrity in case of need" with the help of a "reserve army, made up of fit men on a regional basis"; [13] the intellectuals, "genuine freedom of culture"; [14] the Christians, "a new flowering of that faith . . . social transformation . . . redemption, fraternity and equality"; [15] and the government bureaucrats, the opportunity "to unionize themselves in order to defend their rights and their professional dignity." [16] These campaign promises are difficult to reconcile with Napolitano's argument with his party's skeptical Christian Democratic opponents: "It is . . . totally misleading, and we must say so frankly, to demand or to expect us to do some sort of about-face with respect to our ideological and political traditions and positions." [17] Refusal to break decisively with the Stalinist past and the bold articulation of new platforms have an air of unreality about them and create a problem of credibility that Europeans would find difficult to live with.

The legacy of Communist takeovers which came on the heels of reverses at the ballot box in Eastern Europe in 1945-1947 still influence judgments about the Eurocommunists as fair players in the democratic political process. Although Marchais, Berlinguer, and various PCI spokesmen have asserted their willingness to relinquish power in case of an electoral defeat as a ruling party, doubts still persist. In any case, Carrillo's and his Eurocommunist colleagues' deep preoccupation with the questions of the "international correlation of forces" and occasional references to "patriotic wars" of national defense do at least hint at the possibility that a Communist party, upon its defeat at the polls, might, with the help of the pro-Communist volunteer militia, seek to remain in power and, if necessary, summon external assistance from like-minded foreign powers. The Eurocommunists' collective silence about Cuban and Soviet involvement in African civil wars, PLO terrorism in the Middle East, and the Sino-Soviet war by proxy between Cambodia and Vietnam tends to support this inference.

Despite the image of monolithic unity, the Eurocommunist parties are heterogeneous entities and are made up of people with diverse backgrounds and commitment to the parties' goals. "Leadership," as R. Neal Tannahill points out, "is one of the most important factors determining the policies of the Communist Parties of Western Europe, but at the same time, it is one of the most difficult concepts to grasp in a generalized form." [18] The same is true for these parties' hard-core militants, dues-paying members, circle of ad-hoc supporters, and even more so for the 18-20 million anonymous Western European voters who cast their ballot for Communist candidates. As the data on pro-Communist votes for the mid-1950s and the 1971-75 period indicate, the percentage of Communist electoral support has remained steady at the 10 to 10.5 percent level over the years. However, the combined percentage of votes cast for the four Communist parties of Latin Europe at the last election prior to 1978 is exactly 20 percent, or twice as high as the 15-nation Western European average for 1971-75. [19]

Although the size of Communist electoral support seems substantial, especially in Italy and France, the membership turnover is remarkably high in the latter party. The paradox posed by the size of the electoral support that is eight to thirteen times higher than the estimated membership of the four Latin European parties attests to their considerable organizational strength as well as to corresponding weakness of the

[15]

conservative, socialist and liberal parties in these countries. Eurocommunist electoral platforms have been quite successful in capitalizing on growing working-class and middle-class estrangement from the postwar political order of Europe. Still, the Eurocommunists have yet to achieve a decisive break-through and prove, to the satisfaction of the absolute majority of the electorate, their worth as the sole governing party. This has never happened at any free election anywhere in the world, and, short of a total collapse of Western European party politics as we know it today, is not likely to happen in the foreseeable future.

Nevertheless, Eurocommunism, both as a manifestation of the rapid transformation and of the threatening breakdown of traditional political authority in southern Europe and as a foreign policy dilemma for the Atlantic community, is likely to be with us for some time. Unless the underlying causes of the malaise of liberal democracy are diagnosed early and accurately, there is a chance that the authoritarian essence of Eurocommunism and the danger it poses to the freedom of Western Europe might be overlooked by those seeking to treat the symptoms instead of the root causes of this new political reality.

In sum, the purpose of this volume is to inform four kinds of readers with interest in international affairs and concern about the European situation in particular. They are, first, responsible officials of the U.S. government and others of the foreign-policy community professionally concerned with planning and decision-making; second, the academic community, including scholars, teachers, and students of world affairs; third, that segment of the general public which is interested in and reasonably well informed about foreign affairs, a body of people growing in number and in importance as public support becomes ever more essential to the successful conduct of policy; and fourth, officials and general readers in Europe and in the Soviet Union with an interest in knowing the nature and directions, and even variety, of American thinking on such subjects as communism, Europe's future, and détente. It is the authors' and the editor's hope that this book will aid all four types of readers to learn more about and perhaps contribute to the solution of the shared concerns discussed in this book.

NOTES

1. Santiago Carrillo, *"Eurocommunism" and the State*, (London: Lawrence and Wishart, 1977), p. 103.

2. "Who Will Rule Europe in 1995?" *The Economist*, November 29, 1975, p. 17.

3. *Ibid.*, p. 16.

4. Anthony Crosland, *Social Democracy in Europe* (London: Fabian Society, 1975).

5. See, for example, contributions by Richard Lowenthal, Bogdan Denitch, Jean-Pierre Worms, and Robert E. Lane to a symposium on "European Social Democracy—New Problems, New Prospects," in *Dissent*, vol. 24, no. 3 (Summer 1977), pp. 248-96.

6. Cf. Neil McInnes, *Euro-Communism*, The Washington Papers No. 37. (Beverly Hills and London: Sage Publications, 1976).

7. Carrillo, cited, p. 101.

8. *Ibid.*

9. V. I. Lenin, *Selected Works*, vol. I (Moscow: Foreign Languages Publishing House, 1960), pp. 485-597.

10.   Carrillo, cited, p. 98.

11.   Giorgio Napolitano, "A Government Party," *The Italian Communists,* no. 6 (November-December 1976), p. 15.

12.   Luciano Lama, "Talking Straight to the Workers," in *ibid,* pp. 34-39.

13.   Carrillo, cited, pp. 70, 73.

14.   *Ibid.,* p. 34.

15.   *Ibid.,* p. 32.

16.   *Ibid.,* p. 56.

17.   Napolitano, cited, p. 16.

18.   R. Neal Tannahill, "Leadership as a Determinant of Diversity in Western European Communism," *Studies in Comparative Communism,* vol. IX, No. 4 (Winter 1976), p. 350.

19.   *A Report on West European Communist Parties,* Prepared by the Foreign Affairs Division of the Congressional Research Service, Library of Congress. (Washington, D.C.: U.S. Government Printing Office, 1977), p. 4.

ONE

Postwar Western Europe: The Cradle of Eurocommunism?

Pierre Hassner

Once again, "a ghost is haunting Europe: the ghost of communism." But is it the same Europe? And is it the same ghost?

It seems that after six decades of drifting farther and farther to the East, communism is about to return to those developed lands where the founding fathers expected it. It is a different kind of communism, older and weary, just as its birthplace.

Still the question remains. When the crisis between Romania and the Soviet Union started, someone remarked that the communization of the Balkans had led to the balkanization of communism. This seems to be true. On a global scale and, from the vantage point of Yugoslavs, Eurocommunism might appear as the most recent stage in a process that began with their own rift with Moscow. By the same token Eastern

Europe itself seems more Communist than balkanized. Could it be that the Europeanization of communism to which the optimists in the West look forward, should be more superficial or transitory than the communization of Europe which the pessimists fear as its result?

The answer, of course, depends on the interaction between three basic variables: the evolution of the international environment, that of West European societies, and that of the Communist parties themselves. Certainly the third is not just a result of the other two; and the crux of the problem lies precisely in the lag between the spectacular transformations of European societies, the greater stability of the military balance and of diplomatic alignments, and the even greater resilience of the Leninist model of organization and, very likely, the Leninist conception of power among Communist parties.

The pessimists fear that if and when these parties do indeed gain access to power this may turn out to be the decisive factor. On the other hand, it may well be that they will never arrive there unless they undergo a change which would go beyond words and opportunistic tactics.

The optimistic version is precisely that they are undergoing this change anyway, not through their own deliberate decision, but as an effect of détente, of the deterioration of their relations with Moscow, and of their interpenetration with Western society.

The real question, then, is that of the relationship between tactics, strategy, and evolution. Is there a smooth, even unconscious, transition from each to the next one? Leninism is above all an instrument for the conquest of power: Could it be that, in the West, in order to reach power, one has to stop being Leninist, or is it enough to stop appearing to be so? Or, alternatively, if harsher times lie ahead, does Leninism suddenly recapture a relevance which it had been losing? Does the problem lie in the need for parties which are no longer revolutionary to adapt to situations which are becoming so again?

The present situation would seem in most cases to present a meeting between two equally ambiguous developments that seem to be evolving in opposite directions: that of changing parties which no longer quite correspond to the revolutionary model without having yet become democratic; and that of social and economic conditions which, though no longer enjoying the stability of the 1960s, are not ripe for revolution.

More generally, one could speak of a balance of competition or crises. At the broadest level, this takes the form of the coincidence between the crisis of the capitalist system and that of the Communist model. Internationally, the United States' leadership is no longer either exercised or accepted as it used to be in the years of "Pax Americana." This, in turn, has contributed to turn the non-Communist left toward more neutralist positions and toward a greater willingness to form coalitions with the Communists. Conversely, the decline in the image of the Soviet Union has made it more imperative for the Communist parties to detach themselves from Moscow; and this, along with détente, has contributed to legitimizing them as bona fide participants of the Western political process. At the same time these changes have created new difficulties. The Western parties do not dare make a complete break with Moscow, yet, at the same time are compelled to share Moscow's declining popularity without being able either to identify with it or to propose a credible alternative model which would be neither the Soviet nor the Western one.

In terms of legitimacy and of efficiency there is a coexistence between the crisis of capitalism and a crisis of Marxism in terms of its incapacity both to explain the capitalist crisis and to provide an attractive model of socialism. Each side finds it difficult to turn to its advantage the contradictions and failures of the other.

Finally, in terms of political institutions and organization, the same paradox obtains in West European societies. The horrors of Stalinism and the popular attachment to constitutional democracy force at least the Western European Communist parties to proclaim their allegiance to political pluralism and to the institutions of the liberal democratic state. This, however, is occurring just at the time when these institutions show new signs of paralysis and of irrelevance to the real world of economic crisis and social struggles. Leninist parties are therefore tempted to moderate their evolution toward social democracy, and are inclined to maximize the comparative advantage of their "organizational weapon," which, again, jeopardizes Communist gains in legitimacy and political acceptability.

All this adds up to an impression of fluidity and unpredictability. One can discern contrasting trends and dilemmas more so than the direction of events and likely outcomes.

Thus the situation is both new and old. In fact, it may be argued that since the late 1960s we have been witnessing a return to a transition period which has many characteristics in common with the years 1945-47. As then, the strategic, diplomatic, social and ideological lines are visible but not clearly drawn. In Western Europe one awaits for the verdict of Italian elections, one wonders whether the French and Italian Communists really want to come to power, whether France will have a neutralist policy, and one is as much at a loss in attempting to prognosticate about the evolution of Spain and Greece as to predict the superpowers' intentions for the future of Europe.

The rough coincidence between geographic situation, international alignment, and domestic regime which obtained after

1947-48, was shattered twenty years later when the Paris and the Prague springs brought into the open the possibility of revolutions in the West and of the diminution of Soviet rule in the East. While the reassertion of Soviet power and the attempts at forced integration have limited these risks in Eastern Europe, the nature of the regimes, as shown by the case of Poland, is still subject to explosions. In the West the possibility of further divergences between domestic evolution and international structures has been further underlined and reinforced by specific national events and trends. The historical or political decline and fall of traditional European ruling elites have been exacerbated by general crises and their manifestations, such as the simultaneous spreading of inflation, unemployment, and the effects of the global energy crisis.

Ever since 1968, every year or two has brought a new signal that the postwar order, especially in Western Europe, was reaching its end: 1971 spelled the end of the Bretton Woods system; 1972 spelled the end of a certain type of direct confrontation between the West (in particular, the United States and Germany) and the Soviet Union; 1973 is remembered by the rise in oil prices; 1974-75 saw major changes in Portugal and Greece, and growing evidence of the possible ungovernability of France and Italy without the Communist party. The crisis of Social-Democratic parties linked to a persistent general crisis (as in England) and to the erosion of power (as in Germany and Sweden) is another, less spectacular but possibly no less important sign.

These scattered examples do show, however, that while Western Europe as such shares some general structures and a general crisis, its social, economic and political problems have, even during the twenty years of apparent international and ideological immobility, been profoundly different according to regions and to nations. Behind the wall of arms and of words, profound social processes were at work; they have produced in terms of political regimes and the disappearance of right-wing dictatorships a narrowing of differences as well as a widening of the gap between the stable and the unstable, the rich and the poor, the powerful and the weak.

To the extent that a geographic division—which is necessarily at least as rough as the historical division we have sketched—makes any sense, one can distinguish between three Western Europes: (1) *Northern and Central Europe*, with an economy more developed, culturally of predominant Protestant tradition, where the Communist parties do not represent an important force, and politics is being dominated by Social-Democratic or conservative parties; (2) *Southern Europe* (Spain and Portugal, Greece and Turkey, if we might regard the latter as a Western European country), where, by geographic situation, economic level, and social conditions, the political regimes have stood somewhere in between industrialized Northern Europe and the Third World. Their politics have been dominated by the effects of civil wars, by the role of the military, by alternations of military rule and limited parliamentary democracy. Communist parties have been banned in most of them most of the time; the Communists' strength has been based more on their role in clandestine action than on their popular support. As far as Eurocommunism is concerned, the Southern European Communists' contribution is less that of serious candidates for power than that of examples of alternative Communist strategies—as demonstrated by the Greek party of the interior versus the party of the exterior, the Carrillo line versus the Cunhal one. (3) For our purposes, *France* and *Italy* are *the* two central countries in every sense of the word. They share some of the characteristics of both other groups of countries, with France being closer to the North in terms of economic development and administration, and Italy to the South. Both have been parliamentary democracies since the war and both share the unique characteristic of being blessed or afflicted with mass Communist parties which attract between 15 and 35 percent of the electorate and have a plausible prospect of participating in government in the future.

While the differences between the recent evolution and the likely future of the two countries and of the two Communist parties are extremely significant, and while the fate of other countries like Germany may be even more crucial to the fate of Europe, it is fair to say that much of the interest in European Communism in the age of détente is based on concern with developments which are primarily French and Italian.

The differences between the special situations of the Communist parties in these two countries and in the rest of Western Europe are apt to make us skeptical about the determining effect of global international factors. The differences in social structures and political evolution between the two countries themselves compared to the common features in the respective importance of their Communist parties are apt, in turn, to make us skeptical about the determining effect of national socio-economic factors. However, we shall briefly examine both sets of forces and constraints leading to the present circumstances. We shall look first at how they have been affected by the international context, then at the evolution of West European societies themselves, finally at the prospects they offer for the evolution and the role of the Communist parties.

The Age of Détente?

If we are, indeed, in the age of détente, it does not necessarily follow that détente is the most significant reality of our time, nor that it is a decisive factor in the rise or the transformation of Western European communism; or that, *a contrario,* it was the cold war which had previously prevented or contained this evolution. This is not the place to discuss whether détente is a reality or an illusion. There is no doubt that its claim to be the main characteristic of our age has sharply diminished since 1973. In retrospect, it may well turn out to be a much more fragile claim than that of the "nuclear age," which does designate a permanent feature of our world even though the socio-economic problems linked to energy and demography, to the crisis of the international economic order, or to the nature of industrial or post-industrial societies have acquired a greater saliency.[1]

If one speaks of short-run phases rather than of long-range ages, it seems fair to limit the period of détente proper, in the broadest sense both of the notion itself and of its primacy on the international scene, to the years 1969 (or, even more precisely, 1971) to 1973. However, this applies to détente mainly as a process of negotiation raising hopes of transforming the nature of world politics. One can take, however, a more modest and a more long-range view of détente as a condition or as a situation rather than as a policy, or as a process involving perceptions and attitudes at the level of society, rather than strategies and agreements at the level of diplomacy.

This more basic, negative, and psychological sense concerns the relaxation of tensions, the erosion of the cold war perceptions and attitudes, and their consequences upon the domestic and international politics of Western countries. For this reason, it is the common ground upon which the respective and divergent politics of détente seem to rely as their starting point if not as their cause. The problem can be seen in retrospective as well as in prospective terms; it applies to the pre-détente as well as to the post-détente age. It concerns the relation of attitudes toward the international environment and toward the internal politics of Western Europe, or, in less subjective terms, the relation between international conditions and constraints on the one hand and internal structures and processes on the other. Here again, some kind of a rough division into periods, regions, and dimensions seems in order. If the influence of the external environment, particularly of the cold war and of détente, upon domestic evolution, particularly upon the role of Communist parties, is meant in a direct causal way, then it applies essentially to the pre-1948 and, to a lesser extent, post-1968 periods, and to Mediterranean rather than to Northern Europe.

Much ink has been spilled over the attitude of Western Communist parties, particularly the French and the Italian, in 1944-45.[2] Did they or did they not want to come into power? Was their moderation (shown in agreeing to disarm their paramilitary organizations and in accepting the framework of the bourgeois state and seeking the alliance of de Gaulle or of the Catholic Church) the expression of their national character or of a strategy decided in Moscow? In 1947 did they voluntarily leave the French and Italian governments as a consequence of the new Soviet attitude, or, on the contrary, were they expelled upon orders from Washington?

These questions cannot be answered in a satisfactory way, and certainly not in a few paragraphs. To this writer, a few generalizations on this critical early period do seem, however, more likely than the opposite assertions: (1) The postwar situation in Western Europe was not revolutionary, and the order which emerged was not, as in Eastern Europe, superimposed by an alien power upon a recalcitrant social reality but was, rather, the expression of this social reality itself and, broadly speaking, of the political preferences of the populations.

(2) In 1947, the Communist parties (certainly the Italian

one) would have preferred to continue participation in their respective governments. Their withdrawal, however, was the effect neither of a sudden and brutal order from Moscow to them nor of equally sudden and brutal orders from Washington to the Italian Christian Democrats or the French Socialists to throw them out. Rather, it was the fruit of the preferences of the latter parties, which did reflect, however, a logic of separation—the logic of the falling Iron Curtain and the cold war, the proclamation of the Truman Doctrine and the founding of the Cominform, the announcement of the Marshall Plan and its rejection by the East.

(3) An obvious exception is Greece. There, geographic location and the trends of domestic development were obviously at odds with one another at the end of the war. Foreign intervention from the Communist side (particularly from Yugoslavia) and, even more directly, from Britain and the United States determined the outcome of the civil war and the nature of subsequent regimes.

While it would be false to claim in the case of the Spanish and Portuguese dictatorships that they were saved from their own people by Western intervention, it does seem plausible that one international trend (the defeat of the German and Italian fascist regimes) might have swept them away if another emergent international trend (that of the split between the West and the Soviet Union and of America's search for allies against communism) had not given them a new element of legitimacy and a new margin of tolerance. Conversely, while it is not détente which caused the deaths of Salazar and Franco, it did contribute to the new feeling of isolation of their regimes and facilitated the emergence of successor regimes that are willing to accept the risks involved in admitting the Communist parties to the competition for power. But we are, then, speaking of indirect and diffuse influences, rather than of direct and compelling action.

In this more general sense, it is obvious that the external environment, of being a part of the Western security and economic system, has played a decisive role in the evolution of Western Europe as a whole. But to analyze it one needs to distinguish among the dimensions of European reality and to understand the discrepancies and interactions between structures and processes.

In Europe, the two universal distinctions of domestic versus international politics, and of diplomatic and strategic interaction versus social and economic interdependences are further complicated by the direct relationship of the continent to the central nuclear balance between the two superpowers. Through the physical presence of Soviet and American troops and nuclear weapons, Europe is the continent of bipolarity, which in terms both of military balance and of territorial borders has given it a stability unknown to other continents. By the same token, bipolarity has contributed to freezing abnormal political situations and to sharpening the dilemmas of security and change. It becomes necessary, then, to use the analytical device of tripartite division, between (a) the strategic-territorial system, based on the division and balance between the two alliances led by the two superpowers; (b) the actions and reactions of states; and (c) the evolutions and revolutions of societies.

One of the central contradictions of the European situation has been between, on the one hand, the fixity or rigidity of the system which has remained essentially bipolar, and, on the other hand, the attempts of governments to maintain, acquire or recover their diplomatic flexibility and the efforts of societies and populations to pursue their own logic of autonomous development and mutual interpenetration. Put another way, the essential dialectic of state and society (which, at the global level, becomes that of the interstate system and of transnational society) must, particularly in the European case, lead to further differentiations in terms both of independence versus interdependence and of stability versus change. In both respects, one should distinguish, within the interstate dimension, between the constraints of the nuclear-territorial system and the policies of states, and, within the dimension of society, between socio-economic structures and developments and cultural, ideological and, ultimately, political attitudes and behaviors.

While all these dimensions are obviously always present, it may not be too artificial to assign a certain prevalence to each of them for a specific period. In this sense, the cold war may be seen as corresponding to the prevalence of the system and hence of the logic of division between two camps and of unity within each of them. The period between 1962 and 1968 saw the brief flourishing of diplomatic flexibility—with the Gaullist attempt at a return to the classical European balance and with various attempts at finding an "alternative to partition." And the period since 1968 meant the confirmation of the status quo, but, at the same time, a challenge to it at the societal level.

In a way, the impossibility for any state to escape from the constraints of its geographical situation—be it Portugal or Romania—has been confirmed by economic interdependence. But even in this area increasing conflicts within the two camps (between the United States and the European Community or between Greece and Turkey) challenged the assumption of common interests, and increasing contacts between West and East challenged the notion of two antagonistic systems. More important, the respective crises of each alliance system have challenged the primacy of the global conflict.

Because they tended to ignore ideology and domestic politics, the diplomatic attempts of the French and Romanian mavericks were based on the autonomy of interstate relations, and on the specific common interests of middle powers against the two superpowers. These had the effect of depriving the opposition between communism and liberal democracy of its primacy, or at least of its sacred character. Even though de Gaulle, like Kissinger after him, emphasized the distinction between the U.S.S.R. as a great power and communism as a domestic threat, they deprived themselves of the traditional argument for excluding the Communist parties from the normal political game as instruments of the Soviet threat.

But the most complex and contradictory relationship is between the East-West conflict and the other conflicts and alignments within and between the countries of the Western alliance. In the last period, the East-West conflict has definitely lost, if not its crucial ultimate importance, at least its immediacy and sense of urgency. This, indeed, is what the trend we have called "détente as a situation" as opposed to "détente as a policy" [3] has been about: not the disappearance of the cold war or the resolution of the East-West conflict, but a psychological and negative reality—that of a decrease in tension and attention directed to the other side, and of an increase in tension among Western nations, forces, elites or social groups, and attention to domestic problems.

The cold war has not disappeared, but it has become one cold war among many. A subtle dialectic is at work: It is not détente which has created the conflicts between Paris and Washington, between North and South, between center and periphery, between Athens and Ankara, between the young and the old, between the Right and Left, and between the employed and the economically marginal strata of society. On the contrary, many of these conflicts were always there, or had been growing during the cold war years, but were kept dormant or silent by the primacy of the cold war. Others have emerged with greater strength in recent years, either through biological accident or through the economic and socio-cultural

[31]

crisis of the West, through the revolt of the oil producers, or through the paralysis of modern democracies. But if these new threats have seemed more immediate or more dramatic than the Eastern one, the consequently changed perception of the latter has, in turn, contributed to liberating forces of conflict that were held in check by the perception of an external threat.

The reinterpretation of East-West relations and that of intra-Western conflicts tend to reinforce each other through well-known perceptual mechanisms. The downgrading of military considerations was prompted both by their lack of credibility to new generations and by the new urgency of other problems. This, in turn, has contributed to the upgrading of economic or territorial conflicts between allies, to political conflicts between Left and Right (as in France), or between the forces favorable to moderation and the "opposite extremisms" (as in Italy), and in both cases, to an emergence of their Communist parties out of their previous isolation.

The basic East-West division which had justified this isolation has not gone away. Détente as a situation is based on the erosion of the old perceptions but has not led to an alternative international or European system. Détente as a policy has consisted in expectations or strategies that hoped to build upon the new psychological situation either in the direction of a new balance of power more favorable to the independence of small and middle powers (this was the "Gaullist" and Romanian view) or in the direction of gradual convergence through increasing toleration and through the erosion of borders. The latter was the "change through rapprochement" conception common to Brandt, Berlinguer and Kádár. Détente may also be viewed as a rapprochement at the top between the leaders of the two alliances based on their firm control of their respective systems (the Kissinger-Sonnenfeldt version). Or, as the Russians see it: controlled integration in the East and controlled disintegration in the West. Or, as the logic of Carillo's thesis has it: socialist Western Europe rising in opposition to both superpowers and attracting Eastern Europe away from the Soviet Union.

None of these policies seems really to be working, because the psychological consequences of détente and communication seem too strong to be neatly confined to interstate relations or to one half of Europe, but not strong enough to destroy the realities of the division of Europe and of its power structure, including, in particular, American economic and Soviet military superiority on the continent. The international environment is presenting increasing challenges to détente through the new self-confidence and activism of the superpowers, in the military area for the Soviets and the ideological one for the United States. On the other hand, domestic problems in Western Europe are more pressing than ever and do not permit a return to the priority of defense and to the exclusion of the Left.

Different formulas for partial conciliation are possible. One, practised in particular by the Left, from the Italian Communists to the French Socialists and even the German Social-Democrats, follows what might be called reaction to "cognitive dissonance" through eliminating new perceptions or integrating them to obsolete ones. Thus, the support of détente for domestic reasons leads either to ignoring the objective changes (e.g., in Soviet military power or attitudes) or to finding in them, consciously or unconsciously, yet another reason for détente and hence for the blurring of ideological opposition. This is what "Finlandization" may ultimately mean: adopting the most reassuring interpretation of Soviet behavior precisely because one is not reassured.

An opposite formula is beginning to be used by the Right: the Conservatives in Britain and the Christian-Democrats in Germany are using the crisis of détente and the growing perception of the Soviet danger as an instrument against their Social-Democratic adversaries, whom they accuse of being blind to the hard realities of defense and ideological confrontation. The argument based on the international danger is likely to be increasingly used by the Right in France and in Italy. In these countries the Communists' persisting links to Moscow and the Socialists' penchant for neutralism or pacifism lend more credibility to charges of this kind than in the German and the British cases. Conceivably (for instance, in the case of an invasion of Yugoslavia), this might make the difference for the domestic evolution of these countries. From the crisis of détente policies through the crisis of détente as a psychological situation, one would come to a crisis of the Left within the domestic political struggle of Western countries, and to a halt in the integration of Communist parties.

Neither of these two opposite developments, both of which have some basis in existing trends, is, however, very likely. Except in the most extreme case, conservative governments would have to continue détente in the limited sense of military negotiations and economic cooperation with the East, and hence find it difficult to make the argument that contacts with Berlinguer are more unacceptable than with Brezhnev. Unless they resort to fascist regimes or measures, the conservatives would continue to need the support or the toleration of the unions and of the working class. Conversely, left-wing governments, even including Communists, would need (whether they would admit it, as Berlinguer did on June 15, 1976, or not) protection against Soviet power. Even more importantly, they would have to find (as shown by the cases of Chile and Portugal) some accomodation with a predominantly capitalist Western environment. And this means accommodation with great powers like the United States and the Federal Republic, the multinational corporations, the objective realities of international interdependence and of national demands against a drop in consumption.

All West European governments will be faced, then, with a series of contradictions (between defense and détente, or between international interdependence and domestic social policies). In these contradictions—except in the most extreme cases involving a drastic change in the structure of the continent—the international environment acts (with varying degrees of effectiveness) as a constraint or a brake, or as a diffuse and indirect influence rather than as a direct cause of national developments through the deliberate action of foreign powers.

This is only valid, of course, unless economic problems and, in particular, the energy crisis assume such dimensions that the political processes of some more vulnerable European countries become directly subjected to those who finance their budgets. There are elements of a situation of this kind in Portugal. However, Western powers and financial institutions are by no means the only ones, or even the most directly, involved. In Italy, one can discern trends toward a kind of "Maltification" with Libya acting (as in Malta) as a financial substitute to Western influences; or it may be that Saudi Arabia and Iran will exert their own financial influence in a conservative or anti-Communist direction. But even in such extreme cases, the leverage at the disposal of foreign economic intervention or financial diplomacy is largely determined by the degree of vulnerability of the recipient countries, which, in turn, depends upon their economic, social and political evolution.

Western Europe: Victory and Paralysis

To generalize in a few pages about the effect of East-West relations upon the evolution of Western Europe is difficult enough; to do the same about the evolution of Western European societies themselves is next to impossible. What is there in common between the evolution of Sweden and of Spain, or to take two countries that belong to the same group in the threefold division presented above, of West Germany and Great Britain? Yet clearly they all, albeit in various degrees, have been subjected not only to the same geopolitical constraints but also to common socio-economic trends like the phenomenal growth of GNP and of international trade in the 1950s and early 1960s , and the crisis of the late '60s and '70s, whether under the impact of external factors like the Vietnam-induced American inflation, the end of the Bretton Woods monetary system, or the increase in the price of oil. Yet the importance of these general trends as compared to specific national factors is hotly debated.[4] Even those who emphasize the general character of the crisis or the transnational character of capitalism agree that the impact of the same phenomena can be profoundly different on countries which are at different stages of economic development, or have different social structures and political regimes.

Indeed, not only is the relationship between the economic, the social and the political dimensions different from country to country, but within each of these dimensions one sees contradictory trends toward integration and disintegration, homogenization and differentiation, co-optation and marginalization, convergence and conflict, polarization and de-polarization. And the cycles of each may be analogous from country to country but not necessarily synchronized.

This is particularly striking in the case of the three southern candidates for the European Community, which look forward to the virtues of affluence, European integration, and centrist liberalism or social-democracy at a time when those countries that already have them are more or less turning their back on

[36]

them. Among the latter countries themselves, a particularly perverse combination of convergence and divergence is threatening. For the European Community and, perhaps, for the whole Western system to function, it is desirable that economic situations should be complementary rather than analogous, but that social and political orientations should be converging rather than conflicting. Yet, we are threatened with a synchronization of economic phases: with everybody suffering both from inflation and from unemployment, everybody wanting to increase exports and to decrease imports, and with a parting of political ways. Germany and Britain seem to be going toward the right, and France and Italy toward the left.

Despite lags and gaps, explosive contradictions and no less explosive coincidences, it is not altogether artificial in 1978 to suggest two broad generalizations about the Western European economic, social, and political order. For the first time this order is universally accepted, in the sense that all existing regimes pay at least lip service to it and no active and explicit challenge is directed against it. And second, nowhere does it seem to succeed positively, in terms of either efficiency or legitimacy, either in providing economic security and political leadership or in promoting communication and community among citizens.

In the whole of Western Europe the principle of a pluralistic and open society is accepted by all significant political forces. This involves above all the system of constitutional democracy with several parties competing for, and alternating in, power, which everybody, including the Eurocommunist parties, claims to be accepting. But it also involves its economic and social counterparts. These are a mixed economy where both state intervention and market competition play a role, albeit in differing proportions; some form of interest-group pluralism, rather than a polarized society dominated by one class or a solidarist one based on the negation of conflicting interests; and, finally, an open economy and society based on the acceptance of the European Community or of some other form of interdependence with the international environment.

The other side of the coin is no less obvious. All Western European countries may be accepting constitutional democracy, but in not a single one, today, does the system provide a stable majority. All are ruled by fragile coalitions and, if polls and by-elections are to be believed, most of these coalitions no longer represent a majority of the people. Even more importantly, in all countries the ability of parliaments to control governments and of governments to fulfill their traditional functions (like keeping law and order) or their new ones (like providing jobs and social services and, more generally, managing their economy) seems severely limited to the point of impotence. In most cases, governments are increasingly passive mediators or messenger-boys between the unfulfilled demands of organized groups represented in particular by the trade unions, and those of the transnational environment represented by international institutions, foreign states, or private banks.

As a result, the temptation or the necessity of escaping from these pressures or constraints leads to powerful trends away from international competition and away from the European Community. The latter, like parliamentary government, has its legitimacy eroded by its lack of effectiveness. This goes hand in hand with the flight from liberalism: the general consensus on pluralist democracy shows many signs of being highly conditional or provisional. The failure of political parties to solve the economic crisis may well lead to a return of authoritarian, military, or conservative rule in Portugal or Spain. It may, in France and in Italy, justify the predictions of those who—in spite of left-wing or Eurocommunist claims of allegiance to pluralism—see, in the coming to power of a left-wing coalition based on a *programme commun* or even of a national coalition based on *compromisso storico,* the potential for a decisive change of regime, from a liberal to an authoritarian one. Even in Britain, the successive failure of parliamentary government and of government by social contract to handle the economic situation may end up by challenging the existing institutional consensus, which so far has been as remarkable by its resilience as by its paralysis.

It is necessary to explore this ironic or contradictory situation of what may be loosely called the Western European model, of its victory and of its crisis—by looking in a slightly more dynamic way both to the origins of the paradox and to its possible developments and consequences.

THE PRESENT DISAFFECTION: ROOTS AND CONSEQUENCES

In a book whose title is as ironic as the situation it is dealing with, *Plaidoyer pour l'Europe décadente,* [5] Raymond Aron uses three subtitles which point to three aspects of this paradox: "Europe mystified by Marxism-Leninism," "Europe unaware of its superiority," and "Europe victim of itself." Much of his analysis points to the same phenomenon we are discussing, that of Europe becoming the victim of its own successes, of prosperity and liberalism giving rise to expectations and demands which may ultimately undermine them. But the general slogan of the book is "two specters are haunting Europe—freedom and the Red Army"; and its practical conclusion is that the alternative to the present order can only be a fundamental change for the worse—to which even partial reforms may be contributing. This would seem to make Aron vulnerable to the charge of being both too optimistic about Europe's present successes and too pessimistic about the effects of possible changes.

In fact, the constraints of Western, post-industrial societies may be such as drastically to limit both the ability of liberal democracies to satisfy their citizens and the viability of radical alternatives, whether utopian or totalitarian. The question then, is that of the meaning of the present disaffection with the existing system, or its roots and consequences. A case can be made that it should be seen not as the negation but as the continuation of the successes of the 1950s and '60s. Seen in this perspective, what horrifies many conservatives and thrills revolutionaries in the guise of the crisis of the West, of capitalism, or of democracy would appear as the further fulfillment of precisely those trends which constitute their main virtue or their very essence. Where conservative pessimists see a crisis of the system, optimist reformists see a sign of health or of recovery. The crisis, in the optimists' view, would be not that of the system itself but that of illegitimate, obsolescent, or at least exclusive elites or classes. If they are replaced or lose their monopoly of power or wealth, this would be a sign of health rather than of sickness, or at least it would represent a recovery and an improvement of the Western system.

In terms of the political and constitutional order, this argument is certainly tenable. One could argue that the essence of Western liberal democracy is an agreement on the rules of the game, the central one being that of alternation in power based on free elections. In this sense, the system is in crisis as long as such alternation cannot take place. This had been the case, in postwar Western Europe, because of the existence of important forces which one might call "anti-system," whether of the Right or of the Left, whether in power or as challengers whose accession to power would have changed the nature of the regime.

Spain, Portugal, and, for a time, Greece, were in the first case, through their right-wing dictatorships. In France, and Italy, the domination of the left-wing opposition by an anti-system Communist party has enabled the Gaullists and the Christian Democratic party to remain indefinitely in power by lack of a democratic alternative. A third, more vague and socio-cultural element common to both types of cases has been seen in a more "ascriptive" conception of power, as an attribute or a property, characteristic of more traditional regimes, where a transfer of power is considered not as a normal functioning of democracy but as a total loss leading to a total change of regime. If, instead, each side becomes committed to the democratic rule of replacement through elections as a normal event, one may say that a permanent crisis of the system has been cured, or that progress in Western democracy has occurred.

In Spain, Portugal and Greece, this is definitely so, since one of the most remarkable aspects of the post-dictatorship period has been how, whether through a smooth transition in Greece and Spain or through a chaotic period in Portugal, the Western model of democratic government seems to have emerged as the preferred choice, rather than a Communist or a Third-World-like military regime. For France and Italy, however, the optimistic case rests on the assumption that the Communists no longer dominate the Left because of the rise of the Socialist party in France; or through changes in their conception of the conquest and exercise of power in Italy; or that the conservatives are ready to leave power peacefully if the electorate so decides.

None of the three conditions is certain to be fulfilled. This is why in Italy the preferred formula seems to be the gradual co-opting of Communists into the power structure rather than a clearcut change of majority and of government; and in France it may well be that the Left either does not make it to power or is eliminated by a right-wing reaction.

Whatever its gradualness and its setbacks, there is no doubt about the process itself, however. The process involves the twin and converging aspects of the gradual exhaustion of ruling elites and of the emergence of an alternative elite whose trend to "de-radicalization" makes it at least potentially a candidate for inclusion in the normal political game and for integration in West European society.

Inclusion and integration may, actually, be the key words of the postwar system in the social and economic areas, even more than in the political one. Indeed, one may argue that some of the current political phenomena—like the democratic transformation of Spain or the Communist claim to participation in power in Italy—are best seen as attempts of the political dimension to catch up with the social and economic gains. The spread of modern industrial and consumer society had already brought Spain into Western Europe and was making the isolation imposed by the Franco regime more artificial every day.

The growing integration of rural strata into the industrial working class and of the industrial working class into the world of mass consumption calls, in a country like Italy, for a double integration: an adaptation of the forces which represent the working class to the realities of modern society and their inclusion in positions of power and responsibility within a system which cannot function without the active consensus of the major unions.

At any rate, the story of the twenty-five years after the war is indeed, all over Western Europe, that of the inclusion of ever larger segments of the population into the structures of production, consumption and education of modern society. Nobody has described this movement more eloquently in the case of Italy than the Communist leader G. Amendola, whose affirmation that "Never have so many Italians had it so good" created a kind of scandal. He backed it up by a series of well-known figures, showing that with a threefold increase of the GNP per capita between 1957 and 1973 (i.e., a median annual increase of 4.6 percent) there occurred a four-fold increase in the consumption of meat, a five-fold increase in the number of high school and university students, a five-fold increase in the number of persons enjoying social security, and a six-fold increase in those enjoying retirement benefits.[6] The dramatic diffusion of consumer durables (cars, television sets, refrigerators, washing machines, etc.) is known to all.

In general, given the massive decline in agricultural population, it is fair to say that the last generation in Western Europe has seen a considerable homogenization in standards and styles of living, with an unprecedented increase of the numbers included in urbanized and relatively educated modern society, characterized by at least some participation in mass private consumption and in the benefits of the welfare state. To that extent, the central idea of President Giscard d'Estaing in his book, *Democratie Française*—i.e., that the dualistic opposition between bourgeoisie and working class has been superseded by the emergence of a huge amorphous middle class which is both homogeneous and pluralistic, along various cleavages of interest instead of class conflict—is true enough, as long as one looks at consumption rather than at production, and at life-styles rather than at political attitudes.[7]

In terms of occupational structure, the Italian sociologist and economist P. Sylos Labini has documented the general resilience of the middle classes, within which one must distinguish between the decline (and, often, the proletarianization) of the small self-employed bourgeoisie and the increase of the white-collar employees working in services and particularly in the public sector (and tending to integrate parts of the new more technical working class). He puts the middle classes at a level of about 50 percent of society, which he finds surprisingly stable over the years and in comparison with rather different nations like Italy, Great Britain, France, Spain, Japan, the United States, Argentina and Chile. Meanwhile, of course, the agricultural population declined everywhere, whereas the size, trend and composition of the industrial working class were more variable according to stages of growth and national pecularities (27 percent in Spain; 33 percent in Italy in 1971 from 13 percent in 1886; 27.8 percent in France from 17.7 percent in 1886; as compared to 22 percent in the United States from 24.7 percent in 1890).[8]

The conclusion does seem to follow, then, that the persistence of a pluralist structure based on mobility and bargaining within a certain social consensus and the trend both toward the integration of the working class in society and toward the strengthening of its role were bound to push the Communist parties toward adapting and political society toward accepting them.

Internationally, one can argue in similar terms that the problems of the European Community stem from its successes: from the liberalization of trade and the creation of a single market, which today, in times of crises, produces a protectionist backlash; from the application of the southern countries for membership, which is yet another testimony to the success of the Community and another step along the road mapped by Jean Monnet and his followers, namely, progressive extension of the Community through the inclusion of whoever wanted to join the common enterprise.

In each of these areas, however, it is just as easy and

necessary, if not to argue the other side of the case, at least to show the other side of the coin. On the most general level, one can show for the key trends of the Western system like alternation, inclusion, integration, what Raymond Aron did in an earlier work, *Progress and Disillusion,* for values like freedom, equality and universality: namely, that at a certain point in their success they become self-defeating or bring forth counter-reactions.[9] From a political and, even more, from a social and economic point of view, the developments of the 1950s and early '60s have produced new contradictions and new problems. And the effects of external factors, above all the international economic crisis, combined with these earlier or permanent factors to produce either new deadlocks or new dilemmas. The central aspect may be the contradiction between the political model of competition for alternation in power within a consensus on the rules of the game, and the social reality which may either impose deeper cleavages and more bitter struggles tending toward civil war, or require a more substantive and more inclusive consensus tending towards national coalitions.

To take a second look at the examples already cited, it is by no means certain that in the three former southern dictatorships the model of competition between two or several parties is safely legitimized. In each, it is put on probation by the strains of a severe economic crisis. In Greece, due in great part to the unique role of Mr. Caramanlis—itself a rather Gaullist version of the Western model—no alternative seems in sight. In Portugal, the military alternative to a weak Socialist government incapable of handling a chaotic situation is very much present indeed. And we should note that the present Portuguese formula, while based on free elections and on the primacy of the strongest political party, constitutes at the same time a combination of minority government and of national coalition (through general passive acceptance), which has some kinship with the Italian situation and may constitute a precedent for a future French solution should the Left win and then split.

In Spain, while the role of the army is less visible, the economic crisis is no less threatening. Although the results of the recent elections do seem to be leading to a classical pattern of alternation in power between center-right and center-left, the elements of tacit national coalition between the two main parties and including even the two smaller parties of Santiago Carrillo on their left and Fraga Iribarne on their right are unmistakable.

Finally, Italy, France and Great Britain offer three classical examples of the crisis of the traditional Western model. In Italy, at least for the time being, what is being demonstrated is the impossibility of one half of the country to govern without the other half. The de facto grand coalition controlled by the two major parties may lead, in conformity with the Italian tradition of *trasformismo,* to the co-opting of the Communists within the power system of the Christian Democratic party and to their subsequent emasculation. Or, it may lead to the break-up of the Christian Democratic party and to the emergence of the PCI as the de facto leader of the coalition. Finally, following the West German model, it may lead to a separation, once the PCI has been either legitimized or weakened, or both, by the grand coalition, followed by a struggle between the Left and Right. The last outcome is not impossible but is by no means the most likely of the three. The Italian preference for continuity and compromise between political forces, though conducive to a new polarization between the left and right parties and their grass-roots (or marginal strata) followers who are not included in the deal, seems to reinforce rather than to disrupt these traditional trends.

In France, the classical model may also be in trouble but for exactly the opposite reasons: not for lack of division but for lack of consensus. The Left does propose a clear alternative to the Right; but, despite a mutual recognition of common rules of the game, the political polarization and, in particular, the claim of the Left (including the Socialist party) to bring about a "break with capitalism" and to "change life" have resulted in the actual advocacy by the Communists of measures whose logic is nationalist and bureaucratic, state-oriented and protectionist. Since the consequences of Communist intentions imply a break with the international environment, the Gaullists and Chirac will resist it. Thus, it is likely that, whether the Left fails or wins, or gains power just long enough to provoke an economic disaster and bring back the Right, the dream of national union shared by President Giscard and by a majority of Frenchmen has even less chance of happening than the Anglo-American model of orderly alternation in power. Curiously, while in Italy the political elite is essentially united and the country very deeply divided, in France political elites are polarized and the country has much less deep and violent divisions.

Even in England a paradox—both similar and different—appears when one compares the evolution in relations between political parties and among social forces. Until recently it has seemed to be the model both of bipartisan alternation in power and of the "social contract" of unions, employers and governments. The problem lies in the contradiction between the two: though electoral trends tend to make a return of the Conservative party into power inevitable, the necessity of a social contract makes the trade unions the arbiters of British politics and particularly of Labour party politics. The continuing gravity of the economic crisis seems to put the viability of both aspects into question just as much as their coexistence. The social contract seems to be failing, and the two major parties, especially Mrs. Thatcher and the left-wing of the Labour party, seem to be undergoing a rather un-British ideologization. The trend, then, would seem to be toward a polarization along French lines, both ideological and class. Yet, the gravity of the crisis and the willingness of the British people (alone in Europe) to accept staggering losses in living standards make the other extreme, that of a national coalition on the basis of a war-like emergency situation, just as conceivable.

Only in the Federal Republic among major countries does the model of democratic competition for power seem to run its normal course. Even there, although in much milder form than in Britain, there are rumors of grand coalition among the three political parties and of the growing alienation of the unions from the SPD and from the capitalist system. But Germany has yet to feel the full impact of the economic crisis. If, as some predict, it is heading for serious trouble in this respect and should, as a consequence, become isolated internationally, its domestic political stability may, like that of Britain, be less taken for granted than it has recently been.

The root of France's problem is essentially political and stems from its traditional ideological division and from the additional bipolarization imposed by the Gaullist system upon a relatively "centrist" society. In virtually all other countries it is the social and economic crisis which, in the short, dramatic run or in the conceivable future, puts into question the stability of an otherwise accepted political structure. Ultimately, even for France, any evaluation of the political future, including the evolution and role of the Communist party, depends upon an evaluation of the roots and consequences of the prosperity of the 1950s and '60s and of the present crisis, of the return of the former or of the worsening of the latter.

Prophecies about the future and determinism about the past are certainly inappropriate here. In particular, it would be wrong to see the present situation as the inevitable outcome of the very factors which created the earlier successes. Yet it *is* important not to underestimate the uneven pace and contradictory character of the process of integration and inclusion of new masses of people into modern, industrial or affluent societies, about which Western politicians from Giscard d'Estaing to Amendola have been so optimistic. When seen in the light of the present crisis, the analysis of the "economic miracles" of the preceding period points to three kinds of features which challenge the optimistic assessment. First, as was pointed out in particular by Professor Nicholas Kaldor,[10] the expansion of the 1950s and '60s was based on low salaries and stable and relatively low prices of raw materials, particularly of energy. The former was canceled by the explosion of salaries throughout the capitalist world but particularly in Western Europe in 1968-71; the latter, by the increase in raw materials prices after 1971 and, most dramatically, by the energy crisis of 1973.

Second, during the years of economic "miracles," each of the positive phenomena (increase in consumption and in social services, in urbanization, in social mobility, in education, in free trade, etc.) has had its negative aspects, counterparts or consequences. The positive side has created new expectations, the negative side has created new tensions.

Third, when economic conditions change, whether through inner dynamics or external circumstances, the expectations remain and tensions are exacerbated. Western European societies thus combine the problems of affluence and those of poverty, the dissatisfaction created by the successes of technocracy and by its failures.

[49]

The first consideration points toward a Marxist explanation: The prosperity of the developed would seem to be based on the exploitation of the underdeveloped, i.e., of the cheap unqualified labor migrating from the countryside and of the raw-material producers. Whether or not one accepts this interpretation with its theoretical and moral implications, it does seem to contain a kernel of historical truth, namely, the exceptional (or, at any rate, unique for the time being) character of the decades of uninterrupted growth and of moderate inflation. In particular, what emerges from this new, retrospective look is the crucial character of the immigration of unskilled labor from the countryside (as in Italy) or from the less developed Mediterranean countries (as in Central and Northern Europe). Even more striking is the importance of the period 1968-71 as a watershed from the social point of view. The wage explosion of industrial countries which took place in 1968-69 in Japan, France, Belgium and Holland, and in 1969-70 in Germany, Italy, Switzerland and the United Kingdom remains, according to Kaldor, largely unexplained. But its consequences are enormous, not only in relations with the United States (where it has been much less sudden and violent, so that now the costs of labor in several European countries are as high as American ones) but for the general evolution of these countries themselves. From a general point of view, one may note that the socio-cultural crisis and the economic one, the revolt of the students and the change in the rules of the game by the working class are more closely linked than is usually assumed. In France, the May revolt succeeded a period of decline in real wages and of youth unemployment and produced the wage increases of the Grenelle agreement. In Italy, the *autumno caldo* of 1969 started both the "creeping May" of the universities and the sharp jump of the working class from one of the lowest paid and least protected to one of

[50]

the best paid and best protected in Europe. While the "Italian miracle" was based in large part on the comparative advantage of Italian industry in terms of labor costs, Italy today is the only country which is going through the economic crisis both, like France, with yearly increases in real wages and, unlike France, without significant losses in employment. It is precisely the most specific features of the Italian case which give the most telling indications about the general problems faced by West European societies.

Left-wing commentators have pointed out that if the Italian working class has been successively the weakest and the strongest in Europe, it was in great part because of the southern Italians whom the industrial north has used as unskilled workers instead of Algerians or Turks.[11] In a first phase, the high proportion of new nonintegrated workers has made for greater organizational weakness and for a permanent "workers' reserve army." In a second phase, their integration and their combativeness, despite cultural shocks and conflicts, increased much more rapidly than that of often non-European aliens who, in other countries, did not speak the language and could always be sent home; on the other hand, the availability of new reserves tended to dry up both because of the crisis and because of their absorption by the parasite public petty bureaucracy. The result was a much greater bargaining power for the unions and the workers in general.

This analysis covers only half of the truth and is quite insufficient to explain why, after 1969, the capitalist defenses crumbled so markedly to the point of accepting not only spectacular wage increases but also laws like the *statuto di laboratori*, which make it virtually impossible to fire anybody. Political fators like the role of the Socialists in center-left government should not be underestimated in this respect. The contribution of the migrants from the south to the northern working class is obviously a double-edged sword. Their militancy and their situation are more volatile than those of genuinely integrated skilled workers. The increased strength of the working class implies new responsibilities for the unions or for the PCI, and these responsibilities imply a new integration as well as a constant rebellion or overbidding by more militant groups. Thus the sequence is the PCI being overturned on its left by the unions, the unions by the factory councils, the factory councils by the ultra-left, and the ultra-left itself by more or less spontaneous or more or less conspiratorial ultra-ultra-left groups. It is not by chance that Italy is by far the country where the ultra-left has the most serious working-class following.

The atmosphere of constant conflict is not confined to the factory. The imperfect integration of the immigrants has made of Milan and Turin the most tension-ridden cities in Europe and, increasingly with the crisis, the result has been the proliferation of an explosive *Lumpenproletariat* at least as much as a strong working-class. The problems are strikingly similar at the universities. The rapid inclusion of a million students, many of rural or working-class origin, often from the south, has led to the creation of an intellectual *Lumpenproletariat* without any prospects either for real study or for finding a job.

Sylos Labini points out that

in the grave crisis Italy is going through, the problems of two groups emerge ever more clearly: that of the intellectual sub-bourgeoisie and that of the urban and rural sub-proletariat. The problems of both groups converge into the big and anguishing problem of employment, whose gravity lies not so much in its dimensions as in its structure. While in the north and center of Italy the rate of adult male unemployment is very low, it is notably higher in the south and for women and young people with a diploma.

Unemployment threatens to increase even further with the return of emigrants from other economically depressed Western European countries.

The lesson is clear: Industrialization, urbanization, increased access to higher education and to mass consumption have produced or increased new disequilibria between north and south, between center and periphery, between men and women, employed and unemployed workers and bourgeoisie on one side, "marginalized" *Lumpenproletariat* and *Lumpenbourgeoisie* on the other. As Suzanne Berger has shown, industrial growth, far from eliminating the traditional sectors, maintains them and relies increasingly upon them (through such devices as second jobs, home labor, occasional labor) as safety valves in times of crisis to disguise unemployment or circumvent labor laws.[12]

Instead of one disappearing bipolarity, there are several recurring bipolarizations! Until recently, Italian analysts would juxtapose the productive Italy of labor and profit to the unproductive Italy of rent and parasitism. Today, the fashion is to contrast two societies: the integrated one of those who have some capital or a job (represented by the agreements of business and unions, as well as of the Christian Democrats and the PCI) and the "marginalized" one of those who have neither and who are the source of anarchic violence from the right and left. Of course, all three Italies of productive work, of parasitism and clientelism, and of unemployed strata oscillating between despair and utopia coexist and interact.

These Italian characteristics exist in some fashion in all Western societies, particularly in those of the south. The Communist leader Pietro Ingrao, in his new book *Masse e*

[53]

Potere, asks whether the Italian case is the fruit of retarded development or "the exasperated and paradoxical anticipation of problems which are also maturing in other countries." [13] Obviously it is both, the common problems being exacerbated in Italy's case by the contradictions between its accession to the levels of salaries, consumption, number of students, and hence of aspirations, of the more developed countries and its keeping the productive and administrative infrastructure of lesser developed ones. The former governor of the Bank of Italy and present head of Italian businessmen, Dr. Guido Carli, has defined as schizophrenic this situation of extreme backwardness in certain respects combined with extreme modernity in terms of values, ideologies and aspirations: "the most advanced feminist movement in Europe, the strongest Communist party in Europe, the most combative trade unions in Europe, the most revolutionary student movement in Europe, the highest number of graduates in Europe." [14]

But schizophrenia is also the best label for the situation of most West European countries and of Europe as a whole. The same ambiguous relationship between center and periphery, between modernity and tradition, between integration and marginalization, between fragmentation and interdependence, between paralysis and mobility, the same contradictions between aspirations and constraints characterize relationships within the European Community and between the latter and the candidate-member countries.

Indeed, it is this international and, in particular, European dimension which adds perhaps the most decisive touch to the respective schizophrenia of the various countries. This is so not solely because the disappearance of favorable international conditions (in terms of raw-materials prices, etc.) expose the incompatible character of the aspirations of various social groups, which even inflation can no longer hide by projecting them into the future. But today the contradictions between the demands of security and of competition, of a protective and potentially protectionist welfare state and of an open and potentially transnational economy, produce unsolvable dilemmas for each European government. As the Italian sociologist A. Pizzorno puts it: "The question is what can be the political consequences of a type of crisis where organized groups are in a position to support their claims with great force, while capital keeps its freedom to choose how much and where to invest, and whether to remain in the country or to leave it."[15]

In face of these contradictions, various societies, parties, and governments are wavering between equally unsatisfactory answers. They all have to do with the role of the state, caught between the pressures of the various national or subnational groups and those of the international and transnational environment. The two main forms of the general dilemma can be seen as a horizontal and a vertical one.

The horizontal form of the dilemma is expressed in its simplest terms as between nationalism and internationalism, or between protectionism and free trade, or between independence and interdependence. It is particularly vivid for southern, dependent or peripheral countries; or for countries like Italy (which exports both workers and capital) and France (two countries whose growth has been mainly led by exports, which the crisis makes both more necessary and more inaccessible); or for Britain which exports capital but survives through foreign loans. In most countries, the horizontal dilemma takes the form of the choice between a more Europeanist or a more nationalist orientation, with the latter having more cultural connotations in the case of southern countries, where it stands for a rediscovery of traditional roots or for an identification with the Third World. This is particularly frequent among young intellectual and military elites as opposed to the preference of the majority for Europe, liberal democracy, and welfare capitalism. In France, it would represent a mixture of Gaullism and of state-centered socialism.

The vertical dilemma can be said to be between various combinations of corporatism and populism, as well as of centralization and fragmentation. The two elements, mentioned above, of protectionism or self-closure from the international environment, and of an increased role of the state, recall the doctrine and practice of corporatism, as put forward by fascist regimes. But, to make it complete, a third element goes together with this emphasis on a conflictual or neo-mercantilist attitude toward the external economic environment: it is the minimizing of conflicts of interest, or of class struggle, within the nation itself. This emphasis on national solidarity collides, however, with the other, more current meaning of the word "corporatism," i.e., the organized defense by particular groups of their specific interests as against a general or class interest.

The conciliation between these two trends (and both are real) can only come through organized bargaining at the top between unions, business, professional interest groups, and state bureaucracies to replace the parliamentary political process, the mechanisms of the market, or violent class struggle. This is the logic of the social contract, of wage and income policies, of historical compromises, and of national coalitions. But, in turn, it runs up against populist or spontaneist reactions directed against big government bureaucracy, against the state, against taxes, against welfare systems (as in Sweden or Germany), in the name of local participation, or of ethnic groups, or of grass-root militants or branch unions, or "autonomous" movements organizing other social categories.

[56]

Again, the most lucid analysis of the phenomenon and its possible consequences is by A. Pizzorno:

> Not only are the various categories of workers better organized but the new phenomenon is that so also are other entities outside the labor market proper: students and other youth groups, certain groups of unemployed, groups of tenants and of homeless, etc. Hence a diffuse, uncoordinated conflictuality of a corporative kind which, paradoxically, is more effective when it is dispersed. Any single group has become capable of frustrating decisions of general policy which hurt its interests, but not of proposing effective alternatives. Capable of occupying universities or factories but not ministries, police barracks or other places of real power. (But is there still a Winter Palace to occupy? And even if there was, who would care to move in?) Meanwhile, the practical result is that the course of the economy continues to favor the stronger classes.

From this description which, again, is certainly colored by the specific Italian situation but is potentially relevant to other countries, Pizzorno turns to speculations about the future:

> In turn, dispersed conflictuality feeds the growth of *guerriglia* among marginals and creates the conditions for a right-wing authoritarian regime. There are solid organized forces which militate against this eventuality, but they are weakened by the continuation of the crisis, which tends to loosen the ties between the leaders of big organizations and their grass-root militants.

[57]

However, the authoritarian regime could not solve the problems either. Economic interdependence would have its effects on the *guerriglia,* and the spiral of disorder would soon return, as shown by the Argentine case.

Only one formula seems, then, conceivable for imposing the necessary sacrifices in conditions of equality without sacrificing democratic freedoms: that of an emergency government based on specific agreements of limited duration between the main social and political forces. Although this solution is primarily Italian, it does seem to me to have a general value if the crisis continues. For the problems of consensus, polarization and fragmentation, and of their negative or positive, passive or active, coercive or peaceful forms are affecting all countries in one way or the other.

The degrees of consensus, of polarization, and of fragmentation vary from country to country. Still it is possible to distinguish three types of combinations corresponding (1) to the classical Western model and to its practical realization before the crisis and in the central and northern countries, (2) to the present crisis, and (3) to its possible outcomes.

Among forms of consensus one can distinguish the basically conservative consensus of the "end of ideology" period, the negative consensus on "not rocking the boat" based on the fragility revealed by the crisis, and the new positive consensus around an emergency program of sacrifice or austerity which may, according to Pizzorno, be the only way out.

Among forms of polarization, one would have the bipartisan one (within a framework of consensus about the system); the "cold civil war" one of forces that no longer recognize a common legitimacy yet are encamped before each other in fear of common disaster throught the escalation of violence; and finally the peaceful or violent revolution, with one side

[58]

replacing the other and changing the nature of the regime.

The decentralized or dispersed element in society takes the forms of (a) interest-group pluralism in the pre-crisis model, (b) the fragmentation of protest described by Pizzorno in times of crisis, and (c) violent anarchy or "war of all against all" in the "Latin-Americanization" scenario he projects for the future.

The combination of conservative consensus, of political "imperfect bipartism" or alternation, and of interest-group pluralism was characteristic of all North and Central European countries before the crisis and, in its imperfect form, excluding the Communists, in France and in Italy. The combination of negative consensus and of the fragmentation of protest is characteristic of most countries today—certainly of Italy but also to some extent, at least, of many others from Portugal to Britain. France is the exception here, at least at the political level, where it is following more the "cold civil war" model. Some fear a violent future revolution and others look forward to it. Many Frenchmen believe in a peaceful break with capitalism; but, again, it is likely that even for France the only alternative to anarchy is some kind of a new consensus which would unite energies and impose sacrifices. The question remains whether this would happen, as President Giscard wishes, under the hegemony of the middle classes or whether, as in the Communist version, the "union of the French people," which should exclude only a "handful of monopolists," should take place under the hegemony of the working class represented by its "avant-garde."

While different outcomes are likely for different countries, the most decisive question may well be (even in the case of a new emergency consensus reached in each of them) whether they will be directed against each other, as in the Heilbroner scenario of conflicting authoritarian nationalisms using each other as scapegoats, or whether they can converge into a common European historical compromise or social contract.[16]

WHITHER THE COMMUNIST PARTIES?

If it is true that the main problem in Europe today is neither social revolution nor the management of capitalist affluence but, rather, what the Italian Communists call "social recomposition," or the re-establishment of a measure of unity and control to counteract the inequalities of uneven development and the anarchy of "dispersed conflictuality" and to bring about greater acceptance of solidarity and austerity, then the perspectives of the Communist parties may well have to be seen in a new light, both in France and in Italy. The PCF and the PCI have, several times in postwar history, missed the boat by misjudging the character of ongoing developments or by understanding it too late. This is particularly obvious for the French party, which, in 1956 and 1968, missed the opportunity of de-Stalinization and let itself be outflanked by the unexpected renaissance of the Socialist party. By contrast, the PCI has, ever since the war, pursued its long march of interpenetration with Italian society and has accelerated it after 1956 by starting to move away from Moscow's dictates. In doing so, the PCI put itself in a position to profit fully from the decline of the Socialist party and to pre-empt any possible revival of the latter on the French model.

In their interpretation of the evolution of Western capitalism, however, both parties have had their share of partly common, partly divergent misinterpretations. Neither (nor, for that matter, any other Communist party) believed in the postwar economic recovery. The PCI was caught by surprise by the Italian economic miracle just as much as was the PCF by the modernization and growth under the Fourth and Fifth Republics. Where they differ is that the PCI drew the lessons of this failure and progressively rallied to all the themes of the Italian center-left and of the Western model of liberal capitalism: growth, competition, the market, free trade, European integration, acceptance of NATO in the name of détente. The explicit formulation was an alliance with the modern, productivist strata of Italian and European society, represented by Fiat's Giovanni Agnelli, in order to perfect the modernization process. The trouble is that, at the time the PCI was rallying to the system under the claim of wanting to help run it in a more efficient and democratic way, the system itself was already in deep trouble. While the PCI expected to share the benefits of the economic miracle, of European integration, and of détente, the three are more or less grinding to a halt and the Communists have to share the burden and the risks of promoting austerity, coping with anarchy, facing international isolation through the weakness of European institutions and the suspicion of both superpowers.

For the first time, however, the lag between the real situation and the Communists' adjustment to it seems to be sharply reduced, at least in the domestic area. Not only that, but if the main problem today is that of the alternative between voluntary consensus and violent anarchy and the more equal sharing of inevitable sacrifices, the Italian Communists have been in the forefront of all European political organizations in proposing a revision of priorities in these directions. Since the winter 1976-77, they have shifted their emphasis toward the themes of "social recomposition" (aimed both at controlling the spreading anarchy and lawlessness and at correcting the economic imbalances of development) and of a new economic model. The new model is based on a combination of austerity, increased planning with cuts in public expenditures, and the maintenance of market stability, as well as a reorientation of consumption and of exports. This strategy is based on collective and national priorities within the framework of an open economy and coordinated efforts to find supranational solutions to the problems raised by transnational capitalism. While nothing proves that they have the detailed conceptions or will have the practical power necessary to translate these broad directions into reality, the Italian Communists have succeeded, though at some cost in their relations to the marginalized strata and their own working-class base, in establishing their credibility as the main promoters of the new attitudes needed to face the crisis and build a new consensus.

The response of the PCF to a changing situation has been very different. Unlike the PCI, the PCF leaders never agreed before the crisis to recognize either the benefits or the constraints of economic growth and of international competition, but chose to cling to Marxist predictions of inevitable crisis and impoverishment and to demagogic demands for indiscriminate tax increases and nationalizations. While their emphasis on "state monopoly capitalism" and on the *union du peuple de France* was their way of calling for a new national consensus to include most of the bourgeoisie, their particular twist was the underlining of the role of the state (today in the service of "monopolies," tomorrow in the service of the people) and the insistence upon their own role as an avant-garde. When the crisis came, they could claim that they had predicted it all along and that they were better prepared to handle it, both doctrinally and organizationally, than their Italian comrades who, on both levels, were victims of their own opportunism.

Yet, conversely, the PCF's own sectarianism prevented it from having a chance to play the leading role in a new, post-crisis consensus. As for the contents of this consensus, in spite of paying lip service to pluralism, of accepting the existence of Western organizations and of courting all social strata, both the ultimate rigidity of their doctrinal position and the boundless opportunism of PCF tactical slogans combine to deprive the party's socio-economic stance of credibility. The PCF proclaims in the same breath that the poor conditions of the French economy are the product of the general crisis of capitalism and that the energy crisis or the need for austerity are inventions of the ruling exploiters, that getting rid of them and putting the state in the hand of a left-wing majority would enable France to escape the general crisis and avoid any sacrifices, provided there is an increase in nationalizations, redistribution, and protectionism.

This would certainly seem to indicate that a Communist-inspired consensus in France could not rely on conciliation either with private business or with the international capitalist environment, including the Common Market or even a SPD Germany. It is only in the case of a sharpening of the crisis, both domestically and internationally, that they could hope to wrest first place in the Left or in the country, in opposition or in government, from a wavering, co-opted or divided Socialist party and to lead the resistance against "reactionary plots" or "imperialist pressures."

Despite the novelty of the situation, we are back, then, to the initial dilemma between the Europeanization of Communist parties or the communization of European countries. It is clear that neither in France nor in Italy can one return either to the golden days of capitalist expansion, or to the golden days of revolution, either to the early 1960s or to 1917. Everywhere, the only chance for the Western system to survive is to find a new legitimacy and a new efficiency while keeping a pluralist basis. This has to mean a new role both for the state and for citizens, and a new sense of community and of equality. These can only be reached through a deep democratic transformation of liberal and socialist ideas and of national and European institutions. In principle, both major Communist parties are aware of this dilemma. The Italian Communists have no wish to become classical social-democrats and the French Communists have no illusions about the possibilities of a Leninist revolution in today's Western Europe. Yet, the two alternatives clearly delineated by the Spanish and Portuguese parties, respectively—of gaining legitimacy by wholly accepting the West European consensual framework and breaking with the Eastern heritage, or of counting on Leninist tactics and organization to gain power at the top—are bound to reassert themselves for the more complex and ambiguous Italian and French parties in time of crisis.

Both in France and Italy, national preferences and traditions are combined with broader trends concerning Western European society. In the long run, beyond whatever can be achieved or risked in terms of emergency coalitions in Italy or electoral struggles in France, either the positive evaluation of Western developments made by the Italian party before the crisis will come to pass and the French party will, with less success, have to follow the Italian road; or else the French view of irreconcilable conflict within capitalism and between nations is confirmed, and it is the Italians who may have to imitate the French in going back to a harder and more exclusivist line, both organizationally and nationally.

More generally, if constitutional democracy, economic prosperity, and European or "trilateral" integration recover from their respective crises in the West, then the fate of Western Communist parties is likely to be that which Richard Lowenthal predicted in the early 1960s in his famous essay,

"The Prospects for Pluralistic Communism": away from Leninism either toward social-democratization or toward becoming utopian sects.[17] If, on the contrary, the trend in the West is toward more bitter conflicts and disintegration, trade wars, and civil strife, then today's Eurocommunist parties may either recover their traditional role as leaders of the working class in an intensified social struggle, or themselves become the strongest, or at least the toughest, elements in authoritarian and nationalistic regimes, which would represent a kind of unanimistic or left-wing fascism.

In both of the latter cases, either in opposition or in government, their Leninist, centralist or authoritarian features would be maximized, as opposed to the pluralistic features associated today with the notion of Eurocommunism. On the other hand, neither right-wing nor, even less, left-wing nationalist or authoritarian regimes can isolate themselves, at least in Western Europe, from the pressures of the international economic environment. The very crisis which may have provoked their retrenchment may also make its success more difficult since it increases the vulnerability of dependent countries, unless they are willing to go all the way in the Cambodian direction of self-sufficiency at the price of merciless repression and brutal structural change. There is no doubt that unless some form of consensus, which would be both as free as today and more egalitarian at the national and European level, can arrest the vicious spiral of crisis, the two ultimate forces which will survive are the strength of the authoritarian form of organization embodied in Leninism, and the strength of the manipulative and dominating form of interdependence embodied in multinational corporations and international finance, as denounced by Harold Wilson in a famous speech.

Solzhenitsyn presented *Lenin in Zurich* as a prelude to the victory of communism in the East. If democratic socialism and European integration fail, the fate not only of Eurocommunism in the West but also of Western Europe as such may well be decided by the decisive battle between the epigones of Lenin and the gnomes of Zurich.

Notes

1. Cf. J. Smart: "The Great Engines: The Rise and Decline of a Nuclear Age," *International Affairs,* and Daniel Bell, "The Future World Disorder," *Foreign Policy,* No. 27 (Summer 1977).

2. Two brief and recent overviews in English on this ongoing debate are the chapters by Donald Blackmer, "Continuity and Change in Italian Communism," pp. 21-53, and Ronald Tiersky, "Alliance Politics and Revolutionary Pretensions," pp. 420-56 in Donald L.M. Blackmer and Sidney Tarrow, eds., *Communism in Italy and France* (Princeton, N.J.: Princeton University Press, 1975). The most recent contribution is L. Marcou, *Le Kominform* (Paris: Presses de la Fondation Nationale des Sciences Politiques, 1977), pp. 51-71.

3. Pierre Hassner, "Détente and the Politics of Instability in Southern Europe," in J. Holst and U. Nerlich, eds., *Beyond Nuclear Deterrence: New Aims, New Arms* (New York: Crane, Russak & Co., 1977), p. 42.

4. See, for instance, in Italy the debate between P. Sylos-Labini and L. Maitan in L. Maitan, *Dinamica delle classi sociali in Italia* (Rome: Savelli, 1975).

5. Raymond Aron, *Plaidoyer pour l'Europe décadente* (Paris: Robert Laffont, 1971).

6.   G. Amendola, *Gli anni della Republica* (Roma: Editori Riuniti, 1976).

7.   Giscard d'Estaing: *Democratie Française* (Paris: Fayard, 1976).

8.   P. Sylos-Labini, *Saggio sulle classe sociali* (Rome: Laterza, 1975) pp. 63-75 and 161-68.

9.   Raymond Aron, *Les désillusions du progrès* (Paris: Calmann-Levy, 1969).

10.   Nicholas Kaldor, "Inflation and Recession in the World Economy," *The Economic Journal,* December 1976.

11.   Maitan, cited, pp. 26-27. See also D. Grisoni and H. Portelli, *Luttes ouvrières en Italie de 1960 à 1975* (Paris: Aubier-Montaigne, 1976).

12.   Suzanne Berger, "Uso politico e soppravivenza dei ceti in declino," in L. Cavazza and S. Graubard, eds., *Il caso italiano* (Rome: Garzanti, 1974), pp. 219-313.

13.   P. Ingrao, *Masse e potere* (Rome: Editori Riuniti, 1977), p. 9.

14.   G. Carli, *Intervista sul capitalismo italiano* (Rome: Laterza, 1977), pp. 48-49.

15.   A. Pizzorno, "Prospettiva Crisi," *Panorama,* March 18, 1977.

16.   Robert Heilbroner, *An Inquiry into the Human Prospect* (New York: Norton, 1974).

17.   See also Richard Lowenthal, "Communism as an Historical Force," *International Journal,* vol. 32, no. 1 (Winter 1976-77), pp. 1-19.

[T W O]

The Italian
Communist Party:
The Modern Prince
at the Crossroads*

Norman Kogan

There is a specter haunting Western
European Communism; it is the specter
of Eduard Bernstein.[1]

If there is one thing that does not bother
us, it is to be accused of revisionism.[2]

It was in 1956 that Palmiro Togliatti, Secretary General of the
Italian Communist Party (PCI) publicly announced the strategy of the "Italian way to socialism," and the doctrine of

"polycentrism."[3] The announcement marked no new and drastic shift in the party's domestic strategy; rather, the doctrine threatened the organizational essence of the international Communist movement, for it rejected the role of the Soviet Union as the leading state and the Communist Party of the Soviet Union (CPSU) as the guiding party of that movement. While Togliatti would later beat a minor retreat on the literal meaning of polycentrism, abandoning the idea of organizing regional groupings of Communist parties, he affirmed the independence of the Italian and other parties. The following year, on his return from an international conference in Moscow, he emphasized that the Italian party bears sole responsibility for its own policies; what it shares with the international movement are ideals and ultimate visions. Neither the history nor the power position of the Soviet Union can be ignored, but they are not controlling over other Communist parties.[4]

In domestic affairs the Italian party had embarked on its own strategy from the time that Togliatti returned from Moscow in 1944. It was a strategy of broad alliances, with all forces willing to work for common goals, and in the last years of World War II even the monarchy was included. It was a strategy of inserting the PCI's presence in all sectors and areas of Italian society to influence and in the long run to control these sectors. It was a strategy that recognized that large portions of the Italian population were influenced and led by other major organizations and movements, socialism and Catholicism, and the Church and political parties identified with these movements. These agencies, it was assumed, were not necessarily hostile to many of the goals promoted by Communists, and the populations they represented could be influenced

*The research on which this chapter is in part based was made possible by a grant from the University of Connecticut Research Foundation.

[69]

for or against the PCI and its goals. It was incumbent on the Communists not to isolate themselves from the larger society to ensure that the population would not be directed against them in the first place, and perhaps it could be organized to support the PCI's objectives in more optimistic contexts.[5]

The choice of this strategy reflected two overriding conditions, historical and geographical. The experience of fascism had demonstrated the capacity of anti-Communist political movements to isolate the traditional left in Italy and to rally substantial popular support against it. The struggle against fascism had emphasized the importance of collaboration with non-Communist forces to survive and finally emerge victorious. The preference for collaboration had gotten Communist leaders into trouble with Moscow as early as the 1920s.[6] These were the lessons of the days of bitter exile. They led to the Unity of Action Pact with the Socialists, dating from 1934. The next year it was Togliatti, together with Georgi Dimitrov, who originated the popular front strategy at the 7th Comintern Congress.[7] These lessons also led to the creation of the Italian General Confederation of Labor (CGIL) in 1944, merging the Catholic, Socialist, and Communist labor movements into one confederation headed by Christian Democratic, Socialist, and Communist trade union leaders. Strategies of anticlericalism and of religious conflict were rejected. In 1947 the PCI voted to include the Lateran Accords in the new Constitution of the Republic. It was decided to build not an elitist cadre party, but a mass party in which everyone who was willing to support the party's immediate, concrete goals would be welcome. Over Stalin's objections the decision was made that a party member did not have to be a knowledgeable and believing Marxist-Leninist.[8] The Communists thus supported the creation of the 1948 Constitution of the Republic that incorporated a mixture of liberal democratic, Catholic, and socialist principles. None of these positions necessarily made Italian Communists into believing liberal democrats or Catholics, but it did accustom them to working and living in a society where pluralities of doctrines, groups, and behaviors could be assimilated into their everyday modes of operation.

If their reading of history induced them toward this strategy, the facts of political geography confirmed it. Italy is a peninsula of Western Europe that juts into the Mediterranean Sea; the American and British navies dominated that sea. Within a few weeks after the end of the war in Italy, Togliatti went to Milan, the center of the partisan resistance in the north, to inform his comrades that the party would have to follow the legal, not the revolutionary, way to power. There were over one million Anglo-American troops in Italy, and Winston Churchill had demonstrated a few months earlier in Greece that he would not hesitate to crush a revolt. Italy was not located where a Red Army could engage in successful counter-intervention. Even the most orthodox of Communists would have to recognize that a successful revolutionary strategy in Italy could come only after the balance of forces in Europe had shifted decisively and irrevocably in favor of the Soviet bloc. In the meantime the party would have to operate under the conditions that prevailed.[9]

The PCI was a member of all the Italian cabinets formed by the Committee of National Liberation from April 1944 to May 1947. Its leaders, such as Togliatti, were ministers and undersecretaries. Others, such as Ambrogio Donini, were appointed ambassadors. While the war was going on, the main goal of the Communists was to promote the Italian war effort at the side of the Allies, urging the unity of all anti-fascist forces in the struggle against the Nazi occupation of central and northern Italy. Behind the German lines the Communists quickly became the largest force in the partisan resistance.

[71]

When the fighting ended, reconstruction of the country was the highest priority, and only the United States was in a position to give significant help.

In these circumstances the Communists endorsed American aid for Italy's economic rehabilitation. After they were eliminated from the cabinet in May 1947, this endorsement did not change immediately. Togliatti wanted to accept Marshall Plan aid but submitted to Soviet opposition when the Russians decided to launch their campaign against it. Reluctantly the Italian Communists adjusted to the cold war after 1947, publicly following and supporting Soviet foreign policy in the wider world, while trying to maintain and pursue their domestic strategy in Italy. They refused to follow Soviet and East European criticisms and demands for a revolutionary offensive at home.[10] Their main domestic objectives were to maintain and defend their presence and alliances in all areas of Italian life. In this effort they suffered two significant defeats: elimination from the government and the splitting of the trade union movement. When Alcide De Gasperi excluded the Communists and Socialists from the cabinet, they were also gradually weeded out of positions in government service. By 1949 the Italian General Confederation of Labor had been split and two independent anti-Communist confederations had been created: one Catholic, *Confederazione Italiana dei Sindacati Liberi* (CISL); the other social democratic and republican, *Unione Italiana di Lavoro (UIL)*.

Defeat was far from total. The Unity of Action Pact with the Socialists was maintained in their joint opposition in parliament. The Socialist trade unionists remained in the CGIL with the Communists. In many parts of Italy the two parties continued to collaborate in local governments, municipal and provincial, as well as in numerous cooperatives and front organizations. The presence of Communists in the arts, sciences, mass media, and professions continued to expand. At the trade union level, efforts were made to collaborate with the rival confederations on concrete bread-and-butter issues for their members. In the 1950s these efforts had limited and sporadic success. At the parliamentary level, while denouncing the government and its foreign and domestic policies from the floor of the chambers, the Communists made deals and played the game of parliamentary politics behind the closed doors of the committees.[11] In short, during the peak of the cold war period the country was not as drastically fractured as surface appearances would indicate. The Communists had deep roots in Italian society; they were not a sect of ideologues deposited in the country by a foreign power, and they could not be driven into a narcissistic isolation.

The Position of the PCI in Italian Life

Socialism developed in Italy in the 1870s and 1880s, emerging from the declining Mazzinian tradition of the Risorgimento. In its earliest period Italian socialism was predominantly libertarian in philosophy, influenced by the activity of Bakunin in the peninsula. In the 1890s Marxism replaced anarchism as the dominant socialist doctrine. The Italian Socialist Party (PSI), founded in 1892, rapidly established strongholds in growing industrial centers of the northwest, where Italy's first industrial revolution was getting its start in the 1890s. Unlike many other European socialist movements, however, the PSI also sank roots in the countryside, particularly in the Po Valley among the landless peasants and in central Italy among the sharecroppers. These were zones where Mazzini's influence and anticlericalism were strong. By the first decade of the twentieth century Socialists were elected to the Chamber of Deputies. The establishment of universal male suffrage in 1912 increased the number of Socialist parliamentarians, and the conversion of the electoral system to proportional representation after World War I further expanded the size of their parliamentary delegation. The party won 35 percent of the total vote in the 1919 parliamentary election, making the PSI the largest party in the country, with the largest group in the Chamber of Deputies.[12]

At the end of the nineteenth century, European socialist thought had been brought to the attention of Italian intellectuals through the works of Antonio Labriola. Quickly the Italians themselves began to make their contribution to the elaboration of Marxist ideology. A revisionist school grew up during this period, when revisionism was percolating through German and Austrian Marxism.[13] Italian revisionism became the basis of a major battle between reformists and revolutionary maximalists for control of the PSI during the first decade of the twentieth century, a battle that split the Socialists into separate camps.[14] Temporary reunification after the war led to the 1919 electoral success, but by 1921 the party was again divided. The Italian Communist Party was born of a schism at the Leghorn Congress in January of that year. It was not long before the Communists themselves divided on the question of how to meet the growing fascist threat. While Italian liberalism was collapsing, the revolutionary purist, Amadeo Bordiga, first Secretary General of the Communist party, continued to insist that bourgeois liberalism was the real enemy. The wing of the party led by Antonio Gramsci finally gained control in 1924, but by that time the opportunity for free party activity was fast receding. Mussolini banned all parties but his own in January 1925.

Communist and other political leaders went into exile or were reduced to silence. Inside Italy the Communist party, alone of all the parties, was able to keep a small underground organization in existence. In exile, mainly in France, the Communists went through periods of collaboration with, or isolation from, other anti-fascist organizations, especially the Socialists. Moscow was dictating policy, but the Italians were happiest when they were able to collaborate with fellow anti-fascists, unhappiest when submitting to Soviet demands for separation. World War II and the leading role the Communists played in the resistance to the Nazi occupation of Italy provided them with the domestic base to emerge at the war's end as a major inheritor of the Italian Marxist and revolutionary tradition.[15] In the 1946 election to the Constituent Assembly the PCI received 19 percent of the vote to the PSI's 20 percent. In the 1948 parliamentary election the PCI pulled ahead, quickly establishing itself as the leading party of the Left, while the PSI went through schism and decline.

The PCI not only had absorbed and transformed the socialist tradition but had taken over a large part of the PSI's electoral and geographical base. From the first postwar elections it became clear that the Communists were running best in the old socialist strongholds of the pre-fascist period, the central Italian regions of Emilia-Romagna, Umbria, Tuscany, and the Marches, plus the working-class neighborhoods of the industrial cities of the northwest. Communist party membership was derived in large measure from former socialists or the sons of socialist parents. Party membership grew quickly, from 10,000 members in 1943 when Italy surrendered to the Allies to over a million in 1948, to reach a peak of more than 2 million by 1955. After 1955 membership declined to approximately 1,600,000 in the mid-1960s. It began to grow once more in the 1970s; at the end of 1976 the party claimed over 1,800,000 members organized in approximately 12,000 sections throughout the country. This is the largest membership

[75]

of any non-ruling Communist party in the world. An estimated 250,000 to 300,000 of the members can be considered militant activists.

The overall growth of the Communist electorate, as distinguished from membership, was slow and steady until the 1970s, when it took an upward spurt. The other two major parties, the Christian Democratic party and the Socialist party,

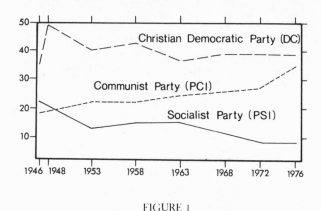

FIGURE 1

*Trends in the Electoral Strength of the Three
Major Italian Parties, 1946-1976*

Sources: Data for 1946-72 were taken from Mario Caciagli and Alberto Spreafico, Eds., *Un sistema political alla prova* (A Political System Under Trial), Bologna, Il Mulino, 1975, page 61, Table 7. Data for 1976 were from election election results published in the Italian press; see, for example, *Corriere della sera* (Milan), June 23, 1976. Points in the figure represent percentages of total vote polled by the respective parties in the 1946 Constituent Assembly election and in subsequent elections to the Italian House—elections with the broadest voter franchise. In 1948, the PCI and PSI ran on a joint ticket, which polled 31 percent of the vote. In 1968, the PSI united with the Social Democrats under the banner of the Unitary Socialist Party (PSU), which polled 14.5 percent of the vote.

By permission from Giacomo Sani, "The PCI on the Threshold," *Problems of Communism*, November-December 1976, p. 28.

TABLE 1

1972 and 1976 Elections, Chamber of Deputies

Party	Percentage of Popular Vote in 1976	Number of Seats in 1976	Percentage of Popular Vote in 1972	Number of Seats in 1972
Christian Democratic	38.7	262	38.7	266
Communist	34.4	228	27.1	179
Socialist	9.6	57	9.6	61
Social Democratic	3.4	15	5.1	29
Republican	3.1	14	2.9	15
Liberal	1.3	5	3.9	20
Neo-Fascist	6.1	35	8.7	56
Radical *	1.1	4	—	—
Proletarian Democracy *	1.5	6	—	—
South Tyrol Peoples	0.5	3	0.5	3
Other	0.3	1	3.5	1
	100.0	630	100.0	630

* New parties in 1976.

The PCI vote in 1976 totaled approximately 12,600,000.

Source: Corriere della Sera, June 23, 1976.

were strongest in the years immediately after the war and have declined or remained stable since then. (Figure 1 traces their electoral fortunes after the end of World War II. Table 1 gives the results of the 1976 election to the Chamber of Deputies, comparing party percentages and numbers of seats to the results of the 1972 election.)

Since the 1976 election, trends in public opinion appear to have benefited the PCI. A public opinion poll taken in April 1977 by the firm Demoskopea showed Communists leading Christian Democrats for the first time. In response to the question "If an election were held today, for which party would you vote?" a national sample of the electorate answered as shown in Table 2.

TABLE 2

*Results of an April 1977 Public Opinion Poll of Relative
Party Preferences, and Actual Percentages
in Election of June 20, 1976*

Party	Survey Responses, April, 1977 (Percent)	Election of June 20, 1976 (Percent)	Difference in Percentage Points
Christian Democratic	35.4	38.7	−3.3
Communist	36.2	34.4	+1.8
Socialist	9.6	9.6	—
Neo-Fascist	6.7	6.1	+0.6
Republican	4.0	3.1	+0.9
Social Democratic	2.9	3.4	−0.5
Liberal	1.2	1.3	−0.1
Proletarian Democracy	1.7	1.5	+0.2
Radical	1.3	1.1	+0.2
Other	1.0	0.8	+0.2

Source: Panorama, May 24, 1977, p. 43.

The growth of PCI electoral strength has been geographical as well as numerical. It still runs best in its central Italy strongholds, but its growth in other parts of the country, especially in the south, has been so marked that today it can truly be said to be a national party. (Table 3 illustrates this development.)

The policy of the PCI over the years has been to extend its appeal to all sectors of the Italian electorate, not merely to workers, peasants, or intellectuals. This is the natural out-growth of its strategy of presence and of alliances.[16]

By the 1970s it was apparent that the party was making

gains especially among younger age groups. Figure 2 shows the results of a 1975 survey that tends to support Giacomo Sani's description of the PCI as a catch-almost-all party.

A large part of the PCI gain in the 1976 parliamentary election came from young first-time voters, the voting age for electing deputies having been lowered to eighteen.[17] Table 4 shows the relative support for the PCI by age group.

The growing attractiveness of the PCI to the voters is the result of their altered perception of the attributes of the party. In the 1950s and 1960s popular suspicion of the party was based on one or more of the following beliefs:

a) it is the enemy of religion;

b) it is not committed to the rules of representative democracy, no matter what it says about the democratic way to socialism;

c) it is the agent of a foreign power (the USSR);

d) it is ready to use violence to gain its ends;

e) its internal cohesion and discipline (democratic centralism) is dangerous to the country;

f) it is the enemy of private property.[18]

In the late 1960s and early 1970s these negative perceptions began to recede. A sample survey taken in 1973 showed that 55 percent of the respondents thought Catholicism and communism were compatible. More than half of the non-Communist respondents no longer considered the party to be undemocratic. In a Doxa poll published on September 1, 1976, 75 percent of the sample no longer considered the PCI a serious danger to freedom, although 45 percent of the non-Communist respondents still harbored some reservations.[19] That same poll also indicated the positive virtues attributed to the party.

TABLE 3

Increase in the Electoral Strength
of the PCI by Region, 1946-76

Region	Difference between PCI's percent of vote in 1946 and in 1976	Rate of increase (in percent)
Northwest		
Piedmont	+ 14.6	70.2
Liguria	+ 10.7	37.7
Lombardy	+ 11.5	57.2
Northeast		
Trentino-Alto Adige	+ 5.1	63.0
Veneto	+ 10.1	73.7
Friuli-Venezia-Giulia	+ 13.4	101.5
Central		
Emilia-Romagna	+ 11.0	29.3
Marche	+ 18.1	83.0
Tuscany	+ 13.9	41.4
Umbria	+ 19.3	68.9
South		
Lazio	+ 21.8	154.6
Campania	+ 24.9	336.5
Abruzzi-Molise *	+ 23.0	227.7
Puglia	+ 17.0	115.6
Basilicata	+ 20.3	156.0
Calabria	+ 20.8	170.5
Sicily	+ 19.6	248.1
Sardinia	+ 23.1	184.8

* While Abruzzi and Molise formed separate regions in 1976, they constituted a single region in 1946. Therefore, they are treated as one region for purposes of this particular analysis.

Sources: Calculated by the author on the basis of data in Giorgio Galli, Ed., *Il comportamento elettorale in Italia* (Electoral Behavior in Italy), Bologna, Il Mulino, 1968, p. 334, and in official reports of the results of the June 1976 election, published, *inter alia,* in *Rinascita* (Rome), July 2, 1976, p. 8.

By permission from Giacomo Sani, "The PCI at the Threshhold," *Problems of Communism,* November-December 1976, p. 30.

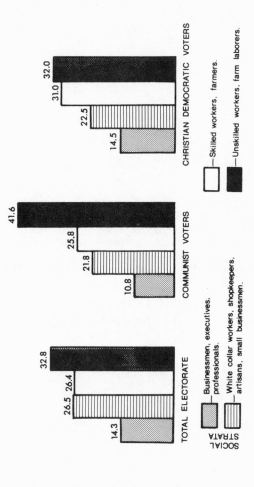

FIGURE 2

Social Composition of the Italian Electorate, 1975 (in percent)

Source: The three profiles were prepared on the basis of 1975 survey data made available to the author by Giovanni Sartori and Alberto Marradi. Respondents were assigned to social strata by the author on the basis of their occupation or that of the head of the household.

By permission from Giacomo Sani, "The PCI at the Threshold," *Problems of Communism,* November-December 1976, p. 31.

TABLE 4

Support for the PCI in Different Age Groups, 1975 [a]

Age in 1975	Percentage Favoring the PCI	Number of Cases
65 and over	17.4	132
55-64	23.6	178
45-54	25.6	281
35-44	27.5	258
25-34	41.1	265
20-24	43.5	407
18-19	47.5	181
16-17	52.0	150
All age groups	35.5	1852

a. Data from the Sartori-Marradi study (1975).

Source: Giacomo Sani, "Mass Support for Italian Communism: Trends and Prospects," paper presented at the conference on "Italy and Eurocommunism, Western Europe at the Crossroads?" June 7-9, 1977, p. 21 (mimeographed).

With a large number of respondents giving "no answer," the following scores were registered by non-Communists:

Communists	Percent
a) are honest	45
b) have many good ideas	60
c) are "simpatici"	34
d) are against violence	43
e) are competent	65

The altered perceptions of the PCI by the mass public are the product of changing characteristics of Italian society, the changing behavior of the mass media of communication, and

[82]

the changing policies of political elites, as well as the changes in the party itself. Since World War II, Italy has gone through a second industrial revolution. Between 1950 and 1970 it had one of the highest rates of economic growth in the Western world. As a result, what was largely a rural, agricultural society in 1945 is an urban, industrialized, services society today. Only 15 percent of the labor force was left in agriculture, forestry, and fishing by 1976. There have been vast movements of people, from the countryside to the city and town, from the south to the north, and from Italy to jobs in other European countries or overseas. There has been a growing secularization of society, with a decline in the political authority of the Church.

Since the late 1960s the mass media give the PCI much more coverage. The Christian Democrats no longer have exclusive control over the state radio and television networks, as many independent television stations were legalized after 1973. The press gives extensive coverage to the declarations of PCI leaders and interviews prominent Communists frequently. *L'Unità*, the Communist daily paper, has the third-largest circulation in the country on weekdays and the largest on Sunday.

The political culture of the country has changed. In the last fifteen years most intellectuals have been attracted to leftist causes. Leftist sympathies are apparent in the independent (non-party or non-Church) press and in the editorials in leading magazines. In the civil and military bureaucracies and in the professions, groups and factions with leftist sympathies no longer hide their viewpoints. In the secondary schools and universities leftist teachers are in a large majority, and their student bodies have predominantly leftist leanings. This climate of opinion can be exploited by a number of leftist parties, but the PCI has undoubtedly been the main beneficiary.[20]

[83]

Furthermore, non-Communist elites have been in constant contact with PCI leaders for over a decade, and this contact has become apparent to larger segments of the population. After the 1976 election, parliament was organized in public, collective negotiations by all the "constitutional parties," including the Communist; only the neo-fascists, radicals, and proletarian democrats were excluded. The PCI received the presidency of the Chamber of Deputies, four committee chairmanships in the Chamber, and four in the Senate. In these circumstances it is not surprising that the mass suspicion of the party has declined, that the party can hardly be viewed as anti-system. Nevertheless, hostility to the PCI remains in various segments of the electorate, particularly among many rank-and-file Christian Democrats.[21]

COMMUNISTS AND SOCIALISTS

In 1977 the PCI had four times as many supporters as the PSI (Table 2). In 1946, by contrast, the two parties had been approximately equal in electoral backing, the PSI being slightly larger (Figure 1). This drastic reversal of fortunes was as much the result of Socialist deficiencies as of Communist capabilities. The two parties, it must be remembered, had signed the Unity of Action Pact in 1934. Broken in 1939 as a result of the Nazi-Soviet Non-aggression Treaty, the pact was renewed in 1941 after the German attack on Russia. At the end of the war the Socialist leader Pietro Nenni persisted in supporting the agreement. In his view the success of fascism and Nazism in Italy and Germany were the result of division in the working class: "When Socialists fight Communists, reaction triumphs." [22] Differences of opinion on this subject led to the first schism within the Socialist party when in

January 1947 Giuseppe Saragat took an anti-Communist minority out of the party to form what came to be called the Italian Social Democratic Party.

In April 1948 the PCI and PSI presented a combined slate in the parliamentary election. In the superheated apocalyptic atmosphere of "Christ vs. anti-Christ, Rome vs. Moscow," fed by the Czech coup d'état of February 1948, the Christian Democrats won their greatest election victory of the postwar period. Many more Communist than Socialist deputies were elected on the combined slate, indicating the effects of the Social Democratic withdrawal the previous year and the greater discipline of the Communist voters. When the Italian General Confederation of Labor split in 1949, the Socialist trade unionists remained with their Communist fellow workers rather than follow Christian Democratic, Social Democratic, and Republican workers into the new competing labor confederations.

In foreign policy, Socialists agreed with Communists to oppose Italian membership in NATO, Western European Union, and the European Coal and Steel Community. In 1952 Pietro Nenni received the Stalin Peace Prize (which he returned after 1956).

The two parties ran separate slates in the 1953 parliamentary election, and the PCI margin over the PSI grew, as indicated in Figure 1. After the election the Socialists began to develop a more individual stance. By 1955, Socialist leaders were indicating that their opposition to NATO was declining. In 1956 the strains between the two left parties were exacerbated sharply. Publication of Khrushchev's speech of February 1956 on Stalin's crimes and the invasion of Hungary in October led to open PSI condemnation of Soviet communism, and the Italian Communists lamely defended Russian behavior. Nenni asserted that democracy was as important as socialism;

true socialism could be only democratic. By 1957 the Unity of Action Pact was effectively dead. That fall the Socialist parliamentarians voted for ratification of the treaties establishing the European Investment Bank and Euratom, and abstained on the European Economic Community. The PCI parliamentarians voted against all three, but with hesitation. Under the influence of their Socialist collaborators, the CGIL trade union Communists were becoming interested in the possibilities which the European market opened to Italian labor. Party discipline and loyalty to Moscow's opposition to a European Community prevailed, this time at least.

After 1956 the prospect opened for Socialist participation in Christian Democratic cabinets and for reunification of the two Socialist parties. A number of years were to elapse before either of the two objectives would be gained, with the Communists doing everything they could to prevent their realization. By the early 1960s Socialists were entering coalitions with Christian Democrats at the local level. In 1962 the PSI started to vote for national Christian Democratic governments, and in December 1963, Socialists entered the cabinet. The next month a group of left-wing Socialists broke away from the PSI to form the Italian Socialist Party of Proletarian Unity (PSIUP). Except for this small splinter party, the Communists were effectively isolated at the national level.

The center-left coalitions, based on combinations of Christian Democratic, Socialist, Social Democratic, and Republican parties, lasted off and on from 1963 to 1975. The coalitions' lives were troubled by disagreements over policy and patronage, personal ambitions and rivalries of leaders, and electoral disappointments. The expectation that electoral support would be attracted away from the PCI was contradicted by the continued slow growth of the Communists (Figure 1). The reforms that were to justify the existence of the coalitions

[86]

came hard and infrequently. In 1966 the PSI and PSDI reunited, but two years later in the 1968 parliamentary election revealed that the two parties together fared worse than when they ran separately. They split once more in 1969. By the early 1970s the Socialists were pronouncing the center-left experiment a failure. Their problem was to find an alternative.

The PCI persisted in its strategy of alliances in spite of rebuffs. During the center-left period, local governments controlled by coalitions of the left parties declined in number but never disappeared. After 1970 their numbers increased as Socialists switched alliances away from Christian Democrats back to Communists. Figure 3 summarizes this history for provincial governments; a parallel record exists for municipalities.

When regular regional governments were established in 1970, the Communists emerged as the largest party in three regions, Emilia-Romagna, Tuscany, and Umbria. The PSI accepted the PCI invitation to join in the formation of governments for these regions. After the 1975 regional elections the regions of Liguria, Piedmont, and Lazio were added to Communist-Socialist control. By 1976 almost all the major cities from Naples northward were under left-wing administration, and in many of them Social Democrats and Republicans were joining the coalitions. As of June 1977, no Christian Democratic local party organization had accepted Communist invitations to participate in a local left-wing government, but a Christian Democrat had agreed to serve as speaker of the regional council of Emilia-Romagna.

In pursuing its alliance strategy the PCI has been very generous to the Socialists. The latter have received more positions, and more important positions, than their numerical strength warrants. Socialist mayors, provincial presidents, and even regional presidents hold office, even though the PCI polls

FIGURE 3

Leftist Vote and Control of Italian Provincial Governments, 1951-75

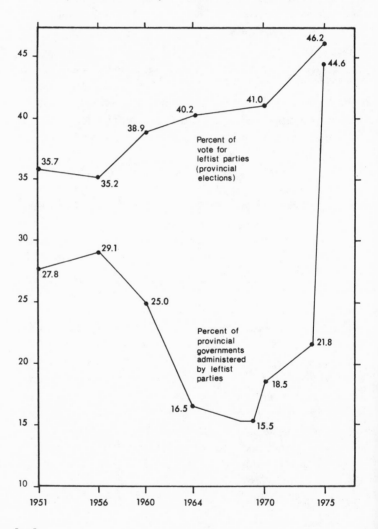

many more votes than the PSI. In Tuscany, for example, the president of the region is a Socialist although the Communist vote is three times that of the PSI. Communists follow the same policy in the trade unions, cooperative leagues, cultural groups, and other nongovernmental organizations.

After 1972 the Socialists were insisting that the problems at the national level were so serious that Communist participation in government was essential to any kind of solution. By 1975 many PSI leaders were calling for a "left alternative" to replace Christian Democratic rule. Neither their poor election return of 1976 (9.6 percent of the vote) nor PCI policy gave the Socialists much room for hope.

In the postwar period Italian socialism has not provided an effective attraction for the voters. Government policies have been partly influenced by the PSI presence in various coalitions. It is in their long and difficult relationship with the Communists, however, that Socialists have made their greatest impact, for the evolution of Communist ideas and programs has reflected the Socialist presence.

Notes to Figure 3:
* Leftist is defined to include the PCI, PSI, PSIUP, and other minor left-wing parties.
Years noted are those during which nationwide provincial elections were held. Control of governments can change between elections, however, because (a) some provinces hold their elections in other years or (b) the provincial coalition may fall.

Source: Martha H. Good, "The Italian Communist Party (PCI) and Local Government Coalitions: From the Center-Left to the Historic Compromise," paper presented at the Annual Meeting of the Midwest Political Science Association, April, 1977 (mimeographed).

THE EVOLUTION OF COMMUNIST DOCTRINE: POLITICS, RELIGION, ECONOMICS

The years between 1947 and 1956 were extremely uncomfortable for the PCI. The events in Eastern Europe in 1956 caused even more discomfort: Khrushchev's secret speech on the crimes of the Stalin era, the Hungarian revolution in the fall, and the reaction of Socialists and Communist intellectuals opened the road to a more serious and critical rethinking of the relationship between socialism and democracy. Italian communism from its very origins has been led or influenced by intellectuals, inside or outside the party apparatus. Amadeo Bordiga, Antonio Gramsci, Palmiro Togliatti, Enrico Berlinguer, to list party secretaries general, fit this category. Luigi Longo is the only secretary general who can be called a worker in origin, and even he entered the apparatus in his youth to spend most of his life in the party organization, not in a factory. These people have the training and disposition to interpret Marx and Lenin for themselves, rather than to rely on Moscow's fiat.[23] They came from a tradition that reflected the humanism of the Italian heritage and the liberalism of Benedetto Croce, who dominated Italian culture in the first half of this century. Gramsci emphasized the crucial role of the educated man and the creative intellectual and rejected a crude determinism. Togliatti, even while a high functionary of the Comintern apparatus in the 1930s, could argue, in the words of Fritz Fisher:

It is necessary for each of us to establish continually the balance between the intellectual and the man of action, within the individual who gives to his thought perspectives for the future; in this way only can we educate the party in its totality to reach an analogous equilibrium. If the Communist intellectual neglects this duty, soon the party will be led only by organizers, by manipulators, and tacticians.

Fisher concludes: "His antipathy was directed to those functionaries who considered Marxism a closed system, a catechism in which all the basic problems had already received their definitive answers." [24]

A large part of the organizers and professionals who run the party comes from the middle classes. Among the PCI parliamentarians, individuals from middle-class backgrounds outnumber former workers three to one.[25] It is not surprising, therefore, that Khrushchev's revelations would open the door to a ferment that would carry the party far beyond its previous positions. The assertion emerged that the Italian road to socialism was the democratic road to socialism, and its implications would have to be worked out in subsequent struggles and debates over many years. Bringing a mass party around to accepting these implications would be even more difficult and is far from complete. But for practical working politicians the order of priorities is, first, domestic politics and, second, foreign policies. For Marxist and Italian intellectuals as well as for practical politicians, sooner or later theory has to be brought into a working relationship with practice by the party leadership.

The evolution of the PCI's doctrines was gradual but persistent. The economic boom of the late 1950s led Giorgio Amendola, a leading member of the party's Executive Board or *direzione*, to call for "creative research . . . on the economic development of the capitalist world."[26] Agostino Novella, president of the CGIL, at the 1961 Congress of the World

[91]

Federation of Trade Unions (WFTU) urged the separation of the trade union movement from political party control, even though the two should remain friends.[27] By 1962 Togliatti was wondering publicly if the traditional class struggle made sense in the advanced countries of the West.[28]

Already in 1961 the Communists were openly asserting that if they came to power they would retain parliament and the multiparty system, although they hedged by limiting the parties to those that had accepted the goal of a socialist society.[29]. They called for a probing historical analysis of the Stalinist corruption of socialist democracy, and raised questions about abandoning democratic centralism and using majority and minority votes.[30]

In an editorial written for *Rinascita,* dated August 25, 1962, Togliatti endorsed reformism. He proclaimed that the party accepted the method of gradual reforms, on a democratic basis, but with the goal of achieving a truly socialist society. His differences with the Social Democratic parties of Western Europe, he asserted, were not over the method of reform but over their abandonment of socialism as the final goal.

The ferment stirred up in the Catholic world by Pope John XXIII and Vatican Council II stimulated renewed Communist efforts to understand and narrow the differences with the Catholic community. At the 10th Congress of the PCI in 1964, Togliatti recognized that "not only can the aspiration for a socialist society gain ground in men who have a religious faith, but also ... this aspiration can find a stimulus in a religious conscience facing the dramatic problems of the contemporary world." [31] In his final political act, the memorial he wrote to Khrushchev just before his death at Yalta in August 1964, he called on international communism to pay attention to the forces of religion and to the Church, and to recognize their concern for and potential contribution to the cause of the working class.[32]

Luigi Longo succeeded Togliatti, and under his leadership the trends already set in motion continued. At the 11th Party Congress in 1966 he stated, "Just as we are against the confessional state, so are we against state atheism. And is it not possible, is it not necessary to seek together points of agreement and of collaboration so that we may succeed in building together a new society?" [33] Gradually the exclusion of nonsocialist political parties from competing in a socialist society was dropped. By the end of the 1960s the following propositions were the accepted principles, as set down by the authoritative leaders and party organs.

The line on which the PCI moves is that of the Italian way to socialism, which has for its objective—as has been indicated in the last four congresses of the party—the construction of a socialist democracy which will put an end to the exploitation of labor, effectively guarantee the social equality of all citizens, in the fullness of their democratic rights, and create conditions of the free development of their personality outside of any constriction resulting from poverty, exploitation, tyranny or the political and social domination of exploiting classes. . . . The objective of the Italian Communists is to arrive at socialism with the union of all working and democratic forces, secular and Catholic, with a plurality of contributions that parties, organizations, political and social forces can bring to the conquest as well as management of the socialist state.[34]

The Socialist Italy for which we struggle must be a free, independent and sovereign country, without foreign mortgages and conditioning, a country in which political choices will be determined always and only by the will and in the interests of the workers and the people, and

[93]

this—and only this—will be the fundamental rule which will guide the construction and administration of the new society. This is our strategic choice. Reaffirming it and deepening it, we create not only links but unitary relations to advance on this road, with the goal of a socialist society rich in democratic articulations, based on a popular consensus, on the direct and active participation of the masses, on the laic, non-ideological character of the state. An objective, that is, of a socialist society, decentralized, non-bureaucratic, in which religious liberty, the freedom of culture, of science and of art, the freedom of information, of expression and circulation of ideas, will make socialism in Italy; with the presence of a plurality of parties and social organizations committed to a free and democratic dialectic of differing positions, something qualitatively different from the experiences hitherto known and fully corresponding to the traditions and the will of our people.[35]

This summation of what we can consider the conquests and legacy of the "bourgeois" democratic revolutions is now accepted as the patrimony of a Marxist party. In affirming the non-ideological character of the state, there is an implicit rejection of the doctrine that the state is an instrument of a ruling class. Rather, it must protect the rights of all competing interests and classes, even if the goal of the competition is to eliminate "exploiting" classes. The Communists assert that the "hegemony of the proletariat," which will be discussed later, is not to be imposed by the state.

But who comprise the exploiting classes? Here politics merges into economics. It would be easy for an orthodox Marxist to identify exploiters as all those who derive income from property rather than from their labor, or from the efforts of their brains rather than their hands. Such definitions would immediately cast most of the Italian population into the ranks of the enemy. For a party committed to a mass strategy, required to compete in free elections, straining for alliances and presence in all areas of Italian society, the object is to minimize, not enlarge, the ranks of the enemy. Early in the postwar period Togliatti excluded small owners, self-employed artisans, white-collar and professional people, small and then middle-size industries and their owners and managers from the ranks of the class enemy. In subsequent years the enemy would be limited to the large, private monopolists. Since a substantial and increasing share of large firms in Italy were publicly owned or controlled, this left very few enemies indeed.

In recent years opposition in principle to the remaining large private firms and even to foreign multinationals has disappeared. It has been replaced with the proposition that they are neither good nor bad, *per se*. It is what they do or do not do that counts. If they produce in the public interest, as defined by the public authorities, there is nothing to criticize. As the Italian Communists became committed to democratic programming instead of command planning, they and especially their economic experts could foresee the positive role that private capital, native and foreign, could play.[36]

In a new study of the role of multinationals, several important conclusions were reached by the authors:

> Without exception, Communist leaders say that their proposed policies, and their conception of economic planning, do not exclude a role for foreign direct investment. Indeed, they note that it would not be possible for Italy to push ahead for long with further industrial development

were the sources of such investment to dry up, or even markedly diminish.[37]

They quote one Communist leader on the limits that private firms must respect:

> "We cannot permit firms to do exactly as they like; to make foreign exchange deals as they may desire; or basically to go their own way without any interference from state authority. The state must have a policy. Economic development requires that investments and other basic processes come under greater supervision and control than has been the case so far." [38]

Recently some of these controls have been spelled out. Lucio Libertini, a member of the PCI Central Committee, writes:

> We don't believe that the multinationals are an invention of the devil. On the contrary, they are an essential structure of capitalism, and in the current phase of development they express at the same time an objective tendency to the unification of the world market, which in itself is neither capitalist nor socialist.
>
> On the basis of this judgment we have no thought of eliminating the multinationals from our country alone. And even less do we want to discourage foreign investments. A policy of autarchy and isolationism would truly be crazy. We want to negotiate realistically with the multinationals about their presence in the Italian economy; which means to give and receive effective and certain guarantees. The following problem is very important: we can no longer permit the multinationals, particularly in certain sectors, to sell in our country a product fabricated essentially outside of Italy.

I would like to cite, in this regard, the example of the electronics and information industries, a decisive sector for the development of the world economy. In this sector it is useful for Italy to pass a law which would oblige the large companies to produce in our country a given percentage of the goods they want to sell in our market. I remind you that similar laws now exist in the United States, Sweden, and Japan.[39]

These judgments have been reinforced by the Communists' growing disillusionment with the real alternatives operating in the world around them. First, the increasing inadequacies of the public sector in Italy, its inefficiencies, its redundancies, and its political clientelism destroyed any great enthusiasm for further public takeovers or nationalizations. Second, the failures of Soviet planning, the bureaucratic rigidities, the waste, the distortions of resource misallocation cooled the appeal of a command economy. In their judgment the Soviet system did not work; it not only would not work in Italy but did not work in Russia. In an interview with James Reston, Sergio Segre, head of the International Affairs Committee of the PCI's Central Committee, remarked, ". . . Nobody in the West believed any longer in 'the Soviet model' as an answer to the West's problems." [40] His colleague Lucio Libertini writes:

A new economic policy does not require new nationalizations. The extension of public property in Italy is very large, certainly much larger than in the other European countries. The real problem is its reorganization, and its concrete management for a policy of balanced development and full employment.

We believe that experience has demonstrated both the failure of total planning, which degenerates into bureaucratic paralysis, and the inexistence of a perfect, competitive market, which can maintain equilibrium and utilize resources in an optimal way.... Therefore democratic planning is necessary, which could define and guarantee space for entrepreneurial initiative. We know that the prospect of an effective democratic programming is a new frontier, not yet explored. But it is the facts that launch us on this historic challenge.[41]

While accepting a mixed economy with a continuing substantial private sector, especially at the level of small and medium-size enterprises, Communists have to avoid being called traitors to socialism or being charged with having abandoned the quest for social justice for the masses. The outcome of these conflicting motivations has been the slow and careful elaboration of a new goal, "socialization of the rewards, not socialization of property." These are the words of Luciano Barca, the principal economic theorist of the PCI and a member of its *direzione*.[42] What socialization of the rewards means has still to be spelled out. It does not mean expropriation of profits. It could mean replacing the present regressive tax structure with a more progressive tax system, employee participation in shareholding, increasing the proportion of gross national product going to wages, the extension of the cooperative movement, or trade union participation in shareholding.

Redefining socialist goals is the work of theoreticians, but the Communist leaders today must concentrate on current economic and political crises. So they say that they do not know what the future socialist society will really be like; all they do know is that all historic and current models are inadequate. Marxism is not a dogma frozen in the past; there is still time and room for creative Marxists to think out new solutions to problems that historical Marxism could not have anticipated. Socialism is a process, not a utopian end-point after which all change ceases; as a process it requires creative rethinking to meet new conditions, not a tired repetition of past slogans. In Libertini's words, "We are not interested in orthodoxy in respect to the classics of Marxism. Marxism is critical thought, which evolves with reality; it is not a dogma. We will never engage, therefore, in a war of citations with anyone, we will not dispute over this or that phrase of Marx." [43] In line with these ideas Communist leaders tend to call their party a party of Marxist formation rather than a Marxist party—a change which has also opened up member-ship to individuals who do not wish to be considered Marxists.

Economic Doctrine in Action

The rethinking on the nature of the state and of political processes, as illustrated above, has ended up in the assertion of the indissoluble link between democracy and socialism, al-though not necessarily its observance in practice. The rethink-ing on the nature and problems of the economy has led to the decline of traditional Marxist modes of economic analysis. They have been replaced by the use of contemporary post-Keynesian methods of analysis—by what is called, in the United States, the "new economics." Italian Communists writing about the current economic crisis have made this conversion apparent in the way they appraise the issues and discuss the several kinds of solutions and their feasibility, and in the way they write about controlling inflation, relieving unemployment, resolving balance-of-payments difficulties, managing the public debt.[44] Although no longer believing that solutions to these problems can be found in Marx, they are neither committed neo-Keynesians nor monetarists, nor adherents of any academic theory. In effect, they are eclectic learners and borrowers from any source. In broadening the basis of their analysis, however, they have, until recently, shied away from endorsing one of the major panaceas of the European Left, co-determination. The opposition to co-determination is grounded in the disinterest of the Italian trade union confederations, and in the reluctance to share responsibility for and to defend decisions made mainly by management. In another sense, there is the historic experience of the workers' councils immediately after World War II that often demonstrated that workers in a given plant or firm could be as selfish and indifferent to the welfare of other workers in other firms as were the bosses. Marxist ideology may idealize the noble proletarian; Italian skepticism has its doubts.

The PCI has substantial, though fluctuating, influence in the trade union movement. After the schism of 1949 this influence was limited directly to the CGIL, which remained the largest of the three labor confederations. The other confederations were influenced indirectly by the necessity of adapting their strategies to the moves and positions of the CGIL. During the 1950s and early 1960s the relations of the confederations alternated between rivalry and occasional collaboration: rivalry at the political and confederation level, collaboration at the plant or industry level on bread-and-butter issues. The affiliation of the confederations to the political parties and the dependence of the non-Communist ones on American financial support both served to exacerbate tensions.

After 1965 CISL was moving toward autonomy from the Christian Democratic party, instructing its officers to choose between holding office in the union or office in the government or in the party. The final break came in 1969. UIL adopted the same policy. These moves were directed toward the reunification of the labor movement, which necessitated breaking party control. Inside the CGIL the Socialist trade unionists had clearly expressed their desire for greater autonomy, especially during the period of reunification between the PSI and PSDI. The consequence was that the CGIL congress of 1969 voted also to make union and party office-holding incompatible for the same individuals.

The stage was set for labor reunification. It appeared probable in 1972 but did not materialize. Instead, a federation of the three confederations was constructed, committed to the autonomous development of trade union policies on traditional labor goals but also to the affirmation of a labor position on the broader political, economic, and social issues of the day.[45]

Party influence on labor has not disappeared just because the formal links have been cut. But none of the parties, including the PCI, has been able to dictate the policies of unions in recent years. The aggravation of the economic crisis in the 1970s—especially the high rate of inflation caused in part by very large wage increases—has induced the Communist leadership to try to regain influence over trade union policy. In the fall of 1976 and spring of 1977 the PCI was engaged in a major effort to bring the trade union federation into line, and Berlinguer was preaching austerity to all the Italian people.

Communist political and economic leaders have to approach Italy's economic crisis from a position of weakness. The levers of command are not in their hands. Control of the private and the very large public sectors is in the hands of either private entrepreneurs, few of whom are Communists, or Christian Democratic politicians. In the postwar period the Italian economy has become increasingly dependent on foreign trade, and the rate of increase has accelerated in the 1970s. By 1976 it was close to 35 percent of GNP. Italy has always been deficient in key raw materials and in important foodstuffs, and growing prosperity aggravated the deficiencies by increasing

[101]

the demand. Since 1969 and 1970 the terms of trade have turned against Italy and other exporters of finished goods. Foreign debt grew; by 1977 Italy owed $18 billion to foreign lenders. To pay for imports and to service the debt, Italy has to export more than ever in a situation where its competitors are fighting for the same markets. So the lira is devalued to sustain exports, but this aggravates inflation at home.

Communist economists know very well that if Italian producers are not efficient and competitive there will be no wealth to distribute in Italy. They know that if the Italian economy is not attractive to investors, domestic or foreign, no new jobs will be created. Increasing government investment has not had much effect in raising the efficiency of production; in fact, it has substantially heightened the rate of inflation by expanding the money supply. Subsidizing existing unprofitable public and private firms, covering the growing deficits of regional, provincial and local governments, and of nationalized state and semi-state agencies further add to the public debt, which is met by borrowing from government-controlled banks and by printing money. More inflation. Public employees and the organized workers in large firms are protected by indexing. The automatic wage increments, readjusted on a quarterly basis, push wages up. Still more inflation.

The rise in worldwide prices of raw materials, especially petroleum and foodstuffs, the wage increases obtained by organized labor coupled with indexing, and the large government budgetary deficits (from 13 to 15 percent of GNP in 1976) financed in substantial part by printing money are the three major causes of Italy's current economic malaise. No Italian government, of whatever coloration, can do much about the first these causes. To bring wages under control requires the cooperation of Communists because they still have more influence with the trade unions than anyone else. To cut the

public debt by reducing public spending requires the cooperation of the Communists because of their role in many of the
local governments and because of their involvement in the
demands for substantial, justifiable, but very expensive reforms. Communists are telling the workers they have to work
harder but earn less (in real terms). They are telling the
unions that their demands for the reform of health and sanita-
tion, education, public housing, and public services in general
have to be cut back because they are very expensive. They are
insisting that workers can be laid off only when there are other
jobs to go to.

Political wisdom says that in a competitive political situation, Communists, like Christian Democrats, find it hard to
impose sacrifices on unwilling people. Together they may risk
it so that neither can gain advantage at the expense of the
other. In October 1976, they jointly imposed a limited austerity program on the country, but without facing the hard
choices. The Communists do not want to be accused of
sacrificing the interests of the worker. The PCI endorses
austerity only if all sectors of society, all income groups, are
required to make sacrifices. But no Italian government, even
with indirect Communist support, has the power, the efficient
bureaucracy, or the receptive population to enforce generalized sacrifices. The Communist leadership may recognize that
the only solution that is more than temporary is to institute an
effective incomes policy. In Italy, however, an incomes policy
means wage freezes, while speculators, manipulators, opera-
tors, self-employed professionals take care of themselves. Even
under another name an incomes policy will be difficult to
enforce, but only through the cooperation of Christian Democrats and Communists is it remotely possible.

For years the Communists have claimed they are a responsible party, a party of government. They eschewed wild pro-

posals in parliament that would produce a cheap propaganda gain even when certain that there was no chance of their passage. As an opposition party they claimed that their input into legislation on the floor of parliament and within the committees was intended to improve it, not sabotage it. At the local level they have tried to provide a model of efficient, honest administration that has made an impression on the public. In recent years even these local Communist governments have started to go bankrupt as they have expanded municipal services and subsidized unprofitable transportation systems. Now, maintaining this posture of responsibility requires political sacrifices that will test their claims. Competing parties, especially the Christian Democrats, have been generous to all claimants for a share at the public trough. It remains to be seen whether the Communists can say no in these circumstances, especially when they do not bear primary responsibility.

FOREIGN POLICIES: IDEOLOGY AND NATIONAL INTEREST

During the early postwar period, the PCI supported the foreign policies of the Soviet Union, resisting only on those issues that had direct negative effects on internal developments and the party's domestic operations, For example, the PCI stood up for the *Italianità* of Trieste at the time when Soviet Russia was backing the most extreme Yugoslav territorial claims against Italy in that border area. In 1947 Togliatti wanted to support Italy's acceptance of the Marshall Plan aid proffered by the United States but succumbed to Soviet demands for out-and-out opposition to the plan. These were the years when alignment with Soviet foreign policy directives produced negative political results at home. The Communist opposition to the Marshall Plan led to the splitting of the CGIL, the elimination of Communists from jobs in the public service, the Papal excommunication of 1949. In the early 1950s the PCI opposed the first hesitant steps toward European integration, the European Coal and Steel Community and the European Defense Community. It led the attack on Italy's membership in NATO.[46] The Italian Communists were in a very uncomfortable position in those years, but their sense of loyalty to and identification with the Soviet camp led them to suppress their unease.

Still, this opposition was tempered by a realistic sense that the NATO commitment represented a strong and necessary support to the Italian government, which it was foolish to deny. On July 4, 1953, four months after Stalin's death, Togliatti called on De Gasperi and informed him:

> In the current parliamentary situation we know we cannot ask you to denounce the Atlantic Pact. We want Italy to assume the role of an initiator of activity for peace. It should not be just one of fourteen NATO countries but should take a concrete initiative for one step, and then another, to help détente. . . . A gradual disarmament for all of Europe can be faced. Europe, not just the West. Europe doesn't end at the Rhine, or the Elbe, but at the Urals. . . .
> De Gasperi objects: No initiative can be taken outside the Atlantic Pact. You cannot ask us for a rupture.
> Togliatti retorts: Correct. A rupture cannot be the premise of détente.[47]

The Italian-Yugoslav diplomatic settlement of the Trieste dispute in 1954 led to a rapid improvement in relations between the Communist parties of the two countries and endorsement by the PCI of Yugoslav nonalignment. This was not an anti-Soviet move, because after 1955 Khrushchev was engaged in a policy of reconciliation with Tito.

Events in Eastern Europe in 1956 laid the foundations for the assertion of an autonomous Italian way to socialism, which could extend to an independent foreign policy. Expressions of independence in foreign policy, however, were slow in coming. Although Communist trade union leaders in the CGIL were intrigued by the possibilities for Italian labor built into the provisions of the treaty that created the European Economic Community (EEC), party discipline prevailed and in the autumn of 1957 all PCI members of parliament voted against ratification of the Treaty of Rome. The subsequent benefits of the EEC to Italian workers and to the Italian economy could not be ignored, however, and in 1961 at a meeting of the World Federation of Trade Unions, CGIL leaders openly endorsed this instrument of potential European integration. In the same year the PCI proclaimed its approval of the EEC over the opposition of the parties of the Soviet bloc and of the French Communist party.[48] It was the first open deviation from Soviet foreign policy positions and the first step toward association with the "Western" camp. From this time Communists wanted to be included in the Italian parliamentary delegation to the European Parliament at Strasbourg, but only in 1969 did they attend.

The next public expressions of dissension came over the relations of parties within the Communist world. The emergence of the Sino-Soviet schism in the early 1960s, accompanied as it was by the mutual denunciations and castigations of the two powers, put the PCI in an ambivalent position. On the one hand, it was the direct object of attacks from its Chinese comrades over the issue of revisionism. On the other hand, it upheld not only the right of the Chinese to establish and pursue their own policies but also the right of fraternal Communist parties to criticize each other publicly. While deploring exaggerated language on all sides, the PCI firmly opposed Soviet efforts to mobilize the international Communist movement in order to pronounce a collective anathema and excommunicate the Chinese.[49] The long and bitter dispute, however, has demonstrated the extreme difficulty of getting the principle of diversity accepted in the movement, although the principle was asserted by Togliatti as early as 1956. Only with the East Berlin Conference of European Communist Parties in June 1976 might it be said that diversity has been institutionalized.[50] Subsequent Russian back-tracking, the Soviet interpretation of proletarian internationalism, casts doubt on this achievement.

The Soviet invasion of Czechoslovakia in August 1968 was probably the critical turning point in foreign policy for the PCI. It led to an open criticism of the Soviet Union that was not withdrawn despite the protests of many local and section leaders of the party. It led to a rethinking of the international situation in Europe and the larger Western world. For almost twenty years the PCI had opposed NATO and Italy's membership in it with the slogan "Italy out of NATO and NATO out of Italy." Now the alliance was seen to have virtues formerly unperceived. In the usual pattern, the shift in position was neither immediate nor announced to the world. Gradually the old slogan disappeared from circulation. In 1969 the NATO treaty came up for renewal, as provided for in its own terms. Instead of making an issue out of renewal the Communists let the occasion pass, but hardly from neglect or oversight. By 1972 the word was being circulated quietly that the party had no objections to the alliance. In 1973 Berlinguer could say publicly that Italy and Europe had to be equally friendly to both the United States and the Soviet Union.[51] In September 1974 the PCI publicly announced its acceptance of NATO, and the position was reaffirmed at the Party Congress of March, 1975. In a programmatic speech Secretary General Berlinguer expressed his concern about the weakening of the role of the West

> in which we Italians also live, as a people and nation and as Italian Communists. We have said and we repeat that we do not raise the question of withdrawal from the Atlantic Alliance, but we have also said and repeat that while remaining in this Alliance, we can and must work in favor of détente, which necessarily implies not pitting ourselves against either the United States of America or the Soviet Union.[52].

In effect the PCI had reversed its alliances without specifically saying so. At the same time it has linked this reversal to the pursuit of détente, postulating a goal in which military alliances are superseded and become irrelevant. How can this fundamental change be explained? How do the Communists justify the shift?

Probably the most important explanation is the primacy of domestic policy, the achievement of the goal of the PCI's entry into the government of the country.[53] In the geographical and political distribution of forces outside and inside Italy, this goal can be reached only in alliance with other parties that have a stake in the independence and security of the nations of the Western world. Acknowledging this stake as part of the price for achieving their goals, the Communist leaders accept the quid pro quo between foreign and domestic policies.

But this is not the only reason. Berlinguer is not going to announce publicly that he and his colleagues engage in reversals of alliance for crass motives of pure power. There are other factors and they are equally real. The peace of Europe depends on a balance of power between two alliance systems in which the United States and the U.S.S.R. play pivotal roles. For Italy to pull out of one of theses alliances upsets the international equilibrium and threatens the peace. As a responsible party, the PCI does not want to precipitate a war that could devastate Italy and Europe. In addition, the Italian Communists have been engaged in a long struggle to develop an Italian way to socialism. The destruction of "liberal" communism "with a human face" in Czechoslovakia by the Warsaw Pact countries in August 1968, followed by the assertion of the Brezhnev Doctrine, has driven home the lesson that the Italian way to socialism is impossible in a Europe dominated by the Soviet Union. In Berlinguer's words, "I feel safer on this side." [54]

Détente contributes to lessening the dangers of war in a world of military blocs. While the Communists (and the Socialists and Christian Democrats, too) say that the elimination of blocs is the only sure guarantee of peace, they consider this elimination a prospect for the twenty-first rather than the twentieth century. They have no expectations of a withering away of blocs in any foreseeable future. Reiteration of this distant goal makes it easier for the rank and file to swallow the reversal of alliances that is so recent. Meanwhile, détente serves more immediate and realistic ends. Throughout the postwar period the foreign trade policy of Italy, endorsed by all parties, has been to trade with all countries, regardless of ideological or political prejudices.[55] The intensive cold war era hindered and obstructed this policy, although it did not halt it.

An atmosphere of détente permits trade and investments to flow more freely across ideological divisions. The dominant powers in the principal military blocs can be more relaxed over political and economic experiments conducted by the smaller nations inside these blocs, such as an "historic compromise" in Italy. International frictions, such as those tearing apart the nations of the Eastern Mediterranean, can be kept from escalating and spreading. Reducing the risk of war between the two blocs reduces the necessity to choose between them in the event of a serious crisis. It must be appreciated that large numbers of Italian Communists, especially those with many years of activity in the party, have psychological and emotional ties to the Communist world; in a crisis their instincts and feelings would be torn.[56]

The Atlantic Alliance and the European Community have the potentiality for rivalry and antagonism, as well as for cooperation. Italy's policy has been to emphasize the complementarity of these two groupings and to minimize hostilities. It has not hesitated to follow nationalist policies when its interests dictated. It has refused to follow all attempts, such as those instigated by de Gaulle in the 1960s, to set Europe against the United States. While trying to avoid the necessity for choice, when that was no longer possible, Italy chose the Alliance over the Community.[57] The entry of the Communists into the Italian parliamentary delegation to the European Parliament in 1969 saw something of a change of tone, a change that appeared in the speeches of the principal Communist delegate, Giorgio Amendola, who seemed to follow a Gaullist line setting Europe against America. In subsequent years, however, as the gradual shift in favor of accepting NATO developed momentum, the Gaullist line declined. The nationalist tone remained, nurtured mainly by the necessity to assert

[110]

independence from the Soviet Union, secondarily by resentment against continuing American attacks against the party and its domestic ambitions.

The repeated Communist assertions of national independence, for the party and for the government, raise questions about the nature of the commitment to the European Community. There is a contradiction between national assertions and the federalist ideal. The Communists have announced their acceptance of European federal institutions; they strongly support increasing the strength of the European Parliament, and have endorsed direct popular elections to the Parliament, now scheduled to take place in 1979. At the same time they have no expectations that true federalism will be achieved.

The European Community is important economically, symbolically, and politically. Other members of the EC are Italy's most important trading partners. The organization creates rules protecting Italian workers in other EC countries. It provides credits and loans to help tide over balance-of-payments deficits. Though the money may come from West Germany and the United States, it looks better to Italians, including the PCI, to have it processed through the EC. The Communists' presence in the European Parliament helps legitimize their claim to be a Western political party, an integral part of the Western world.[58] At Brussels and Strasbourg they forge links with other political parties, and the CGIL does the same with other Western trade union organizations. After 1979 the Communists would like to create a broad left parliamentary group at Strasbourg, not only with the French Communist party but also with the German Social Democratic party, the British Labour party, and the French Socialist party, for they have assiduously cultivated relations with these parties in recent years. They provided good offices in establishing

[111]

contacts between the German Socialists and East European Communists that contributed to the success of Willy Brandt's *Ostpolitik*. They did all they could in an unsuccessful attempt to persuade the left wing of the British Labour party to support the European Community. The closer their relations with the European socialist movement, the more they neutralize hostility to their domestic advances in Italy; in turn the socialists help guarantee their adherence to the Western camp. At the end of 1977 the PCI announced that it wished to establish an ongoing study and consultative arrangement with the Socialist parties of Northern and Western Europe.

While establishing as close a relationship with the West European socialist and labor movements as they will permit, the PCI continues to participate in the international Communist movement. The schism between the Russians and Chinese opened up more room for maneuver for other parties. It bolstered the assertions of the PCI that the movement can survive only by accepting diversity, which eventually the East Berlin conference of June 1976 institutionalized.

By that time, however, the PCI had assigned highest priority to its relations with other West European Communist and Socialist parties, rather than with the CPSU.[59] The denunciations of the Warsaw Pact invasion of Czechoslovakia provided an initial common ground. Gradually, contacts among the Communist parties of Western Europe increased, and by 1973 regular conferences were being scheduled. Within a few years, it might be argued, a strategic alliance among the Italian, French, and Spanish parties had emerged, marked by the joint Italian-Spanish declaration of July 1975, the Italian-French declaration of November 1975, and the common declaration of all three in Madrid in March 1977. All these declarations affirmed principles reiterating many of the positions of the Italian way to socialism. There has emerged a

[112]

commitment to promote common action among European Communist and Socialist parties.[60]

None of this implies the establishment of a European regional Communist center. Highly national parties, all rejecting the doctrine of a guiding party, are not going to accept subordination to a regional entity or to each other. But they recognize they have common problems and have proclaimed a number of common aspirations. The Italian party moved earlier in this direction, the Spanish party has in certain respects moved farther. Continuing movement appears likely since it is in the interests of these parties to proceed, for it pays off domestically in their long struggle for power. The result is likely to be even more strained relations with the CPSU in the future.[61]

The PCI's acceptance of NATO raises questions as to the limiting terms or conditions of the commitment. How do the Communists define Italy's obligation to the alliance? They no longer ask for the elimination of NATO bases from Italian soil, or the exclusion of NATO submarines and surface vessels from the Mediterranean Sea. For a brief period in the early 1970s they toyed with the idea of neutralizing the Mediterranean, calling for the withdrawal of all navies not of riparian states. As this would have reversed a Soviet naval buildup in progress for over a decade, the Russians naturally rejected the call. In all probability the PCI leaders expected this negative response and could use it to rationalize their acceptance of United States naval vessels in the area. Peace, after all, depends on maintaining the balance.

The Communists have no new military strategies to propose for NATO or for Italy.[62] But they do assert political conditions. The most important is that NATO members must not intervene in the internal affairs of other NATO members, meaning that the United States should stop interfering in

[113]

domestic Italian politics. They also argue that Article 2 of the North Atlantic Treaty calls for the strengthening of free institutions, which means that United States political leaders should not have supported regimes like those of the Greek colonels, Salazar, and Franco.

In addition, Italy's Communists emphasize the geographical limitations of the NATO commitment. It does not apply outside the area of the member countries, which means they are under no obligation to defend, support, or endorse the policies, commitments, and behavior of their allies in Asia, Africa, Latin America, or the Middle East. Thus the Communists can continue to be hostile to United States policies in the Third World. They have expended considerable effort to establish good relations with revolutionary movements, whether Communist or non-Communist, in many countries of the Third World. Italian dependence on OPEC oil has reinforced a tendentiously pro-Arab posture. While saying they recognize the right of Israel to secure and defensible boundaries, the PCI backs political movements, such as the PLO, that deny this right.

Except for the petroleum-producing countries, the direct interest of Italian Communists in the underdeveloped countries is limited. They know they cannot guide revolutionary movements in those countries: not only are their means limited, but they reject the concept of the guiding party. Their ideas of Eurocommunism provide no model for these countries since they define Eurocommunism as the communism of advanced, industrialized societies. Their attitudes and policies toward the Third World are not much different from those of other Italian and European parties. In October 1973, it was a Christian Democratic government in Italy and a Social Democratic government in West Germany that blocked American efforts to use their territory to aid Israel during the Yom Kippur war. Because the PCI's outlook on most Third World issues parallels the Russian viewpoint, this area of foreign policy provides an avenue of retreat to the Soviet camp if the "opening to the West" is a failure. If Berlinguer can reverse alliances once, he or a successor can reverse them a second time. There is nothing in the Italian diplomatic tradition of the twentieth century to prevent it. But non-Communist Italians also have inherited that same tradition. It is to the interest of Italy's allies not to encourage or provoke another reversal.

PRAGMATISM AND IDEALISM: THE DILEMMAS OF THE MODERN PRINCE

It is a long-standing judgment of Italian political historiography that the masses of the Italian people throughout the period of Italian unity have remained "outside the state." The Kingdom of Italy, the outcome of the Risorgimento, was governed by a "liberal oligarchy" with which neither the Catholic faithful nor the peasants and workers could find any meaningful identity. The Vatican opposed the Kingdom and enjoined the eligible faithful from participating in its political processes. Workers and peasants were excluded from its workings, but even after the extension of the suffrage they were not effectively absorbed into the political system.

Not surprisingly, then, culture more than the state and its political structure provided whatever unifying elements existed in Italian society. It is also not surprising that the emerging Catholic and socialist political movements in the twentieth century would share a hostility to the state and its liberal oligarchy, however little else they shared. The social

[115]

base for a revolutionary tradition was clear. Mussolini could negotiate a reconciliation between state and church in the Lateran Accords of 1929, but this would not automatically bring the Catholic masses into a patriotic association with the political order. Nor could he have more than temporary success in evoking a genuine enthusiasm for his regime on the part of peasants or workers.

The resistance movement of World War II and the postwar democratic republic that emerged were supposed to bring the Italian people into the state, to eliminate the distinction between legal Italy and real Italy. The 1948 constitution reflected a mixture of liberal, Catholic, and Marxist principles. The major parties, Christian Democratic, Communist, and Socialist, dominated the political competition, leading either the government or the opposition. These parties claimed to speak for the Italian masses, yet in 1955 a Christian Democratic president of Italy, Giovanni Gronchi, could condemn the political and social order that left large sections of the population estranged, "those working masses and middle classes whom universal suffrage has conducted to the doorstep of the state's edifice without introducing them effectively to where political direction is exercised." [63]

The domination of the Italian state by Christian Democrats for more than thirty years leaves no reason for the beneficiaries of this rule to be hostile to it or to feel left outside. But the attitude of the Catholic masses toward it remained open to speculation. During these same years, however, the Communist leadership has appeared to develop a strong commitment to the political institutions of the republic, if less so to its economic arrangements or social behavior.[64] The party is an accepted member of the "constitutional arch." It is not treated as an anti-system party, whatever lingering uncertainties or

[116]

hostilities may remain among various groups of non-Communists about its intentions. Its leadership participates in the state. Yet the attitude of the Communist masses toward that state also remains open to speculation.

Given the long and deep-seated hostility of the masses toward the state, it is understandable that Italian Communists continue to claim they are revolutionaries. Their critics to the left charge they have abandoned the revolution and betrayed the proletariat. Their critics to the right and in the West assert that their revolutionary goal remains the imposition of a dictatorship of the proletariat and a command economy. Critics in the East claim the Italian road to socialism is all right as long as the PCI is not in power, but not afterwards. In response to these criticisms the PCI leadership denies bad faith, and insists that its commitment to democratic socialism is a strategic choice, not a tactical maneuver to disarm its adversaries politically and psychologically. In the words of a member of the Central Committee, Vincenzo Galetti,

> When we think about a lay state, neither atheistic nor confessional; when we refuse to give privileges to one ideology as against another; when we fight for social, political and state pluralism; when we speak of a democratically programmed mixed economy; when we struggle to establish an open relationship between representative democracy and "direct" democracy at the base—in all this we are already prefiguring our own conception of socialism. . . . It may seem superfluous to set all this down; but it is not, if one thinks of the many times when, in discussing with leading comrades of the Communist Parties of socialist states the Italian situation, the tactics and strategy of the workers and democratic

[117]

> movement in our country, we have often been told that all this is very well at present, in the struggle to win power, but that afterwards ... afterwards nothing. We reject all forms of opportunism because we know that tomorrow we shall have only what we have been able to gain today, through our struggle.[65]

From the perspective of a non-Italian observer, there appears to be little that is typically revolutionary in the preceding statement. But Italy in the relatively recent past has been an ideological and a confessional state, a one-party state, even though the Italians knew better than to take official ideologies, official churches, and an official party too literally. When the Communist leaders respond to the critics on their left, they assert that the goals they seek would achieve a fundamental change in the structure of society and produce new human beings with different value systems. These, they claim, are revolutionary ends, to be reached through the gradual modification of institutional and social structures.[66] The means, in other words, are in the historic reformist tradition of Western socialism.

Increasingly, Communist theoreticians have emphasized the Western and Italian roots of their Marxism. They argue that their vision is linked to the thought of Marx and Engels, Antonio Labriola, and Antonio Gramsci, all products of Western culture and traditions. East European versions of Marxism become more and more alien. Some Italian Communists verge on the repudiation of Leninism. In the words of a leading member of the Executive Bureau of the party, Giorgio Napolitano,

> We are well aware of the fact that today we affirm a conception of the relationship between democracy and

socialism which cannot be identified with that elaborated by Lenin. But we have elaborated our conception without separating ourselves from the method of Lenin and by adhering to historic conditions which have profoundly changed: which were not, in effect, even foreseen by Lenin.[67]

Lucio Lombardo Radice argues that revisionism is the method of Lenin. "We are all revisionists or, if you like, Marxist-Leninists in the sense that we have all adapted, changed or ignored the texts according to the demands of the concrete situations in which we found ourselves." [68] If Lenin could be a revisionist and in turn become subject to revision, so can Gramsci, and Lombardo Radice admits that his party's program is a revision of Gramsci's.

> The modern prince, the myth-prince, cannot be a real person, a concrete individual; it can only be an organism ... This organism is already provided by historical development and it is the political party ... The Modern Prince must and cannot but be the preacher and organizer of intellectual and moral reform, which means creating the basis for a later development of the national collective will towards the realisation of a higher and total form of modern civilisation.[69]

The higher form of modern civilization is now defined as democratic socialism. It is clearly distinguished from the dictatorship of the proletariat, a phrase that gradually disappeared from circulation in the 1950s. It is also distinguished from social democracy, but here the distinction is vague. What it means in the long run is still unknown, by Communists as well as by questioning outsiders. If Lenin did not foresee the profound changes of modern history, neither can they. They admit, at least, that they cannot provide a blueprint for utopia, but predict it will be different from any Communist or Social Democratic systems now extant. They recognize that Social Democratic parties and regimes in Northern and Western Europe have done much for the workers; they have provided welfare and security and redistributed incomes. But their efforts have been directed toward making the neo-capitalist system, whatever that may be, work better, rather than toward changing the structure of the system. Democratic socialism must exercise controls over the direction of investments and the purposes of production without imposing a command economy. It appears to be more in the nature of establishing guidelines that are enforceable and of shifting more production to public goods and less to private goods. The differences from social democracy are subtle indeed.

Protestations of good faith by responsible leaders of important parties have to be taken seriously but do not have to be swallowed whole. Ambiguities and contradictions about the democratic way to socialism persist, and they nourish the skepticism of critics to the right and in the West. Three unresolved issues produce concern: the failure to break openly with the practice of democratic centralism within the party, the continuing references to the "hegemony of the working class," and the absence of an open split, as distinguished from public disagreements and criticism, with the Soviet camp.

While there is a level of public debate and disagreement inside the PCI that is found in few if any other Communist parties, the Leninist injunction against factionalism is still enforced. Different tendencies within sections of the leadership and the rank and file exist and are not particularly hidden, but the degree of discipline is still formidable, especially when compared to the pathological factionalism of the other Italian parties.[70] The negative experience of the others is the standard justification offered for retaining democratic centralism; but the practice did not emerge as a response to developments in the larger party system, being instead an inheritance from the Bolshevik tradition. Romano Ledda, co-director of *Rinascita*, calls it a Jacobin conception of the structure and strategy of his party, and admits that the development of the concept of pluralism implies the revision of democratic centralism.[71] Altiero Spinelli says the Bolsheviks inherited it from the pre-World War I German Social Democrats. In any case, there is no reason to expect that democratic centralism will be abandoned any sooner than that military alliances will be dissolved.

Gramsci created the phrase "hegemony of the working class" as a substitute for the dictatorship of the proletariat. There are probably as many explanations of its meaning as there are individuals to explicate it. It appears to contradict the commitment to democratic socialism and pluralism. For skeptics it is merely a euphemism for the dictatorship of the proletariat. Others less skeptical call it the dictatorship of the proletariat by consensus. It might mean that there are limits to pluralism, that only forces labeled as socialist or progressive would have liberty of action in the future democratic socialist society; it could also mean achieving the ideal of eliminating the social distinction between workers of the brain and workers of the hand, between intellectual and manual labor.

Franco Rodano, the former "Catholic communist," [72] defines hegemony as the opposite of domination. It means giving direction to a society which permits the free expression of various claims by social groups so that the claims are satisfied without coercion.[73] Giorgio Napolitano asserts that hegemony rejects the imposition of power by one group since no one party or group can claim exclusive representation of the working class. Other parties, Socialist and Catholic, as well as non-party groups such as free trade unions, cooperatives, various social organizations, also play a role in expressing the legitimate needs of the working class.[74] Lombardo Radice defines hegemony as constructive leadership in society by the proletariat, not to dictate to society, but to head it.[75] Rodano claims that hegemony means transforming value systems, replacing individualistic, privatist, selfish bourgeois values by the solidarist, altruistic values inherent in working class culture that naturally puts the common good above individual gain.[76] This is another version of the myth of the noble proletarian. It may satisfy a philosopher-theologian, but the practical Communist politicians who have to run things prefer to rely on the bourgeois values of the carrot and the club.

The possible incompatibility of the commitments to both democratic pluralism and hegemony of the working class remains a problem to be resolved in the future. Present threats to democratic processes are very real. The rising tide of terrorism in Italy, both politically and privately motivated, has led the Christian Democratic government to introduce bills that would permit preventive arrest under limited circumstances, wiretapping, police interrogation without the presence of a defense lawyer, administrative closing down of command posts of suspected terrorist groups, and reform of the security forces. Both the PCI and the PSI have been reluctant to approve these bills, but as the level of violence increases their reluctance declines.[77] When the terrorism reached a peak of ferocity in the spring of 1978 with the kidnapping and subsequent execution of Aldo Moro by the Red Brigades, the PCI demanded that the government hold firm. It insisted on no negotiations with the terrorists and demanded more stringent application of police measures. After Moro's death it was ready to endorse further changes in the security laws that might further restrict the civil liberties of extra-parliamentary political groups. For several years the PCI has presented itself as a party of law and order, and its commitments to democratic law and order are now being put to the test.

It is most unlikely that the PCI leaders would initiate an open split with the Soviet camp although they might provoke their own excommunication; but it would be unwillingly. Their strategy has been to avoid sharp and irreversible breaks in both domestic and international operations with their putative allies and presumed enemies. The high value placed on détente in part reflects this preference for a political context that reduces the necessity for making irrevocable choices. Since they do not control the world around them, situations arise in which they cannot equivocate. In 1947 they refused to launch a revolutionary offensive in Italy despite the exhortations of their East European comrades. In the early 1960s they refused to join the Soviet Union in its efforts to outlaw the Chinese comrades, the violent Chinese attacks upon the Italians notwithstanding. They publicly condemned the Warsaw Pact nations for invading Czechoslovakia in 1968. In the following year they quietly began the shift that by 1974 led to the open acceptance of NATO. At the Conference of European Communist Parties in East Berlin in 1976, Berlinguer specifically rejected the Soviet version of proletarian internationalism and insistently reiterated the national independence of each party.[78]

While the Berlin conference may have formally institutionalized diversity in the international Communist movement, it was not long before the Soviet leadership reverted to its traditional interpretation of proletarian internationalism.

[123]

Growing attacks on Eurocommunism by Russian and East European parties in 1977 spared the PCI directly by hitting at the more outspoken, but weaker, Spanish Communist party. The PCI might have to react vigorously to protect its credibility at home and defend a policy that dates back at least twenty years. How far such a reaction may go is speculative and would depend on whether the polemics escalate or recede. It might lead to the revival of Togliatti's polycentrism, which he dropped after raising it in 1956.

The avoidance of irrevocable breaks is to some degree an Italian way of dealing with problems. It is a highly political way, since one never knows when a present enemy may be a future friend. It also reflects the continuing gap between the advanced positions of the leadership and the more traditional attitudes of the rank and file. Many oldtimers in the party, in the base and also in the leadership and apparatus, have a lingering identification with the Soviet Union that cannot be discounted.[79] When *L'Unità* printed a summary report of Berlinguer's interview in the *Corriere della Sera,* in which he gave his two reasons for accepting NATO, it reproduced his statement on the balance of power but omitted his admission that "I feel safer on this side." [80] He was not being censored by his own official party newspaper; he was recognizing that many of the readers of *L'Unità* were not yet ready for such an admission. If it did not appear in the party organ, they might not be aware of it, or in any case it would not be authoritative for them. This withholding of information does not, of course, prepare them for changes of policy, and perpetuates the gap between the leadership and a base still affected by years of pro-Soviet and anti-U.S. propaganda. Recognizing the gap, the leadership subsequently published the complete text of Berlinguer's interview and other statements on foreign policy in an attempt to update the information base of middle- and lower-level party officials. In 1976 and 1977 a considerable effort was made to raise the consciousness of the cadres in the whole area of international affairs.

Very few Italians, even in hostile factions of the Christian Democratic party, charge that the current Communist leadership is dishonest in the pursuit of its present policy of "historic compromise." Some argue that if the Communists were to come to power, the current leadership would be replaced by a hard-line, pro-Soviet group. Where this group is and who composes it is hard to determine. Differences exist between those who emphasize the parliamentary approach and those who argue that it must be supplemented by mobilizing the masses to achieve party goals.[81] Mass mobilization, however, does not mean a direct assault on the system, since no important Communist leader believes that an objective revolutionary situation has existed in Italy since World War II. Nor, in spite of the terrorism, do they believe that Italy is in a revolutionary mood or even in a pre-revolutionary phase.[82]

In fact, the historic compromise is based on an opposite estimate of the situation. There was a real fear, aggravated in the early 1970s by the resurgence of neo-fascism, the rise of political violence based on a strategy of tension, and threats of military coups, of a reactionary overthrow of the parliamentary republic. Large sectors of the Italian population outside the network of Communist-directed organizations, still influenced by the Catholic Church and the Christian Democratic party, are potentially available to support progressive programs but are not likely to be detached from their cultural and political identifications. In the immediate postwar period Togliatti had thought a strong and long-lasting alliance with the Catholic world was possible, a mirage which the year 1947 brought to an end. The PCI then hoped it could detach the Catholic masses from the Christian Democratic party, and this strategy had some, but limited, success. Next an effort was made to separate the left-wing factions of the Christian Democrats from the rest of the party. This also failed.

With the rising threat of reaction in the early 1970s, the effort shifted to achieve an alliance with the whole Christian Democratic party, including its conservative factions, and to obtain an indirect *placet* from the Church. After 1972 the Socialist party was already arguing for bringing the PCI into the governmental majority to strengthen thereby the country's efforts to deal with its economic and political crises. Berlinguer's fear that those non-socialist sectors of society which could be mobilized for progressive policies could also be frightened into attacking and destroying progress is the heart of his argument for the historic compromise. The key to survival and to a future is to reassure the growing middle classes that they need not fear social degradation and therefore react in a hostile and antidemocratic manner. His goal is to avoid the polarization of Italian society and politics, because a responsible party cannot engage in dogmatic sectarian extremism and because in a situation of polarization the Left could only lose. In the fall of 1973 Berlinguer felt that a similar development of middle-class fear and hostility had provided the conditions for the military coup that destroyed the Allende government in Chile. Chilean events reinforced the preoccupation with military threats on the Italian peninsula.[83] By 1976 he proposed a government of national unity incorporating all the constitutional parties, even the small, conservative Liberal party, to isolate the anti-parliamentary extremists. From Berlinguer's point of view even a left-wing majority, unless it were lopsided, would be insufficient to scotch the

[126]

danger of an antidemocratic inversion. For all these reasons, if Italy's difficulties were to be aggravated further by continuing inflation and unemployment, the PCI's preference would be to cool down rather than heat up a crisis of the parliamentary regime. In line with this strategy the PCI rejected Socialist proposals for a left alternative. Although it failed to obtain a government of national unity, it abstained in the parliamentary vote in August 1976, which brought a minority Christian Democratic cabinet to office. This abstention was essential for the survival of the minority cabinet. In July 1977 it joined the other constitutional parties in publicly negotiating new agreements with the government on economic and internal security policies. In January 1978 it made a major effort to obtain a government of national unity in which it would participate. The effort failed, but in March 1978 the Communists became part of the parliamentary majority supporting the minority cabinet. Since major policy-making was being conducted through negotiations among the leaders of the five parties constituting the parliamentary majority, a de facto or shadow government of national unity was in actual operation.

A different outcome is conceivable. Broad alliances of differing and suspicious parties may be unable to reach agreement on the policies required to manage intractable problems. The failure of a weak and overloaded government, supported by or including the PCI, to meet the claims of the people may lead the PCI to conclude that the democratic way to socialism, and indeed the parliamentary republic itself, can no longer work. Since the Communists are the best organized and most highly integrated of the political parties, they might take the gamble of striking for power and, if successful, impose a more orthodox Communist way to socialism. Such a gamble would mean reversing the judgments and strategies of decades. It

[127]

would risk the reaction of the national police and the armed forces, which the Communists do not control as of 1977; and the presence of NATO forces in the area would be a further discouragement to such a gamble. If Soviet power were to return to Yugoslavia and Albania, however, NATO's influence would be diminished and the PCI's perplexities and uncertainties increased. To reduce the temptation, the other parliamentary parties will have to remain vigorous and effective. So will the Socialist parties of Western Europe, with which the PCI has tried to establish close ties, and they might use these ties to protect the Communists from themselves.

Domestic crises, however, present the PCI with its greatest difficulties for the future. There are the difficulties with the trade unions as the party tries to promote austerity. There are the internal party opponents to whom the whole strategy of historic compromise is wrong. There is the extra-parliamentary left, charging betrayal of the revolution and appealing to a restive, embittered youth facing or experiencing unemployment. There is the prospect that the problems of Italy are not amenable to resolution and that the party will be judged a failure. And the emergence of the American human rights campaign threatens the atmosphere of détente within which the PCI has tried to manage its relations with both groupings.

Prophecies of catastrophe, however, discourage constructive thought and action. The evolution of the PCI's "democratic road to socialism" is an indicator of the continuing power of the democratic ideal. The loosening—and, in a real sense, disintegration—of the Soviet camp is an indicator of the continuing power of the national ideal. The Communists insist they are a national, not a nationalist, party and have no nationalist goals on the pattern of earlier twentieth-century integral Italian nationalism. For the time being, the PCI

[128]

continues to pursue both ideals. Although the latter, the national ideal, is more clear and unambiguous, the democratic ideal is harder to pin down and to forecast. In 1964 and 1965 Giorgio Amendola, a key figure in the development of PCI policies, argued that in Italy and Western Europe communism in its traditional sense and social democracy had both failed. What was needed was a new party of the working class "neither Communist nor Social Democratic." At that time he was proposing a merger in Italy with the Socialists and those Social Democrats who might be amenable.[84] The merger never occurred. Instead his own party, without a change of name, has become, or moved to become, the new party he was calling for. Like anything new, it retains elements of its own past as well as the novelties that distinguish its newness. To judge the relative weight of each is a problem for itself as well as for others.

It is to the interest of these others, the non-Communists both domestic and foreign, to encourage the continuation of this long and difficult evolution. The changes which have taken place are the result primarily of the developing internal political, economic, and social conditions of Italy. To a lesser extent they are a product of the balance of forces at the international level. The largest contribution of the others, therefore, will be to re-enforce those conditions and stabilize that equilibrium.

NOTES

1. Kevin Devlin, "Prospects for Communism in Western Europe," in R. V. Burks, ed., *The Future of Communism in Europe* (Detroit: Wayne State University Press, 1968), p. 21.

2.   Paolo Spriano, in an interview with Lanfranco Vaccari, *L'Europeo,* July 16, 1976, p. 14. Spriano is a member of the Central Committee of the PCI and a major historian.

3.   Palmiro Togliatti, "Democrazia e socialismo, autonomia e internazionalismo," interview in *Nuovi Argomenti* in 1956; reprinted by the PCI as an addendum to *Almanacco PCI '76.*

4.   Norman Kogan, "National Communism vs. the National Way to Communism—An Italian Interpretation," *The Western Political Quarterly,* September 1958, pp. 660-72.

5.   Harald Hamrin, *Between Bolshevism and Revisionism: The Italian Communism Party, 1944-1947* (Stockholm: Swedish Institute of International Affairs, 1975).

6.   Joan B. Urban, "Moscow and the Italian Communist Party: 1926-1945" (Ph.D. dissertation, Harvard University, 1967); also Joan B. Urban, "Italian Communism and the 'Opportunism of Conciliation,' 1927-1929," *Studies in Comparative Communism,* Winter 1973, pp. 362-96.

7.   George Urban, "A Conversation with Lucio Lombardo Radice," *Encounter,* May 1977, p. 9.

8.   In the middle of the 1950s it was estimated that of approximately 2 million party members probably no more than 25,000 or 30,000 could be described as Marxist-Leninists.

9.   Norman Kogan, "Italian Communism, the Working Class, and Organized Catholicism," *The Journal of Politics,* August 1966, pp. 531-32.

10.   Eugenio Reale, *Nascita del Cominform* (Milan: Arnaldo Mondadori Editore, 1958).

11. Franco Cazzola, "Consenso e opposizione nel parlamento italiano. Il ruolo del PCI dalla I alla IV legislatura," *Rivista Italiana di Scienza Politica*, March 1972, pp. 71-96.

12. Norman Kogan, "Socialism and Communism in Italian Political Life," in E. R. Tannenbaum and E. P. Noether, eds., *Modern Italy, A Topical History Since 1861* (New York: New York University Press, 1974), pp. 102-22.

13. Enzo Santarelli, *La revisione del marxismo in Italia* (Milano: Feltrinelli Editore, 1964).

14. Giuseppe Mammarella, *Riformisti e rivoluzionari nel Partito socialista italiano 1900-1912* (Padua: Marsilio Editori, 1968).

15. Charles F. Delzell, *Mussolini's Enemies: The Italian Anti-Fascist Resistance* (Princeton, N.J.: Princeton University Press, 1961).

16. Stephen Hellman, "The PCI's Alliance Strategy and the Case of the Middle Classes," in Donald L. M. Blackmer and Sidney Tarrow, eds., *Communism in Italy and France* (Princeton, N.J.: Princeton University Press, 1975), pp. 373-419.

17. Giacomo Sani, "Mass Support for Italian Communism: Trends and Prospects," mimeographed paper prepared for the conference on "Italy and Eurocommunism, Western Europe at the Crossroads," June 7-9, 1977, pp. 4-8.

18. Giacomo Sani, "Mass Level Constraints on Political Realignments: Perception of Anti-System Parties in Italy," *British Journal of Political Science*, January 1976, pp. 1-31.

19. Giacomo Sani, "The PCI on the Threshold," *Problems of Communism*, November-December 1976, p. 35.

20. Sani, "Mass Support for Italian Communism: Trends and Prospects," pp. 17-19.

21. *Panorama,* May 31, 1977, pp. 47-48.

22. Pietro Nenni, "Che cosa vuole il Partito socialista," *Una battaglia vinta* (Rome: Leonardo Editore, 1946), p. 18.

23. R. Neal Tannahill, "Leadership as a Determinant of Diversity in Western European Communism," *Studies in Comparative Communism,* Winter 1976, p. 354.

24. *L'Espresso,* February 4, 1973, pp. 18-19.

25. Neil McInnes, *The Communist Parties of Western Europe* (London: Oxford University Press, 1975), pp. 66-67.

26. Quoted in Pio Uliassi, "Italy: The Politics of Uncertainty," in Jeanne J. Kirkpatrick, ed., *The Strategy of Deception* (New York: Farrar, Straus and Co., 1963), p. 306.

27. Alexander Dallin, ed., *Diversity in International Communism* (New York: Columbia University Press, 1963), p. 502.

28. Kogan, "Italian Communism, the Working Class, and Organized Catholicism," p. 538.

29. Dallin, *Diversity in International Communism,* p. 435.

30. *Ibid.,* pp. 429-35.

31. *Tesi del X Congresso* (Rome: Riuniti Editori, 1963), p. 666.

32. The text of Togliatti's memorial is printed in *Rinascita,* September 5, 1964, pp. 1-4.

33. Quoted in *Il Crociato*, February 12, 1966.

34. From the resolution of the Political Bureau, or *direzione,* of the PCI at the peak of the Czechoslovak crisis, July 17, 1968. Reprinted in *Almanacco PCI '76,* pp. 251-52.

35. From the address of Luigi Longo, Secretary General of the party, to the 12th Congress of the PCI, 1969. Reprinted *ibid.,* p. 252.

36. Eugenio Peggio, *La crisi economica italiana* (Milan: Rizzoli Editore, 1976), pp. 96-97. Peggio is the director of the PCI's economic study bureau, CESPES, a member of the Central Committee, and, since August 1976, Chairman of the Budget and Finance Committee of the Chamber of Deputies. See also his "Le Società multinazionali e la sinistra europea," *Politica ed economia,* nos. 2/3, 1971, pp. 23-24.

37. Joseph LaPalombara and Stephen Blank, *Multinational Corporations and National Elites: A Study in Tensions* (New York: The Conference Board, 1976), p. 104.

38. *Ibid.,* p. 105.

39. Lucio Libertini, "The Problem of the PCI," mimeographed paper presented to the conference on "Italy and Eurocommunism, Western Europe at the Crossroads," June 7-9, 1977, pp. 3-4. Libertini is also Chairman of the Committee on Transportation of the Chamber of Deputies.

40. *New York Times,* June 10, 1977.

41. Libertini, "The Problem of the PCI," p. 3.

42. Personal interview with Barca.

43. Libertini, "The Problem of the PCI," p. 6.

44. For illustrations of this proposition, see issues of *Rinascita* or the reports of the PCI's economic study bureau, CESPES. Examples can be found in the intervention of Luciano Barca at the roundtable on the Italian economy sponsored by the Movimento Gaetano Salvemini on March 17, 1976. "Crisi economica e crisi politica," *Quaderni del Salvemini,* no. 22, pp. 15-22; also Peggio, *La crisi economica italiana.*

45. Peter Weitz, "The CGIL and the PCI: From Subordination to Independent Political Force," in Blackmer and Tarrow, eds., *Communism in Italy and France,* pp. 541-71.

46. Norman Kogan, *Italy and the Allies* (Cambridge: Harvard University Press, 1956), pp. 134-41, 204-208.

47. In 1953 Giulio Andreotti (prime minister in 1977) was undersecretary to the prime minister. He was present and took notes at this conversation; he published them in a book, *Intervista su De Gasperi* (Bari: Laterza, 1977).

48. Norman Kogan, *A Political History of Postwar Italy* (New York: Frederick A. Praeger, 1966), pp. 146-47.

49. On the relations of the PCI to the international Communist movement, see Donald L. M. Blackmer, *Unity in Diversity: Italian Communism and the Communist World* (Cambridge: The M.I.T. Press, 1968).

50. Kevin Devlin, "The Challenge of Eurocommunism," *Problems of Communism,* January-February 1977, p. 3.

51. Speech of Enrico Berlinguer to the Central Committee of the PCI; reported in *La Stampa,* February 8, 1973.

52.   Speech of Enrico Berlinguer to the 14th National Congress of the PCI, March 18-23, 1975; reprinted in *The Italian Communists,* Foreign Bulletin of the PCI, March-May 1975, p. 103.

53.   Giuseppe Mammarella, *Il partito comunista italiano 1945-1975* (Florence: Vallecchi Editore, 1976), p. 232.

54.   For a presentation of these two arguments, see the interview with Berlinguer published in the *Corriere della Sera,* June 15, 1976.

55.   See the speech of Christian Democratic Foreign Minister Attilio Piccioni in 1962. Italian Information Office, *Italian Report,* July, 1962, pp. 19-22.

56.   Urban, "A Conversation with Lucio Lombardo Radice," p. 10.

57.   Primo Vannicelli, *Italy, NATO, and the European Community: The Interplay of Foreign Policy and Domestic Politics* (Cambridge: Center for International Affairs, Harvard University, 1974), pp. 47-51.

59.   Devlin, "The Challenge of Eurocommunism," p. 20.

60.   *Ibid.,* pp. 9, 18.

61.   Neil McInnes, "Euro-Communism," The Washington Papers, 37 (Beverly Hills: Sage Publications, 1976), pp. 77-78. See also, *The New York Times,* June 24, 1977.

62.   See Ciro Zoppo, *The Defense and Military Policies of the Italian Communist Party* (Santa Monica, Calif.: The Rand Corporation, 1977).

63.   Giovanni Gronchi, *Discorsi d'America* (Milan: Garzanti Editore, 1956), p. 39.

64. Robert Putnam, *The Beliefs of Politicians: Ideology, Conflict and Democracy in Britain and Italy* (New Haven: Yale University Press, 1973), pp. 191-95.

65. Vincenzo Galetti, "Il punto cruciale: la democrazia socialista," *Rinascita*, March 12, 1971, as translated and quoted by Kevin Devlin, "Radio Free Europe Research," mimeographed, March 19, 1971, p. 7.

66. Mammarella, *Il partito comunista italiano 1945-1975*, p. 242.

67. Giorgio Napolitano, *Intervista sul PCI*, ed. by Eric J. Hobsbawm (Bari: Giuseppe Laterza e Figli, 1976), p. 130.

68. Urban, "A Conversation with Lucio Lombardo Radice," p. 19.

69. Antonio Gramsci, *The Modern Prince and Other Writings* (London: Lawrence and Wishart, 1957), pp. 137, 139.

70. It has been argued that there is as much discipline inside the factions of other parties as there is within the PCI as a whole, and since the factions are the real source of power in the party system, the PCI does not differ significantly from the other parties in this respect. This argument, however, is more apologetic than substantial.

71. Interview with Ledda by Lanfranco Vaccari, *L'Europeo*, July 16, 1976, p. 13.

72. When the Allies liberated Rome in 1944, a small group of Catholic intellectuals calling themselves Catholic Communists emerged from the underground. They called themselves Communists who derived their ideology from holy scriptures, not from Marx. During the following year Pope Pius XII forced them to disband. Most of them moved into the left wing of the Christian Democratic Party; a few, including Rodano, joined the PCI.

73. Franco Rodano, *Sulla politica dei communisti* (Turin: Editore Boringhieri, 1975), pp. 44-45, note 18.

74. Napolitano, *Intervista sul PCI,* pp. 72-73.

75. Urban, "A Conversation with Lucio Lombardo Radice," pp. 21-22.

76. Rodano, *Sulla politica dei communisti,* pp. 40-41.

77. Marino de Medici, "Recent Developments in Italy," paper presented at the conference on "Italy and Eurocommunism, Western Europe at the Crossroads," June 7-9, 1977.

78. *L'Unità,* July 1, 1976.

79. Lombardo Radice reflects this lingering identification. See his statement in Urban, "A Conversation with Lucio Lombardo Radice," p. 13.

80. *L'Unità,* June 25, 1976.

81. Mammarella, *Il partito comunista italiano 1945-1975,* pp. 251, 264.

82. Interview with Sergio Segre by James Reston, *The New York Times,* June 8, 1977.

83. The proposal for an historic compromise emerged in three articles in *Rinascita* entitled "Reflections on Events in Chile," September 28, October 5, and October 29, 1973.

84. Kogan, "Italian Communism, the Working Class, and Organized Catholicism," pp. 541-42.

[THREE]

French Communism, Eurocommunism, and Soviet Power

Ronald Tiersky

In the turbulent decade after the "events of May" 1968, history worked, somewhat surprisingly, to offer French communism a third chance to share national power. In its first two government experiences, the French Communist party *(Parti communiste français,* PCF) came and went quickly and spectacularly: first as a partner in the Popular Front (though not participating in the cabinet) and then as a ministerial party in the Liberation and Tripartite governments at the end of World War II. Following consolidation of the cold war in 1947-48, the PCF became for two decades a sort of alien outpost of Communist power, France being both a key member of the Atlantic military alliance and a bastion of Western bourgeois political-cultural civilization. The postwar division

[138]

of Europe, in short, seemed to consign French communism—if not immediately to the famous "dustbin of history"—then to a progressive and ultimately terminal debility.

During the cold war years this prediction seemed in most aspects in the process of realization. From the PCF's moment of greatest strength in 1944-46 it thereafter declined organizationally across the board. After 1947 the Communists were excluded and isolated from French political and public life generally, and in the 1950s even the top leadership disaggregated partially, disoriented by political failure, internal dissension, and the near-fatal illness of Maurice Thorez, the central leader since 1934. In response the PCF organized itself as a "counter-society," a sectarian and millenarian political enclave whose grandiose plan for remaking society would have mattered little were it not for the party's perplexing continued electoral success (about one-fourth of the vote up to 1958) and for fears concerning French Communist "fifth column" allegiance to the opposition camp in an East-West conflict.

Beginning in the late 1960s, however, the French Communist party started to show signs of new life both strategically and organizationally. Nonetheless, at the time General de Gaulle resigned the presidency in April 1969, no observer could have reasonably predicted that in less than a decade the PCF desire for widespread nationalizations in industry, and for a generalized "rupture" or break with liberal capitalism, would have some serious chance of directing government policy. This is because no one could have predicted the successful post-1968 resurrection of the French Socialist party (formerly known as the SFIO, after 1969 known as PS) on the basis of radical economic policies, nor the PCF-PS "Common Program" governmental alliance signed in June 1972. The PCF's strategic potency in the 1970s, in short, was

[139]

derived from its surprising program alliance with an unexpectedly revivified Socialist party.

Yet the signs of new life in French communism even before the 1978 elections were not entirely unambiguous. Strategically, for one thing, the alliance with the Socialist party, even though anything but harmonious, was clearly easier to maintain in opposition than it would have been with the immeasurably greater problems of actually governing. Moreover, in spite of the relative lack of burdens in opposition, negotiations to update the 1972 left-wing program broke down in September 1977, with the March 1978 legislative elections—and a possible left-wing victory—directly in view. The disunited left-wing parties then suffered a striking defeat in these elections, and the idea of a Communist-Socialist government is now implausible.

It seems evident, then, that the political and strategic obstacles in the way of a formal Communist entry into French government remain formidable and have undoubtedly even increased again in 1977-78. Not the least of these impediments, to be sure, result from the radical Communist strategy itself, conceived from a Leninist attitude toward allies, and implemented with unpredictable and violent tactical turns when the leadership believes the party's interest can be served. In short, despite certain successes after 1968, PCF strategy after 1978 remains faced with fundamental hostility in French society as a whole, including even the PCF's former Socialist party allies. A second ambiguity in the PCF's success of the 1970s attached to the party's remarkable organizational growth. In particular, an extraordinary increase in the party membership and in the number of factory cells was largely misleading (for reasons to be discussed later on), and Communist growth was on the whole of much less political significance than its absolute values seemed to indicate. Furthermore, in a longer-range view, social structural evolution in the past decade has emphasized certain tendencies which narrow increasingly the social bases upon which French communism traditionally had hoped to prosper. With its political strategy founded unchangingly on a dogmatic proletarian perspective, the French Communist leadership in the 1970s seemed to find only traditional "industrial" responses to "post-industrial" questions, its reactions exclusively anti-capitalist when the problem is more the increasing power and autonomy of the state from *any* meaningful social control.

President Valéry Giscard d'Estaing, on a state visit to the United States in May 1976, predicted the "historic decline" of French communism. By this he did not mean its disappearance, but rather a progressive weakening of PCF influence to the point at which the Communist party would no longer be necessary to an alternation of political majorities. As French politics and political sociology settle into some new focus following the mesmerizing elections of spring 1978, the major conclusion we want to reach here is some assessment of Giscard's prediction: Is French communism, on balance, in the ascendant, or can one support the hypothesis of its "historic decline"? The answer at first glance would seem to require a "standard" inventory of "standard" indicators. However, despite even the PCF's Leninist fireworks of 1977-78, one must consider a more complex problem and a more complex possibility as well: that the decline of French communism is indeed underway, but in the sense of a long-term and still very incomplete transformation into "Eurocommunism," an autonomous, liberalized and, need one add, long-awaited Communist adaptation to West European society and politics.

The passionate controversy in recent years over whether the French and other so-called Eurocommunist parties have "really changed" reflects in its inconclusiveness the character

[141]

of the phenomenon itself. The PCF, the PCI, and the PCE have gainsaid, however haltingly and unsystematically over a period of two decades, the goal of a violent proletarian revolution and a rigidly Soviet-style society. The PCF today calls for a "French road to socialism," meaning a non-violent, democratic and, on the whole, gradualist strategy which would issue in a pluralist egalitarian society, a "socialism in French colors." Yet the explication of these concepts leaves serious doubts that French Communist goals have become compatible with liberal politics, or constitute a genuine democratic vision. This is implied, for example, in the continued assertion of a PCF vanguard role derived from the historical laws of class conflict, justifying permanent Communist leadership of the regime and of society. Similar doubts are provoked by the perpetuation and defense of "democratic centralism" within the party, as we see again in internal party controversy after the 1978 elections. On the other hand, in recent years the French Communist leaders have vigorously asserted their autonomy from Soviet control, and, as discussed below, a point of no return was apparently reached suddenly in late 1975. This public defection from unconditional loyalty to the Soviet Union was hailed at the time by many observers as the sign of a decisive PCF turn toward Eurocommunism. Indeed, after rejecting this label for more than a year thereafter, the PCF Secretary General Georges Marchais adopted it himself after the Spanish-Italian-French "Eurocommunist summit" meeting in March 1977.

As an ideal type, one may define Eurocommunism, paraphrasing William Griffith, as various combinations of three elements: autonomy from the U.S.S.R., domestic democratic reformism, and regional Europeanism. The analytical problem, then, is to define the distance between the policies of any one party and the ideal-type concept. In general, today one must say that *no* Communist party is unambiguously Eurocommunist. Moreover, there remain major differences in structure, strategy, and policy among the Eurocommunist-oriented parties themselves—differences very likely as, or more, important than the similarities. In the French case, for example, the move away from Soviet control within the international Communist movement has taken the form not so much of a positive regional Communist view with the putative Eurocommunist comrades as a strident French chauvinism. This strongly nationalist communism in the PCF, moreover, transcended the question of relations among Communist parties to develop "Gaullist"-style positions as well on such state policy questions as European integration and national defense. In 1975-78, the PCF therefore seemed to be often more "Gaullo-Communist," as Pierre Hassner termed it, than "Eurocommunist." To be sure, Eurocommunism and Gaullocommunism are concepts, not realities: that is to say, they do not "manifest" reality but are rather analytic categories imposed on social practice by the observer in order to organize it and, thus, to understand it. Keeping this in mind, one can comprehend current contradictions in French Communist policy as the burden of finding a workable and politically advantageous strategy within a triangle of Soviet power, Gaullocommunism and Eurocommunism.

The French Communist party today thus remains in the process of an unavoidable internal and international evolution whose general character and goal remain a mixture of incompatible types even after almost two decades. Communist behavior in the breakdown of the Common Program alliance in 1977-78 demonstrated that elements of the Soviet heritage still give this mixture its distinctive character, yet also added still new dimensions to the ambiguities of PCF behavior and intentions. Although we now have the answers to some ques-

[143]

tions long posed—that of the party's decision-making autonomy in particular—it is impossible to reconcile French Communist criticism of East bloc repression (of civil and political rights, of trade union rights) with its own practice of "democratic centralism" and its own behavior as alliance partner. It is too facile to conclude that "nothing has changed" in French communism; but neither can one yet conclude that the essential has changed.

And so long as French communism's democratic credentials remain unconvincing, its strong presence on the French Left will make the *débloquage* of French political life—that is, the creation of a legitimized political alternative on the Left—an extremely dangerous undertaking.

The French Communist Tradition

Soviet Alignment

Historically speaking, the best-known element of French communism has been its "unconditional loyalty" to the Communist Party of the Soviet Union (CPSU). This loyalty meant both support of Soviet foreign policy (acting as a "national detachment" of an international movement centered in Moscow) and emulation of Soviet methods (Stalinism). The current public fascination with Eurocommunism makes it worth insisting that, despite minor nuances and certain hesitations from time to time, the French Communist tradition of "unconditional loyalty" meant, simply, extreme PCF responsiveness for three decades to directives from Moscow.

Before the Second World War, the PCF was controlled by the Soviets both informally and through the direct administration of the Third International, or Comintern.[1] In the 1930s, for example, the PCF Secretary General Maurice Thorez had no more say about French communism's role in international Communist strategy than did the foreign Comintern "advisors" attached to the French party.[2] Under Thorez, Secretary General until 1964, the French Communist party became the most thoroughly Stalinized of the major non-ruling parties. And one of the party's major preoccupations was to prevent the emergence of an original national doctrine and strategy, such as Antonio Gramsci had produced for Italian communism. Indeed, the PCF leadership sought to merit its reputation in the international Communist movement as the "eldest daughter of the Church."

Thus unconditional loyalty to the Soviet Union and Stalin produced doctrinal poverty, not to say insipidness, in French communism—often manifested in politically foolhardy and morally corrupt endorsements of Soviet policies transferred by the PCF with bureaucratic rigidity to the native soil. For example, the PCF leaders almost destroyed their own party in 1928-33 by accepting Soviet instructions for an ultra-leftist "class against class" policy. They came even closer in 1939 by supporting the Nazi-Soviet Pact, which led not only to illegality and decimation of the party but, incomparably worse, to a legitimation of Hitler's intention to attack France. More recently, French Communist support of the Soviet "Zhdanov line" in 1947 led the PCF into an extraordinary insulated political ghetto for more or less two decades, in the process blocking many chances for political and social reform in society-at-large.

Maurice Thorez lived eight years past the 20th CPSU Congress in 1956, yet at his death in 1964 the PCF still lacked any coherent and realistic strategy for achieving its own goals. It still hesitated to rethink its unconditional loyalty to Soviet power and to begin de-Stalinization. This abysmal situation was only partially obscured by sublimation in a "personality cult" of Thorez, itself yet another derivative of "unconditional fidelity" to Soviet Stalinist theory and practice.

Ouvrièrisme

In the "personality cult" in the PCF, Maurice Thorez was represented as the *fils du peuple,* a celebration of working-class social origins which implies the second major aspect of French Communist tradition, *ouvrièrisme* or dogmatic proletarianism.[3] Unlike other Western European Communist parties (the PCI in particular), the PCF historically organized its ideological cosmology around a brutal and in some ways terrorist doctrine of proletarian supremacy. To be sure, *ouvrièrisme* was a powerful French tradition predating the PCF by a half-century. But it was brought to fetishist extremes by the PCF bureaucracy, as part of its hero-worship of the Soviet myth.

In positive terms, *ouvrièrisme* is a dogmatic priority to working-class social characteristics in party ideology, policy, and leadership. The PCF's revolutionary theory traditionally assigned an exclusive role to the industrial manual working class as the social vanguard of the struggle for socialism. The absence of a French Gramsci—i.e., an influential party theorist attempting to come to terms with the sociological realities of a highly industrialized society—was expressed here in a refusal to adapt the rigid simplicities of Soviet dogma to the complexity of French conditions: for example, in the a priori rejection of concepts like the "historic bloc," which might have rendered French Communist doctrine more credible, as well as opened the possibility of new alliances somewhat larger and, first of all, somewhat earlier. In terms of social origins it is true that many of the early PCF leaders—Thorez and the union leader Benoît Frachon for example—did indeed arise from working-class backgrounds. Soon, however, the PCF became dominated by an elite made up largely of men who had been workers for a short time at the beginning of their careers before becoming full-time "professional revolutionaries," i.e., party bureaucrats. The present Secretary General, Georges Marchais, was a metal worker and *Confédération générale du travail* (CGT) union militant in the aeronautics industry before joining the party at the age of 27. Since becoming leader, Marchais has sought to acquire a certain veneer of "bourgeois" political culture, and his public personality—originally very consciously *ouvrièriste*—is no longer quite so much in contradiction with the non-Communist political and social world in which he increasingly operates. Nonetheless even today Marchais remains far from accepted as a potential national leader in what remains a basically middle-class, conservative society.[4]

A complementary aspect of the *ouvrièriste* tradition in the French Communist movement has been a deep distrust of intellectuals. This means both intellectuals as an independent group (i.e., independent of party control) and the individual intellectual's interest in the free discussion of ideas, in speculation, and in resistance to dogma. Intellectuals in the French Communist party have been in the past often accused of arrogance, of political lassitude, and of unwillingness to abdicate personal or "bourgeois individualist" views in favor of "correct working-class positions." The PCF political bureaucracy, perpetually at odds with the intellectual corona at the margins of party activity, has thus been able to retain or tolerate only a few intellectuals of general renown over a long period.[5]

A last element of *ouvrièrisme,* perhaps the most important in terms of legitimizing the Communist movement in society, has been the genuinely working-class-dominated sociology of the membership, the electorate, and the Communist "world" in French society generally. The PCF, in other words, has traditionally sought to be a "working-class party" in its social composition as well as "the party of the working class" in its policies.[6] Although only a small percentage of French workers embrace Communist doctrine and join the party, the PCF can legitimately claim to be more working class in its membership and electorate than any other party. In the 1920s, i.e., before the Popular Front, the PCF was a small party (30,000-40,000), most of whose members were indeed active manual workers. Since the Resistance, Liberation and Tripartite years, however, the PCF is better described as a party of working-class families (about 60 percent of the membership in the 1960s, including wives of workers and former or retired workers) than of workers on the job (about 40-45 percent today). The large PCF electorate at the Liberation and during the Fourth Republic (around one-quarter of the vote) was perhaps 40 percent working class. In the Fifth Republic, with an electorate about one-fifth smaller in percentage terms than during the Fourth Republic, the Communist vote has been slightly over one-half working class, and the PCF generally receives about one-third of the total working-class vote. In the Communist-dominated CGT, about four in ten still do not vote for the PCF.

In short, despite the considerable authentically working-class element in PCF organizational and electoral strength, French communism has long strayed in practice from the original Comintern exhortations and from its own dogmatic proletarian pronouncements. Today, of course, an increasing social diversity in French communism could become one of its greatest strengths.

Organizational Narrowness

The traditional PCF organizational strategy "elevated its small membership into a virtue, recalling the Leninist precept that strength lies in discipline and discipline is found in a devoted cadre of pure revolutionaries." [7] This strategy of localized and intensively cultivated strength—*encadrement,* as Sidney Tarrow and others have termed it in contrast to the Italian Communist strategy of attempting to be "present" everywhere in society—was the result of several factors.

Not the least important of these was the original geographical concentration of the Communist membership and electorate from the time of the Communist-Socialist split in 1920. To the extent the PCF leaders have always chosen the path of least resistance, i.e., the path of least innovation, this intensive emphasis on cultivating the original areas of Communist strength needs no further explanation. The greatest organizational bastion of French commonsim has always been the "Red Belt" working-class suburbs of Paris. For example, the Paris-area Seine Federation traditionally has accounted for one-fifth to one-third of the entire membership and after the 1971 municipal elections more than half the 59 towns with more than 30,000 population in the Paris region were Communist municipalities (this was even increased in the 1977 elections). The other geographic concentrations of French Communist influence have been in the southeast (a region historically "red": Radical Socialist in the nineteenth century, Socialist at the turn of the century, and then Communist) and in the *Massif central* where the PCF vote is "largely an institutionalized protest vote inherited from the anti-Parisian radical-

[149]

ism of the past." [8] The Paris dominance is explained, as Tarrow puts it, by the fact that the "PCF is strongest where the proletariat has the greatest proportional weight within its organizations." [9] This organizational fief in the Parisian working-class areas of course strongly reinforced the dogmatic *ouvrièrisme* in French Communist doctrine, and both in turn reinforced the bias toward *encadrement* in organizational strategy. A third reason for the *encadrement* mentality is the fact that the PCF embraced the Jacobin centralizing tradition in French political culture, merging it with Leninist doctrines that were themselves conceived as a Jacobin heritage. In sum, over the years weakly organized geographical areas in French communism were allowed to become weaker, and the strong areas were more intensively cultivated.

The failure to reach beyond Paris and two provincial areas was paralleled by a similarly narrow approach to mass and "front" organizations. Though in certain periods one or another mass organization might have been emphasized for circumstantial reasons—such as the Peace Movement during the cold war when all other PCF organizations were largely ineffective—historically only the CGT, the Communist-dominated union confederation, has regularly received an established priority in organizational and strategic calculations. The CGT is easily the strongest French union, with between 2 million and 2.5 million members, two to three times as many as the Socialist-leaning CFDT and the independent FO. It has been by far the most important Communist influence outside the party and the union could well be considered the real source of the party's own strength in the postwar period. This has been most true no doubt during times of political isolation—e.g., the cold war years—somewhat less so during periods of détente and alliance possibilities. In any case, the singular success of Communist influence in the union movement (qualified as it has been by the relative weakness of the labor movement as a whole in France—only 20-25 percent of French workers are unionized) is at once another expression of the *encadrement* mentality and of proletarian dogmatism.

To sum up, the traditional *encadrement* bias in French communism emphasized control over growth, stability over dynamism and stasis over process. Necessarily, the question was raised repeatedly by both critics and friends as to whether the PCF bureaucracy had not become "inoculated" against extending the organization to the point where it could face the inevitable "contamination" risks of seeking national power in a serious way. Indeed, in the late 1950s and early 1960s many observers concluded the PCF was locked permanently into immobilism and stagnation. Some even went so far as to question whether the PCF leaders really were interested in national power at all, arguing they were satisfied with being the "government party of the opposition," and the strongest party in a Left permanently out of power. Many of the PCF leaders, we now know from memoirs and biographies, indeed despaired of gaining power.[10] They believed the only realistic policy for French communism was to "maintain the organizational weapon intact" while waiting for the Soviet system to demonstrate its superiority to capitalism, as Khrushchev boasted in the late 1950s. The PCF claim to be a revolutionary vanguard party was, in short, increasingly open to contradiction. At the same time, various domestic and international factors combined to push the French Communists toward a break with the past. Power interests thus merged with external pressures—above all, after the political lessons of "May 1968"—to move the PCF finally toward serious organizational and doctrinal innovation.

[151]

The Revolution of Tradition?

The events of 1977-78 demonstrate again that it is impossible yet to speak of a "new" French communism. Nonetheless, given all the changes in the past decade, one cannot deny a partial—that is, fundamentally still only a potential—transformation. An efficient way to develop this argument is to inventory certain significant changes in the three key elements of French Communist tradition discussed above, and to examine external effects at the international and national levels. In conclusion one can then situate the PCF within what I have called above the Eurocommunist-Gaullocommunist-Soviet power triangle.

The International Dimension

Between November 1975 and June 1976 the PCF leadership moved unexpectedly and decisively (i.e., publicly) to consummate a decade-long shift toward autonomy from Soviet influence over its decision-making processes. Were this decision-making autonomy now to be combined with a repudiation of general alignment with the "socialist" (i.e., Soviet) bloc countries in international relations, one could conclude that the historic transformation from loyalism to independence was complete. However, the PCF bureaucracy remains bound dogmatically to the Soviet Union in a shared perception of world politics divided into decadent and rising systems. This residual Soviet ideological leverage counsels prudence: Bureaucratic autonomy is not quite the same thing as political independence, and the current PCF decision-making autonomy

[152]

ought not to be seen as either absolute or necessarily permanent. Rather, the 1975-76 break, analyzed below in detail,
should be understood as a shift in a relative balance, and the
sudden PCF assertion of autonomy has not gone uncontested
by the Soviets. An ideological and political struggle continues
today in the international Communist movement, a more
complex, widespread and multi-layered power struggle than
ever before, based on negotiation and consensus rather than
domination of one party by another. In this new situation, as
we shall see, the decision thus far on both sides in the French-
Soviet relationship to refuse an irreparable break results as
much from mutual power interests as from idealized conceptions about socialist fraternal community.

On the French Communist side, the gradual movement
since 1956 toward giving priority to its own interests over
Soviet interests is related politically to the seizing of decision-
making autonomy. However, neither autonomy nor pursuit of
self-interest means that French Communist policies need to be
always different from, let alone opposed to, Soviet policies.
Indeed, however strong PCF-CPSU disagreements may be—
about relations among Communist parties in the international
movement, the conduct of détente, or the nature of socialism—
the French party, to serve its own interests (as they are still
defined in the "two camp" framework), must, of necessity,
remain supportive of the general foreign policy line of the
U.S.S.R. In other words, the PCF tradition of monolithic
loyalism has given way to a new policy which (1) distinguishes
the French Communist party both from strictly Soviet loyalist
parties (mainly in Eastern Europe) and from other autonomist
parties (i.e., essentially here the Eurocommunist PCI and
PCE but also in some ways the Yugoslav party), but which
(2) is still based on the belief that the future of world socialism
is linked to the expansion of Soviet-linked power. Thus it is

[153]

misleading to conceive of the international Communist movement after the 1976 East Berlin Conference as being divided into two homogenous camps of Soviet-aligned and autonomist or Eurocommunist parties. Instead we do better to postulate a series of partial, complex and changeable alliances among different groups of Communist parties, on different issues or types of issues, a complicated set of relations in which the French Communist party has assumed an increasingly idiosyncratic role.[11]

The PCF foreign policy still takes its departure from the Soviet-originated conception that world politics is dominated by an historical rivalry between two camps: the "imperialist" camp on the one hand, led by American capitalism worldwide and West Germany in the European Community (and by Brazil, Iran, and Zaire in other areas); and the camp of "peace, national liberation and socialism" on the other hand. In the latter camp Communist countries and the non-ruling parties are allied with "progressive" movements in the less-developed countries. This broad agreement on the basis of international relations is then nuanced by the PCF. For example, at preparatory sessions to the 1976 East Berlin Conference, the PCF, along with the Spanish Communist party, accused the Soviet Union of excessive moderation in its relations with the West, of being too mild in its ideological denunciations of capitalism, too weak in its support of socialist change in Western Europe, and in general more interested in what it can get from great-power détente than in its role as international revolutionary vanguard. The danger, so far as the PCF is concerned, is that this policy tends to legitimate the theory and practice of spheres of influence and therein the West European social and economic status quo. By implying that social progress in Western Europe is as much or more a consequence of détente as of class struggle, the Soviet Union works against the West European Communist power goals,

(The Portuguese Communists share this opinion; the Italians do not; the Spanish may have changed their opinion since 1975.) French Communist demands for greater Soviet aggressiveness have had minor ramifications outside Europe as well: A good example is PCF criticism of the U.S.S.R. for its very weak support of the Palestinians against the Syrian military offensive in Lebanon in the fall of 1976.

Historically, the turns of Soviet foreign policy have commanded the destiny of French communism. This continues to be true in the new era of PCF autonomy, but in a different and paradoxical sense. The Soviet great-power interest in political accommodation and increased economic exchange with countries of the Atlantic Alliance increases the pressures within the PCF for autonomy, while at the same time détente continues to be an important and perhaps even a *sine qua non* condition of a successful PCF alliance policy domestically. This is to suggest that a Soviet move away from détente might well confront the PCF leaders with a drastic choice, one which could result either in a completion of the national transformation of French communism or, on the contrary, in some kind of new compromise with Soviet influence.

Historically, the first chance to reconstruct French communism as a fundamentally national institution came with the Popular Front alliance in the 1930s. Indeed, many observers, and no doubt many of those who rallied to the PCF then, believed the party was out to rejoin the national political community it had deserted in December 1920.[12] During the Popular Front era the PCF was transformed from a small, sectarian, radical revolutionary organization—30,000 members, 12 parliamentary deputies, and a splinter labor union adjunct, the CGTU—into an organization of broad dimensions, operating in political alliance with moderate parties at the national level. By 1937 the PCF had over 300,000 members, 72 deputies, and was part of the parliamentary coalition supporting the government led by the Socialist Léon Blum, a government which also included the Radical Socialist party, the liberal-secular conscience of the Third Republic. There was even a Communist-Socialist negotiation about reunifying the PCF and the SFIO, while the huge Socialist CGT and the tiny CGTU actually did merge—the first step in Communist takeover of France's most important labor union.

The national reconciliation that was theoretically possible in the Popular Front was however rejected by the Communists. Rather than embrace national and liberal values, the PCF leaders asked the SFIO to adopt bolshevism, and they tried to subvert both the SFIO and the CGT in the reunification plans. In other words, by the time of the Popular Front (1936) the "bolshevization" of French communism was already completed under the local Stalinist triumvirate: Maurice Thorez, Jacques Duclos, and Benoît Frachon.

In the resistance movement and at the Liberation the French Communists were faced with a second opportunity to reject the Bolshevik frame of mind. There were many reasons why they might have done so—most of all, the inclination to give in to political success. For one thing, the PCF was almost consistently a ministerial party between 1944 and 1947; for another, the Communist and Socialist labor union forces, which had split at the beginning of the war, were now reunited once again in the CGT. There was even renewed talk of merging the PCF and SFIO outright. In 1946 the PCF even became the largest electoral force among all French parties, a distinction it held thereafter throughout the Fourth Republic. Of particular interest, during the summer of 1946 the PCF and the Christian Democrat (MRP) Premier Georges Bidault both called for internationalization of the Ruhr and for French annexation of the Saar region; the significance was that the PCF therein opposed (only temporarily as it turned out) Soviet propositions made by Molotov.[13]

Beyond all this, the French Communists had a large stake in the first draft constitution for the Fourth Republic (defeated in May 1946, 53 to 47 percent). Though generally a forgotten episode today, this rather radical first draft proposal was of extraordinary potential significance because it resulted from Communist-Socialist alliance (of *frères ennemis*, to be sure) which, during months of negotiation, imposed its views on the more moderate Christian Democratic party (MRP). The Socialist party (the old SFIO) at this time agreed more or less to the same conception of political alliance which later underlay the 1972 left-wing Common Program between the Communist party and the new Socialist party (PS). (We may note in passing that defeat of this first draft constitution, contrary to all pre-election polls, was the first rejection of a referendum in French history.)

In November 1946 Maurice Thorez gave a startling interview to *The Times* of London in which he advocated the doctrine of separate national roads to socialism. With hindsight it is clear that this apparent endorsement of national Communist politics was but another Soviet-coordinated policy; the German KPD had taken this line as early as June 1945, as had the Czech and the Hungarian parties. By the time Thorez and the French took it up, the theme was already being extended throughout Europe and Scandinavia.

In 1947 the PCF reverted publicly to type, turning its back once again on national reconciliation. After the Cominform was created that year, the French Communists accepted the cold war and the "Zhdanov line" theory of "two camps." Ever more the "eldest daughter of the Church," the PCF supported ruthlessly Stalin's purge of "bourgeois nationalist"—i.e., Titoist or autonomist—tendencies in the international Communist movement. The French "Marty-Tillon Affair" was the PCF's own limited version of the show trials in the East bloc.

Stalin's death in 1953 and Khrushchev's denunciation of the "personality cult" three years later at the 20th Soviet Party Congress left the old-guard PCF leadership, and Maurice Thorez especially, in the curious position of being more royalist than the new king. Given the traditional thorough-going Stalinism in the PCF, it was hardly surprising that Thorez did everything possible to resist de-Stalinization. The PCF Secretariat at first simply denied the authenticity of the Khrushchev "secret speech," while Thorez and the few other privy PCF leaders even tried to prevent the Central Commit-tee as a whole from finding out that it had not been a Western fabrication.[14] When Khrushchev was quickly obliged by the forces he had unleashed to backtrack on liberalization, choos-ing to crush the Hungarian revolt by force in November 1956, the PCF leadership was only too happy to support him in the strongest and most unequivocal terms: "After two weeks of political confusion, the cause of socialism is triumphing in Hungary ... [I]t would have been inconceivable that the Soviet ... army not answer the appeal [for help] ..."

From the beginning of his tenure it was obvious that Khrushchev could not hope to wield Stalin's authority vis-à-vis the foreign Communist parties, and this, of course, only encouraged Thorez's resistance to de-Stalinization all the more. Moreover, when the Sino-Soviet conflict developed in the late 1950s, Thorez even showed signs of favoring the Chinese, because they had rejected outright both Khrushchev's denunciation of Stalin and his policy of peaceful coexistence. Thorez, however, was at that point threatened in his own party by a Khrushchev-oriented faction, very strong among Communist youth and whose main leaders in the party were Marcel Servin and Laurent Casanova. Finally, a cynical bargain was struck: In exchange for Thorez's support in arranging a temporary rapprochement with the Chinese at the 1960 Conference of 81 Parties in Moscow, Khrushchev gave Soviet permission to purge the "Servin-Casanova group." Thus Khrushchev was able to bring the French party back to alignment with Soviet power; and when the Sino-Soviet conflict became uncontrollable, the PCF was among the most anti-Chinese of the non-ruling parties. From the Soviet point of view, however, the unintended cost of Thorez's support was the legitimization of an independent French negotiating position. Thus, PCF loyalism henceforth was always somewhat ambiguous in its depth, though the surface pattern was broken only years later.

Nonetheless, the PCF acceptance of Khrushchev and the 20th Soviet Party Congress line—with whatever reticence—brought something new and quite significant into the French Communist strategy at the national level. This idea of a "peaceful transition to socialism," adopted by the non-ruling Communist parties as a vanguard-theory corollary of the Soviet great-power diplomatic strategy of "peaceful coexistence," obliged the PCF to make a more serious attempt to find political allies at the national level. In short, post-1956 developments in the international Communist movement combined with a weak domestic position to push the PCF toward a consequential policy of political alliances, the result of which was to begin finally a certain nationalist transformation of the French Communist tradition.

Maurice Thorez died a Soviet loyalist in 1964, but his preparation of Waldeck Rochet as successor suggests that he had already in his own mind decided the advisability of adaptation. In 1959 he had half-seriously proposed a joint program with the SFIO, and in 1962 had endorsed unilateral Communist concessions to win informal electoral cooperation with the Socialists. At this point Thorez was already seriously ill, and the leadership transition already under way. Indeed, following Thorez's hesitant first steps, the 1964-69 stewardship of Waldeck Rochet solidified the commitment to change the party.

The 17th PCF Congress in May 1964 was a watershed, for at this point the hesitations about committing party doctrine to a national, i.e., an idiosyncratically "French" strategy for socialism seemed to give way. The Congress adopted a multiparty alliance strategy as a permanent goal (though still insisting on Communist party hegemony within the alliance), and forthrightly proposed a "minimum" joint program with the Socialist party. In 1965 the PCF supported François Mitterrand, then an independent Leftist, for President against General de Gaulle, from the first ballot, with no *quid pro quo.* Two years later the PCF was rewarded by Mitterrand and his allies with formal (i.e., public) cooperation in the 1967 legislative elections.

The success of this 1967 alliance strengthened an incipient trend in French politics toward not only electoral but also political bipolarization, because one result of Gaullist domination of Fifth Republic institutions was to push the Socialist party into unambiguous opposition. In 1968 the PCF leaders chose to play it safe during the "events of May," maintaining their "peaceful" strategy and the goal of alliance with the Socialists. Then in August 1968 the PCF Politburo took the unprecedented step of breaking solidarity with Moscow by publicly condemning the Soviet-led invasion of Czechoslovakia. Nonetheless, in spite of the new direction gradually sketched out in 1964-69 during the tenure of Waldeck Rochet, the PCF wavered for eight years more before making a definitive assertion of autonomy from Soviet control.

For one thing, Rochet's weak personal authority in the

party allowed the Stalinist traditionalists to maintain certain of their positions, and in some ways even to reconsolidate them. The inner-party struggle here between rearguard Stalinists and what we can now call "Italianizers" goes far to explain the great ambivalence apparent in PCF policies during this period. For example, direct criticism of the U.S.S.R. remained a virtual taboo, and condemnation of the invasion of Czechoslovakia was rendered ambiguous by PCF complicity in the subsequent "normalization" of Czech-Soviet relations. At the 1969 world conference of Communist parties the PCF once again adopted a pure Soviet perspective regarding the central issues: the Sino-Soviet split and the question of "unity" in the international Communist movement (i.e., loyalty to the U.S.S.R.) The PCF criticized the Polish government's methods in repressing the December 1970 Gdansk riots, and also spoke out against certain judicial procedures used against Soviet dissidents. But in these cases the French Communists refused to see anything more than leadership "errors"; it was in their view certainly not a problem in the regime as such.

Thus, until the PCF suddenly adopted an "autonomist" position at the November 1975 preparatory meeting for the 1976 Pan-European Conference of Communist and Workers' Parties, it remained without any doubt basically a Soviet-aligned party, willing to shoulder the traditional burdens of "proletarian internationalism." Moreover, in contrast to the long and persistent evolution in Italian communism, steadily maintained rather than opportunist in response to particular events, the French Communist movement toward autonomy has responded above all to the national political calendar. For this reason the PCF leaders have been unable effectively to refute those critics who say their compromises with liberal democratic doctrine are tactical and perhaps even hypocritical. Ironically, it is likely that the PCF evolution toward party autonomy and pluralist doctrines would have become self-sustaining in any case. But in the event itself the 1975-76 turning point was reached under the stimulus, in large measure, of the possibility of national power, which developed suddenly between 1972 and 1974.

The extraordinary significance of having drawn the Socialist party into a joint governmental program in June 1972 became fully clear to the Communists themselves and to outsiders only as the Socialist electoral surge in 1973-74 suddenly gave the left-wing alliance a clear chance of winning a national majority. After François Mitterrand's near-victory in May 1974 against Giscard d'Estaing, the Communists operated on the assumption that the Left could take power in the next elections. However, the motivation to move more quickly toward compromise with the Socialists was blunted by the very fact that the latter in 1974-75 seemed to have become the strongest electoral force on the Left and in France as a whole. Moreover, PCF support of the Portuguese Communist party (PCP) after the revolution in April 1974 further complicated French Communist maneuverings. In 1974-75, as the preparatory meetings began to plan the Pan-European CP conference, criticism of the Socialist party domestically and support for the PCP internationally thus had become keynotes of French Communist policy. For a year after the first preparatory meeting in October 1974 the PCF supported Soviet-sponsored proposals for the conference's declaration, drafted by the host East German SED party, which made an uncritical reaffirmation of "proletarian internationalism," i.e., Soviet loyalism (and, in context, support for the PCP). After bitter conflict between the autonomist (Yugoslav, Italian, Romanian, Spanish) and loyalist factions, the Soviet-aligned parties appeared to concede finally at the October 1975 meeting. Jean Kanapa, the French Communist delegate to these meetings said at this time that the PCF would reluctantly agree to the kind of limited joint declaration wanted by the autonomist parties. However, at the November 1975 meeting the loyalist parties reneged, and the PCF surprisingly sided with the autonomists. At almost the same time, Georges Marchais and PCI leader Enrico Berlinguer signed a separate bilateral declaration in Rome, endorsing generalized Communist party autonomy, the peaceful and democratic national Communist strategies, and calling for a new form of socialism which would respect basic civil, political and religious liberties. Non-Communist political analysts had begun to talk of "Eurocommunism" following a similar PCI-PCE joint declaration in July 1975, and the PCF now appeared to be joining the new trend. We shall return to Eurocommunism further on. The point here is simply that in the last months of 1975 the PCF leadership seems to have taken a fundamental decision about its relations with the Soviet Communist party.[15]

Given the PCF's tradition, it would be precipitous to believe that French Communist autonomy is necessarily permanent, and that an authentically national reconstruction of French communism is now inevitable. Nonetheless, even the most cautious observer cannot fail to attach considerable significance to French Communist behavior in this regard since November 1975. The decision to drop the "dictatorship of the proletariat" doctrine at the 22nd PCF Congress in February 1976 was in this sense more a symbolic act than a policy innovation: It crystallized doctrinal alterations of the previous decade and dramatized the new PCF autonomy both from Soviet ideological authority and Soviet leadership in the international Communist movement. Marchais's well-publicized decision not to attend the 25th Soviet Party Congress a few weeks later—contrary to a long-standing tradition—then further emphasized the PCF's determination to join the autonomist ranks, as did Marchais's behavior at the international East Berlin conference, finally held at the end of June 1976.[16] At this meeting the PCF "Gaullocommunist" style was quite marked: Marchais seemed intent on flaunting a certain party chauvinist arrogance, which set the PCF off from even the other autonomist leaders, the PCI's Berlinguer and the PCE's Carrillo. Then in March 1977, Marchais and Berlinguer met with Santiago Carrillo in Madrid in what non-Communist observers termed a Eurocommunist summit meeting, and at this point Marchais began to apply the Eurocommunist term to himself.

Since the three major Eurocommunist parties disagree on important issues such as European integration, and since there is as yet no joint Eurocommunist program or strategy, the PCF embrace of Eurocommunism can be misleading unless one understands that for them it refers basically still to the battle with Soviet influence and with the Soviet Union as a model of socialism. The PCF's Eurocommunism, in other words, is not yet a genuine West European vision. Its touch-stone is rather a criticism of Soviet theory and practice which still falls far short of a socialist idea appropriate to liberal democratic society.

Just before the 22nd Congress Marchais said that, "There is no democracy and liberty if there is no pluralism of political parties, and if there is no freedom of speech . . . We consider that the principles we enunciate concerning socialist democracy are of universal value. It is clear we have a disagreement with the Soviet Communist party about this question." [17] This statement surely implies that the U.S.S.R. is not a democracy; if it is not a democracy, and if democracy and socialism are inseparable, then the next deduction would seem to be that the Soviet Union is not a socialist society. However, despite preparation of the ground for what would be a fundamental doctrinal change of considerable practical consequence, there is no sign that any such move is envisaged at this point although there is increasing pressure from outside the party, and some from within, to face this issue. Furthermore, a break with the Soviet Union does not follow necessarily from the fact of autonomy. There has even been a certain backtracking on the entire question from time to time. For example, the major PCF foreign policy spokesman Jean Kanapa replied as follows to Dezsö Nemes, a conservative Hungarian Communist who "questioned the credibility of our policy" of giving up the "dictatorship of the proletariat" doctrine: [18]

... we do not question the historical necessity of the dictatorship of the proletariat in those countries which have resorted to it. Nor do we question the fact that one may in the future consider it necessary in other countries ... [At the 22nd Congress] We spoke only for France and for our time.

In the same vein, Marchais has gone so far as to say that not only other "socialist" parties but also "capitalist" parties could exist in socialism as the PCF would practice it; but he continues to assume, nonetheless, that socialism once attained is "irreversible," leaving one to wonder whether he understands the implications of his own beliefs.

PCF behavior toward the end of the preparations for the Pan-European conference was probably the best example of the idiosyncratic Gaullocommunist-Eurocommunist ambivalence in which the party has settled since the move to autonomy in late 1975. In March 1976 the PCF submitted a separate working paper to the negotiating parties. The document criticized both the Soviets and the Italian Communists for their failure to exploit to the full the "general crisis of

[165]

capitalism"—the former out of "diplomatic" motives (great-power rather than revolutionary vanguard preoccupations) and the latter for domestic political advantage (in order to promote the "historic compromise," which the PCF leaders apparently considered too moderate a policy). Arguing from the position that radical change is possible in Western Europe even today, the PCF working paper went on to make the audacious criticism that the draft resolutions for the conference suffered from a "lack of class analysis" of the relation of forces on an international scale, in that they limited discussion of the contradictions in "imperialism" to an analysis of the difference of opinion between Western hawks and doves. The PCF also opposed the proposal to drop "proletarian internationalism" and to substitute "internationalist solidarity" as the slogan for describing relations within the international Communist movement. Its argument was that party bureaucratic autonomy, which the PCF supports, should not weaken party revolutionary solidarity, i.e., unity in the international Communist movement (including material help) in national struggles for power. One supposes that the PCF leaders were fearful lest autonomy delegitimize "fraternal" support such as had occurred in Chile, Portugal, and Angola. Like de Gaulle, the PCF leaders thus seemed intent on playing a second-rate power position into first-rate influence through the force of personality or party idiosyncracy. Like de Gaulle, they seemed to be giving lessons to everyone from a position of weakness. Like de Gaulle, they bowed ultimately to greater force and interest.

The French Communists continued to raise strong objections up to the final meeting, even withholding agreement to attend the conference at all. The decision to stage the conference finally at the end of June 1976 was thus in a sense imposed on the PCF, a multilateral snub of its Gaullocommunism by Soviet loyalists and autonomist parties alike.

The change in the PCF attitude toward Eurocommunism is another expression of the limits on a strictly national or Gaullocommunist policy. During the two years when Marchais rejected the term, he was nonetheless anxious to underline the convergence of PCF and PCI positions. For example, Marchais was much more interested in signing the joint PCF-PCI declaration of November 1975 than was the PCI leader Berlinguer, calling it an "historic" event. (And indeed this was true in that the November 1975 declaration signalled publicly the end of Soviet loyalism.) When Marchais finally began to use the term following the Madrid summit meeting of March 1977, he implicitly admitted the PCF interest in *appearing* Eurocommunist whether or not this is true, and whether or not Eurocommunism exists at all. Thus the French Communist embrace of Eurocommunism to this point has been largely a matter of image-building and "ideological struggle," window-dressing for an already established policy, which is itself the important point. At the most, the PCF has attempted to use the Eurocommunism label to its own advantage by stressing the "positive" connotations (democratic policies and reformism) as opposed to the "negative" rejection of Soviet authority. (The Soviets have argued that for a Communist party to call itself Eurocommunist is to step onto bourgeois ideological terrain. French Communist behavior leading up to the September 1977 split with the Socialists indicates that such arguments by foreign "comrades" may not have gone entirely without effect.) In short, it is unlikely that any important PCF policies have changed because of the discussion about Eurocommunism. For example, the PCF's shift in April 1977 accepting direct elections to the European

Parliament would have no doubt occurred in any case, all the more so in that the PCF did not decide to support European integration by this move, but sought rather to do what it could to limit supranationalism by making its support conditional on a commitment against it in the French electoral law. The national priority in PCF policy was evident again in May 1977 when the Communists gave up their opposition to the French strategic nuclear force. In doing so, the PCF dealt a serious blow to prospects for a Western European integrated nuclear deterrent—after all, no Western European government can be expected to consent to French Communist veto over use of the European Community's weapon of last resort.

In sum, the PCF decision to become Eurocommunist has been doctrinal image-making of little practical consequence. It is more like the decision to abandon the "dictatorship of the proletariat" doctrine than the assertion of decision-making autonomy, which had considerable practical effects. If Eurocommunism is in part a commitment to West European Communist regionalism, it seems likely that its development as joint action and a joint program is dependent on the degree to which politics in Europe become European politics. That is to say, Eurocommunism as yet is not a regional Communist organization, and could become so only if political calculations for all parties in Western Europe are regionalized in the event of further integration. Given the potential costs of precipitous action by the Western European Communist parties (e.g., provoking undesirable Soviet or non-Communist reaction), it would make sense to move toward organized regional Eurocommunism only to the extent that significant new power contests develop at the European Community and West European levels. For the moment, of course, the Communists are not hard pressed in this regard, although one should not underestimate the potential significance of direct election of

[168]

the European Parliament. Moreover the disagreements between Eurocommunist parties—much exacerbated by the PCF's behavior in the past year—may both prevent a regional Communist convergence and incite more working relationships between certain Communist and certain Socialist parties across national boundaries.

The PCF's relations with other West European Communist parties remain essentially bilateral, despite the several multilateral party meetings held since the innovating Brussels Conference in January 1974. PCF-PCE relations, for example, have been rather formal and hesitant, following a very clouded past during the PCE's exile when the PCF, as a Soviet-aligned party, gave precious little help to Santiago Carrillo in his struggle with Soviet influence.

PCF-PCI relations are probably fated to be strongly competitive. Despite a certain rapprochement after summer 1975, and the Marchais-Berlinguer meetings of November 1975, June 1976, and April 1977, the two major West European Communist parties probably cannot avoid a permanent struggle for leadership of Western European communism. Ever since the personal rivalry between Maurice Thorez and Palmiro Togliatti during the Second World War in Moscow, PCF-PCI relations had until recently always been rather hostile. Up through the 1950s the French party was dominant in the sense that both placed greatest importance on status within the international movement and here the "natural grace" of the "eldest daughter of the Church" could hardly be equaled. This attribute was enhanced by the fact that France has been more important in Soviet great-power calculations than Italy has been. Emergence of the "Italian way" as the leading ideological influence in Eurocommunism therefore has been a consequence of the shift to the priority of national power over international allegiance in Western Communist party calculations generally. In this regard, furthermore, the PCI seems to have a key advantage: it is far more extensively rooted in Italian society than the PCF is in French society. In the nature of politics conceived as a struggle for power, the PCF leaders therefore are obliged to inveigh against Italian Communist influence in Western European communism, all the more so in that the PCI's consistency and moderation place into question French communism's more radical perspectives.

To be sure, the PCF's acceptance of Eurocommunism allowed a certain increase in relations with the Italian and Spanish Communists, but its immoderate behavior in French domestic politics in 1977-78 had a new chilling effect, the consequences of which are likely to be durable.

The National Dimension

Given the geostrategic situation of France, and assuming that the PCF leadership seriously wants power, there is for a party with one-fifth of the vote no realistic alternative to a policy of sustained alliance with other parties. Furthermore, the PCF's alliance policy can be broadened or narrowed, with the fundamental condition that it must—as throughout PCF history—be based first of all on a coalition with the Socialist party. Within the Communist-Socialist-Left-Wing Radical "Union of the Left" alliance, the PCF after 1974 was clearly an electoral minority. The risk of policy domination and perpetual junior-partner status inherent in this situation was a major tension in the rupture of the alliance in fall 1977.

Before the alliance broke down, it had seemed that the Communists' chance to counter the new Socialist electoral superiority would arise only if the Left succeeded in taking power. In such a case, the PCF might benefit more than the PS from the nationalizations a left-wing government would undertake, by "colonizing" the new state industries with its union supporters in the CGT. The increased union strength would then increase the PCF electorate. Today, the Communist hopes would seem to rest on the possibility that the Socialist party will split or will lose public support because of inner-party factionalism. In any case the new troubles on the French left have manifested again the Communist belief that socialism in France can only be synonymous with a dominating role for the Communist party and implementation of its program.

SOCIOLOGY AND ORGANIZATIONAL STRATEGY

During the past decade the Communist political strategy and certain tendencies in the evolution of French social structure combined to provoke a number of remarkable departures from the traditional PCF *ouvrièrisme* and *encadrement* organizational style.

One of the most striking characteristics of French communism's social bases since the Liberation has been the dominance of the public sector of the economy in furnishing membership, electorate, militants, and even to some extent the top party leadership.[19] The civil service status *(fonctionnaire)* of workers in state services and nationalized enterprises—with the guarantee of job-security and protection of union and political activity—allows both the PCF and the CGT to operate more effectively there than in private enterprise. For example, the Communist electorate, as a general rule, increases in proportion to the size of a factory (public enterprises are large almost by definition). And the CGT obviously finds

[171]

it easier to organize and to mobilize workers with job security than those in the private sector, who must reckon with the French *patronat,* i.e., owners and managers in private industry, many of whom are not yet beyond a certain "savage capitalism"—for example, capricious hiring and firing, or unofficial and even illegal restrictions on union activity. In any case, the PCF's disproportionate public sector organizational strength weighs heavily on the Communist analysis of society, of the contemporary working class, and of class solidarities.

First of all, the civil servant bias in PCF support has been one important factor modifying the *ouvrièriste* conception of capitalism defined as the struggle between workers and owners of private enterprise. The new theory, while less dogmatically proletarian in tone, is not, however, significantly less Manichean than the old. The French Communist version of "state monopoly capitalism" (first consecrated as the revised general theory of advanced capitalism by the 1960 Moscow Conference of 81 Communist and Workers' Parties) simply merges the state-as-owner with the *patronat,* arguing that there is, more or less, no difference in interest, purpose or intention between the two. While it may be seen as encouraging that PCF doctrine has begun to exhibit some curiosity about changes in the role of the state in advanced Western societies, it must be said that the new version of "us and them" is still rather poor theory, which has been thus far only slightly better politics. In fact, it is possible that the traditional PCF tendency to cultivate its strengths rather than to correct its weaknesses—here meaning to increase further the genuine Communist power base among state industry workers (they have *fonctionnaire* status)—is, as a practical matter, a more compelling reason for the present Communist goal of extensive nationalization than is the doubtful Communist vision of a "peaceful transition to socialism." In 1973, for example, the PCF won more votes (33 percent) in the public sector than any other party, but its 27 percent score in the private sector was less than the right-wing parties'. In consequence, one can argue with some substance that the *ouvrièrisme* in French communism is giving way gradually to a *fonctionnarisation* of the organization and strategy.

The "state monopoly capitalism" theory, which alleges that more and more social categories will perceive themselves oppressed by capitalist concentration, justifies abandonment of the narrow organizational focus traditional to French communism. The result, however, has been no more than an ambivalent version of the PCI strategy of "presence" everywhere in society and endorsement of the broadest possible "social" alliances between the working class and other classes and groups whose interests are said to merge in the development of late capitalism. Here is the basis for what the PCF calls a "Union of the French People," a proposed alliance of all those groups whose interest is "anti-monopolist," a "crushing majority of the people." This translates in political terms the post-Allende judgment that any Popular Front government will require much more than 51 percent (let alone the minority support behind Allende's coalition) to impose its policies on the capitalist class. Thus the French Communists argue they are not trying to divide France in two, as the political bipolarization indicates. They claim to be remaking a new grand consensus which exists "objectively," i.e., in a convergence of social and economic interest, but has yet to be realized "subjectively," i.e., politically. The PCF today therefore attempts to appeal far beyond the working class to almost all groups in society, arguing that an "anti-monopolist" interest is sufficient reason to favor the "Union of the Left" alliance and, indirectly, the Communist party. Yet the PCF simultaneously continues its claim to be an intransigent working-class party,

[173]

the practical contradiction being evident. Ironically the Socialist party has been able to criticize the PCF's ideological competence by saying the "Union of the French People"-"Union of the Left" ambivalence stems from incompetent class analysis, a prelude to policy confusion and political demobilization. The PS has juxtaposed to it the doctrine of a "class front," which, though less violent in its imagery of class antagonisms, is more insistent on strict class solidarities as the basis of socialist politics.

The empirical evolution of the French occupational structure toward "post-industrialism"—i.e., numerical predominance of the service sector—renders progressively more ambiguous the significance of the private sector "industrial proletariat," both socially and politically. This incontrovertible sociology provided another incitement to revision of the "dictatorship of the proletariat" doctrine at the 22nd Party Congress in 1976: ". . . [the proletariat] today signifies the core, the heart of the working class . . . While its role is essential it does not make up the totality of the latter, and, even more so, of salaried workers as a whole . . ." [20]

It is probable, however, that the most pressing reason for this doctrinal turn away from Leninism lies elsewhere than in the interest of "scientific socialist" analysis of society. (There would be continuity in this: In the 1950s—in the face of an economic boom—Maurice Thorez had argued the continued validity of Marx's theory of ever-greater impoverishment of the working class!) Stated most crudely, one can say that the French Communists required a new alliance attitude and democratic-pluralist doctrines once they decided to break out of the cold war political ghetto. These innovations required ideological dressing in turn, however appropriate they might have been objectively: Lenin, a master at the extraction of "correct" theory from "necessary" practice, would have understood.

Nonetheless, as opposed to other Eurocommunist parties which have given up ideological pronouncements about the exclusive role of the working class and the Communist party, the French Communists are still rather blunt "vanguardists": The struggle for socialism means "first of all the necessity that the working class has a directing political role . . ." Moreover, "the possibility of building socialism in France is linked to the Communist party's capacity to exercise a directing influence in the popular movement . . ." [21]

The PCF analysis of French society categorizes 44.5 percent of the active population as working class in 1976, and asserts that 45 percent of its 94,000 new members in 1975 were working class.[22] This "coincidence" would indicate that in the future the party will continue to claim only that "the working class is the most numerous" occupational group, thereby justifying again that its "directing political role" in French socialism should not be described as a dictatorship, even of the majority. This may prove not to be the case, however. Contrary to most analyses of French society, the PCF defines the working class so as to be able to argue it is growing: 3 percent between 1968 and 1976. To make such an argument, the PCF has extended the definition of working class to include certain white-collar categories which others have called the "new working class," and still others have called a "post-industrial" class. From time to time, moreover, the PCF's "extended hand" to the rest of the potential "Union of the French People" (55.4 percent of the salaried population in 1976, according to its own estimate) still communes with a threatening *ouvrièrisme*. At the 22nd Congress, for example, Marchais told these potential comrades: "Naturally your interests are not always identical with those of the workers. We don't hide the fact that we defend, and will always defend, the latter." A few minutes later in the speech he concluded nonetheless that the rest of France has "nothing to fear" from the alleged social destiny of the working class.[23] It is not easy to know whether this was ingenuous or disingenuous.

In sum, even the newest, most audacious PCF attempt to demonstrate an understanding of democratic pluralism and to reach out further among non-working-class groups in society has been nullified by its refusal to abandon a worn-out doctrine of the chosen people. And the rather obvious artificiality of the PCF's new look is a not inconsiderable part of the explanation for the party's continued electoral stagnation.

Electoral Politics

Until the 1977 municipal elections, the hesitant and ambivalent turn away from *ouvrièrisme, encadrement,* and Soviet loyalism in the previous decade had failed completely to justify itself at the ballot box, where the current account in PCF strategy is now balanced. As shown in Table I, in the previous national elections (1973) the PCF received 1.3 percent less of the actual vote than in 1967 and also did less well than in 1962. Furthermore the changing relation of the percentages of registered and actual voters demonstrates that the Communists had not benefited from abstentionism as consistently as one might have thought, the last negative case being again the 1973 elections.

The trend against the Communists was extended in a series of eighteen legislative by-elections held in 1974-76, and again in the March 1976 cantonal elections. In the cantonals the PCF won 22.8 percent at the first ballot, which represented

TABLE 1

The PCF National Vote Since 1945

Year	PCF Vote	Percentage of Registered Voters	Index	Percentage of Actual Voters	Index
1945	5,005,336	20.3	100	26.0	100
1946a	5,199,111	21.0	103.4	26.1	100.3
1946b	5,489,288	21.9	107.8	28.6	110.0
1951	4,910,547	20.0	98.5	25.6	98.4
1956	5,532,631	20.6	101.4	25.7	98.8
1958	3,882,204	14.2	69.9	18.9	72.6
1962	3,992,431	14.4	70.9	21.7	83.8
1967	5,039,032	17.7	87.1	22.5	86.5
1968	4,435,357	15.7	77.3	20.0	76.9
1973	5,085,108	17.0	83.7	21.4	82.6
1978	5,787,436	16.8	82.7	20.6	79.2

Note:
Totals for metropolitan France. 1945-56 totals are Fourth Republic elections; 1958-73 are Fifth Republic.

no progress (the PCF gets a slightly higher first ballot cantonal vote than in legislative elections because it runs more candidates than other parties in these local elections). In the 18 by-elections PCF candidates improved previous first ballot scores in only five districts, and made the run-off (i.e., defeated the other left-wing candidates at the first ballot) only four times, losing all four. The PS, on the contrary, while running candidates in but 15 of the 18 by-elections, gained each time and won four new seats altogether.

The Communists, however, did seem to gain in one area. And that was the ability to rally votes at the second ballot in favor of a PCF candidate. Previously the rule was uniformly that a Socialist candidate would get more Communist votes in a second-ballot situation than the reverse, but the trend was broken in the Yvelines in November 1976. At the time this seemed still a very minor innovation, and some electoral analysts predicted that eventually the two-ballot, single-member constituency system would localize PCF electoral strength even more, because the Socialist electorate seemed likely to expand further in areas controlled by the Communists. It was significant at this point that the PCF leaders talked not so much about imposing the Communist vanguard role in the "Union of the Left" alliance as they took up the PS line of a few years earlier—when the latter was the weaker electoral force—that the Left coalition "must be balanced" to succeed.

Given this background, the March 1977 municipal elections seemed potentially a watershed in the strategic success of French communism, beyond reinforcing the strong swing to the left at that point and the general bipolarization in recent French electoral politics. First, the Left alliance as a whole took control of most large French cities. In the 39 cities over 100,000 population, the Left went from 12 to 22 controlling positions. In the 221 cities over 30,000 population (the municipal electoral law changes at 9,000 and 30,000 population threshholds), the Left went from 97 to 157 controlling positions, well over two-thirds. Second, the Socialist party, continuing the trend of a decade, once again gained more from PCF-PS electoral cooperation than did the Communists. Of the 157 left-wing victories in cities over 30,000 population, the Socialists were stronger than the Communists in 81 (the PS controlled 47 of these cities before the elections), meaning that the mayor would be a Socialist. The Communists, who began the elections with 50 controlling positions in cities over 30,-000, ended with 72. Thus the Socialists outdid the Communists not only in absolute but also in relative gains. In the 581 cities with populations of between 9,000 and 30,000 the Socialists again won more than the Communists.

In general the Left gained 618 major municipalities (i.e., with populations above 9,000) from the ruling Gaullist-Giscardist-Centrist coalition, in the process more or less doubling its geographic reach and wiping out the Center generally in the large cities. This result extended the electoral-political bipolarization further down into local politics. The winner-take-all electoral system worked to magnify fairly modest but across-the-board shifts in the vote (generally less than 5 percent) into an unexpected tidal-wave victory for the Left. The left-wing gains were thus somewhat fragile, and all the more so as their significance depended on continuation of the PCF-PS alliance, which was anything but assured, as events of fall 1977 have shown. It is noteworthy in retrospect that in the 35,000 small towns (below 9,000 population; about 32,000 French municipalities have less than 400 population) a much greater stability appeared overall. In short, the Left in 1977 profited disproportionately from an electoral system which magnifies small vote differences into large institutional victories: To be sure, this simply reversed the previous pattern of conservative, and especially Gaullist, favoritism in such a system. And it is no surprise therefore that Giscard d'Estaing's supporters now raise the possibility of changing the electoral system.

The most important result of the 1977 municipal elections however, could have been the second ballot breakthrough of the Communist party. In the large cities, the left-wing parties ran joint lists, and on the second ballot non-Communist left-wing voters did not hesitate to elect lists where the Communists dominated and where the candidate mayor was a Communist. For the first time the PCF benefited equally in this regard from electoral alliance with the Socialists, and the

Communists now are part of 90 more ruling municipal coalitions in large cities than before (157 as against 67). Of equal or perhaps even greater potential importance, the Communist party electoral geography expanded radically along with that of the Socialists (although, again, to a lesser extent). All this of course gave the PCF a mechanism to organize in new areas, a matter of considerable significance because the party had not gained votes in the previous 15 years through other means: Neither détente, nor the Socialist party decline in the 1960s, nor the PCF's doctrinal innovations, nor autonomy from the Soviet party, nor even severe unemployment and general economic recession had increased the Communist electorate. For the moment it seems still true that, beyond a well-established limit, discontented sections of the French electorate will not shift to vote for the PCF as they might for other parties. Rather the Communists have been obliged to organize constantly just to maintain their vote. The 1977 municipal elections thus have given the PCF one opportunity to reverse its electoral stagnation, and in this sense the PS decision to run joint lists with the Communists may have certain lasting consequences. While the PCF-PS alliances at the local level may or may not last (and many have already broken down), the increase in Communist geographic implantation could have some long-term effect on the French electoral landscape. Communist organizational efficiency, once entrenched, was shown in 1977 in the fact that all 50 PCF large-city (over 30,000) municipalities were re-elected on the first ballot, and all with increased majorities.

Thus, altogether, a PCI-style strategy of gradually penetrating French society and politics was enhanced by the 1977 elections, encouraging in the PCF leadership a long-term perspective that previously had been less clear. (Compare the Socialist/Communist/Left-wing Socialist electoral evolutions

FIGURE 1

*Percentage of Votes of the Socialist and Communist Parties in Italy and France (1945-76) *

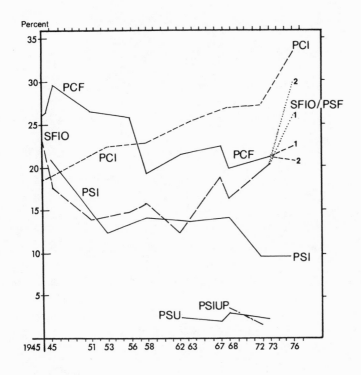

Notes:
   1. Cantonal elections (March 1976).
   2. IFOP poll (March 1976).
   * I am indebted to Mr. Stefano Bartolini of the European University
Institute (Florence) for permission to reproduce this graph.

[181]

TABLE 2

Five Indicators on the Hypothesis of the "Historic Decline" of French Communism

Year	PCF Membership	Workplace Cells	Percentage of National Electorate	L'Humanité[a] Readership	Percentage of Adult Population	Percentage of Population Favorable to PCF Participation in Government
1962			21.7			
1964						31 (June)
1966						38 (February)
1967	± 350,000	± 5,000	22.5			40 (January)
1968			20.0			48 (February)
1969	380,000		(21.5)[b]	534,000	1.5	(69)[d] (December)
1970				522,000	1.5	(60)[d] (December)
1971		5,172		592,000	1.6	
1972	390,000	5,348		607,000	1.7	
1973	410,000	5,681	21.4	562,000	1.5	
1974	450,000	6,575		569,000	1.5	(See Note e)
1975	500,000	8,072		660,000	1.8	
1976	543,000	± 9,000	(22.8)[c]	496,000	1.3	44 (January)
1978	± 630,000	± 10,000	20.6	593,000		

Notes:

a. Data collected by the *Centre d'étude des supports de la publicité*, an independent organization whose studies are used to determine prices of newspaper advertising space. The statistics given are general readership, as opposed to sales. The 1977 figure was 670,000. In the column next to readership (in absolute terms) is the percentage of total French adult population, a more relevant measure since population is increasing.

b. The first ballot score of PCF candidate Jacques Duclos in the 1969 presidential election, not strictly comparable to the national PCF electorate in legislative elections.

c. PCF first ballot score in the 1976 *cantonal* (county) elections to the Departmental Councils, not strictly comparable to legislative election results. As explained above, the PCF *cantonal* vote is generally slightly higher than in legislative elections.

d. Percentages for 1964, 1966, 1967, 1968, and 1976 are responses of those "favoring" PCF ministerial participation. Percentages for 1969 and 1970 are responses of those who "would accept" PCF ministerial participation—i.e., the question was put differently, resulting in strikingly different scores. Sources: For 1964, 1966, 1968 and 1969, see Tiersky, *French Communism . . .*, pp. 306-307. For 1970 and 1976, see *Sondages*, 1971 (1-2), p. 73, and 1976 (3-4), pp. 28-29.

e. A somewhat comparable question was put in an October 1974 poll (*Sondages*, 1975 (3-4), p. 51): "If the Communist Party were to participate in the government, would this be a good or a bad thing?"

	A Good Thing
For the economy	37
For social matters	54
For individual freedoms	25
For national independence	23

in France and Italy, as shown in Figure 1). Furthermore, unlike the PCI, the PCF in 1977 seemed in a position to pursue "presence" and national power simultaneously, whereas during the past two decades the Italian Communists were obliged through the force of circumstance to follow a strategy in two steps.

(In lieu of a detailed analysis of the left-wing split and defeat in the March 1978 elections the Postscript on p. 196 offers a judgment of why the PCF took the line it did in 1977-78, jeopardized its gains, and for the most part betrayed its genuine reforms of the past decade.)

MEMBERSHIP AND WORKPLACE ORGANIZATIONS

These electoral results help clarify the ambiguity surrounding the striking Communist party organizational evolution in recent years, shown in Table 2. The PCF was an organization of 225,000-300,000 in the early 1960s. This was the postwar low point, at the bottom of a steep decline from the temporarily inflated membership during the early postwar years. After the "events of May" 1968 the party's size increased slowly but steadily.[24] But the major gains of recent years began only in 1973-74. The yearly enrollments announced by the party were 48,000 in 1972; 80,000 in 1974; 94,000 in 1975; and 108,000 in 1976. Assuming a 10-15 percent turnover each year in the old membership, the PCF at the end of 1976 had more or less doubled its size since the 1960s, essentially in the past few years. In terms of workplace cells the increase has also been striking: about 58 percent between 1973 and 1976 (from 5,681 to about 9,000).

However complicated the evaluation of organizational growth may be, these arithmetic gains have been quite remarkable in and of themselves. France is a country known traditionally for the reluctance of its citizens to join voluntary associations; and while a closer examination results in a complex judgment, the recent Communist success in a planned wholesale expansion is a striking affirmation of its dedication and efficiency in organizational work. (Similarly in early 1977 the PCF announced a plan to double the sales of *L'Humanité* and to expand the general readership, both of which have apparently met with some success.)

It is arguable, however, that the tremendous membership increase in absolute terms after 1973 has been largely artificial, because it is the result first of all of a policy decision in the party bureaucracy, rather than of some kind of socio-popular gold rush toward the Communist party. That is to say, the greatest part of the increase no doubt has resulted from a decision to give up the traditional *encadrement* preference for a small and tightly controlled organization. In its place the PCF leaders have taken up a policy of enrolling sympathizers in the party, if only to the extent of getting them to accept a party card—another "Italianization" of French Communist practice. The reason for the policy change is obvious, given the link between current PCF strategy and organizational style: The only road to power for the PCF is through the ballot box. The PCF always receives more votes where it has more members and militants to organize the electorate. Therefore the party needs more members, who will be converted—so the intention goes—into militants after a certain time.

This decision to extend the French Communist organization is self-evidently a major gamble by the leadership. It is not likely that should the PCF become an authentic mass party, its leaders could ever hope to turn back, i.e., recreate a "small" party. Furthermore a mass party whose membership has joined in the process of its "democratization" would be a poor vehicle to try to maneuver toward a seizure of power, on the off-chance the leadership should want to return to the old strategy at some future point. In other words, the choice of a "peaceful transition to socialism" strategy and a mass party organization is, in almost all foreseeable circumstances, a permanent choice.

At present, two conclusions are possible concerning the new French Communist organizational strategy. First, up to 1977 the general "audience" or societal influence of the Communist party was not increased much, if at all, by the striking arithmetic increase in membership. The change was far more a realignment among the different strata of the Communist "counter-society"—i.e., sympathizers became members—than in the relation between the "counter-society" and the rest of French society. In this sense the membership increase has not yet given the PCF a greater "presence" in society, as one can see in the combination of stagnation and set-back the PCF suffered in the 1974-76 elections, and again in the 1978 election. If the membership or workplace cell increases manifested a general and authentic increase of Communist influence, then the PCF's electoral scores should have been similarly affected to some extent. Yet, as pointed out above, up to 1977 the PCF failed to gain votes from *any* of the causes one might have predicted. Moreover, as shown in Table 2, in 1976 the percentage of French people *favorable* to PCF ministerial participation had not increased beyond the figures for 1966-68. Of more significance, the percentage of *non-Communist Left* voters favorable to PCF ministerial participation was significantly lower in 1976 than in 1968 (58 to 70 percent). While part of this decline is due to the fact that the Socialist party has attracted large numbers of moderate and presumably more anti-Communist voters in the past few years, the problem remains that the PCF's ministerial pretensions are less widely accepted by its necessary ally's electorate

[186]

than before. Paradoxically, then, it may be the case that, not Socialist decline, but rather Communist alliance with a stronger Socialist party is the most promising way to increase the Communist presence in society.

Second, to enroll large numbers of Communist sympathizers as members has created "new-old" cleavages within the membership,[25] and has surely reduced the relative level of militant activism and responsiveness to leadership directives in the party as a whole. This internal discussion may be part of the explanation for the striking drop in readership of the party newspaper *L'Humanité* in 1975-76, as indicated in Table 2. Beyond this, even assuming the decline to be somewhat overstated, it is clear that *L'Humanité*'s general readership is now not much greater than the party membership itself, a marked change from earlier periods.[26] However this may be, given the political stagnation of French communism in the 1950s and 1960s, there is considerable political logic in "Italianizing" the movement. The voluntarist organizational expansion in the PCF is a strong indicator that the leadership up to 1977 had decided to bid for national power, and was no longer satisfied to be "the government of the opposition." The PCF remains much less a reflection of its society than are other French political parties and its only hope of gaining power is still its organizational apparatus rather than the popular appeal of its policies. As Giovanni Sartori has put it, political parties not only "reflect" society (as the Marxists emphasize), they also organize it (as Lenin understood as well or better than anyone).[27] Some parties are kept in power despite corruption, incompetence and inefficiency because they reflect well the societies they govern. Other parties cannot gain power because their program and organization are inappropriate.

A further ambiguity in the membership increase is the

difference between its absolute and relative significance in demographic terms. Joining a political party is on the whole an act of youth. The facts that the 18-35 year age groups in France are now larger than in the 1960s, and that in 1975 three-fourths of the new recruitment occurred here, suggest that the increase in the *rate* of Communist recruitment is less significant than the absolute increase would indicate.[28]

A third ambiguity in organizational growth concerns the workplace cells. The total number is not as significant necessarily as the number and geographical distribution of the enterprises in which the PCF is organized (the PCF does not disclose the latter data) or the degree of activism. The problem is similar to that of Communist municipal strength: localized and intensively cultivated strength may manifest a political ghetto and *encadrement* mentality. The Communists gain little from having a 70 rather than 60 percent majority in certain "red belt" municipalities. Likewise, they gain relatively little from increasing the number of factory cells in a place where they are already strong. And one suspects that much of the new workplace cell strength is precisely of this type: CGT union activists were switched, beginning in 1973-74, to party work, and organized the new members (already sympathizers for the most part) into more cells in enterprises where the PCF was already well established.

Finally then, the important political question is whether the somewhat artificial increase in organizational strength will be transformed into organic growth: Will the national Communist electorate increase? Will the PCF be able to reach beyond its sympathizers to enlarge its influence and mobilization capacity in French society, rather than simply redistribute roles within the Communist world, much as it already exists? In short, will the PCF's great organizational shift away from *encadrement* and *ouvrièrisme* merely delay the "historic decline" of French communism, or will Giscard d'Estaing's prediction be disproved?

INTELLECTUALS AND INTERNAL DISSENT

The PCF leadership has moved away from its tradition of Soviet alignment, *ouvrièrisme,* and *encadrement* both in search of national party goals and because of a general evolution within the international Communist movement. Despite remarkable changes in organization and doctrine, however, this development remains an unfinished revolution in the French Communist mentality. For many reasons, the PCF may find it in its interest to maintain this ambiguous position in French politics for some time to come.

One barometer of the limited "openness" in French Communist strategy and organizational style is the political leadership's attitude toward party intellectuals and toward open internal debate in general. In the past few years there have been several tense stop-and-go experiments with "liberalizing" policies, such as permitting journalists and the general public to visit cell meetings, publicizing disagreement over the 22nd Congress decision to abandon the dictatorship of the proletariat doctrine, and even announcing the number (very small!) of votes against it or in abstention at the preceding federation meetings. None of this, on the other hand, has yet gone very far toward legitimizing internal dissent from leadership policies, or at least its authentic and continuously guaranteed expression within the party. And while "democratic centralism" in the PCF is in certain respects undoubtedly less rigorous than ever before, the leadership in no way intends to

[189]

make of the party a liberal organization; to the contrary, democratic centralism is today once again exalted as the foundation of party unity and efficiency, one of its central distinguishing characteristics as a Communist party.

Within this general situation it is apparent that party intellectuals now have more room—and are even encouraged in certain directions—to express nonconformist positions than in the 1960s. But this kind of artificial liberalization has happened before. It is of infinitely greater significance that some of the debate this time centers on the question of the connection between democracy and socialism, and is tied to formal party criticism of East-bloc policy regarding political, civil, cultural and religious liberties. Nonetheless, as in earlier periods of more open internal discussion, the extent of disagreement and nonconformity seems to be rather strictly controlled by the political leadership. Thus, its eventual significance remains to be seen, because the bureaucracy could probably even today enforce a hard-line policy once again, as we have seen in the recent election. The persistent criticism of East-bloc regimes over democratic rights, however, could well develop a momentum of its own which the political leadership would not be able to manipulate without inciting losses of support and prestige greater than it would be willing to bear.

One of the most encompassing problems of internal discussion in recent years centered around the decision of the 22nd Congress to give up the dictatorship of the proletariat doctrine. In 1969-70 the nonconformist intellectual Roger Garaudy violated democratic centralism in order to raise publicly his suggestions for reforming PCF doctrine toward "Italian" or Gramscian conceptions. Whatever the top leaders thought privately at the time about moving away from dogmatic proletarianism, they rejected Garaudy's attempt to appeal outside the party's traditional channels. At the 19th Congress in 1970 Garaudy was destroyed politically within the party and later was excluded outright. In 1976, on the contrary, the leadership publicized inner-party opposition to abandoning the dictatorship of the proletariat doctrine in debates before and during the Congress, and permitted one of Louis Althusser's disciples, Etienne Balibar, to publish a book arguing that this amounted to betraying Leninism. Balibar's criticism was answered soon in books by Jean Elleinstein, a controversial PCF historian who in the past few years has acted often as a trial balloon for the Marchais leadership, and by others.[29]

A public controversy among Communist intellectuals was thus joined, designed to give publicity to the new legitimacy of limited nonconformity. Elleinstein, for example, makes a point to note that since the Garaudy affair no one has been excluded from the PCF over questions of dissent (though some have quit and some have received lesser internal sanctions). He also says that his book was written and published without authorization or clearance by the political bureaucracy, which—even were it true—of course confirms by implication the continuing general censure in the party. When, in December 1976, Elleinstein urged the PCF leadership to rethink the general question of democratic centralism, he apparently overstepped an important boundary. A few days later he published an open letter in *Le Monde,* in which he backed away from both his idea and, more importantly, his right to speak.[30] In short, at all important levels French Communist intellectuals are still required to act as if bound by the Leninist-Stalinist notion that politics is a brutal zero-sum conflict with everything at stake— an increasingly inappropriate attempt to justify subordinating the freedoms of inquiry and expression to political decisions of a party bureaucracy.

[191]

CONCLUSION: POWER REALITIES AND FRENCH COMMUNIST
GOALS

Despite the seductive imagery of "Eurocommunism" and of
a "socialism in French colors," the PCF theory and goal of a
permanent "directing influence" in politics continues to contrast sharply with the liberal principles of other major French
parties. At the same time, the French Communists have
relatively little chance of achieving their goal. On the one
hand, in its doctrine the PCF is caught between the analysis of
"state monopoly capitalism" as an inherently international
phenomenon and the argument that an irreversible break is
possible in France—a potential new version of "socialism in
one country." On the other hand, and more importantly, the
PCF in practice is confounded by rather evident geostrategic
and historical-cultural facts of life.

But these kinds of contradictions between goals and real
possibilities—though still of the essence—are old stuff in French
communism. What was new—or at least increasingly apparent—in the 1968-77 period was that the PCF leaders seemed
prepared to act as if socialism were not inevitable. Thus for
many the insoluble problem of knowing what the PCF leadership "really wanted" had become secondary, either because
the PCF had become revisionist in fact, or because the important point was how the Communists acted, no matter what
they believed. (It was often added that perhaps the Communists themselves were no longer certain of their own intentions.) This was the justification for François Mitterrand's
argument that the Socialist party's problem was not so much to
worry about the sincerity of PCF commitments to democratic
pluralism, as it was to create conditions which obliged them to

act "responsibly." The meaning of the PCF's raising the stakes and intransigence in 1977-78 is precisely to throw into question this assumption that the Communist leaders would make the necessary compromises as a government party. To the extent that the Communists were responsible for the split, or could have prevented it with concessions, the fact that the alliance cracked *before* rather than *after* the elections is portentous, given all the PCF had invested in the *union de la gauche* for over a decade and thus risked in destroying it. This is true even if the PCF leaders had simply concluded that the Left alliance was most likely to be defeated in 1978 and were cutting their losses in order to avoid greater damage if the major strategic option were to fail again. It is the Leninist mentality, the leadership capacity for unpredictable radical zig-zag, which is at issue.[31]

Whether or not an alliance on a left-wing program is resurrected, the general potential for PCF governmental influence remains strong enough to warrant concluding remarks on two foreign policy questions in the light of what has just been said.

Before the split, it seemed clear that the Communist goal in the 1978 elections was victory: but not so much a victory of the *union de la gauche* (in which the Socialist party influence was dominant), as a victory of the Common Program (in which the Communist responsibility was greater) considered as a binding contract which the left-wing parties were to implement more or less literally. The Communists insisted above all on the "contractual" obligation to nationalize, which would have served them both organizationally and ideologically. Given this priority concern with domestic policy (i.e., read the party's own power goals), it appeared highly probable that the PCF leaders would do everything to avoid serious problems in foreign policy—at least until the domestic reforms of the Common Program had been pushed as far as the Socialists could be driven.[32] PCF declarations indicated that the major potential foreign policy problem for them would be the extent to which European Community policies, structures, and pressures worked against radical domestic changes— in general, the central Communist objection to plans for further European integration. The PCF's opposition to European integration in principle therefore could be modulated in a trade-off: a conciliatory Communist policy toward the EC in exchange for a hands-off EC policy toward the French left-wing alliance. Given the Common Program economic and financial policies, however, it is questionable whether an EC-French Left government crisis would have been avoided. In short, the Communists either were not terribly lucid regarding the consequences of their policy, or were prepared for a more radical confrontation than appeared to follow from their actions over the past years taken as a whole.

The same tensions crystallized in PCF defense policy. The Communist endorsement of the *force de frappe* in May 1977 seemed at first to be simply a ringing affirmation of the party's new nationalism, an attempted further legitimation of its governmental aspirations. Yet the new policy called for giving up the targeting of the French nuclear force against cities and the East bloc and also for a collective decision-making process, which, together, would have neutralized totally its credibility. This weakening of the French defense thus seemed to imply a fundamental choice: either a return to open dependence on NATO—which the Communists could hardly have had in mind—or working toward a general renunciation of France's reciprocal obligations in the Atlantic Alliance. The PCF leaders rejected such judgments, saying they were not interested in questioning membership in the Atlantic Alliance, at least for the present. But of course the long-term PCF goal

[194]

remains to disengage France progressively from the Alliance. Communist endorsement of the *force de frappe* thus turned out to be in its details once again a sign either of political obtuseness or of preparation for a radical confrontation, and the burdens on PCF-PS cohesion and on the Common Program's feasibility were significantly increased.

The present situation remains ambiguous at two levels. At the national level, the PCF's Eurocommunist and Gaullocommunist tendencies do not constitute either social democracy or liberal nationalism. At the same time, situational factors and the PCF's undeniable internal evolution in recent years have worked to make Communist governmental participation no longer unthinkable. Whether or not the PCF-PS alliance is reconstructed, the fact of having moved the PS so far to the left in recent years must be seen as a striking testimony of French communism's tenacity in French society, and of the political will of its leadership. Yet the split in the French Left has raised new (or, rather, old) questions about the PCF leadership's intentions and its strategy.

At the international level, the PCF declarations of autonomy and nonalignment are confounded both by the persistence of two blocs in Europe and by the schismatic tendencies in the international Communist movement. Conceivably these together could eventually force the PCF to oppose Soviet power—i.e., both Soviet "socialism" and Soviet foreign policy—openly and consistently. The Soviets would no doubt like to reclaim or at least to split the PCF in the event French Communist maneuverings should fail decisively in the next few years. But a general PCF return to Soviet alignment would probably require a sudden and massive disaster for the French Communists, which, paradoxically, the PCF may have avoided in 1978, even if at the expense of a potential left-wing victory. Thus Western interests have much to gain if the

Eurocommunist tendencies in French Communism are maintained, and Western leaders must ponder carefully the potential incentives and pressures which might move the French Communist party more decisively away from a discredited tradition.

*   *   *

POSTSCRIPT, MAY 1978

The outcome of the elections of March 1978, and, above all, the French Communist responsibility in determining the Common Program and then causing the defeat of the left-wing alliance, would seem to confirm the analysis of party strategy and organizational problems presented in this chapter. The reasons for the Communist-Socialist conflicts over program and power relationships are clear from what has been said above. The left-wing split itself was also foreseeable; it was less easy to predict that the rupture would occur *before* the elections, in order to cause a left-wing defeat, rather than as a *result* of the elections, in order to break up a governing alliance.

The limits of the study of politics as a science (i.e., as a task of prediction) are evident. What one could not know—a key variable—was the PCF leadership's evaluation of the changing *conjoncture* in 1977-78. Moreover, it seems likely that this evaluation changed, or at least did not become irreversible, until perhaps January 1978.

My earlier judgment,[33] that the PCF leaders probably believed there was more to gain by winning than by losing, proved to be wrong, or perhaps the belief changed in fall and winter 1977. Finally, they decided that a defeat was the necessary price to "safeguard the party." That is, almost certainly the PCF leaders came to believe that the March 1978 elections might constitute the "historic defeat" of the party electorally, with the Socialist party taking the defecting Communist votes and assuming permanent hegemony on the Left. They feared finding the Socialist party at 27-30 percent of the electorate (as opinion polls indicated) and the PCF around 18 percent, heading toward the 15 percent symbolic "historic decline" level set by President Giscard d'Estaing. While splitting the alliance could not guarantee keeping the Communist electorate, it almost certainly would frighten off Socialist votes, defeat the Left, and thus prevent the PS from consolidating itself as a governing party. The PCF is used to permanent opposition and has shown it can survive without power. This is far from certain in the Socialist case, for the PS has rebuilt itself above all as a party of government.

What the French Communist leadership showed in the 1978 electoral campaign once again is its political cynicism. It cares essentially only about the strength of its own party, and defines this as the measure of gains on the "road to socialism." This is a Stalinist oppositionism, which is derived from, and reproduces, a "fortress" mentality, a brutal conservatism whose main purpose is to secure one's own position even as it is camouflaged in traditional rhetoric about "safeguarding the revolutionary instrument." Clearly, the PCF attack on the Socialist party in 1977-78 had less to do with genuine disagreements over how much business should be nationalized than with a brutal and cynical test of party strengths.

In short, the French Communist leaders demonstrated once again in 1978 that they still refuse resolutely to come to grips with the real problems of French society, and that—the least one might ask—they refuse to see the benefit of policies for change other than their own. As in 1968, their policy is "no revolution but 'the' revolution"—that is, no change but 'their' change. That is, no change. French politics, as I have written before, remains blocked in a dilemma centered on the nature of the French Communist party. There are two conceivable solutions: Either the PCF must change, or else a part of its social bases must fall away, or be cut away from it. The Socialist party strategy in 1972-78 was reasonable, if dangerous; unfortunately it was also not successful. Nonetheless, the pressures on the PCF have been increased.

NOTES

1.   The best short discussion is in Annie Kriegel, *Les communistes français* (Paris: Editions du Seuil, 1970), chap. 10 and passim.

2.   Principally the Czech Eugen Fried, known as Clément, and also for a short time Ernő Gerő (Singer), who after 1945 was the number two man in the Hungarian Communist party under Rákosi. See Philippe Robrieux's excellent biography, *Maurice Thorez: vie secrète et vie publique* (Paris: Fayard, 1975).

3.   A notable example of this is Thorez's ghostwritten autobiography, *Fils du peuple* (Paris: Editions sociales, 1939, 1949 and 1960).

4.   At the moment of his rise to the top, Annie Kriegel commented: "Georges Marchais is *truly* a copy of the model young Communist, exactly like the dream hero of the (PCF) Young Women of France twenty-five years ago: A plain young fellow with an attitude of 'up and at 'em,' thick set, the hands of a worker, . . . a friendly smile— sure of himself, of his comrades and of the Party which has taught him so much and given him everything." *(Op. cit.,* p. 144.) This description would have fit few other West European Communist

party secretary generals. Furthermore, Marchais cannot avoid slipping back into the proletarian cult mood from time to time in public, as during a spring 1976 television debate with former Minister of Industry Jean-Pierre Fourcade. Fourcade at one point questioned the PCF's competence in economic and financial matters. Marchais became immediately quite agitated and aggressive: "I didn't graduate from the National School of Administration, if that's what you mean . . . Yes, I'm a worker." Marchais then launched into an extended tirade against elitism and in praise of the working man, a spontaneous outburst which the party press then played up heavily for a week. Although this sort of posturing outburst is still popular inside the party, it is generally avoided in public, and neither Enrico Berlinguer nor Santiago Carrillo would likely have taken the bait the way Marchais did.

5.   The writer and poet Louis Aragon is probably the best known of these. Some interesting recent memoirs by ex-PCF intellectuals: Pierre Daix, *J'ai cru au matin* (Paris: Robert Laffont, 1976); Dominique Desanti, *Les staliniens: Une expérience politique, 1944-56* (Paris: Fayard, 1975); and Paul Noirot, *La mémoire ouverte* (Paris: Stock, 1976). The actress Simone Signoret has, in *La nostalgie n'est plus ce qu'elle était,* recalled the relations of herself and her husband, actor-singer Yves Montand, with the Communist "world" in France, and the World Peace Movement internationally. On the history of French Communist intellectuals, see David Caute, *Communism and the French Intellectuals* (London: André Deutsch, 1964) and Richard Johnson, *The French Communist Party Versus the Students: Revolutionary Politics in May-June 1968* (New Haven: Yale University Press, 1972).

6.   Bertrand Badie makes an interesting use of the distinction in *Stratégie de la grève: Pour une approche fonctionnaliste du Parti communiste français* (Paris: Armand Colin, 1976).

7.   In "Communism in Italy and France: Adaptation and Change," in Donald L.M. Blackmer and Sidney Tarrow, eds., *Communism in*

Italy and France (Princeton, N.J.: Princeton University Press, 1975), p. 606.

8.　*Ibid.*, pp. 100-102.

9.　*Ibid.*, p. 603.

10.　See Robrieux's biography of Thorez and Daix's memoir, cited above, for example.

11.　See Lilly Marcou and Marc Riglet, "Du passé font-ils table rase? La conférence des partis communistes européens," in the *Revue française de science politique*, vol. 26, no. 6 (December 1976), pp. 1054-79.

12.　In December 1920, at the Congress of Tours, the Socialist party split over whether or not to join the Third International, creating the Communist-Socialist separation. It is not germane here that the Popular Front tactic was agreed upon in Moscow, if not actually thought up by Soviet Comintern leaders. Nor is it important to argue about whether a repatriated PCF would more likely have been a form of national Leninism (one could argue this is a self-contradiction) or a social democratic revisionism.

13.　Former Communist Pierre Daix writes of this episode: "... everyone could see the Party was acting as a national party, ..." *op. cit.*, p. 172.

14.　On the camouflage vis-à-vis the Central Committee see Robrieux, op. cit., chap. 8, and Jean Pronteau and Maurice Kriegel-Valrimont (CC members in 1956): "Le rapport? Quel rapport?" in *Politique-Hebdo*, March 11-17, 1976. Recently the PCF admitted its top leadership had lied for 20 years on this matter by acknowledging that its delegation to the 20th Soviet Party Congress (Thorez, Duclos, Georges Cogniot, and Pierre Doize) had been given a copy of the secret speech at the time. See the PCF Politburo declaration in *L'Humanité,* January 13, 1977, p. 4.

15.   There is evidence that the PCF leadership believed the Soviets had not supported the Portuguese Communist party sufficiently; a similar opinion exists about Soviet help to the Allende government and the Chilean Communist party.

16.   The PCF in between refused to attend a May 1976 conference—one month before the pan-European conference—on Marxist-Leninist theory, attended by 45 parties including the PCI and PCE.

17.   See *L'Humanité,* January 15, 1976.

18.   "A propos d'un article d'un camarade hongrois: Le passé n'a pas réponse à tout," *France nouvelle,* October 4, 1976, p. 20.

19.   See a summary of relevant data in Neil McInnes, *The Communist Parties of Western Europe* (London: Oxford University Press, 1975), p. 73.

20.   From Marchais's speech to the congress, *Cahiers du communisme,* February-March 1976, p. 44. The blue-collar working class was about 32 percent of the total salaried population in the past few years.

21.   *Ibid.,* pp. 44 and 60.

22.   *Ibid.,* pp. 47 and 149.

23.   *Ibid.,* pp. 45, 54, and 56.

24.   The relation between the political crises of 1968 and longer-term changes in Communist strength remains to be studied in detail. Badie (op. cit., esp. pp. 181-95) makes an interesting contribution.

25.   The PCF press for the past two years has been filled with leadership admonitions about "distrust" of new members—to the point of not issuing a party card to many who sign membership forms—and of "elitist" and "sectarian" attitudes at the rank-and-file level (some of which is probably snubbing of unskilled and immigrant workers by the skilled worker militants who have traditionally controlled the factory cells). The PCF organizational secretary, Paul Laurent, has said there can be, however, no question of a "pause" in recruiting, even though "The more we recruit . . . the more problem areas will arise in the organization. This is obvious." (L'Humanité, September 21, 1976, p. 6.) According to very incomplete figures given out by the PCF, the new members in 1976 were about 20 percent students and about 40 percent workers. The latter were not divided into skilled/unskilled, nor was the percentage of immigrant workers given.

26.   In response to this decline the format of L'Humanité was changed in January 1977 to make it less distinguishable from other French papers. In addition, the party pledged to make reporting more truthful and more complete, for example, printing all the facts known about a given story and reporting certain kinds of stories previously ignored for political reasons. One L'Humanité official was even quoted in the paper as saying that several members had complained to him that they had to buy Le Monde to be well-informed. The PCF press in general has undergone considerable changes in format of this type in the past year or two, designed to reinforce the party's attempt to create a new public image.

One might add that the correlation between readership of the party press and general Communist influence in society is no doubt weaker today than before. This is because Communist ideas now penetrate society through the Union of the Left mechanisms (e.g., the Common Program) and even through the PS, to the extent the Socialists are obliged to discuss or even adopt Communist positions. The key example here is legitimation of the Communist proposition for a broad and concentrated strategy of nationalization since 1972.

[202]

27.   See his development of this point, with interesting references to West European Communist parties, in "From the Sociology of Politics to Political Sociology," in Seymour Martin Lipset, ed., *Politics and the Social Sciences* (New York: Oxford University Press, 1969), esp. pp. 80-87. Sartori extends the analysis in his important work, *Parties and Party Systems: A Framework for Analysis* (New York: Cambridge University Press, 1976), the first volume of two.

28.   The line of reasoning is Annie Kriegel's, though the argument is somewhat different. See *Le Figaro*, October 8, 1976, p. 6.

29.   See Etienne Balibar, *Sur la dictature du prolétariat* (Paris: Maspero, 1976); Jean Elleinstein, *Histoire de l'URSS* (Paris: Editions sociales, 1972-75), 4 vols.; *Histoire du phénomène stalinien* (Paris: Grasset, 1975); and *Le P.C.* (Paris: Grasset, 1976); and Jean Fabre, François Hincker and Lucien Sève, *Les communistes et l'état* (Paris: Editions sociales, 1977).

30.   See *Le Monde*, December 12-13, 1976, p. 27. Since the 1978 elections, on the other hand, Elleinstein has adopted a dissent of personal integrity.

31.   For a general statement of PCF foreign policy in English, see Jean Kanapa, "A 'New Policy' of the French Communists?" *Foreign Affairs*, January 1977, pp. 280-95.

32.   The repercussions of a general PCF turn-around would transcend French politics. As Robert Legvold rightly asserts in this volume, the PCF shift consolidated the possibility of Eurocommunism and French communism probably holds the key to its future. A French defection would attack the core, i.e., the content of Eurocommunism, and would do so because of frustrations with a political strategy that the PCI and PCE will also face.

33.   "Western Policy Towards the French Left," *Survival* (London), October 1977.

[203]

[FOUR]

The Domestic and International Evolution of the Spanish Communist Party *

Eusebio M. Mujal-León

A new era opened in Spanish politics with the death of Francisco Franco in November 1975 and the subsequent democratization of the country's political structures undertaken by his successor, Juan Carlos de Borbón. Elections for a 350-member Chamber of Deputies and a 248-member Senate in June 1977 paved the way for the adoption of a Western European-style parliamentary system, and in late 1978 Spaniards overwhelmingly approved a new constitution.

* I should like to acknowledge the support of the Social Science Research Council during 1977 and 1978. Thanks are also due to Emilio Fontela of the University of Geneva and to Amando de Miguel of the University of Barcelona (Autónoma) for their comments and suggestions on an earlier draft of this chapter.

[204]

After nearly four decades of authoritarian rule, hitherto repressed political and social groups are demanding a place in the new democracy—none more insistently than the *Partido Communista de España* (PCE) which, until its legalization in April 1977 functioned as perhaps the best organized and most effective opposition force in the country. The political significance of Spanish communism extends beyond the borders of Spain however. In the course of the last decade, the PCE has dramatically changed its international posture, going from unconditional supporter to prominent critic of Soviet domestic and foreign policies and becoming in the process a vociferous exponent of what has come to be termed Eurocommunism. With full-fledged Spanish Communist entry into the Spanish political arena only a recent event, it is an appropriate time to stand back and review the recent history of the PCE with a view to assessing its future course.

THE HISTORICAL DIMENSION

It has been a long journey but, nearly forty years after the end of the Civil War, the PCE has entered the politics of a democratic Spain. The PCE does not emerge from a lengthy internal exile with a tight, sectarian organization, disdainful of bourgeois political parties and institutions, and with a political base that focuses on a narrow sector of society. That may be the image one has of how an until recently clandestine Communist party should operate—particularly after the recent experience in Portugal—but it does not fit the reality of Spanish communism. Already a mass party with more than 200,000 members, the PCE has for some time now based its policies on the need to convince others on the Left and all but the party's most irreconcilable enemies on the Right that, although ad-

[205]

vocating a radical restructuring of Spanish economic and social institutions, it intends to abide by the rules of the democratic game.

That the Spanish Communists emerged from clandestinity the best organized force in the country is not surprising. Communist parties have traditionally been able to cope with the rigors of illegality much better than have other political groups. Juan Linz, a noted student of authoritarian regimes, has observed that such regimes characteristically face no serious challenge from moderate and liberal elements.[1] By discouraging political involvement and by periodically undertaking feeble efforts at internal liberalization and reform, the Franco regime managed, in fact, through the 1960s and early 1970s, to neutralize and/or co-opt most of the emerging oppositionists. Of the traditional organizations of the Spanish Left—and here we allude primarily to the Anarchists, the Socialists and the Communists—only the last were able to adapt to clandestinity with any efficacy. The others atrophied organizationally, becoming essentially emigré groups with little implantation in Spain. Their absence created a vacuum on the Left which the Communists, with the unwitting help of a regime which insisted that the slightest evidence of dissent was the product of Communist infiltrators, did not hesitate to fill.

The PCE's fortunes, however, were at a low ebb in the decade and a half after the defeat of the Republican forces in 1939.[2] Its leadership was in exile, torn by personal squabbles and totally dependent on Moscow; its militants and organization decimated in Spain. Once the bright star in the Comintern galaxy, the PCE was not even invited in 1947 to the founding session of the Cominform. The party had expected that with the end of World War II the victorious Allies would turn on Franco and re-establish the Republic. The anticipated intervention never materialized: the cold war and the exigencies of Soviet-American global rivalry permitted Franco to weather the storm his close identification with the defeated Axis powers had brought. By 1948 the PCE was forced to admit that the opposition could not on its own defeat Franco. The party disbanded the guerrilla movement it had organized during the 1940s and which at one time it had expected would catalyze the overthrow of the regime.[3] Internationally, the party loyally followed the twists and turns of the Stalin line, finding plenty of "Titoist traitors" in its ranks after the Soviet-Yugoslav break, denouncing the pro-Western orientation of other opposition groups, and sparing little in its adulation of the Soviet leader.[4] To make matters worse, from the PCE's point of view, its erstwhile Civil War allies, the Socialists and Anarchists, would not forgive what they considered the Spanish Communist betrayal of the revolutionary cause and condemned the PCE to suffer what Ignacio Fernández de Castro has perceptively called an *exilio dentro del exilio*.[5]

Under these circumstances, it would not have been surprising to see the PCE turn inward and adopt extremely narrow and dogmatic policies. That this did not happen is in no small part due to the fact that in 1956 control of the party changed hands. Conflict had been simmering within the PCE since the early 1950s, becoming more marked after Stalin's death in March 1953, and finally erupting in late 1955 with the admission of Spain to the United Nations.[6] A majority of the leadership wanted to launch a massive international campaign to comdemn acceptance of Spain as a U.N. member as yet another betrayal of the antifascist and Republican cause by the West. Others, grouped around a former head of the *Juventudes Socialistas Unificadas*,[7] Santiago Carrillo, opposed that course, arguing it made little sense in the existing situation to undertake such an effort which was, in any case, destined to fail. Disagreement over the specific policy issue, however,

masked a more fundamental difference in political style between the younger, more dynamic elements and the older
members of the leadership. The differences, while exacerbated
by personal antagonisms, were more than the product of a
generational cleavage. By 1956, they had reached a crisis point
and, ostensibly over a breach of party discipline on the U.N.
issue, Carrillo and his supporters were on the verge of expulsion. Fortunately for them, the 20th CPSU Congress with
Khrushchev's condemnation of Stalin and his cult of personality and the first truly important political demonstrations
in Spain since the end of the Civil War intervened within a
few weeks of each other. Dolores Ibárruri, Secretary General
of the PCE since 1942 and the *grande dame* of Spanish
communism, then decisively shifted her support to Carrillo
and those who argued for more open and adaptive policies.
Carrillo would not be elected Secretary General until the 6th
PCE Congress in 1960 (with Ibárruri elevated to the largely
honorific post of party President), but by the spring of 1956
he had assumed a dominant role in the party's affairs and had
begun to shift its orientation and organizational focus from
Prague and Moscow to Paris and Rome.

It was at Carrillo's instigation that the PCE on the twentieth anniversary of the Civil War issued a call for National
Reconciliation.[8] Although the appeal was in the tradition of
previous efforts, such as the *unión nacional* (1941) and the
frente nacional antifranquista (1953), to coalesce a broad alliance of forces against the regime, it nevertheless represented
an important break with the past. The appeal expanded the
scope of the PCE's alliance targets to include "democratic"
Catholics and even Falangists and suggested a peaceful overthrow of the regime would come in a relatively short space of
time.

[208]

The Domestic Strategy of the PCE

The call for National Reconciliation and subsequent appeals (like the one in 1968 for a *Pacto para la Libertad*) centered on the idea that the overthrow of the regime and the establishment of political democracy could be a relatively peaceful process. Because the Franco dictatorship was, in the PCE's view, not the dictatorship of the bourgeois class as a whole but only of a "monopolist" stratum, it would be possible to rally a broad, socially heterogeneous front against the regime around a minimum program calling for a provisional government, the establishment of fundamental political and civil liberties, amnesty, and elections to a constituent assembly. With such a broad coalition in tow, there would be no need for a classic armed uprising.[9] The PCE did not look to the armed forces to play an active role in this enterprise; its efforts were aimed at insuring the military's neutrality or, what was the same thing, its disengagement from the regime during the crisis.[10]

The Spanish Communist leadership, most notably Secretary General Carrillo, coupled this moderate approach to the question of how to transform the regime with the view that the downfall of Franco was imminent and would set the structural conditions for the forces of the Left to eliminate what the PCE described as the existing state monopoly capitalist system.[11] The theoretical justification for this assessment followed from the Communist analysis that Spanish capitalism had developed unevenly. After 1939, Spanish capitalism had attained a degree of concentration which had, in effect, established a state capitalist system in the country; but, alongside this economic superstructure characteristic of advanced industrial societies,

[209]

there stood a backward society where the elimination of the feudal remnants in agriculture and the abolition of an autocratic, centralistic political structure (accomplished in most European countries by the "bourgeois-democratic" revolution in the eighteenth and nineteenth centuries) remained the order of the day. This combination was, in the PCE's view, explosive. It meant that not only the working class, which was harshly exploited, but also the peasantry, which wanted agrarian reform, as well as the "non-monopolist" sectors of the middle class, whose conflict with the state monopoly capitalist system was reinforced by the failure of the regime to complete the "bourgeois-democratic" revolution, could be galvanized to oppose the "financial oligarchy and latifundist aristocracy" which had triumphed in the Civil War.[12]

The year 1956 had seen the first sustained, nationwide political demonstrations and strikes of the Franco era. The new leadership, which had come to a position of dominance within the party arguing that the Franco regime had an extremely narrow base of support, took these developments as confirmation of its thesis that the overthrow of the regime would soon occur. It organized mass actions in May 1958 and June 1959 and exhorted its militants and sympathizers throughout Spain to prepare for the *huelga nacional*.

Life, as Marxists are fond of saying, rendered its judgement. The regime did not fall, and, in retrospect, it is evident that the party leadership seriously misjudged the depth of the economic and social crisis of the late 1950s and early 1960s and the extent to which it could be overcome by the government's Stabilization Plan in 1959. Indeed, the leadership never openly admitted its erroneous assessment, holding until late 1976 to the notion that the regime could not reform itself. As a result of the miscalculation, the party leadership, and primarily Secretary General Santiago Carrillo, had to spend a great deal of time and effort over the course of the next decade explaining why its over-optimistic predictions had not materialized and fending off the attacks of assorted leftists (dissident members of the leadership like Fernando Claudín and Federico Sánchez,[13] supporters of the various *Frente*(s) *de Liberación Popular*, Maoists and Castroists) who rejected the party's analysis and the notions of extended interclass collaboration which it had espoused so insistently after 1956. But, while the party leadership's assessment of the implications of the changes taking place in Spanish society were overdrawn, in the longer run the belief in the imminence of the downfall of the regime and its inability to reform its structures had some felicitous results. It encouraged an activist posture on the part of the PCE and forced the leadership to consider seriously how to insure a broad base of support for the party in a democratic Spain. In the pages that follow, those efforts are analyzed in the context of the policies the PCE adopted with respect to the Catholic Church and its subculture, the labor movement, and the nationalities issue in Spain, as well as the revisions the leadership felt compelled to make in the party's ideological matrix.

The PCE and Spanish Catholicism

Catholicism has traditionally functioned as one of the bulwarks of opposition to change in Spanish society. The Church supported the insurgent Nationalist cause during the Civil War, lending that struggle overtones of a crusade in defense of Western civilization. After 1939, Franco granted it a privileged institutional position within the regime and in August 1953 codified the relationship in a Concordat with the Vatican.[14]

[211]

Over the course of time and, particularly, under the impetus of the Second Vatican Council in 1964, however, that stance changed perceptibly. The Church began to disassociate itself from the regime, shedding the role of fundamental ideological and social pillar, and, by Franco's later years, the hierarchy's public posture (except in a few, generally irrelevant cases) approached that of critical neutrality. Official Church-state relations reached their nadir in February 1974 when the government sought to arrest and exile the bishop of Bilbao for publicly demanding greater civil rights for Basques. The shift went much further elsewhere in the Church. Among priests in worker neighborhoods and in areas where Basque and Catalan nationalism was high, among Catholics involved in the labor movement through the *Hermandades Obreras de Acción Catolica* (HOAC) or the *Juventud Obrera Católica* (JOC), and among intellectuals where Marxists ideas found fertile ground, an openly anti-regime and anti-capitalist orientation became the norm.

The PCE was one of the first opposition organizations to perceive this phenomenon and to appreciate its significance for the future. Already in 1956 the party in its call for National Reconciliation had made a special point of encouraging Communist-Catholic contacts, and Dolores Ibárruri had declared membership in the party was open even to priests.[15] The process accelerated during the 1960s, fueled by the participation of both Communists and Catholics in the *Comisiones Obreras* (CC.OO.) and by the re-evaluation on the part of many Catholic intellectuals (like Enrique Miret Magdalena, José María Diez Alegría, Jose María González Ruiz, or the group known as *Cristianos por el Socialismo*) of traditional Catholic dogma condemning Marxism and philosophical materialism. Clearly, the Communists did not hesitate to exploit what Santiago Carrillo has called the guilt complex many

[212]

Catholics have about the Church's identification with the regime and the tacit assent given to its repressive measures by the hierarchy.[16] However, it is also apparent that the PCE developed over the 1960s a perception that the Catholic-Communist alliance could not be a temporary option, that the active collaboration of the Catholics as a specific social sector, not only in bringing about the overthrow of the regime but later in building the socialist society, was vital in a country where the Catholic subculture was so firmly implanted. Santiago Carrillo clearly articulated this view when he declared that socialism would come to Spain with a crucifix in one hand and a hammer and sickle in the other.[17] The adoption of such a policy met with some resistance in the party.[18] The Spanish Communist leadership, however, has ordered all party organizations actively to recruit "believers," and in early 1975 the Executive Committee emphasized that Catholics had the "same rights and duties" as other members and could aspire to the highest posts in the party.[19] In the summer of 1976 an article in the communist newspaper *Mundo Obrero* went so far as to declare that agreement on "the highest philosophical questions" was not a prerequisite for a Catholic entering the party.[20]

The Spanish Communist strategy toward the Catholic world has also been concerned with preventing the emergence of a strong, anti-Communist Christian Democratic party in Spain. In this enterprise, the party has been helped by the ideological diversity so evident among the various Christian Democratic groups in the country as well as by the personal differences which separated, until recently, the most prominent Catholic personalities.[21] The Communists assiduously courted Ruiz Giménez since the early 1960s in the hope that he and his associates, grouped around the magazine *Cuadernos para el Dialogo,* would prevail in the internal bickering and

[213]

move to create a "progressive" Christian Democratic party. Such a party could join with the Communists and Socialists, decisively shifting the balance of forces in the country in favor of the Left. Despite their efforts, in early 1977 Ruiz Giménez entered into an alliance with Gil-Robles and formed the *Federación Demócrata Cristiana*. Other Christian Democrats helped found the *Partido Popular* and eventually joined Adolfo Suárez in the *Unión de Centro Democrático*. The FDC suffered a devastating defeat at the polls in June 1977, receiving less than 2 percent of the national vote and not electing a single deputy, and many of its members switched to the UCD in the months thereafter.

The Communists and Labor

Traditional, conservative forces had supported Franco during the Civil War to retain their hegemony over Spanish society, preferring to deal with an emerging working class not by co-opting it but by brutally repressing it. Their victory appeared complete a decade and a half after the Civil War with the virtual disappearance of the traditional working-class organizations, the Socialist *Unión General de Trabajadores* (UGT) and the Anarchist *Confederación Nacional del Trabajo* (CNT), and their replacement by the vertically organized *Organización Sindical* (OS). But, in the 1950s, a process of modernization began that radically transformed the face of Spanish society: in the span of something over two decades, Spain changed from an agrarian and rural country with over 49 percent of the active population engaged in agriculture into an industrialized and urban one where in 1975 this percentage had dropped to approximately 26.[22] Economic expansion led millions of Spaniards to imigrate over the course of those years

[214]

to urban centers like Madrid and Barcelona and to cities in the Basque country, thus setting the structural conditions for new sources of labor conflict and dissent. In the late 1950s, the Spanish economy experienced a period of relative decline during which strike movements, although formally outlawed, reappeared. It was in the context of this movement that the first commissions of workers, the precursors of the now well-known *Comisiones Obreras* (CC.OO.), appeared in Asturias. These disappeared, however, as soon as the conflict which gave rise to them subsided. Ironically, it was the government's decision in 1958 to stimulate economic recovery by changing the structure of the collective bargaining system that gave the movement a shot in the arm. Whereas prior to that year the Ministry of Labor had set the wage guidelines for industry, now employers and employees could opt to negotiate contracts at the factory level.[23] This development energized the role of posts like those of *jurado de empresa* and *enlace sindical* which formed part of the official syndical structure but had been open to plant-level elections since the early part of the decade.

The party had scant opportunity in the years immediately following the Civil War to expand its audience although in 1948, when the leadership abandoned the guerrilla struggle, it instructed its militants to be active in the regime's syndicalist movement, combining, insofar as they could, legal and illegal activities. It was the changes in the collective bargaining scheme in 1958 that gave the PCE the opening it needed. After an initial and unsuccessful attempt to harness the nascent *Comisiones* to the party, through a largely ephemeral vehicle known as the *Oposición Sindical Obrera* (OSO), the Communist leadership reversed its course and ordered its militants to work within the movement. Initially, the *Comisiones* benefited from an uncertain judicial status: although Communists and others active in the movement claimed the factory assemblies

[215]

as their source of legitimacy, they used where they could the posts of *enlaces* and *jurados* as platforms from which to conduct their activities. The regime at first entertained the notion that it could use the CC.OO. to channel the dissent that the official organization had proved unable to handle. Thus, in 1964 the *Comisiones* of the metallurgical workers held their first meetings under the auspices of the Falange, and in 1966 the movement and the regime coincided in calling for a heavy turnout in the sindical elections. It soon became apparent, however, that the PCE and other leftist organizations were rapidly expanding their influence and giving the CC.OO. a markedly anti-regime character. The government forced the dismissal of hundreds of activists and the arrest of many others. The crackdown led to bitter polemics within the *Comisiones*.[24]

The harsh repression suffered by *Comisiones* activists at the hands of the regime in the late 1960s and early 1970s, however, helped that organization to become *the* national symbol of labor opposition to Franco. Of the traditional Socialist and Anarchist labor organizations, only the UGT retained some of its former influence, but its decision not to participate in the regime-sponsored sindical elections cut if off from the new sources of working-class activism. There was, as well, the *Unión Sindical Obrera* (USO), an organization founded in the early 1960s by Catholic labor activists with some strength in Catalonia, Madrid and the Basque country, but it could not really compete with the *Comisiones* either. Both organizations had tried to maintain classical trade union structures under the Franco dictatorship, but by so doing they placed themselves at a marked disadvantage with respect to the *Comisiones*. Their amorphous structures based on factory assemblies (they claimed to be a *movimiento sociopolítico* representing the "totality of the working class")[25] permitted a much greater flexibility during periods of political adversity.

[216]

The Communists emphasized the importance of maintaining those structures as well as the avowedly supra-partisan nature of their own orientation. What started out a necessity the PCE sought to transform into a virtue. For it, CC.OO. was the prototype of the *sindicato de nuevo tipo,* an original Spanish contribution to the reunification at the national and international levels of the labor movement split after 1917. Supporters and militants of all the families of the Left would be welcome and, for their part, the Communists abjured any hegemonic pretensions, declaring an intention to abandon the traditional Leninist "transmission belt" concept of party-trade union relations.[26]

By the early 1970s, it was evident, nonetheless, that the Communists, despite having to contend with leftist elements from the *Organización Revolucionaria de Trabajadores* (ORT), the *Movimiento Comunista* (MC), and the *Partido del Trabajo* (PT), had a preponderant influence in the *Comisiones* in cities like Madrid, Barcelona, Seville, Vigo, and Vizcáya and held a clear majority in the CC.OO. national executive, the *Coordinadora General.*[27] After national sindical elections in June 1975 showed the *Comisiones* candidates successful in many areas, some members of the PCE, particularly in Catalonia, argued that a takeover of the *Organización Sindical* had become possible and would give the party control of a key institutional lever in the twilight of the Franco era. The issue was hotly debated at the party's second National Conference in September 1975 and, finally, the leadership rejected the idea as premature.[28] But, after Franco's death a few months later, the party moved to use its dominant position within the CC.OO. as a springboard from which to establish a similar hegemony over the entire labor movement. The Communist-controlled *Coordinadora General* intensified its efforts to have the other major unions, the UGT and USO, join in the constitution of a

[217]

united labor confederation. The only hitch was that the proposed merger would not occur on the basis of equality—*Comisiones* would be the axis for the new federation—and, as might be expected, the other organizations rejected the offer. Thereupon, the CC.OO. decided to go ahead on their own, elect delegates at general factory assemblies, claim that these delegates represented the entire factory, and hold the *congresso obrero constituyente*.[29] The move met with such a decidedly unfavorable response (threatening as well to torpedo Communist efforts to effect a rapprochement with the principal Socialist group, the PSOE) that the *Coordinadora* backed down and in the fall of 1976 declared the CC.OO. would become a traditional labor union calling itself the *Confederación Sindical de Comisiones Obreras*. That decision led to the withdrawal of PT and ORT activists, who sought to form their own *sindicato unitario*. More recently, *Comisiones* has had to cope with a reinvigorated UGT, which received a great psychological boost from the Socialist victory in June 1977 and appears ready to challenge the Communist hegemony in the labor movement.

The Communists and the Regional Question

Tension between the center and the periphery has been a constant in modern Spanish history.[30] Although the antagonism between Madrid, on the one hand, and Catalonia, the Basque country and Galicia, on the other, is deeply rooted both in Spanish history and in the different processes of economic development in each area, forty years of autocratic centralism under Franco has aggravated the situation tremendously. After 1939, the regime treated the Catalans and Basques as conquered peoples. For example, the provinces of

[218]

Guipúzcoa and Vizcáya in the Basque country (or Euzkadi as it is called there) lost the fiscal and judicial autonomy they had enjoyed prior to 1936. And, it was not until 1975 that the government finally permitted instruction in the regional languages in public schools, and only in 1977 is it possible for a Basque, Catalan or Galician to use other than a Castilian name on birth records. Such policies engendered great resentment and, as a consequence, the opposition has found its greatest support in those regions.

The Communists have sought to capitalize on this resentment, but, as in other spheres, they have been extremely moderate in their approach. As an unflagging advocate of the Catalan, Basque and Galician peoples' absolute right to self-determination, the PCE had urged the reactivation of the *Estatutos de Autonomia* granted by the Spanish republic in the 1930s. But, to cut short those opponents who would accuse the party of calling for the dismemberment of the Spanish state, the PCE has stressed that it supports the integration of the various regions into a federally structured democratic state.[31] One problem for the Spanish Communists in recent years has been the explosion of linguistic and cultural nationalist feelings in provinces like Valencia, Asturias, and the Canary Islands. Unwilling to put itself on record as favoring self-determination for regions other than Catalonia, the Basque country and Galicia,[32] the PCE has had to withstand the criticisms of radical nationalists from those regions who demand the right to secede from Spain.[33]

Spanish Communist efforts to articulate an effective response to the regional problems facing Spain have also found expression at the level of organization. with the presence of regional Communist parties in the Basque country and Galicia and a formally autonomous *Partit Socialista Unificat de Catalunya* (PSUC). Their efforts in this sphere have brought

mixed results. The Communists have not been overly successful in the Basque country, for example, where the party has
had to deal with the presence of the various ETA *(Euzkadi Ta
Askatasuna)* factions and the numerous *abertzale* (autonomist)
groups. Many younger people in the region, not to mention
their elders, continue to distrust the Communists and see in
the *Partido Comunista de Euzkadi* (PCE) only an extension of
the Madrid-based leadership. Only in the urban areas of
Guipúzcoa and Vizcáya has the PCE, through the good offices
of its activists in the *Comisiones Obreras,* been able to expand its
audience. A similar situation has developed in Galicia where
the PCG's strength is linked to the presence of the CC.OO.
in the industrial centers; the party has had difficulty penetrating in rural, traditionally conservative, areas which are economically still dominated by a *minifundio* system of land
exploitation.

By contrast, it has been in Catalonia, virtually a fiefdom of
the Anarchist movement prior to 1936, that the Communists
and their organization have had the most notable success. The
PSUC, product of a fusion of four groups in July 1936,[34] has
had a leading role in the constitution of several opposition
fronts, such as the *Assemblea de Catalunya* and the *Consell de
Forces Politiques de Catalunya,* and is perhaps the leading force
on the Left in the region. Benefiting from the virtual disappearance of the Anarchist movement and the historic inability
of the *Partido Socialista Obrero Español* (PSOE) to shed its
image as a party with a *visión españolista,* the Catalan Communists have managed to present themselves as an authentically
regional political force; and in the June 1977 elections, PSUC
candidates made a better showing than Communists running
anywhere else in Spain. Despite their success in this enterprise
and their formal organizational autonomy vis-a-vis the PCE, it
can be said without great fear of contradiction that over the

[220]

last two decades the PSUC has functioned *primarily* as an instrument of the PCE's political strategy. Thus, the Catalan Communists have insisted, over the objections of many Center-Left forces in the region, that the issue of Catalan autonomy be negotiated in a broader Spanish context which included the legalization of all political parties in the country.[35] Even its organizational autonomy is limited: the negotiations leading to the entry into the PSUC in 1975 of a dissident leftist Catalan group known as *Bandera Roja* were carried on by Santiago Carrillo, and the PSUC Central Committee was only asked to give pro forma approval to the results.

Strategy and Ideological Evolution

The Spanish Communist leadership has ably exploited the opportunities offered by shifts in the traditional cleavages of Spanish society to lay a foundation for the party's subsequent political activity. The PCE coupled its policies in these spheres with concentrated efforts to overcome the image, held by many and reinforced by decades of regine propaganda, that it was an essentially alien force, national only in a very formal and narrow sense, whose tactical moderation masked an insatiable list for power that would end sooner or later with the assumption of total control on its part. We have already noted that the PCE sought to break this quarantine by reassuring its prospective middle-class allies that they had nothing to fear from the overthrow of the regime and the subsequent establishment of a *democracia política y social*. As an intermediate stage leading to socialism, the *democracia* presupposed state control of the commanding heights of the economy, with the nationalization of privately owned banks and insurance companies, the adoption of agrarian and fiscal reform programs, and a revamping of the central planning apparatus. But, the PCE promised, the pace of structural reforms would be slow, lasting for an extended period of time, and during this and the subsequent socialist stage all expropriated property owners would be fully indemnified.[36]

As part of its efforts to alter the view of the PCE as undemocratic, the Spanish Communist leadership extensively revised its ideological matrix. In partially abandoning traditional Leninist values in favor of more accommodating, pluralistic and consensual values, PCE ideologues were conscious that such a move had tacticaly utility. At the same time, it should not be overlooked that these changes in values went beyond narrowly opportunistic bounds and represented a partial opening up of the PCE. Both elements were present, for example, in the decision to revamp the traditional Leninist scheme that it was the working class in alliance with the peasantry that would play the leading role in the transition to socialism. The PCE believed that such a conception, accurate in the Russia of the early twentieth century, no longer fit contemporary Spain or, more broadly, Western Europe.[37] The declining importance of the agricultural sector in advanced industrial societies when coupled with the steady effects of the scientific-technical revolution (the latter had made science the "central productive force" in the world, declared PCE ideologist Manuel Azcárate in 1971, and would bring about the eventual elimination of any distinction between intellectual and physical labor) [38] made it impossible for the working class to discharge its leading role, together with the peasantry alone. Instead, the leading role in the stage of *democracia política y social,* as well as in the subsequent stage of socialist revolution would be played by what the party called the *alianza de las fuerzas del trabajo y de la cultura,* a term which owed much to the Gramscian notion of a "new historic bloc."

[222]

Labor referred to the working class and the peasantry, relatively easy categories to define. But the forces of culture was a catch-all term which included professionals like lawyers, physicians, scientists and journalists; administrative personnel in industry and government; and members of the university community.[39] According to the redefinition, those forces objectively interested in joining the working class as *permanent* allies on the road to socialism constituted the overwhelming majority of the population. As a consequence, socialism no longer had to be imposed by a tiny minority in the name of the people: The people, expressing themselves electorally, could gradually expand "bourgeois" democratic rights from the political to the economic sphere until socialism was established. That process would take place over several decades, with a minimum of social disruption.

The task of the parties of the Left was to find the right issues and formulas to galvanize the broad currents favoring socialism. Within the ruling coalition, moreover, the Communists promised that all parties would be on an equal footing. Agreed on the fundamentals, they would be free to carry on a lively "ideological struggle" with respect to the best specific measures to adopt at a given moment. Formally abandoning the traditional Leninist forumlation that the vanguard role in the revolutionary process belonged ipso facto to the Communist party and that other parties, if allowed to exist, were to be conceded a clearly subordinate role, the PCE opted for the less dogmatic, but certainly no less elitist, Gramscian notion of hegemony: that the party had to earn its leading role and should, in any case, aspire to function as a directing but not dominant force.[40] Internally, however, the party would retain its democratic centralist characteristics with differences of opinion tolerated and encouraged only so long as they did not crystallize into factional positions.[41] The basic unit of party

[223]

organization, on the other hand, would not be the factory cell but work and neighborhood sections *(agrupaciones)* which would hold public meetings.[42]

The Political Resolution of the PCE's 8th Congress in 1972 described the Spanish Communist vision of socialist society as one in which there would be respect for fundamental political liberties, freedom of information and criticism, freedom of artistic and intellectual creation, the renunciation of any attempt to impose an official state philosophy, and political pluralism into the indefinite future.[43] In advocating such a model of socialism, the PCE has gone quite a distance from Leninism's singular and, one might say, brutal obsession with the seizure of political power. The contemporary Spanish Communist view, more in line with the mainstream of Marxist thought in Western Europe, sees the struggle for political power accompanied by a coincident and long-term effort to transform the ideological and cultural bases of existing society.

The vision of a society where socialism and democracy are complementary notions is, as the Spanish Communists are well aware, extremely attractive, particularly as it is so radically opposed to the realities of Soviet and Eastern European practice. Caution is necessary, however. For the PCE, reality is still defined in terms of the class struggle. When the party asserts its intention to build a pluralist socialist society, it is important to remember that the Communist conception of pluralism is significantly different from the traditional Western one, in which fresh energies and unexpected ideas may spring at any moment from any point or group in society. The fact is that in the socialist society toward which the PCE claims to be moving, the vestiges of class society—of which bourgeois political parties are one example—will eventually have to disappear. A close reading of PCE documents suggests that, both in the later stages of the *democracia política y social* and under socialism, a bourgeois opposition, if tolerated would have its activities carefully circumscribed.[44] An article entitled "Political Liberties and Socialism" is particularly revealing.[45] Its author, Juan Diz, a member of the Executive Committee, gives his approval to the invasion of Hungary in October 1956 but criticizes the Czech intervention in August 1968. The distinction he draws between the two situations are not all that subtle. In Budapest, "the enemies of socialism who were trying to take advantage of existing liberties" were a danger to the existing order; in Prague, they were not.

THE INTERNATIONAL DIMENSION

The Foreign Policy of the PCE

Despite the favorable consequences which flowed from Spanish Communist defense of broad coalition politics in the struggle against the regime and later in the construction of the socialist society, it is clear that the PCE would have had a much more difficult task to establish its credibility as a profoundly national party had it not moved to assume an independent and highly critical stance toward the Communist Party of the Soviet Union (CPSU).

At first—beginning in the mid-1960s but only gathering momentum after the Warsaw Pact intervention in Czechoslovakia in August 1968—the principal aim of the PCE's efforts was to insure the party's organizational independence from the Soviet Union. By the early 1970s, however, the PCE leadership had begun to realize that organizational independence had broad ideological and political implications. Because the prospects for socialism in Spain were inextricably linked to the fate of the European Communist movement, a regional approach

[225]

by the Left to the problem of "socialism and democracy" was not only vitally necessary but also inevitable. The Soviets may have understood this even earlier than had the Spanish Communist leadership, which may explain why in the years after 1968 the CPSU went to such seemingly disproportionate lengths to bring to heel an ostensibly minor, clandestine party like the PCE. Certainly there is something to the notion that Moscow hoped to make of the PCE an example to other independent-minded Communist parties. As a relatively small party, operating under clandestine conditions and with a membership steeped in a tradition of unreflexive support for the Soviet Union, the PCE offered an easy target. But when in February 1974 the Soviet journal *Partiinaia Zhizn'* launched a bitter and apparently unprovoked attack on the Spanish Communists, the Soviets were attacking not just a critic of the Czech invasion or a party that had tenaciously defended itself against attacks by pro-Soviet dissidents but, rather, a party which by late 1973 was the most active exponent of the formation of a rival center for the international Communist movement with its focus in Western Europe. The Soviet blast was, in short, a conscious attack on a party which advocated the creation on a *European* level of that same "socialism with a human face" which the Prague Spring had symbolized and which was viewed, then and now, by Soviet policy-makers as a challenge not only to their system of imperial control over Eastern Europe but also to the political and social hegemony of the CPSU in the Soviet Union itself.

Origins of the Rift

Although it would be appropriate to date the PCE's adoption of an independent position from the party's criticism of

[226]

the invasion of Czechoslovakia, it is nonetheless clear that the Spanish Communist reaction to that summer's events was the result of a complex process heavily influenced not only by the leadership's conscious efforts to make the PCE acceptable to other opposition forces but also by generational and personality clashes.

The PCE's posture had already begun to shift in November 1963 when the Executive Committee, while approving a resolution on the Sino-Soviet split which condemned the Chinese position and voiced support for Soviet calls for an international conference, noted that the party would not go along with efforts at such a conference "to place this or that party [an obvious allusion to the Chinese and the Albanians] among the accused and condemning it." [46] Subsequently the Spanish Communist leadership moved to strengthen its ties with the independent-minded Communist parties of Italy and Romania, and in early 1966, no less a figure than the Secretary General of the PCE, Santiago Carrillo, criticized Soviet violation of what he termed the norms of socialist legality in the cases of two dissidents, Yuri Daniel and Andrei Siniavsky. Just as important in the long run, we may also presume, were the steps taken by the Spanish leader in two books—*Después de Franco, Qué?* (1965) and *Nuevos Enfoques a Problemas de Hoy* (1967)—to disassociate the PCE from what was "purely Russian in the Soviet revolution": the repression of political liberties and the implantation of a single-party state.[47]

Nevertheless, at this point, the Spanish Communist leadership had probably not yet come to appreciate that either the Soviets would not permit individual Communist parties to elaborate and follow through on plans for national roads to socialism or that they might not, in fact, be convinced of the need to reform and liberalize their own system. It was, after all, not so many years after Khrushchev's well-publicized

[227]

efforts to restore the so-called Leninist norms to Communist party life in the Soviet Union and to smooth over the rougher edges of the system so as to make it more responsive to the demands of the general population. It took the experience of Czechoslovakia in 1968 to disabuse the PCE of these notions.

Believing that the renovating dynamism of the post-January Czech communism offered the international movement the opportunity to recover the "ideological offensive" it had lost as a result of the excesses of Stalinism,[48] the Spanish Communists were unrestrained in their support for the Czech reforms. Shortly after the new Prague regime's "Action Program" appeared in April 1968, Santiago Alvarez, a member of the PCE Executive Committee, expressed his hearty approval for the new course and went so far as to characterize Dubček's Czechoslovakia as "the type of socialist society which, given our concrete conditions and experiences, we think we must have in Spain." [49] The spring and early summer of 1968 were certainly a time of exhilaration for the PCE. As one reads the speeches of party leaders and the articles in the party press during this period one is struck by the naiveté of seasoned Communists, their almost child-like belief that if the Soviet leaders could only be made to understand what was really going on in Prague, they would not be opposed, but would support Dubček's efforts.

The invasion found Santiago Carrillo and Dolores Ibárruri on vacation near Moscow. The next morning, these two along with Luigi Longo, Secretary General of the PCI, and Gian Carlo Pajetta, a PCI politburo member, met with Mikhail Suslov. During the conversation, Suslov reportedly turned to Carrillo and remarked will ill-disguised curtness that the latter's objections to the invasion carried little weight: "After all, you represent only a small party." [50] On August 23, *Radio España Independiente,* the Spanish Communist radio transmitter (which was at the time apparently situated in Czechoslovakia, but was subsequently moved to Romania), broadcast the PCE's official condemnation of the invasion, although a majority of the Executive Committee did not gather and approve a formal declaration until the beginning of September.

That the small and clandestine PCE dared challenge the CPSU so openly over Czechoslovakia was noteworthy. What is more significant, however, is that the PCE did not back down from its challenge at all, preferring instead to sharpen many of its initial criticisms. In this regard, it stood in marked contrast, for example, to the *Partido Comunista Português,* which described the intervention as "dictated by the overriding necessity of the defense of the socialist regime in the entire socialist community and of the peace of Europe." [51]

It was not until mid-September 1968 that the Central Committee of the PCE met, probably somewhere in southern France, and voted to ratify the Executive Committee's earlier condemnation of the invasion. The vote, 65 to 5, was overwhelmingly in favor of that condemnation. Yet as an editiorial published in the party newspaper *Mundo Obrero* and broadcast into Spain over the PCE's radio transmitter in late 1968 admitted, the party was, in fact, having difficulty with both "old and some young" members on the correctness of its policy with regard to the Soviet intervention.[52]

The Growth of Internal Dissension

Once the invasion had taken place, Carrillo moved to cast a distance between the PCE and the Soviet Union, but we must not suppose that an irremediable breach had developed between the two parties by that date. The ambivalence of the situation is attested to by the fact that Eduardo García, despite his support for the Soviet invasion of Czechoslovakia, was allowed to retain the post of Organizational Secretary until April 1969, when he was compelled to resign from the Central Committee. It was only later in mid-December when García drafted an *Open Letter* and circulated it among Spanish Communist emigrés in the U.S.S.R. that he and Gómez were expelled for their "factional" activity.

With their expulsion, a protracted battle began: it was led on the pro-Soviet side by old-guard elements rallying around the Civil War veteran and Executive Committee member, Enrique Líster; on the other side, by Carrillo and younger elements. Líster had viewed developments within the party after August 1968 with alarm.[53] Although apparently he had not voted against the resolution condemning the invasion of Czechoslovakia, it is not surprising that he felt uncomfortable with the new line. At first, and probably with Soviet acquiescence, he had hoped to play a mediating role in the conflict, but later Líster joined forces with García and Gómez. The first issue of their newspaper, which appeared a few weeks later (using the name of *Mundo Obrero* but printed in red rather than black), accused Carrillo of "opportunist deviations of the right and of the left" as well as of "systematic violations of democratic centralism."

Realistically, Líster could not have expected a majority to side with him, but he may well have had reason to believe that he could garner a sufficiently large minority to force the Carrilloist elements to temper their growing independent outlook. Unfortunately, from his point of view, two developments foiled his plans: there was, on the one hand, the fact that Carrillo, in control of the party apparatus, had conveniently enlarged the Central Committee for the special plenum convoked to deal with Líster's challenge by co-opting 29 new members; on the other, that the 79-year-old President of the party, Dolores Ibárruri, threw the considerable weight of her prestige in favor of Carrillo. It was Ibárruri's decision, in particular, that settled the issue. Although she has never publicly explained her reasons, we can perhaps speculate that Ibárruri, conscious of her position as the foremost living link with the PCE's historic past and despite long-standing close ties to the Russians, refused to cast her support to a "splittist," and potentially disastrous, effort.

That Ibárruri had refused to join forces with Líster in some ways sealed his fate with the Soviets as well. They were willing to give him money and organizational facilities, particularly in the bloc countries, but he never received the kind of open and unabashed support he demanded and which the CPSU had given other pro-Soviet factions, notably in the Greek and Australian Communist parties. Moreover, Líster did not really have much of a base of support among the Communists in Spain. His support was primarily among emigré Spanish Communist groups in the U.S.S.R., in Eastern and Western Europe, and in Latin America. Important too, although clearly less so, in explaining the Soviet unwillingness to come out flatly in Líster's favor were the links the PCE began to forge after 1968 with other parties in the international movement.

The relations of the Spanish Communists with their Italian counterparts, always close, grew closer after 1968. When open dissident activity broke out in the PCE, the Italian Communists left no doubt as to where their sympathies lay. A few days after the expulsion of the first pro-Soviet faction (the one led by García and Gómez), a PCE delegation headed by Santiago Carrillo visited Rome. Shortly thereafter *Rinascità*, the PCI's political weekly, published an article by Central Committee member Renato Sandri endorsing Carrillo's handling of the split.[54] In October 1970, a few weeks after

[231]

Líster's expulsion, the PCI rendered a similar show of support. Subsequently, the Italians went a good deal further and enlisted the assistance of Vittorio Vidali, Political Commissar of the famous Fifth Regiment which Líster had commanded during the Civil War. In June 1971, Vidali wrote Líster a letter, published in the official *Mundo Obrero,* in which he declared that the dissident activity "objectively served the class enemy." [55] Later in the same year Vidali went to Cuba and took a very active role in defending Carrillo against the dissidents' efforts to win support among the Spanish Communist emigrés there.[56]

The PCE's other staunch ally proved to be the Romanian party. A joint communiqué signed in April 1966 in Bucharest had given a clear indication that the Spanish Communists were making efforts to shift from their traditionally unconditional pro-Soviet stance. It marked the beginning of an era of extremely close ties between the two parties, particularly, Santiago Carrillo and Nicolae Ceaușescu. In June 1969, *Scînteia,* the Romanian Communist daily, published the entire text of Carrillo's speech to the world Communist conference, an honor accorded only the Romanian President, Soviet General Secretary Brezhnev, and PCI Secretary General Berlinguer. In December 1970, it also republished a blistering *Mundo Obrero* critique of Líster's activities.

The closeness of Spanish Communist relations with the Italians and Romanians during these and subsequent years stands in marked contrast to less warm and more formal relations they had with the French party (PCF). No mention was made in the French Communist press of the García expulsion, and it was only several weeks after Líster was expelled from the PCE that *l'Humanité* published a report on the events, citing *Le Monde* as its source. The article alluded to the principle of noninterference as codified in the June 1969

Conference document in explaining why the PCF had "deliberately abstained from publishing the least commentary." [57] Formal recognition of the Carrillo-Ibárruri leadership came only at the end of November 1970—not until it had become abundantly clear that the Soviets were not themselves intending to "recognize" the Líster group.[58] The coolness in relations between the PCE and PCF dated from the May 1968 events. Santiago Carrillo had implicitly criticized the conservative French Communist stance in June 1968 when he decried the all-too-common attitude of "reserve" and "prevention" among Communists with regard to the student movement.[59] Such an attitude, he warned, would lead only to a reduction in the strength and influence of Communist parties. The French leadership, under fire from its "revisionist" wing, could not have missed the volley. When, in the spring of 1969, Carrillo opened the pages of the Spanish Communist theoretical journal, *Nuestra Bandera,* to Roger Garaudy for a study on the "problems of revolution in evolved capitalist countries," he only rubbed salt in the wounds.[60]

Two years after the invasion of Czechoslovakia, the struggle between the regular organization of the PCE and the dissident group moved into high gear. The dissidents, striving to overcome their well-publicized image as nothing more than a Soviet pressure group, embarked on a course aimed at wresting international recognition and displacing the official party. To this end, they held a rump congress in April 1971 and then sought to use Enrique Líster's position as an incumbent member of the Presidium of the World Peace Council to gain entry for themselves at a WPC meeting in Budapest a few weeks later. Acting in concert with Líster, the organizers of the affair, offered the regular PCE delegation, led by Spanish poet Rafael Alberti, a Lenin Peace Prize laureate, joint representation on the Council with delegates from the dissident group. Alberti refused the offer and the delegation withdrew from the Assembly. This bold move met with partial success. Although Líster was not removed from the WPC Presidium, the new World Council posts allocated to Spain were not filled by members of either delegation.[61]

The regular PCE organization responded to the efforts of the dissidents and their Soviet backers on a broad front. Meeting in Belgrade in May 1971, the party's executive Committee declined an invitation to attend the 14th Congress of the Communist Party of Czechoslovakia. At the same time, Manuel Azcárate, PCE ideologist and international affairs expert, published the article "On the Use of Marxist Method." Formally a critique of a document adopted by the Czechoslovak party's December 1970 Central Committee meeting, the article was, in fact, no less than a direct challenge to all Soviet justifications for the August 1968 invasion. "Was socialism in danger?" Azcárate asked rhetorically. "To say yes," answering his own question, "is not only to laugh at truth but also to insult socialism." [62] Then, in June 1971, the PCE followed up these verbal thrusts with a demonstration of the party's mass following: it organized a huge rally at Montreuil Park in Paris, which was attended by some 50,000 people, mostly Spanish immigrants. Finally, in October 1972, the official Spanish Communist party convened its own version of an 8th Congress. The 104 delegates present elected a 118-member Central Committee, a 24-member Executive Committee, and a seven-man Secretariat. Santiago Carrillo delivered the main report in the Central Committee's name. Essentially a reiteration of well-known features of the PCE's position, it coupled a call for solidarity with all 14 socialist countries with an appeal for a new unity of the international movement based on "respect for the independence of each party . . . [and] noninterference, *in word as well as in fact,* in internal affairs." [63] The Congress received fraternal messages from 37 parties, including the CPSU. While the messages from the pro-Soviet ruling parties were circumspect and by no means warm, they did at least acknowledge the PCE to be a legitimate expression of the Communist movement in Spain. This concession so exacerbated differences within the dissident group that its ranks split in late 1972; the group's Central Committee, meeting in January 1973, voted to dismiss Eduardo García, Agustín Gómez, and Alvaro Galiana from their posts on the Executive Committee.

In the meantime, Líster and his supporters (perhaps numbering only several hundred now) went on to convene an Extraordinary Congress in late June 1973 and changed the group's name to the *Partido Comunista Obrero Español* (PCOE). Reduced to relative impotence abroad, the PCOE decided to concentrate its efforts on the struggle in Spain. By early 1974, in one of those ironic twists of Communist politics, it considered entering into an alliance with the *Frente Revolucionário Antifascista y Patriotico* (FRAP), an umbrella terrorist organization formally founded in January 1974 and dominated by the Maoist-oriented *Partido Comunista de España, Marxista-Leninista*. Most recently, the PCOE entered into negotiations aimed at fusing with a group of leftist Communist dissidents, the *Oposición de Izquierda al Partido Comunista* (OPI), who were not pro-Soviet but had left the PCE after the 8th Congress in disagreement over what they considered Santiago Carrillo's preoccupation with allaying the fears of the Spanish bourgeoisie and his disinterest in offering a real, socialist perspective to the Spanish working class.

The CPSU and the Spanish Challenge

That the Soviets may have had their reasons for exercising restraint in their dealings with Carrillo [64] should not obscure the fact that they could only have been daily becoming more concerned with the PCE's determined efforts to devise a theoretical framework within which the party could justify a position of autonomy and independence. For example, an article written by Carrillo and published in *Nuestra Bandera* in the fall of 1968 sought to explain not only the military intervention in Czechoslovakia but the Sino-Soviet conflict in terms of Marxist theory. Carrillo noted the existence of something akin to a "cold war" among the socialist countries and laid the blame for this and other problems dividing Communists at the door of ruling Communist parties, which, he declared, were influenced, as often as not, by "reasons of state rather than proletarian internationalism." While admitting the duty of every Communist to defend the accomplishments of the "socialist community," he insisted that under no circumstances should non-ruling Communist parties become "satellites of one or another socialist state." Blind allegiance would not help the international movement's present difficulties. What was required was not a "directing center or a common discipline" but recognition of the need for each Communist party to elaborate its strategy independently—that is, "to reaffirm its national personality." [65] Carrillo's article, like his speech to the June 1969 Moscow Conference, only suggested the origins of the "present difficulties." He left to others the task of making that fundamental point explicit. With that purpose apparently in mind, *Nuestra Bandera* in 1970 published two essays, one by Juan Diz of the Executive Committee, the other by Ernest Martí of its Central Committee.[66] Both authors attributed the stagnation and crisis of the international Communist movement to the "monolithic and authoritarian tradition" inherited from Stalin.

Particularly demonstrative of the independent role the PCE had come to play in the world Communist movement was the

[236]

visit to China in November 1971 by a delegation headed by Secretary General Carrillo and including four other members of the PCE Executive Committee. The visit marked the first time a non-ruling Communist party had resumed relations with Peking after severing them in the heat of the Sino-Soviet polemics in the early 1960s. Although the Spanish delegation did not manage to meet with any more important figure than Keng Piao, head of the CCP's Central Committee section on relations with foreign Communist parties, Carrillo was more than willing to accept the partial snub. After all, the trip could not help but underscore to the Soviets that the "new" unity which the Spanish hoped to build in the international movement would in no case be based on proletarian internationalism *qua* unconditional loyalty to the Soviet Union. A *Mundo Obrero* article in early December 1971 reiterated the party's position:

> There must be no guiding party or ruling center. No party has the right to impose its views on another or to interfere. Each party has its own forms and methods of action which are different from someone else's. These are general principles we regard as essential to arrive at a new unity—a unity of diversity of the Communist movement and of anti-imperialist forces.[67]

Eurocommunism and the PCE

The PCE delegation's visit to Peking in late 1971 marked the end of one stage in the post-1968 development of the Spanish Communist party, a stage during which the Carrillo group successfully defended its independence vis-à-vis Moscow. During the course of those three years, the PCE had

[237]

been elaborating its own vision of a Spanish road to socialism, primarily in the books and articles of Carrillo and a few other key personalities in the party, but it had been unwilling (perhaps out of caution) publicly to express its conviction that the West European Communist parties had to elaborate a regional strategy and a model of socialism for the entire region. In the months after the Peking visit the PCE's efforts shifted from defensive efforts aimed at blunting Soviet interference, to advocating and marshalling support for a regional popular-front approach. Although the party by no means abandoned its position on crucial issues of the international movement—in fact, it adamantly reiterated its stance on more than one issue—it moved more openly to relate its domestic strategy to a regional Western European perspective.

The Europeanization of the PCE

In the 1950s and early 1960s the PCE had, like other Western European Communist parties, denounced the European Economic Community (EEC) as an instrument of domination by North American and European monopolies and thus rationalized its total opposition to any Spanish association with the Common Market. This assessment derived from a persepctive which considered the world as irrevocably split into two antagonistic and competing blocs, headed by the Soviet Union and the United States respectively. The Czech invasion in 1968, the worsening of Sino-Soviet relations, the Soviet overtures to the Franco regime for diplomatic relations,[68] and Soviet acquiescence to the Spanish government's inclusion in the European Security Conference encouraged the PCE to undertake a thorough re-examination of the motives behind Soviet foreign policy. By 1972, the party leadership had concluded that Soviet support for détente and peaceful coexistence concealed a determination to accept a divided Europe, a Europe in which the Kremlin would for a long time permit American hegemony over the West while retaining its own in the East. Soviet acquiescence to the freezing of the status quo in Europe only pointed up for the Spanish Communists the degree to which *raison d'état* rather than proletarian internationalism had become the motor force behind Soviet policy. At the same time, new perspectives for the transformation of European societies had opened.

In his report to the 8th Congress in 1972, Manuel Azcárate analyzed this situation. In his opinion, there was a favorable climate for the "joint elaboration of strategic choices" among Western European Communists, all of whom would invariably come to share a view of socialism as "the development and broadening of democracy, creating a real workers' power, recognizing the value of political, cultural and scientific liberties and of it as a society that does not give the state an official ideology and which accepts a plurality of parties and the autonomy of the labor movement from any political movement." The "growth of those ideas," Azcárate concluded, "on an international, European level will permit huge numbers of workers and citizens to have a new, concrete and mobilizing image of what socialism can be and what it must be in this part of the world." A Europe where "Communists, Socialists and other forces" worked together, he added, could be called upon to play an important, independent role, forcing a political space in the context of the global superpower competition.[69]

The policy which the PCE has articulated with regard to NATO, the Atlantic alliance, and the presence of United States bases on Spanish territory has been consistent with the broader notion that the parties of the European Left have to make every effort to avoid being destabilizing forces in their own countries as well as on a regional scale. Although the Spanish Communist newspaper, *Mundo Obrero,* in late 1974 called the American bases a "mortal danger for our motherland," the PCE has publicly declared that it will accept their presence in Spain for the foreseeable future or, at least, until Soviet forces withdraw from Eastern Europe. Negotiations for their dismantling should take place, in the Spanish Communist view, in the context of pan-European talks on force reduction. The PCE has shown itself opposed in principle to future Spanish integration in NATO, declaring its intention to campaign against such entry, but the party has indicated it would accept whatever decision a new and democratically elected Cortes adopted. It is unlikely, however, that the Spanish Communists will ever become enthusiastic supporters of that alliance, and there is little chance the party will support increased allocations for defense in the event of Spanish entry into NATO.

It is in the context of PCE efforts to forge a united front of the European Left that we must approach the highly polemical, anonymous article attacking the Spanish Communists which appeared in the CPSU Central Committee journal *Partiinaia Zhizn'* in February 1974. This article singled out four aspects of a report by Manuel Azcárate to a September 1973 PCE Central Committee plenum for harsh criticism: (1) what it called "his incorrect and absurd thesis that there [were]contradictions between the state interests of the socialist countries and the interests of the revolutionary movement"; (2) his invectives against the Soviet socialist system, which, according to the piece, amounted to "spreading all manner of lies about the absence of democracy in the U.S.S.R."; (3) his outlook on the "problem of autonomy and equality of rights of the fraternal parties," which, the article declared, "includes not one ounce of proletarian inter-nationalism"; and, (4) his

[240]

call—"which reeks of nationalism"—for a democratic and socialist Europe. What seemed particularly offensive about the last point was that such a Europe would evidently have "no ties whatever to the present socialist community." [70]

The *Partiinaia Zhizn'* synopsis distorted the Azcárate report in question (as the Spanish were quick to point out), but it by no means misrepresented the PCE's position on certain issues. Specifically, it accurately gauged the intent behind the PCE's call for a European model of socialism: the creation of a European Socialist Community, not under the influence of either superpower, and where democracy and socialism would be complementary. Of all the sins Azcárate could have committed, this clearly disturbed the Soviets the most. The other criticisms, while certainly not insignificant, acquired a special, provocative importance only when coupled with the regionalist perspective. In choosing as their target Manuel Azcárate, the Soviets were attacking the Spanish Communist who, after Secretary General Carrillo himself, was the principal exponent of Spanish revisionism, but it is important to recognize that the vituperation directed at Azcárate may well have been aimed at another target: the PCE's Program Manifesto presented at the September 1973 Central Committee plenum. Certainly, in the years after 1968 the PCE had on more than one occasion criticized what it saw as the fusion of party and state in Eastern Europe, the authoritarianism and bureaucratism exhibited by those societies, and the absence of fundamental democratic freedoms there. With the publication of the Program Manifesto, however, the PCE leadership not only codified those criticisms but pointedly contrasted the PCE's proposed solutions for Western Europe with the practice of the East.

Just what Moscow's motives were in approving publication of the article in *Partiinaia Zhizn'* is, in any case, difficult to assess. The assessment becomes even more complicated when one looks at the joint communiqué issued in Moscow in October 1974 at the end of talks between the two parties.[71] As the communiqué makes amply clear, the PCE representatives' journey to the Soviet Union was no pilgrimage to Canossa. For, while the Russians made a major concession in publicly disowning the splinter Spanish group and "promise(d) by every means an improvement in relations and mutual trust, even when differences exist on certain questions," there were no major concessions by the PCE. Only with respect to the Soviet policy of détente did the Spanish Communists shift their stance and agree that the policy of peaceful coexistence as practiced by the Soviet Union "not only did not restrain the class struggle and the activities of Communist parties in the capitalist countries but on the contrary created more favorable conditions for their development." And yet, even here, caution is necessary; for, the change may have come in response to Soviet assurances that Kremlin policy toward Europe would soon change.

The chain of events poses a major question. If *Partiinaia Zhizn'* in February 1974 had accused Manuel Azcárate (and by implication the Spanish Communist leadership) of "siding with the declared enemies of the Soviet socialist system," why in October did a Soviet delegation sign a joint communiqué with the same leadership group in a "spirit of sincerity and mutual understanding"? What happened in the months after the *Partiinaia Zhizn'* article appeared that could have induced the Soviets to institute such a sharp reversal in policy toward the PCE?

There were, in all probability, two basic reasons for the turnabout. One has to do with developments in the Iberian peninsula. The rapidity with which the Portuguese military overthrew the ultra-conservative regime of Marcello Caetano in April 1974 and the evident deterioration of the Franco government's ability to rule after the December 1973 as-sassination of Admiral Carrero Blanco seemed to confirm something that Santiago Carrillo had been saying all along to the Russians: that the Iberian peninsula had potentially the most revolutionary situation in all of Europe, that the over-throw of the Spanish and Portuguese regimes would create very favorable conditions for the "democratic and progressive" forces of other European countries. The other reason has to do with the all-European Communist conference. The communi-qué was published two days before the opening in Warsaw of a meeting of European Communist parties, the first in a series aimed at finding a formula for agreeing on the terms of a forthcoming meeting. Under pressure to attend from the Italian Communists (who served with the Poles as co-hosts to the meeting), the PCE may have made a formal communiqué with the Soviets the *sine qua non* of its attendance.

The conference of European Communist parties held in East Berlin in June 1976 after two years of hard bargaining saw the public victory of the Eurocommunist bloc. The back-ground and the particulars of the East Berlin conference are discussed in William E. Griffith's chapter on the diplomacy of Eurocommunism. As might be expected, it was Santiago Carrillo who was the most explicit exponent of national communism:

> For years, Moscow was our Rome. We spoke of the great October Socialist revolution as if it were our Christmas. That was the period of our infancy. Today we have grown up . . . We will not return to the past structures and conceptions of internationalism.[72]

Spanish Communist differences with the Soviet leadership had deepened as a result of events in Portugal in the preceding year. At the outset, the PCE greeted the Portuguese revolu-

[243]

tion, seeing in it a prelude to an offensive by the Left throughout Mediterranean Europe. The euphoria quickly dissipated, however, as the Portuguese Communist party, making little effort to conceal its disdain for "bourgeois" political institutions, showed how dissimilar were its views from those of the Spanish on how to exploit the changed balance of forces on the European continent. Relations between the PCE and the PCP had never been particularly cordial, and by mid-1975 they had deteriorated to the point where an anonymous Spanish Communist leader could refer to the PCP as a "phantom of the Stalinist epoch" and could characterize Alvaro Cunhal as a man out of touch with Portuguese reality who, oblivious to changes in the world over six decades, was maniacally determined to repeat the 1917 attack on the St. Petersburg Winter Palace in the Lisbon of 1975. The decree imposing labor unity (January 1975), the banning of the Portuguese Christian Democratic party (March), and the closing of the newspaper *República* elicited quick, negative responses from the PCE. And this was logical enough; for, the Spanish Communists risked seeing their assiduous efforts, aimed at reassuring the Spanish middle classes that their party intended to abide by the rules of parliamentary democracy, undercut by the turn of events in Portugal.

Clearly, the sort of socialist society envisioned by the Portuguese Communists and their radical allies in the Armed Forces Movement (MFA) was diametrically opposed to the *viá española al socialismo*. But what may have particularly disturbed the Spanish Communist leadership was that the Soviet Union, in acquiescing to the PCP's thrust for power in the summer and fall of 1975, may have been doing so, at least in part, to place an obstacle in the way of the PCE and like-minded parties. Santiago Carrillo seemed to imply as much when he warned, in a November 1975 interview with the dissident Italian Communist journal *Il Manifesto,* that no one should

> nourish excessive illusions . . . about the way the U.S.S.R. will react to the formation of socialist countries—or ones in the process of becoming such—not dependent on the U.S.S.R. itself, and which will have a political structure different from those in the Peoples' democracies. There is *no* doubt that the latter will look more and more toward European models of socialism, if we reach that point" [emphasis supplied]. Whether one likes it or not, the socialism in Western Europe will become a pole of reference for the whole working class movement and . . . [we cannot] ignore the fact that this will be viewed with concern in Moscow.[73]

THE PCE AND THE POST-FRANCO ERA

Through the 1960s the Spanish Communists had had little success in building the broad coalition of forces they wanted. Their fortunes changed for the better with the assassination in December 1973 of Spain's head of state, Admiral Luis Carrero Blanco. Carrero Blanco had been widely regarded as the *eminencia gris* of the regime, the man on whom the aged dictator could count to insure the continuation of his system. Whether Carrero could have held the system together is open to question; what is clear, however, is that in the wake of his death the regime entered a phase of slow but noticeable decomposition.

Fueled by an evident deterioration in Franco's own physical condition, the jockeying for position among the various factions of the regime began in earnest. Some, the "aperturistas,"

[245]

held that the democratization of Spanish society within the context of the political structures inherited from Franco was not only possible but necessary in the near future—that it was the only way of avoiding disastrous political and social conflict. Their opponents, the "ultras," represented the most conservative trend in Spanish politics and saw in the slightest deviation from pristine Falangism a betrayal of the ideals for which Franco fought during the Civil War. Carrero Blanco's successor, Carlos Arias Navarro, tried to steer a middle course between these factions, presenting a very modest reform program which called for the establishment of "national political associations" within the context of the existing state party, the *Movimiento Nacional*. The overthrew of the Caetano regime in neighboring Portugal in April 1974 gave his vociferous critics (the most prominent of whom were José Antonio Girón, Blas Piñar, and the group called *Fuerza Nueva*) an opportunity to point to events in that country as confirmation of what would happen in Spain if Franco did not snuff out all attempts at liberalization. Franco's illness in the summer of 1974 exacerbated these tensions and ultimately resulted in the dismissal in October of the leading Cabinet "liberal" Pio Cabanillas, the Minister of Information.

The growing government crisis and the general feeling among politically aware Spaniards that the regime's political structures were anachronistic created a favorable environment for opposition activities. The PCE, convinced that the end of the regime was near, entered into contact with other groups in an effort to form a united opposition front. In July 1974, at a press conference in Paris, Santiago Carrillo could announce the result of those efforts, the creation of a *Junta Democrática*. Described by the Communists as a "temporary convergence of the working class and neocapitalist forces," the *Junta* brought together several opposition parties and personalities, all of whom adopted a 12-point program which called for the establishment of a provisional government, a general amnesty, legalization of all political parties, separation of Church and state, and eventual Spanish entry into the EEC.[74]

Conspicuously absent from the *Junta* were several important opposition organizations like the *Partido Socialista Obrero Español* (PSOE) (which had grown rapidly after militants working in Spain wrested control of the organization and ousted the exile leadership headed by Rodolfo Llopis in 1972), the *Unión Social Democrática Española* (USDE), and various Christian Democratic groups. These organizations had entered into discussions with the PCE concerning participation in the *Junta* but had chosen at the last moment not to commit themselves. Their absence certainly detracted from the scope of the coalition the Communists put together: except for the PCE and the *Comisiones* (and with the possible exception of the PSP), the other organizations and personalities that joined the *Junta* had little real or potential strength. There was, as a consequence, something of the theatrical in the Communist insistence, over the next year and a half, that the *Junta* was the embodiment of the "democratic alternative" to the regime and as such would provide the nucleus for the provisional government that would replace Franco.[75] Creation of the *Junta* was, nevertheless, a significant political victory for the PCE and its moderate policies. It proved to be an ideal vehicle for the Spanish Communists to establish a formal dialogue with others in the opposition and insure that in the post-Franco era the party would be a full participant in the political process. As the first national opposition coalition to emerge in the twilight of the Franco era, moreover, the *Junta* and the groups composing it received an inordinate amount of recognition and favorable publicity. Its representatives travelled extensively, visiting the United States, Mexico, and various European capitals, and successfully presented the organization as the principal opponent of the regime. This was particularly galling to other groups in the opposition, but, then again, they were not to form their own rival organization until June 1975.

Franco died in November 1975. Expecting the rapid disintegration of the regime, the *Junta* adopted a hard-line stance, demanding the self-exile of the newly crowned king Juan Carlos while a referendum was organized to decide the fate of the monarchy and the immediate constitution of a provisional government with the participation of all the opposition.[76] These maximalist objectives were not attainable; for, although the *Junta* and, more broadly, the opposition could and did stage mass demonstrations and call many strikes, it could not offer a coherent alternative to the regime.

For almost a year and a half after his accession to the throne, Juan Carlos and those who hoped to lead Spain through a process of controlled decompression could not capitalize on that weakness. In part, this was due to the fact that the reformers had to overcome not only the resistance of Francoist stalwarts entrenched throughout the state bureaucracy but also the lukewarm attitude of hold-over Premier Arias Navarro, who made little effort to disguise his lack of enthusiasm for Western European-style political democracy. Matters threatened to get out of hand by late spring and early summer 1976 when the Cortes watered down the already weak program Arias Navarro had presented in the king's name. One prominent Christian Democrat, José María Gil Robles, who could hardly be accused of being a radical, warned the king that failure to press forward vigorously would imperil the future viability of the monarchy.[77] Finally, and perhaps in part due to assurances of support he received during a visit to the United States in early June 1976, Juan Carlos moved to break the stalemate. He asked for and received Arias Navarro's resignation and appointed 43-year-old Adolfo Suárez in his place. A man who had made his career in the Falangist bureaucracy, Suárez seemed a most unlikely choice to lead the dismantling of the Francoist political structures. Suárez had, however, the personal confidence of the king and, more importantly perhaps, was young enough to have his political future yet before him. The reform program he announced in September 1976, promising elections before June 1977 and holding open the prospect for the instauration of a parliamentary democracy, received approval of the Cortes in November and was ratified by a referendum one month later.

Suárez' proposal broke the unity of the opposition. The Communist-dominated *Junta* and the *Plataforma* had fused in March 1976 into a single organization, the *Coordinación Democrática* or, as it was popularly called, the *Platajunta*. But *Coordinación* was an unwieldy conglomerate whose members ranged from conservative Christian Democrats to Maoists. When Suárez unveiled his program, the Communists quickly rejected it on the grounds that only a provisional government and not one issuing from the bowels of Francoism was morally qualified to preside over the transition to democracy.[78] The Communists continued to insist on the need for a clearcut *ruptura* with the past and, in this, they had the support of the PSOE, whose leadership, with an eye to future elections and under pressure from its own base, was not willing to be outdone on the Left by the PCE. By contrast, the more moderate elements in the opposition, principally the Christian Democrats and liberal groups, had no difficult with permitting the government to continue in office and preferred, instead, to concentrate on negotiation guarantees that the forthcoming elections would, in fact, be democratic.

Although the Communists would certainly have preferred to topple the regime and thus "conquer" democracy, as political realists they could hardly deny how much the political situation had changed in the span of two years. The party was illegal but no longer clandestine. Its Secretary General had been arrested in Madrid in December 1976 but quickly released, and Communist candidates seemed likely to appear, if only as independents, in the lists for the parliamentary elections to be held six months later.

It was in this context that the extreme Right made a final bid to disrupt the democratization process. In late January 1977, a group of terrorists broke into the offices of Communist lawyers who had been active in defending dissident labor activists. The gunmen lined up the lawyers and shot them. Coming the evening after the kidnapping of an army general by leftist radicals, the action threatened to plunge the country into chaos and possibly lead to a military coup. The Communists responded to the provocation by organizing a peaceful, mass funeral demonstration and calling again for national reconciliation and amnesty, the last even for those who had participated in the crime.

The restraint exercised by the PCE on that occasion put the issue of the party's legalization squarely on the political agenda. In an effort to sidestep the issue, the Suárez government availed itself of a penal code prohibition of groups with "totalitarian" objectives whose policies obeyed an international discipline and referred the matter to the Spanish Supreme Court. In April 1977, however, after some rather tense deliberations, the Court ruled it did not have jurisdiction over a "political" issue and declined to offer an opinion. Suárez could not temporize much longer. Were he not to rule in the PCE's favor, many opposition groups were likely to refuse to participate in the elections, and as a consequence the political reform program would be in jeopardy. Finally, during an Easter holiday weekend when Spain's largest cities were virtually empty, the government announced its decision to legalize the Communist party. The extreme Right predictably called for the military to step in, but, except for the resignation of the Minister of the Navy and some cries of betrayal in the *Consejo Superior del Ejercito*, there were few visible signs of significant disaffection over a move most people understood to be largely inevitable.

The week following the legalization, the PCE Central Committee held its first session in Madrid in nearly four decades. At the conclusion of the plenum, in a move that reflected consummate political opportunism and realism, the leadership approved a motion adopting the present bicolor Spanish flag as the party's own and promising acceptance of a constitutional monarchy. Abandonment of the PCE's traditional insistence on a republican form of government caused consternation among some party members, but the leaders justified the decision on the grounds that polarization of the country into monarchist and republican factions would only serve to give ultra-conservative elements in the military an excuse for intervention. The crisis quickly passed and several weeks later the president of the PCE and Francoist *bête noire*, Dolores Ibárruri, quietly re-entered the country.

On June 15, 1977, after a largely uneventful campaign which officially lasted three weeks, Spain at last held its parliamentary elections. Victory in the contest, as expected, went to the *Unión de Centro Democrático* coalition headed by Premier Adolfo Suárez, with almost 35 percent of the vote, 165 seats in the Chamber of Deputies, and 105 in the Senate; but the PSOE, led by Felipe González, came a close second with nearly 29 percent of the vote, 118 seats in the Chamber, and 66 in the Senate. For their part, the Communists emerged

[251]

as the third largest electoral force in the country, garnering more than 1.7 million votes, 9.2 percent of the national total, and 20 seats in the lower chamber.

Polls taken over the previous two years had almost invariably agreed that the PCE would not receive more than 10 percent of the vote; but many in the party, blinded by the pre-eminent role the PCE had played in the opposition to Franco and gauging by the enthusiasm and size of the audiences drawn during the electoral campaign, had hoped for and expected more. As it was, an electoral law which purported to be proportional but was not, the hangover effect of forty years of anti-Communist propaganda, and the Communist inability

TABLE 1

Results of the June 1977 Election

Party	Vote	Percentage	Deputies
Unión de Centro Democrático	6,220,889	34.7	165
Partido Socialista Obrero Español/Partit Socialista de Catalunya	5,240,464	29.3	118
Partido Comunista de España/ Partit Socialista Unificat de Catalunya	1,655,744	9.2	20
Alianza Popular	1,494,693	8.3	16
Unidad Socialista/Partido Socialista Popular	799,376	4.5	6
Pacte Democratic per Catalunya	498,744	2.8	11
Partido Nacionalista Vasco	286,540	1.6	8
Others *	1,721,581	9.6	6
Total	17,918,031	100.0	350

* This figure includes the votes and deputies of the Coalición Electoral Unió del Centre i de la Democracia Cristiana de Catalunya (167,654 votes and 2 deputies), Esquerra de Catalunya (134,953 and 1), Candidatura de Centro Independiente (67,748 and 2), and Euskadiko Eskerra (58,377 and 1).

Source: Informaciones (Madrid), January 14, 1978.

to wrest the political initiative from Adolfo Suárez in 1976 took its toll. Only in the Catalan provinces, Córdoba, Madrid, Málaga, Oviedo, and Seville did the party receive more than 10 percent of the ballots casts.

PROSPECTS AND CONCLUSIONS

The accommodating, pluralistic, and consensual stance the PCE adopted over the course of the last two decades did not bring the Communists the sort of electoral payoff they had anticipated. The first elections of the post-Franco era, although demonstrating the PCE to be firmly implanted in important sectors of Spanish society and particularly in the working class,[79] were won handily by the UCD and the PSOE. The Communists, who had been convinced their party could easily translate its influence as the best organized opposition force into electoral terms, had to abandon the idea that the PCE would rapidly move into a dominant position on the Left in a democratic Spain and had instead to worry about narrowing the margin which separated them from the PSOE as quickly as possible. Failure to do so would permit the Socialists and the Center to consolidate their hegemony in Spanish politics and make it possible to isolate the PCE.

Communist strategy in the months after June 1977 has been premised on the need to constitute a broadly-based *gobierno de concentración nacional* which would not necessarily include the PCE but would rely on its support in the Cortes. Spanish Communist leaders have defended this position on the grounds that democratic institutions in Spain are still too weak for a polarization of politics into Right and Left to take place.[80] While this posture may reflect a correct assessment of the situation in the country, the underlying analysis also has a

[253]

potent anti-PSOE thrust in the sense that both a condition for and a consequence of success in this venture is preventing the formation of a Socialist-led government.

It is still too early to tell what the outcome of the jockeying among the three major parties will be. Suárez has used competition between the Socialists and Communists (the clearest example is the politico-economic agreement known as the *pacto de la Moncloa,* signed in October-November 1977) to buttress his and the UCD's position, but the *Unión de Centro* is an unwieldy coalition of twelve political parties with Liberal, Social Democratic and Christian Democratic wings, whose base of support may narrow sharply if the government is unable to deal successfully with the manifold economic problem facing the country.

Communists and Socialists will be in stiff competition in many areas of Spanish social life, but their struggle for hegemony on the Left is likely to focus for some time primarily in the labor movement. The PSOE emerged from the June 1977 electoral test a clear-cut winner over Enrique Tierno Galvan's PSP and the *Federación de Partidos Socialistas* (in the aftermath of the victory, PSOE ranks swelled with the inclusion of various Socialist groups including, most notably, in April 1978 the PSP). But only with great difficulty will the PSOE assume the focal role in the politics of the Left its Portuguese counterpart achieved after November 1975.

Communist gains are not likely to be dramatic, but we should not under-estimate their ability (although here, admittedly, a good deal will depend on possible mistakes of the PSOE leadership) to make inroads into areas of Socialist strength. In any case, it can hardly be ignored that many younger Socialists, while cognizant of a historic rivalry with the Communists, nonetheless see the PCE as a natural ally in the struggle for socialism and are likely to press their leaders to collaborate with the PCE on the basis of a common program. The reverse is also true, moreoever, and is an additional reason (aside from an understandable Socialist desire to avoid duplicating the Italian experience) why a Spanish version of the *compromesso storico* is not all that likely.

Spanish Communist political influence will be much greater than might be ascribed the party simply on the basis of the June 1977 parliamentary election results. This is sure to worry some who do not trust the PCE and see many ambiguities in its political evolution. No one can be quite sure of the present intentions of Santiago Carrillo or, perhaps more accurately, of his ability or willingness at a future time of deep social and economic crisis to control and restrain the PCE. The Spanish Communists very likely have, and will for some time continue to have, an instrumental view of parliamentary democracy. Nevertheless, it may be the case that the PCE, finally accepted as a full member of the Spanish political community and constrained by the presence of a strong Socialist party, will find its future options narrowed and itself impelled along the path of democratic reforms.

Such an evolution could lead to change in the centralized character of the PCE organization. Unabashed users of democratic centralism under clandestinity, Communist leaders promised a democratization of party structures once conditions changed in Spain. In the year since its legalization, the party has already opened up significantly. The debates sparked throughout the PCE, but especially in Madrid, Asturias and Cataluña, but the proposal of Santiago Carrillo (and which the 9th Congress meeting in April 1978 eventually approved [81]) to drop the reference to Leninism from the party program and to define the PCE simply as a "Marxist, democratic and revolutionary" organization were probably unprecedented in the recent history of the international Communist movement.

[255]

Carrillo and the party apparatus managed to keep things from getting out of hand; but, as time passes and the intensity of the Spanish Communist quest for democratic credibility and votes increases, they may be compelled to make even greater concessions to those who demand a deepening of internal democracy.

The PCE and its members are not immune to the forces at work in Spanish society. There are new generations of Communists waiting in the wings to assume control of the party. For the present, Santiago Carrillo remains firmly in control. Despite repeated rumors that he is under challenge from one or another member of the leadership (the new Central Committee elected at the 9th Congress re-elected him Secretary General unanimously), there is little chance that he will leave his post until he is ready to do so. Nonetheless, the succession issue, although not explicitly raised at the 9th Congress, will have to be addressed in the PCE in the not-too-distant future. While none of the possible candidates for the post of Secretary General would be likely to change the substance of PCE policy, the change would have its inevitable effect on the party. Carrillo, for better or worse, has been able to impress his own parricular style on the PCE. For him, as for Marshal Tito in Yugoslavia, the PCE and Spain have been too small a stage, and his ideas have always had a European dimension uncommon in many of the continent's Communists. It should not surprise us if a new Secretary General has a less dynamic and articulated view of international and European politics than Carrillo's. On the other hand, the inexorable passage of time and the influx of new blood into the leadership may further undermine the remaining strength of old-line cadres and could thus serve to deepen the evolutionary process in the PCE.

The momentum of the PCE's integration into the Spanish

political system and continuing efforts the party makes to overcome its Stalinist past and the memories of the Civil War may also lead the PCE farther along the road to an open schism with the Soviet Union. Spanish Communist criticism of Soviet domestic policies (in the summer of 1976 *Mundo Obrero* referred to the "totalitarian" socialism in the East) and of the status quo orientation of its European policy have been harsher than those of the PCF or PCI. The results of the tripartite summit of those parties, held in Madrid in March 1977, reinforce that impression. Although it is important not to overemphasize these differences, the fact is the PCE has been the most aggressive exponent of what has been called "Eurocommunism." Indeed, Santiago Carrillo and Manuel Azcárate have been the only Western European Communists in important leadership roles to remark explicitly and favorably on the possible repercussions in Eastern Europe and the Soviet Union of the growth of an independent Western European Communist movement.[82] Carrillo again attacked the Soviet Union with the publication of his *"Eurocomunismo" y Estado.* There the Spanish leader argued that a shift in the system of international relations and the growth of an autonomous Europe was necessary so as "to favor the *transformation* of the Soviet state into a democratic workers' state" (emphasis supplied).[83] The book earned the PCE Secretary General a vituperative personal attack from the Soviet journal *New Times,* which accused Carrillo of putting forth theses "according solely with the interests of imperialism, the forces of aggression and reaction." [84] Publication of the Soviet blast coincided with a meeting of the Spanish party's Central Committee, called to assess the disappointing electoral results. Apparently, the Soviets hoped to take advantage of latent discontent within the party and maneuver Carrillo into a corner; but, if this was their strategy, it backfired. The Central

Committee rallied around its Secretary General and issued a public statement to the effect that an attack on Carrillo and his views was an attack on PCE policies as well.[85] The exchange and the subsequent Soviet refusal to permit Carrillo to speak at the 60th annual celebration of the October Revolution in late 1977 raised the level of polemics between the Soviet and Spanish parties to unprecedented heights. If the Spanish Communist leadership chooses not to press in the direction of a definitive rupture, the primary reason will be the fear that such a move would only serve to isolate the PCE from its French and Italian counterparts and render even more difficult the realization of their political objectives. As it is, a chasm now separates the Spanish Communists from Moscow.

Perhaps to buttress this last point, it may be appropriate to conclude by relating a story, perhaps apocryphal, told me by a Communist leader in the summer of 1975. The incident, he asserted, had taken place at a lunch after funeral services for the deceased French Communist leader Jacques Duclos. Apparently Carrillo and Boris Ponomarev, the CPSU Secretary responsible for relations with non-ruling Communist parties, had both been in attendance and were seated next to or near each other. Invariably, so the story went, the talk shifted to politics and Ponomarev turned to Carrillo and inquired of the Spanish leader with just a hint of sarcasm when one could expect a revolution in Spain. "After all," Ponomarev said, "it has been forty years and we are still waiting." Carrillo, not slow to pick an argument, reportedly turned to Ponomarev and in a scathing rebuttal remarked that he was unsure as to when the revolution would come in Spain, but that he could assure Ponomarev and his colleagues of one thing: "The revolution will take place in Spain before democracy has been instituted in the Soviet Union."

1. Juan Linz, "Opposition in and under an Authoritarian Regime: The Case of Spain," in Robert A. Dahl, ed., *Regimes and Oppositions* (New Haven, Conn., and London: Yale University Press, 1973), pp. 188 ff.

2. For a general survey of this period, see Max Gallo, *Historia de la España Franquista* (Paris: Ruedo Ibérico, 1971), pp. 7-237. On the PCE, Guy Hermet, *Los Comunistas en España* (Paris: Ruedo Ibérico, 1972), pp. 44-52, and Paul Preston, "The Dilemma of Credibility: The Spanish Communist Party, the Franco Regime and After," *Government and Opposition,* vol. 11 (Winter 1976), pp. 69-82.

3. The move came, apparently, at Stalin's suggestion. See Santiago Carrillo, *Demain L'Espagne* (Paris: Editions du Seuil, 1974), pp. 99-100.

4. Hermet, *op. cit.,* pp. 50-51.

5. Ignacio Fernández de Castro, *De las Cortes de Cádiz al Plan de Desarrollo* (Paris: Ruedo Ibérico, 1968), p. 286.

6. Carrillo, *op. cit.,* pp. 107-108. See also Ramón Chao, *Despues de Franco, España* (Madrid: Ediciones Felmar, 1976), pp. 259-60; 268-69, and Enrique Lister, *Basta!* (Paris: n.p., n.d.), pp. 179-80.

7. *The Juventudes Socialistas Unificadas* (JSU) were the product of the fusion of the Communist and Socialist youth movements in April 1936. Before assuming the leadership of the JSU, Santiago Carrillo had headed the Socialist Youth and had played a significant role in the radicalization of his organization as well as the parent PSOE after the abortive Asturias revolt in October 1934.

8. *Mundo Obrero,* July 1956.

9. In 1960, the PCE described the overthrow as coming after a series of well-coordinated strikes—*huelga general política* leading to the *huelga nacional*—which would paralyze the country, but by mid-1976 even this mildly revolutionary approach had been cast aside and the term *ruptura pactada*—meaning a formal agreement between the opposition and reformers within the regime to change the form and substance of government—had entered the Spanish Communist lexicon.

10. See, for example, Fabio Espinosa, "El Ejercito en el Momento Político Actual," in *VIII Congreso* (Bucharest, 1972), pp. 233-49.

11. Santiago Carrillo, *Después de Franco, Qué?* (Paris: Editions Sociales 1965), pp. 15-99.

12. Evidently, the party's scheme had something in it for everyone. It could reassure the Spanish middle classes that with their participation the overthrow of the regime could be peaceful and that in the ensuing *democracia política y social* (akin to the *democratie avancée* of the French Communists) the inevitable constrictions on private property would essentially be directed at the "monopolies." The working class and its allies—destined by force of circumstance, in the Communist view, to lead "bourgeois-democratic" revolution—could be sustained in the struggle by the perspective of structural transformations in the not-too-distant future, accepting a gradual pace, however, in return for middle-class support. For a trenchant critique of the official PCE assessment, see Fernando Claudín, "Dos Concepciones de la Via Española al Socialismo," in *Horizonte Español* (Paris: Ruedo Ibérico, 1966), vol. 1, pp. 59-100.

13. For documents relating to this split, see Fernando Claudín, *Documentos de una Divergencia Comunista* (Barcelona: Iniciativas Editoriales, 1978). A more personal and passionate account may be found in

Jorge Semprún, *Autobiografía de Federico Sánchez* (Barcelona: Editorial Planeta, 1977). Sánchez was Semprún's *nom de guerre*.

14. The agreement established the "national Catholic" character of the regime and gave the Church, among other things, a virtual monopoly on education, subsidies, a clerical immunity from prosecution, censorship duties, representation in civil institutions like the Cortes and the Council of the Realm, and permission for its apostolic organizations to be active in the labor movement independently of the "vertical" sindical structures under the control of the Falange. For thorough and insightful discussions of Church-state relations in Spain, see Alfonso Alvarez Bolado, *El Experimento del Nacional-Catolicismo* (Madrid: Editorial Cuadernos para el Dialogo, 1976) and José Chao Rego, *La Iglesia en el Franquismo* (Madrid: Ediciones Felmar, 1976).

15. Hermet, *op. cit.*, p. 140.

16. Carrillo, *Después de Franco, Qué?* p. 166.

17. *Le Monde,* November 4, 1970.

18. Some of this has come from old-line members who have found it difficult to shed the mantle of anticlericalism, but there have been others who, while agreeing with the tactical and strategic utility of the change, have criticized the lack of intellectual rigor in the Communist-Catholic dialogue and the concessions the Carrillo leadership has felt compelled to make in order to attract Catholics. See, for example, a document distributed for discussion in the Catalan branch of the PCE, the *Partit Socialista Unificat de Catalunya,* in *Materiales,* "La Militancia de Cristianos en el Partido Comunista," 1, January-February 1977, pp. 101-12. An exposition of official PCE policy is Alfonso Carlos Comín's, "Sobre la Militancia de los Cristianos en el Partido. Hacia un Estado de la Cuestion," *Nuestra Bandera,* no. 85, pp. 29-41.

[261]

19. *Mundo Obrero,* March 19, 1975.

20. Not surprisingly, the presence of Alfonso Carlos Comín, a prominent Catholic sociologist and author of an important book entitled *Fe en la Tierra,* on the PCE's Executive Committee, and of at least one priest, Francisco García Salve from the *Comisiones Obreras,* on the Central Committee, has given the party great prestige among politically conscious Catholics. *Mundo Obrero,* July 26, 1976.

21. One could make reference in the 1970s to any number of groups—ranging from the pro-regime *Unión Democrática Española* (UDE) headed by Federico Silva Muñoz, to José Maria Gil Robles' *Federación Popular Democrática* (FPD), right-of-center but in the moderate opposition, and extending at the left of the spectrum to Joaquín Ruiz Giménez's *Izquierda Democrática* (ID)—but they have found it difficult to find a basis of accord.

22. Jose Felix Tezános, *Estructura de Clases en la España Actual* (Madrid: Ediciones Cuadernos para el Dialogo, 1975), p. 47. For a general discussion of Spanish social structure, see Ignacio Fernández de Castro and Antonio Goytre, *Clases Sociales en España en el Umbral de los Años '70* (Madrid: Siglo XXI, 1974).

23. Jon Amsden, *Collective Bargaining and Class Struggle in Spain* (London: Weidenfeld & Nicolson, 1972), p. 62.

24. The Communists, holding to their idea that the regime was in crisis, wanted the CC.OO. to continue to function openly as a parallel organization, ready to take over at the right moment the regime's sindical structure. In the PCE's view, the best way to defend the *Comisiones* was to maintain its character as a mass organization and continue to emphasize the economic over strictly political demands. This fit in nicely with Communist efforts to galvanize a broad front against the regime, but did not sit well with

other leftist elements who wanted the CC.OO. to respond by going on the offensive, adopting radically anticapitalist positions. See the PCE Executive Committee declaration in the *World Marxist Review (International Bulletin),* no. 125 (1968), pp. 40-47 and a biting critique of this tactic by Jerónimo Hernández, "Aproximación a la Historia de las Comisiones Obreras y de las Tendencias Forjadas en su Seno," *Cuadernos de Ruedo Ibérico,* nos. 39-40 (October 1972-January 1973), pp. 57-79.

25.   Marcelino Camacho, *Charlas en la Prisión* (Barcelona: Editorial Laia, 1975), pp. 76-77. Camacho heads the *Comisiones Obreras* and is also on the PCE's Executive Committee.

26.   Nicolas Sartorius, *El Resurgir del Movimiento Obrero* (Barcelona: Editorial Laia, 1975), pp. 55-56. Also Camacho, *op. cit.,* pp. 58-59.

27.   This was confirmed at the June 1976 PCE Central Committee meeting in Rome, at which time almost all the members of the Central Committee were publicly identified.

28.   See the texts in "Segunda Conferencia del PCE," *Nuestra Bandera,* no. 81 (October 1975). Also important because it was a speech to party labor activists is Santiago Carrillo, "Las Tareas del Movimiento Obrero para que el Franquismo Desaparezca También," no. 82, November 1975. It was a special issue with only his speech in it.

29.   Jesus Prieto, "Discordia Sobre la Unidad," *Cuadernos para el Dialogo,* June 19, 1976, pp. 49-50, gives a good overview of the affair.

30.   Carlos Rama, *La Crisis Española del Siglo XX* (Mexico: Fondo de Cultura Económica, 1960), p. 23.

31.   Dolores Ibárruri, *España, Estado Multinacional* (Paris: Editions Sociales, 1971), pp. 42-43.

32.   Santiago Alvarez, "Notas Sobre el Problema Nacional en España," *Nuestra Bandera,* no. 84 (March-April 1976), pp. 19-23.

33.   The rise in anti-Madrid feeling over the last several years has had an impact on the PCE itself: in late 1976, the central leadership had to call the Valencian provincial committee to order for demanding autonomy for that province and the constitution of a provisional government in the area as soon as the *ruptura democrática* had been consummated at the national state level.

34.   The four parties were the *Partido Proletario Catalan,* the *Union Socialista de Cataluña,* the *Partido Comunista de Cataluña,* and the Catalan federation of the PSOE.

35.   See the interview with PSUC Secretary General Gregorio López Raimundo in *Cuadernos para el Dialogo,* September 4, 1976, pp. 21-23.

36.   *Manifiesto-Programa del PCE* (n.p., n.d.), pp. 17-18. The draft version was presented at a Central Committee plenum in September 1973. The second PCE Conference in September 1975 approved the definitive version.

37.   See Santiago Carrillo, "La Lucha por el Socialismo Hoy," in *Problemas del Socialismo* (Paris: Coleccion Ebro, 1969), pp. 20-31.

38.   Manuel Azcárate, "Algunas Consecuencias del Nuevo Papel de la Ciencia," *Realidad* (Rome) no. 23 (June 1972), p. 3. Azcárate, of course, was not the first to advance this notion. Soviet theorists from Lenin on, including Khrushchev in the 1961 CPSU statutes, proposed the elimination of all ideological distinctions between physical

and mental labor and the establishment of an "all peoples' state." The U.S.S.R. was declared to be such a state in the early 1960s.

39. See the pamphlet "Algunos Aspectos de la Alianza de las Fuerzas del Trabajo y de la Cultura" of the Comité de Barcelona del PSUC, February 1973.

40. Santiago Carrillo, "La Lucha por el Socialismo Hoy," in *op. cit.*, p. 43.

41. Santiago Carrillo, *Hacia el Post-Franquismo* (Paris: Coleccion Ebro, 1974), pp. 82-85.

42. Santiago Carrillo, *De la Clandestinidad al la Legalidad* (n.p., n.d.), pp. 64-66. This is the report Carrillo presented to the Central Committee in June 1976.

43. *VIII Congreso del PCE* (Bucharest, 1972), pp. 338-39.

44. On this point, see, among others, Santiago Carrillo, *Nuevos Enfoques a Problemas de Hoy* (Paris: Editions Sociales, 1967) and *Libertad y Socialismo* (Paris: Editions Sociales, 1971).

45. Juan Diz, "Libertades Políticas y Socialismo," *Alkarrilketa* (Paris), vol. 2, no. 2, pp. 13-15. Diz was Azcárate's other name.

46. "Resolución Sobre la Situación en el Movimiento Comunista," *Nuestra Bandera*, no. 38 (March 1964), p. 61.

47. Santiago Carrillo, *Nuevos Enfoques a Problemas de Hoy*, pp. 140-65. The quotation may be found on p. 140.

48. Santiago Carrillo, "The Struggle for Socialism Today," *Nuestra Bandera*, no. 58 (June 1968), p. 41. The notion of a need for a new offensive thrust in all aspects of a Communist party's work is

evident in much of Carrillo's writings and he obviously considers it necessary not only for the PCE but other parties as well.

49. *Mundo Obrero,* May 1, 1968.

50. *Le Monde,* October 23, 1970. This incident is recounted in a lengthy article by K. S. Karol.

51. Radio Free Portugal of September 25, 1968 in *Foreign Broadcast Information Service* (Western Europe), September 27, 1968, p. X2.

52. *Foreign Broadcast Information Service* (Western Europe), January 3, 1969, p. X2.

53. Líster, *op. cit.,* pp. 150-51.

54. "Recent Vicissitudes of the Spanish CP," *Rinascita,* XXVII, February 6, 1970, pp. 10-11.

55. *Mundo Obrero,* July 15, 1971.

56. See his report to the dissident group's Fourth Central Committee plenum in *Nuestra Bandera* (dissident-Paris), April 1972, pp. 68-69.

57. *L'Humanité* (Paris), November 4, 1970.

58. *Ibid.,* November 26, 1970.

59. Santiago Carrillo, "La Lucha por el Socialismo Hoy," *Nuestra Bandera,* June 1968, pp. 11-15.

60. *Le Monde,* February 20, 1969, carried a partial text.

61. *Mundo Obrero* (dissident), June 1-15, 1971.

62. For the content of the article, see *Foreign Broadcast Information Service* (Western Europe), May 28, 1971, pp. XI-2; June 4, 1971, pp. XI-2; and June 14, 1971, pp. XI-2. See also Kevin Devlin's "Spanish Communist Leader on the Lessons of Czechoslovakia," Radio Free Europe *Research* (hereafter RFER), no. 1760, April 5, 1973.

63. *VIII Congreso del PCE* (Bucharest, 1972), p. 16. Emphasis added.

64. There is, of course, no evidence available to substantiate the charge that García and/or Líster received direct subsidies from the Soviet Union. Both Spanish and Italian sources have indirectly made the point, however, and it may reasonably be supposed to have taken place. See *Hora de Madrid* (supplement no. 3) June 1971 which is the organ of the Madrid provincial committee of the PCE and *Rinascita*, XXVII, March 20, 1970, p. 30.

65. "Más Problemas Actuales del Socialismo," in Santiago Carrillo, *Problemas del Socialismo* (Paris: Colección Ebro, 1969), pp. 41-53.

66. See Ernest Martí (pseudonym for Joaquim Sempere of the PSUC Executive Committee), "Ideological Problems and the Cultural Front," *Nuestra Bandera*, no. 64, 1970, as translated in *FBIS*, August 27, 1970, pp. XI-4 and September 3, 1970, pp. XI-4; Juan Diz, "The Antidogmatic Struggle," *Nuestra Bandera*, no. 64, 1970, pp. 73-81. Excerpts of Martí's article may be found in *Le Monde*, November 4, 1970.

67. *Mundo Obrero*, December 10, 1971.

68. In 1969 and 1970 Poland, Czechoslovakia, Bulgaria and Hungary established consular relations with Madrid, and in late 1970 the Polish government authorized coal shipments to Spain at a time when the Asturian miners were on general strike.

[267]

69. It should be noted there was a domestic reason behind this change in the European policy of the PCE as well. Spanish "neocapitalism" clearly favored Spanish entry into the Common Market but had been frustrated in its efforts by the repeated blocking of Spanish entry by European governments until full democracy had been instituted in Spain. The PCE, in effect, offered these groups a deal. If they would join the Communists and other opponents of the regime in forcing a democratization of Spanish political structures, the PCE would drop its opposition to Spanish membership in the EEC once full democracy was instituted in the country. This was a politically astute position: it prevented other forces from branding the PCE an "anti-European" force while the party accepted something that was probably inevitable in any case, the eventual inclusion of Spain in the Common Market. Manuel Azcárate, "Sobre Algunos Problemas de la Política Internacional del Partido," in *VIII Congreso del PCE* (Bucharest, 1972), pp. 183-206. Also of interest is Juan Gómez, "Sobre el Mercado Común Europeo," *ibid.*, pp. 207-16.

70. For the version broadcast by Radio Moscow, see *FBIS* (Soviet Union), February 16, 1974, pp. A1-10. Azcárate's report may be found in *Nuestra Bandera*, no. 72, 1973, pp. 15-30. For particularly valuable discussion of the Soviet article, see Kevin Devlin's "Soviet Attack on Spanish CP," *RFER*, no. 2008, February 27, 1974 and "Spanish CP Stands Firm Against Soviet Attack," *ibid.*, no. 2046, April 10, 1974.

71. *Pravda* (Moscow), October 16, 1974.

72. *Triunfo* (Madrid), July 3, 1976, p. 7.

73. *Il Manifesto,* November 1, 1975, p. 2.

74. *Mundo Obrero,* July 31, 1974.

75. See, for example, the *Manifiesto de la Reconciliación* in *Mundo Obrero,* 3rd week April 1975.

76. *Mundo Obrero,* October 27, 1975.

77. Jose María Gil Robles, "Esquema de un Camino Hacia la Democracia," Madrid, May 1976.

78. See the Central Committee statement in *Mundo Obrero,* September 1, 1976.

79. For a detailed consideration of the PCE and the elections, see my "An Analysis of the Spanish Communist Performance in the June 1977 General Election," in Howard E. Penniman, ed., *Spain at the Polls* (Washington, D.C.: American Enterprise Institute, 1979).

80. See, for example, the speeches Carrillo made to the Cortes in July 1977 and to the PCE Central Committee in September 1977. *Mundo Obrero,* August 3, 1977, and September 15-21,. 1977, respectively.

81. One of the best accounts of what happened at the 9th PCE Congress may be found in the article by Fernando López Agudín, entitled "Un Paso Adelante, Dos Atras," in *Triunfo,* April 29, 1978, pp. 34-36. See also my article in the *Estado de São Paulo (Jornal da Tarde),* May 13, 1978.

82. Carrillo made his first remarks to this effect in an interview with the dissident Italian Communist journal *Il Manifesto,* November 1, 1975, p. 2. Those of Azcárate are in an interview he gave to *Triunfo* (Madrid), July 3, 1976, p. 7.

83. The book was published by Editorial Grijalbo (Barcelona) in the spring of 1977. The citation is to p. 212.

84. "Contrary to the Interests of Peace and Socialism in Europe. Concerning the book "Eurocommunism and the State" by Santiago Carrillo, General Secretary of the Communist Party of Spain," *New Times* (Moscow), No. 26, June 1977, pp. 9-13, at p. 11.

85. *Mundo Obrero,* June 29, 1977.

[FIVE]

Communism and Revolution in Portugal *

Eusebio M. Mujal-León

In early December 1977, after sixteen months in office, the minority Socialist government headed by Mario Soares lost a motion-of-confidence vote in the Portuguese parliament. Approximately two months later, after arduous negotiations, Soares announced the formation of a second government. The *Partido Socialista* (PS) retained a majority of the ministerial portfolios in the new Cabinet, but the government also included representatives of the *Centro Democrático Social* (CDS).

What would have been a normal, indeed ordinary, sequence of events in most other European countries was fraught with significance for this Iberian nation. In the years since 1974,

* I would like gratefully to acknowledge the contribution which a paper prepared by Kenneth Maxwell made to the first part of this essay. The views expressed in this chapter are, of course, my own responsibility.

[271]

Portugal had been convulsed by no fewer than four attempted coups and countercoups, had six provisional governments and two provisional presidents, and on two occasions its people had gone to the brink of civil war.

The agreement signed by the Socialists and the CDS, unthinkable during those turbulent months of the Portuguese revolution, raised more than a few eyebrows. But many hoped that, in so far as the new government could count on a stable parliamentary majority, it might have the base from which to pursue the policies necessary for national recovery.

Things did not turn out that way. Little more than six months later, after demanding and not getting the resignation of the Minister of Agriculture and the alteration of government agrarian and health policies, the CDS withdrew its support from Soares and the government. Efforts to mend the split were unsuccessful, and in a somewhat controversial move the President of the Republic, General Ramalho Eanes, dismissed Soares. Choosing not to convoke early elections, Eanes initiated the search for a new prime minister and after several weeks of consultations entrusted the formation of a government to Alfredo Nobre da Costa, an independent former Minister of Industry. The new government was to have an essentially caretaker role: its principal responsibility was not to permit the economic situation to get further out of hand while the drafting of a new electoral law and the updating of the census took place. Nobre da Costa and his Cabinet lost their first parliamentary test, however. The likelihood is that another independent, better able to draw support from the various parliamentary groups, will hold the line until new elections are held either in 1980 (as scheduled) or earlier.

A realistic assessment of the prospects for the development and consolidation of Portuguese democracy must emphasize the seriousness of the economic and social problems facing the country, and the dangers posed to that democracy by extremist groups of the Right and Left. The situation, although difficult, is still amenable to solution, but much will depend on the willingness of the various political parties to put aside merely partisan interests.

Eventual success in that enterprise will depend to an important degree on the strategy the *Partido Comunista Português* (PCP) chooses to follow over the next few years. As the structures of political authority disintegrated in the aftermath of the April 1974 coup which overthrew Marcello Caetano and the *Estado Novo,* the Portuguese Communists opted for a traditional Leninist approach. In alliance with radical officers in the *Movimento das Forças Armadas* (MFA), the PCP moved to break what it perceived as the weakest link in Western European capitalism and effect a socialist revolution. August and November 1975 saw the culmination and the defeat of those efforts. Thereafter, the PCP followed a much more moderate line, acting with great restraint and premising its policies on the need for alliance with the Socialist party and the constitution of a broadly based *plataforma democrática nacional* whose more limited primary objective would be the defense of political democracy.

This chapter analyzes the role played by the PCP in its domestic environment in the years after 1974. After a brief introduction, the first part focuses on Communist actions and strategy during the initial year and a half of the Portuguese revolution. There follows an analysis of the PCP's efforts in the aftermath of an abortive coup in November 1975 to recapture some of its lost influence. The concluding part of the chapter explores the options open to the PCP in the new, critical phase which the Portuguese revolution has now entered.[1]

Historical Background

Founded in April 1921, the PCP was a small, essentially irrelevant sect for much of the first two decades of its existence. Not Marxist but anarcho-syndicalist ideas enjoyed the greatest influence among members of the Portuguese working class throughout the 1930s. The harsh repression unleashed by the regime of Antonio Salazar (in power since 1929) broke the back of the Anarchist movements and that of most other opposition forces. Only the Communists—organized with small cells as the basic unit and with various levels of intermediate district and regional groups linking the cells together and benefiting from the financial and organizational support given by Moscow—survived this test. As a result, in the years after 1945, it was the PCP which emerged as the dominant force in the anti-Salazar opposition, playing a significant role in the establishment of various umbrella opposition fronts.

The clandestine experience of five long decades had a profound effect on the Portuguese Communist Party. Despite the influence the PCP exerted, its members never numbered more than two or three thousand, and those militants who remained within the country were subject to lengthy jail terms if caught. They led a highly secretive and isolated existence and in many ways were out of touch with the world about them.[2] The experience of Alvaro Cunhal, the Secretary General of the PCP, is illustrative: A man of middle-class origins, Cunhal studied law in Lisbon and joined the party in 1931 at the age of seventeen. Organizer of the Federation of Communist Youth in the Lisbon area, he attended the Sixth Congress of Communist Youth in Moscow in 1935 and upon his return to Portugal became a member of the PCP Central Committee.

[274]

Subsequently, he was arrested three times, spent thirteen years in prison (he escaped in 1961) and an additional fourteen in Eastern European exile. His experience was not exceptional. Figures released at the Seventh PCP Congress in October 1974 indicated that the 34 full and alternate members of the Central Committee had collectively spent over 300 years in jail.[3] That experience steeled the Portuguese Communist leaders and their party, reinforcing a sectarian, *ouvrièriste* perspective in domestic affairs and a reflexively pro-Soviet orientation in the international sphere.

There has been no international issue or event—and this has been true whether we talk about Stalin's break with Tito in 1948, the Sino-Soviet conflict, the invasion of Czechoslovakia, or the more recent pan-European meeting of Communist parties—on which the public posture of the Portuguese Communists has deviated from that of Moscow. We should be careful about the conclusions we draw as to this relationship, however, particularly since they may lead us to overestimate the Soviet role (which is distinct from interest) in Portuguese events in the summer and fall of 1975. There is no doubt that the Kremlin followed those events with great attention. But, as Robert Legvold demonstrates in Chapter 6, the Soviets probably did not have a clearly articulated policy with respect to Portugal, and, in consequence, they probably relied quite heavily on the analyses and judgments the Portuguese Communists made of the situation. Certainly, some analysts and policy-makers in the U.S.S.R. may have wondered about the wisdom of policies which threatened to have a negative effect on détente with the United States; but, in so far as alliance with the radicals in the MFA guaranteed the PCP an important voice in how decolonization in the African colonies was to take place, this may have been a countervailing consideration.

The hardline approach to domestic affairs found expression

at the level of doctrine, particularly with respect to the question of how to overthrow the *Estado Novo*. The analysis presented by the Portuguese Communists was broad and ecumenical: There would be a convergence of social forces, ranging from the proletariat to numerous sectors of the middle classes, against the state monopoly capitalist system which had developed in Portugal. This was all quite similar to the analysis put forth by the Spanish Communists but, whereas the PCE argued after the early 1960s that a change in regime could come about in largely peaceful fashion, the Portuguese Communists always held to the proposition that only a national uprising, in which the military would play an important albeit not dominant role, would bring down Salazar or Caetano.[4] What was more, the PCP doggedly held to the view (first articulated by Bento Gonçalves in the 1930s) that the bourgeoisie was incapable of playing a hegemonic role in that process of change and that such a role would necessarily fall to the working class and, of course, its party, the PCP. [5] Behind the conciliatory, interclass rhetoric lay the Portuguese Communist conviction that their party alone had the dedication and commitment necessary to bring about change in Portuguese society.

One base of Communist support lay in the Alentejo. These were the grain-producing lands south of the Tagus river, where the owners of great estates—76 out of the 113 Portuguese farms with more than 2,500 hectares were in the districts of Evara, Beja and Portalegre, as were 274 of the 375 holdings between 1,000 and 2,500 hectares—still ruled their land as virtually autonomous fiefdoms.[6] The landless agricultural proletariat of the region (similar from a socio-structural point of view to the more backward Andalusian provinces in Spain where anarcho-syndicalism had once been strong) had a long history of militance. An impressive demonstration of the continued vitality of this tradition took place in 1961-62 when general strikes called to protest low wages and to demand agrarian reform paralyzed the entire province of Beja. Communist efforts to organize in the region drew on this popular disaffection as well as the very scale of the units of production. Their size favored mass organization and protected party activists. An index of the importance the Communists attached to the region is the fact that Cunhal is the author of one of the few detailed analyses of the social and economic structures of that part of the country.[7] It is not surprising, given this background, that in the various elections since April 1974 the PCP has received its highest vote totals in the Alentejo.

Another sector where the Communists developed their influence was in the labor movement, especially among workers in the industrial belt around Lisbon and, to a lesser degree, in Oporto. The *Estado Novo* had organized the Portuguese working class into "vertical" syndicates (on the Italian fascist model) in an effort to deflect class conflict and prevent the growth of autonomous labor organizations. The regime, with the aid of the ubiquitous secret police known as the PIDE, had been more or less successful in this undertaking. However, when Salazar suffered a massive stroke in 1968, his successor Marcello Caetano slackened government control over labor and liberalized the rules governing election to positions within the corporatist syndical structures. The Communists seized on this opportunity to penetrate the offical union committees, and in 1970 groups of workers under PCP influence formed the coordinating commission known as *Intersindical*. Prior to the coup of 1974, the Communists were strongly entrenched in the metallurgical and textile sectors and had a growing influence among some service employees, especially the bank workers in Lisbon and Oporto. Indeed, Avelino Gonçalves,

[277]

the Communist Minister of Labor in the first provisional government after the coup, was a prominent leader of Oporto's bank workers.

The Communists also used the electoral opposition front known as the *Comissão Democrática Eleitoral* (CDE), which the government permitted to compete in nevertheless tightly controlled elections for the National Assembly, as an instrument to organize against the regime. Communists, Socialists, radical Catholics, and independents participated in the organization, but it was the PCP which had a preponderant organizational influence. The coalition split in 1969, with Socialists protesting Communist influence in it, but by 1973 the groups had come back together and were united as the MDP/CDE when the coup occurred. The infrastructure developed by the CDE during the last years of the Caetano regime assumed a particular importance in the months after the overthrow of the *ancien régime*. While other groups and personalities left the cover of the CDE to form their own parties and political organizations, many Communists stayed in the movement and used the network it had established as a base from which to take control of local governments throughout the country.

The Coup and Its Aftermath

In the early morning of April 25, 1974, the tanks of the cavalry school in Santarem rumbled into the streets of Lisbon. Within twenty-four hours, Portugal's dictatorship of almost half a century had been brought down. Within twenty-four months, Portugal's presence in Africa, dating back half a millennium, had ended too. No mass movement had brought the old regime down, and the participation of the clandestine political parties of the Left had been negligible.

[278]

It was the army, and specifically a small group of junior officers joined in the *Movimento das Forças Armadas* (MFA), which toppled the dictatorship. At the outset, what had drawn these captains and majors together was a lost sense of purpose, an emotional and intellectual estrangement from their government. These sentiments had been catalyzed by the seemingly endless commitment on the part of the regime to maintain the colonial empire in Africa. Their frustration had initially found expression in professional demands relating to status and privilege, but this changed as it became apparent to the officers that the only way to end the war was to overthrow the regime. Few among them had well-defined political views (of these, some were Marxists and the others had been influenced by the ideology of their erstwhile opponents in the national liberation movements), but most were ready to believe that the armed forces should play a major role in the political process.

In the first months of the revolution, people paid scant attention to the ideas of the MFA. The MFA program, which spoke of a policy favoring "the least advantaged sectors of the population" and defending "the interests of the working classes," was soon promulgated into the transitional constitution of the second Portuguese republic. Most observers preferred, however, to focus on the role and influence of General Antonio de Spínola, the first provisional president of the new republic and author of a controversial book, *Portugal e O Futuro,* published a few months before the coup.

The MFA program and Spínola's book were, in fact, the two key documents of the first phase of the revolution. They set out positions so diametrically opposed (the differences related to the question of immediate decolonization or gradual disengagement in Africa and to the pace and substance of what change was necessary in Portugal), that the conflict could only be resolved by the victory of one side over the other. The disputes over the nature of decolonization and over social and economic change in Portugal were two sides of the same coin, and both had the major Portuguese business monopolies as a point of reference. The latter, like Spínola, regarded the retention of the African territories (particularly Angola and Mozambique) as essential for the economic development of the country, even if this meant continuing to fight the national liberation movements. The MFA, if anything, had made the coup to end the colonial wars, and its most articulate and politicized representatives saw decolonization as having a potent anti-monopolist thrust.[8]

It was one of the strengths of the Portuguese Communists that early on they had recognized the importance of the conflict between Spinola and the MFA. While most other politicians and groups talked of an alliance between Spinola and their parties, Cunhal and the PCP made common cause with the MFA, spoke of an incipient alliance between it and "the people," and emphasized the similarities of the *Movimento's* program with that of the PCP.

Although the Communists had no illusions about Spínola and his objectives, they willingly accepted his request that a party member head the Ministry of Labor. Obviously, Spínola made the offer expecting (not incorrectly as it turned out) that the Communists would best be able to keep wage and other demands by the working class under control. Party leaders certainly understood the risks but undoubtedly felt such an opportunity would not only permit them to consolidate their control over organized labor but also put them in a much better position to cement their relationship with the radical officers in the MFA and to keep an eye on what the military was doing or might do.

The euphoria of the early months disguised for a time the seriousness of the divergences within the Portuguese military.

These grew in intensity over the spring and early summer 1974 and served to bring the PCP into closer collaboration with members of the *Movimento*. It was a tactical alliance, which undoubtedly caused misgivings on both sides. The young officers were, after all, the epitome of the petit-bourgeois radicals whom Cunhal had so virulently denounced in his book *O Radicalismo Pequeno-Burguês de Fachada Socialista*. The officers in the MFA, in turn, appreciated the Communists more for their apparent willingness to follow military leadership and for their discipline and reliability than for their long-term vision of the future of Portuguese society. It was their common opposition to Spinola and his supporters which brought them together.

The conflict between Spínola and the radical officers remained largely hidden from public view until the general and his Prime Minister, Antonio Palma Carlos, overplayed their hand in July 1974. They attempted to force through modifications in the original MFA timetable and therefore allow Spínola to go to the country in an early presidential election. The Council of State thwarted the plan and, as a consequence, in a major blow to Spínola's authority, Palma Carlos resigned. One of the more senior members of the MFA, Colonel Vasco Gonçalves, was appointed in his place a few days later. The new Cabinet contained six military men, three of them members of the Coordinating Committee of the MFA. In an effort to consolidate its position, the *Movimento* set up a special military organization known as COPCON *(Comando Operacional do Continente)* and placed it outside the official command structure.

In late September, Spínola made a last attempt to shore up his own position. Calling on what he described as the "silent majority" to gather in Lisbon, he provoked a major confrontation with the radical officers. Again he lost and this time he resigned from the presidency. In his farewell address to the nation, he warned that it was "impossible to build democracy (when) faced with a systematic assault on the foundations and institutions by political groups whose basic ideology offends the most elementary concepts of liberty."[9] He was replaced by General Costa Gomes, the man who, prior to the coup, had been the choice of many in the MFA for the job.

Struggle within and outside the Military

The Communists attached great importance to the September showdown that pushed Spinola out of the presidency. For one thing, it had marked the first time the PCP and the MFA had gone to the streets together: the party, under cover of the MDP/CDE *(Movimento Democrático Português/Comissão Democrática Eleitoral)* had organized pickets and barricades around Lisbon with the connivance and support of COP-CON. More importantly, the Portuguese Communists saw Spinola's defeat as an indication that the major Portuguese industrialists had lost their political power base and, as a result, that the stage was now set for moving against their economic base through the nationalization of banks and large industrial concerns and the implementation of a thorough agrarian reform. This was the major conclusion of the report Cunhal presented in the name of the Central Committee to the Seventh PCP Congress in late October 1974.[10] The Communists, of course, insisted that such a course would find favor with the overwhelming majority of the population. And they might have been correct. What is much more doubtful is that those sectors comprising the so-called "anti-monopolist" alliance would be in accord with the corollary that it was the PCP as the vanguard of the *povo* and the radicals in the MFA

[282]

which would run the show. If the PCP held back in the fall of 1974, however, it was primarily because the MFA was still not very united after the deceptively easy victory over Spinola.

In response to Spinola's efforts over the first six months of the revolution to dissolve the Coordinating Committee and hence to end the political role of the MFA, the *Movimento* had sought to secure its position within the military by expanding its membership. From a restricted base of 350 to 400 officers, of which a mere of 100 or so were active participants, the MFA grew by September 1974 to encompass some 2,000 officers in all three services. All were still from the regular cadre (the *quadro permanente)* but such a quick growth brought into the MFA both a diversity of opinion and numerous opportunists.

By the end of 1975, the more political officers could be broadly classified into three more or less distinct groups: democratic socialist (with a bias toward Gramscian Marxism), radical populist, and Marxist-Leninist. After March 1975, the last group associated with Prime Minister Vasco Gonçalves, was the most influential. Close to the Communists but not mere executors of Cunhal's will, the *gonçalvistas* established formidable bases of power in the months after July 1974. They dominated the office of the Prime Minister, and this was crucially important because the command structures of the old corporate dictatorship were still centralized there. Particularly important in this context was the Fifth Division, the agency responsible for propaganda and indoctrination. Military men close to the PCP were also influential in the Social Communication and Labor ministries as well as in the commission which had been established to dismantle the secret police. Penetration of the commission gave the Communists and their allies access to voluminous and often-times incriminating files.

The second group on the left, the democratic socialists,

coalesced around the figure of Melo Antunes. Antunes had been a member of the MFA Coordinating Committee from its origins and had been the drafter of the *Movimento's* political program. After he had entered the Cabinet in July 1974, however, his influence within the MFA began to wane as a result of not only the time he devoted to negotiations for decolonization in Africa but also the concentration of power in the office or Prime Minister Gonçalves. He and his supporters saw the armed forces as an essential instrument in the revolutionary process but objected to the vanguard-like notions of Gonçalves. They believed that the MFA had to seek a much broader base of social and political support than that provided by the PCP and its allies. In their view, collaboration with and among all those political parties which accepted the legitimacy of the April 1974 revolution was absolutely essential if there were to be an orderly and peaceful transition to socialism.

A third group stood ostensibly to the left of both Melo Antunes and the PCP-influenced *gonçalvistas:* the populist radicals. This group the fuzzy ideological views but strong support in COPCON regiments stationed in and around Lisbon and among units of the military police. Opposed to all political parties, the PCP included, and enamored of a vaguely defined *poder popular,* the military populists led by Otelo Saraiva de Carvalho counted among their allies a variety of extreme left groups.

·As the political situation in Portugal worsened visibly in late 1947 and early 1975, the interactions among these factions and their relations with the PCP became crucial to Communist hopes of gaining power. In December, Gonçalves and his supporters tried to push through the MFA General Assembly a series of measures designed to institutionalize the *Movimento's* presence in the still-to-be-elected National Assembly. For their part, the Communists, acting once again under the

[284]

cover of the MDP/CDE, organized vigilante groups in Lisbon and arrested prominent industrialists allegedly guilty of economic sabotage. In January, the party took to the streets in support of legislation that would effectively perpetuate Communist control over the organized working class.

This latter mobilization, which the Communists directed at the Socialist party, helped shatter one of the most assiduously cultivated myths of the Portuguese revolution: the supposed unity of purpose between the two parties of the left. When Mario Soares returned from Paris and Alvaro Cunhal from Prague in April 1974, the two leaders had posed together smiling, holding between them in raised salute a red carnation. Representatives of the two parties entered the first provisional government and over the next few months, with the Socialists proclaiming their Marxist credentials and the Communists insisting on the need for broad, multi-class alliances, were downplayed by both sides.

Relations began to deteriorate sharply in late summer 1975, particularly after the Communists supported the decision taken by the Lisbon branch of the MDP/CDE to work toward the transformation of that movement into a formal political party. Tensions grew even more in the aftermath of the frustrated "silent majority" march when the Communists accused the Socialist leadership of harboring sympathies for Spinola. By January 1975 the dispute reached beyond mere party factionalism, and the antagonism underscored how fundamentally different was a political-social model committed to civil liberties and to change within the parameters of a parliamentary democracy from one which sought to establish a single-party state of the Eastern European or Third World types.

Abortive Coup and Radicalization

Amidst a growing polarization in the country and with rumors and warnings of coups and countercoups, Spínola and his supporters launched their abortive coup on March 11, 1975. Poorly planned and executed, the *Putsch* fizzled within hours and Spínola went into exile in Spain and later Brazil. The radicals in the MFA and their Communist allies seized the opportunity afforded them by the event to move against their opponents within the armed forces and among the political parties as well as to enact a series of far-reaching economic measures.

The most important of these measures was the nationalization of the banks and insurance companies. Because of the interlocking nature of the traditional Portuguese ruling establishment, the nationalization of the banks placed in one fell swoop into the hands of the state the major part of the privately owned sectors of Portuguese industry. Since the banks also held mortgages or a controlling interest in virtually every Portuguese newspaper, an additional result was that the state thereby assumed financial control of much of the communications media, including all the Lisbon morning dailies and three of the four which appeared in the evenings. Simultaneously, the new Revolutionary Council of the MFA (heir to the Coordinating Committee) made clear that it would soon promulgate a major expropriation of estates with more than 500 hectares, a measure that would destroy the economic base of the great *latifundia* of the South.

The second series of measures announced by the now dominant military radicals had to do with the military establishment itself. They set aside the various elections held prior to March 11 and expanded the MFA General Assembly to

[286]

240 men, representing the three branches of the armed forces and consisting for the first time of enlisted men in addition to regular officers. The Revolutionary Council also obliged the political parties to sign a pact with the MFA, which assured military supremacy for at least three years, relegated the provisional government to a subordinate position in the new hierarchy of power, and gave to the MFA Assembly a co-equal voice with any future National Assembly in the election of a president. Only the PCP and MDP/CDE were enthusiastic about the agreement; the other parties by and large felt compelled to sign, fearing that otherwise the Constituent Assembly elections scheduled for April 25, 1975 would be called off.

Leading members of the radical faction in the MFA did not disguise their contempt for the "electoralism" of the political parties. Ramiro Correia from the Fifth Division likened the contest to a football pool, and Admiral Rosa Coutinho, former High Commissioner in Angola and a leading member of the Revolutionary Council, publicly called on the electorate to cast blank ballots.[11] Coutinho had on previous occasions decried the absence of an authentically revolutionary Socialist party (neither the PSP nor the PCP fitted the bill as far as he was concerned) and obviously hoped that, if his appeals were successful, this might give the MFA the opportunity to develop a civilian branch and dispense with the other parties altogether. In the end, however, the military radicals were to regret having authorized the elections.

The April 1975 Constituent Assembly Election

The returns underscored that the base of support for the revolution or, at least, that revolution which the radicals had in mind was narrow indeed. The turnout of nearly 92 percent

[287]

TABLE 1

Election Results

Party	April 1975 Constitutional Assembly % of vote	Deputies	April 1976 National Assembly % of vote	Deputies	Candidate	June 1976 Presidential Vote	%	Party	December 1976 Municipal % of vote	Council Posts
PS (Partido Socialista)	37.9	116	35.0	107	Eanes	2,967,414	61.5	PS	33.2	691
					Otelo	796,392	16.5			
PPD (Partido Popular Democrático)	26.4	80	24.0	73	Azevedo	692,382	14.4	PSD (Partido Social Demó-crata—formerly PPD)	24.3	623
PCP (Partido Communista Português)	12.5	30	14.6	40	Pato (PCP)	365,371	7.6	FEPU (Frente Eleitoral Povo Unido: includes PCP, MDP/CDE, FSP)	17.7	267
CDS (Centro Democrático Social)	7.6	16	15.9	40				CDS	16.6	317
MDP (Movimento Democrático Português)	4.1	5	—	—				GDUP (Grupos de Dinamição Unidade Popular)	2.5	5
Voter participation	91.7		83.3				75.4		64.5	

Sources: As Eleições de 25 de Abril: Geografia e Imagem dos Partidos, by Jorge Gaspar and Nuno Vitorino (Lisbon: Livros Horizonte, 1976) for data of 1975 elections. Revista Española de Opinión Pública (Madrid) July 1977, pp. 235, 239, 242, 250-51, and 255, for data on 1976 elections.

FIGURE 1

Portuguese Political Parties

	LEFT		CENTER	RIGHT	
PRP-BR	PCP	PS	PPD (PSD)	PDC	PL
PCP-ML			CDS		
MRPP	MDP/CDE				PP
LCI					
LUAR					
UDP					
MES					
FSP					

ACRONYMS

PRP-BR	Partido Revolucionário Popular-Brigadas Revolucionárias
MRPP	Movimento Reorganizativo do Proletariado Português
LUAR	Liga Unida de Acção Revolucionária
UDP	União Democrática Popular
PCP-ML	PCP Marxista-Leninista
LCI	Liga Comunista Internacionalista
MES	Movimento de Esquerda Socialista
FSP	Frente Socialista Popular
PCP	Partido Comunista Português
MDP-CDE	Movimento Democrático Popular/Comissão Democrática Eleitoral
PS	Partido Socialista
PPD(PSD)	Partido Popular Democrático; as of late 1976, Partido Social Demócrata
CDS	Centro Democrático Social
PDC	Partido Democrata Cristão
PL	Partido Liberal
PP	Partido do Progresso

was one of the highest ever recorded in a Western European national election and it was the moderate Left and Center which led the field. The Socialists garnered 37.9 percent of the vote and the Popular Democrats whom the PCP had sought to

[289]

oust from the provisional government after March 1975 captured 26.4 percent. The Communists obtained only 12.5 percent of the vote and the MDP/CDE, which some wags christened PCP *bis,* trailed even more, receiving a mere 4.1 percent of the total. Abstentions and blank ballots accounted for only about 8 percent of the ballots cast and most of these were in conservative areas where voters could hardly have been supposed to be voicing their support for the idea of a civilian MFA.

The Communists could not have been overly surprised at their showing: surveys taken over the previous two or three months had invariably agreed that the PCP would capture no more than 14 percent of the vote. Indeed, already in the fall of 1974, Communist leaders had begun to warn about the "undemocratic" situation prevailing in many parts of the country and insinuated on a number of occasions that it would be best if the elections were postponed.[12] As it was, the results showed the Portuguese Communists to have a markedly regional base of support, concentrated in the south and in the industrial towns along the lower bank of the Tagus estuary. In Lisbon, the PCP vote reached 19 percent but, as one went northward, the Communist tally dropped sharply with the party lists garnering less than 4 percent in each of the seven Northern districts. By contrast, it was there that the Popular Democrats and the *Centro Democrático Social* did best.

Struggle for Power

The results of the Constituent Assembly elections dealt a serious blow to the hopes of radicals within and outside the armed forces. No longer able to claim a status as the only true representatives of the popular will, the radical factions in the

MFA, the PCP and the multiplicity of extreme left groups had to confront the challenge of the Socialist and Popular Democratic parties, which now could claim a legitimacy emanating from their electoral victory. The conflict between these rival claimants to popular legitimacy, present but not well articulated until the spring of 1975, became explicit in the months after the election. By the end of the summer and again in November, this conflict was to polarize Portuguese society, bringing with it the threats of civil war and a new dictatorship.

The struggle did not turn out to be as one-sided as most observers had predicted. For one thing, neither the MFA nor its leftwing had anywhere near as much unity of purpose as their supporters might have wanted to claim. With the General Assembly of the *Movimento* functioning as the real national parliament, political and party divisions intruded into the MFA with a new virulence after March 1975. As the weeks went by, the chasm separating *gonçalvistas* from military populists and these two from the democratic socialists grew ever broader, eventually immobilizing the General Assembly and leading to the concentration of powers first in the Council of the Revolution and later in a still-born triumvirate composed of Gonçalves, Costa Gomes and Saraiva de Carvalho.

The Communists did not hide their concern about these divisions but they were in large measure powerless to do anything about them. From the outset they had hitched their fortunes to those of the *Movimento* (they were still very much the junior partners in that alliance) and, particularly after their feeble electoral showing, were in no position to back out. Not that the Communists desired to do so. In the spring and summer of 1975, the leaders of the PCP were all the more convinced of the exceptionalism of Portugal, of the proposition that a Western European-style parliamentary democracy was absolutely unviable in this Iberian country. From their perspective, the Portuguese revolution was about to complete its "national-democratic" phase and would soon begin the "revolutionary-democratic" one.[13] The Portuguese Communists believed that the choices would soon enough narrow themselves to either fascism or socialism. It was in this context that Cunhal gave his now famous interview to Oriana Fallaci: "Elections," he declared triumphantly, "have nothing or very little to do with the dynamic of the revoltuion . . . The electoral process cannot but be a marginal complement of this dynamic . . . If you believe that the Constituent Assembly will be transformed into a parliament, you are very much mistaken . . . In Portugal, there will be no parliament."[14]

Such frankness was counterproductive; it helped catalyze domestic and international opposition to the course of the Portuguese revolution. Within the country, this centered in the Socialist and Popular Democratic parties (their representatives resigned from the Gonçalves cabinet in early summer) and in the Catholic Church whose anti-PCP and anti-MFA campaign in the north of the country took on the overtones of a crusade. Internationally, it was the European Economic Community and pre-eminently the Socialist-led West German government which moved to block the possible establishment of a Soviet beachhead in Western Europe.

For a while, that is to say during the months of June and July 1975, there was a certain, even if strained, convergence between the supporters of Prime Minister Gonçalves and those of Carvalho. The Communists, desiring the support of both, hoped the relationship might be cemented, and in late July Cunhal even went to Lisbon airport to greet Carvalho upon his return from Cuba. The honeymoon, if it could be called such, was brief. Those who rallied around the COPCON leader never could forgive Gonçalves for his apparent willingness to become an instrument of the "social-fascist"

PCP, and the proposals they offered at various sessions of the MFA General Assembly (particularly the *Documento Guia da Aliança Povo-MFA* approved in early July) calling for the establishment of neighborhood and workers' councils as channels for direct democracy were aimed as much at the PCP as at the other parties. An open rupture came in early August when Melo Antunes and eight other members of the Council of the Revolution released a document decrying the efforts of a minority to impose a dictatorship. Carvalho cast his lot with them, writing Gonçalves a public letter telling the Prime Minister he had lost the confidence of the people and of the armed forces.[15] Carvalho's decision was of critical importance in forcing Gonçalves' resignation in late August. In so doing, Carvalho parted company (albeit only temporarily) with his followers in COPCON and in the extreme Left groups, who entered into negotiations with the Communists and even formed a short-lived *Frente Unitário Revolucionario* (FUR) in an effort to save the beleaguered Prime Minister.

In all of this, it is fair to say, the Communists did not play a primary role. Their policies during the summer of 1975 consisted essentially of reacting to the initiatives of others.[16] In mid-July, the Communists called for the constitution of a *poder homogeneo revolucionario* excluding the PS, PPD and CDS; in early August, Cunhal made an appeal for broad unity against "fascist and reactionary" forces; then, a short while later, the PCP joined with the ultra-Left in the FUR. These twists and turns in their tactical/political line must have bewildered even their most tested and loyal followers.

In retrospect, it is clear the Communists overestimated the strength of the radicals in the MFA and, equally as important, Vasco Gonçalves' ability to keep the situation in the military sphere under control. They underestimated the resentment that had built up in many parts of the country and the ability

[293]

of the socialists and Popular Democrats in the urban centers, and of the Catholic Church in more rural areas, to exploit this and mobilize the population. Their other mistake lay in thinking that a strategy premised on penetrating the structures of the *Estado Novo* would be successful in the extremely fluid and volatile political environment that came into being after April 1974. In fact, it simply made things easier for the myriad groups of the extreme Left who, presenting themselves as opponents of all bureaucratic entanglements, persistently outflanked the PCP.[17]

Certainly the Portuguese Communists did not view with favor Gonçalves' ouster and the subsequent formation of a new provisional government under Admiral Pinheiro de Azevedo in which the party held only one, relatively minor, ministerial portfolio. Their displeasure, on the other hand, must have been tempered by the fact that the victors in the intramural MFA struggle had not been able to carry through a purge of all radical spokesmen in the armed forces. The weakening of the radical factions, within the MFA, moreover, was not an altogether negative phenomenon from the Communist point of view, particularly since, as far as they were concerned, the political situation in Portugal retained its revolutionary potential. The significant alteration, as Cunhal and his lieutenants saw it, was that the balance of power of the MFA/PCP axis had at last begun to tilt in favor of the party.[18]

This was an extremely important conclusion because in the weeks after the formation of the new government the Communists turned even more than before to a strategy of mass mobilizations and de-stabilization. Unions under PCP influence made extravagant wage claims and the party joined once again with the ultra-Left, this time in fomenting unrest and strikes in military units. The MFA, Cunhal declared at a rally in late October, should resume "its dynamic participation in

Portuguese politics in alliance with the progressive political forces and the popular movement." [19] A month later, *Intersindical* organized a huge demonstration in Lisbon to demand Vasco Gonçalves' return to the government. The situation deteriorated to such a point that the cabinet suspended government operations. Matters came to a head in late November when, ostensibly in response tm an effort to remove Carvalho from his post as commander of the Lisbon military region, some units sparked a short-lived insurrection. There is still no definitive account of those events and of the role played in them by the Portuguese Communists. What evidence is available, however, suggests that PCP leaders had a very good idea as to what was going to take place but prudently wanted to limit official party involvement until it was clear which way things were going to turn out. In the end, they chose not to get involved openly.

NEW COURSE

The failure of the attempted coup of November 25 dramatically altered the complexion of Portuguese politics. The MFA, alliance with which had been the linchpin of Communist strategy, lay shattered with its more prominent radical members purged. The PCP was lucky still to be in the Sixth Provisional Government, but party leaders—although insisting that "the forces and potential of the revolution were enormous" [20]—had to abandon any hopes that in the short term the PCP might come to assume a preponderant role in the political system.

The orientation of Communist policies in this new phase was toward the consolidation and defense of what PCP leaders perceived to be the most significant accomplishments of the

[295]

Portuguese revolution, namely, the nationalizations decreed in March 1975 and the agrarian reform program officially initiated in the summer.

One priority, in this context, was weaning the Socialists away from their incipient alliance with the PPD and CDS and toward one with the PCP. As might be supposed, this was not an easy thing for the Communists to accomplish: although the PS did not relish the notion of establishing closer links with parties to its right, neither had Socialist leaders forgotten the Communist role in the events of the previous summer and fall. They, of course, did not share the Communist conviction that only Communist participation in government would insure the progressive character of that government.

Elections for National Assembly and President

For the PCP, the parliamentary elections of April 1976 were the first hurdle on the road to forging an eventual coalition government with the Socialists. In this regard the elections rendered a mixed verdict. On the one hand, the Communists must have been buoyed by the decline in the Socialist and Popular Democratic vote and the rise in their own. The Socialists went from 37.9 percent in April 1975 to 35.0, and from 116 deputies to 107; the Popular Democrats from 26.4 percent of 24.0, and from 80 to 73 deputies. The Communist total was now 14.6 percent of the vote, up from 12.5 the year before. The new lineup in the National Assembly—107 Socialists, 73 from the PPD, 40 Communists, 40 from the CDS and one from the UDP—indicated that two important PCP objectives, preventing a CDS/PPD majority and of laying the numerical foundation for a Socialist/Communist one, had been attained. It was in the Southern provinces of Beja, Évora and Setúbal where the PCP made its greatest inroads, picking up an average of 6.1 percentage points over its total in 1975. The Communist performance had a less encouraging side however. The PCP fell to fourth place nationally, overtaken by a revitalized CDS which doubled its previous total, from 7.6 percent to 15.9. The absence of the MDP/CDE from this election helped the Communists, but in no province was there a direct and complete transfer of that organization's votes to the PCP banner. In any case, although the election results showed the Communists to be the premier force in the agricultural south, they also demonstrated that the PCP continued to have a markedly regional base of support. The Socialists, although losing votes in most provinces, were still the only group able to claim a truly national presence and as such could still afford to keep the PCP on one side, and the CDS and PPD on the other, at arms length.

In an effort to increase their bargaining leverage, the Communists decided to field their own candidate in the presidential election scheduled for June 1976. The PCP had originally hoped that the Council of the Revolution would achieve a consensus on some well-known, progressive military figure. As it turned out, no such agreement could be reached and two prominent officers, army chief of staff Ramalho Eanes (a key figure in putting down the Nobember 25th coup) and provisional Prime Minister Pinheiro de Azevedo, decided to run. The Communists did not look on either of them with great favor and chose to run in the election as well. The move was not without its risks, but PCP leaders obviously hoped that their candidate would receive a sufficient number of votes to throw the election into a second round and the party could, in exchange for its votes, extract concessions as to the composition of the next government. The scenario was not at all farfetched, but Cunhal and his associates did not count on

Otelo Saraiva de Carvalho and his decision to run with the support of some extreme Left groups in the election as well.

The Communists, forced by Carvalho's presence to stay in the race to the bitter end, suffered a staggering defeat. Not only did Eanes capture nearly three million votes (or 61.5 percent of the total) and win on the first round but Otelo came in second with 16.5 percent. The Communist candidate, Political Bureau member Octavio Pato, came in fourth, behind Pinheiro de Azevedo and with less than half the number of votes the PCP had garnered in the parliamentary elections. Only in the Azores, of all places, did Pato run in ahead of Carvalho. The magnitude of the Communist defeat was most clearly evident in those seven provinces where the PCP had done best in April 1976. There, the losses went as high as 25 percentage points in Setúbal. In the aftermath of the election Communist leaders sought to minimize the damage done—they pointed particularly to the 24 percent combined vote for Carvalho and Pato—but could not disguise the fact that whatever hopes they might have had about coming to some sort of agreement with the Socialists had evaporated for the present. Communist leaders went through the motions the subsequent fall, offering to establish joint lists with the PS for the municipal elections scheduled for December, but they knew ahead of time what the Socialist answer would be. The PCP, in any case, probably preferred to run in those elections without too many encumbrances as its real objective was to recover the ground lost to Carvalho and the extreme Left groups in June. (See Table 1.)

The First Constitutional Government

Soon after the victory, Eanes entrusted Soares, as leader of the largest party, with the task of forming the first constitutional government of the second Portuguese republic. The minority Socialist government was in a unenviable position. Economically and politically, Portugal was in precarious health, victimized by the excesses of the previous two and a half years. Economic problems, which had surfaced already in the final years of the Caetano regime, had been aggravated during the two tumultuous years of the revolution. The sharp increases in industrial wages decreed by the various provisional governments—these went up 39.5 percent in 1974 and 25.0 in 1975—triggered a demand for goods which the Portuguese economy had no way of satisfying without further aggravating its dependence on imports.[21] The drying-up of such external sources of financing as tourism and emigrant remittances did not help matters at all. Public and private investment had dropped substantially as had industrial pi oduction, which stagnated in 1974 and decreased by 4 percent in 1975.[22] The Soares government, economic experts unanimously agreed, would have to find a way to increase productivity and cut down on internal consumption. This would require a series of unpopular measures whose necessity would not make them any more palatable.

The situation was, from a political point of view, only slightly better. The minority Socialist government that Soares headed did not have a stable parliamentary majority. It would be subject to a cross-fire from the parliamentary Right and Left, not to say from the extra-parliamentary extremes as well. The new government had some room for maneuvering, but most observers believed that, sooner or later the Socialists would have to reach some sort of understanding with one or more of the parties represented in the National Assembly.

The Communists, certainly held to that opinion. They also remained steadfast in the belief that the formation of a more conservative, "openly reactionary," government with CDS or PPD participation would simply pave the way for a new

[299]

dictatorship. Portugal, the Communists vehemently insisted, was much further along the road to socialism than any other Western European country.[23] The nationalizations decreed under Vasco Gonçalves and the agrarian reform initiated in 1974-75 had broken the control the capitalist class exercised over the state. Although capitalist relations of production were still *predominant* in the country, these were not decisive because the most important sectors of the economy had come under popular control. At the same time, because of the inherent weakness of the Portuguese middle classes, any return to the previous state-monopoly, capitalist economic system would bring in its wake the elimination of all political liberties. The offensive dimension of this analysis had been emphasized by the PCP in the months after September 1974, and particularly in the wake of the attempted coup in March 1975. It was symptomatic of how much the situation had changed that the party, now on the defensive, had to cement an alliance with the Socialists in order to stave off further defeats.

The formation of a government based on a "presidential majority"—that is, one composed of the three major parties (PS, PPD, CDS) which had supported Eanes in his bid for the presidency in June 1976—was the Communist nightmare. They were undoubtedly correct in assuming that the decisive influence in such a coalition would pass quickly from the Socialists. They were probably also right in thinking that under such circumstances the ouster of the few members of the military Left (like Melo Antunes and Vasco Lourenço in the Council of the Revolution) who remained in positions of responsibility within the armed forces was a foregone conclusion. As it was, the weeding out of undesirable elements from the military in the months after November 1975 had been quite thorough: no fewer than 500 officers had been subject to disciplinary action, as had 80 percent of those officers in the *quadro permanente* who had been delegates to the last MFA General Assembly.[24]

Communist Strategy in the New Phase

The PCP had to engage in a careful balancing act as it pursued an agreement with the Socialists. On the one hand, the Communists needed to be sharply critical of the Socialist government and its policies. This would make the task of organizational maintenance easier, permitting the Communists at once to galvanize and channel discontent. The PCP, however, could not afford to let the dynamics of popular mobilization get out of control. Too intransigent or virulent an opposition to Socialist policies could make the PS more receptive than it already was to overtures from the CDS and PPD. Accordingly, while Communist leaders wasted few opportunities to blast the government and accuse it of following a path of "capitalist, agrarian and imperialist recuperation," they invariably stressed a willingness to negotiate their differences with the government.

Reliance on this two-pronged strategy helped the Communists withstand Socialist efforts to break the hold the PCP had over Intersindical and the influence it exerted among the agricultural laborers in the south.

In the labor movement, the Socialist drive after November 1975 had taken diverse forms. The Socialist group in the National Assembly sponsored a series of bills: one required that syndical membership fees be collected not by the enterprises but by the unions in question, and another made it easier to dismiss workers. Socialist trade unionists also organized a rival movement to *Intersindical* known as *Carta Aberta* after a

[301]

public document they released in early 1976. Composed primarily of unions from the service sector, *Carta Aberta* called for democratic elections in all unions and the convocation of an extraordinary congress. At the outset, its supporters enjoyed a great deal of sympathy among non-PCP labor activists who resented Communist manipulation of organized labor. That atmosphere dissipated as the economic situation worsened and it became more and more obvious that part of the government's economic strategy was to permit prices to rise relative to wages so as to cut down on consumption. Many Socialist labor activists became increasingly disenchanted.[25] The Communists took great pains in the months after November 1975 to keep strictly partisan quarrels out of *Intersindical* and instructed those militants active in the labor movement to concentrate their efforts on galvanizing unity around bread-and-butter issues.[26] This was the essential character of the massive demonstrations *Intersindical* organized in early 1976 and in the spring and early summer 1977. The approach worked. Out of 111 syndical elections held in 1977, the PS lost the leadership of 23 unions and Communist-supported unitary lists won 83.[27] Despite their harsh criticism of Socialist economic policies, the Communists had no interest in forcing an out-and-out crisis. Thus, at the national conference on economic problems organized by the PCP in June 1977, Cunhal made the point that in exchange for concessions from the government the PCP would support "courageous austerity measures" and would undertake to convince *Intersindical* to make only such wage demands as were "possible and necessary." [28]

The Communists used a similar approach in their battle with the Socialists for control of the Alentejo and its agricultural proletariat. Occupations of the great landed estates there had begun in the fall of 1974, but formal decress expropriating those lands and granting a juridical basis to the *unidades colectivas de produçao* (UCP) did not come until the subsequent summer. By late 1975, in any case, approximately 1.2 million hectares of land had been taken over and redistributed. Initially, the Communist party did not have a decisive influence in the region and had to share the initiative with Socialists, extreme Leftists and even COPCON units which on occasion backed up the land occupations by making a show of force. Over time, however, the PCP used its control of the *Sindicato dos Trabalhadores Agrícolas* and its penetration of the Ministry of Agriculture to become the preponderant organization in the Alentejo.

Committed, after November 1975, to break the Communist hold over the Alentejo, the Socialist Ministers of Agriculture issued decrees dissolving the Agricultural Backup and Development Program and cutting off emergency credits to several UCPs until these accounted for how funds already granted had been spent. They ousted Communists from the national ministry and regional Agrarian Reform Centers, cleared lands which had been illegally occupied, and encouraged the formation of a system of cooperatives to compete with the UCPs. The most provocative measure was the presentation to the National Assembly of the so-called Barreto law on the agrarian reform. The bill raised the limit on the amount of land an expropriated landlord could set aside for his own use and set up procedures through which former owners could recover already expropriated properties. The Socialists saw all of the measures as a sort of package which would not only rectify the abuses perpetrated in the past and encourage investment and increase agricultural productivity but also help cut down Communist influence in the region.

The idea was a good one but the Socialist leadership miscalculated the effect some of these measures would have among

[303]

left-wingers in the party (many of them felt the government had given up any real intention of furthering socialist transformations in Portuguese society) und the negative reaction generated by them in the Alentejo. The Communists, for their part, played very effectively on the fears of the agricultural proletariat. They were able in many parts of the Alentejo to make the public see the UCPs as an instrument for guaranteed employment. The directives emanating from Lisbon, the PCP suggested, by emphasizing efficiency and productivity would both lead to the breakup of the UCPs and throw many out of work. Unrest in the region peaked with the presentation and subsequent approval (with PPD votes joining those of the Socialists) of the Barreto law. The Communists certainly played a role in fomenting that unrest—at one rally Cunhal denounced the bill as a "juridical monstrosity" and on another occasion declared it was not "a bill on agrarian reform but a bill for the destruction of the agrarian reform" [29]—but were always careful to insist that they would fight against the measure "within the framework of the institutions and the rights and freedoms granted to the PCP by the constitution." [30] In fact, the party engaged in negotiations with the Socialists up to the last moment in the hope that some arrangement could be worked out.

The battle over the Barreto agrarian reform law was long and drawn out: the Socialists only managed to have the law approved after a last-minute compromise with the PSD (formerly PPD), which, over the objections of party leader Francisco Sá Carneiro, lent its votes to the PS in exchange for an agreement providing for regular consultation between the two parties. Already in April 1977, President Eanes had more or less openly told Soares and his supporters during the course of a speech commemorating the third anniversary of the Revolution that the minority Socialist government did not have an

[304]

unlimited amount of time to make headway against the country's mounting economic and social problems. In the aftermath of the vote, the pressure on the Socialists to conclude some sort of agreement with the principal political and social forces on a short- to medium-term plan for economic recovery became significantly greater.

Few were willing to hazard a guess in late summer 1977 as to what that agreement might look like or which forces would support it. The Socialists remained adamant in their refusal to establish a formal coalition government with any one and the PSD and CDS opposed the inclusion of the Communists in the negotiation process. Isolating the Communists was much more difficult now than in the months immediately after November 1975. The PCP, whether one liked it or not, had an important, even preponderant, influence in the labor movement, and any effort to shunt them aside could bring with it the risk of polarizing the country. Moreover, as we have seen, since early 1976, but particularly after the Eighth PCP Congress in the fall of that year, the PCP had adopted a rather moderate and accommodating stance and thus did not present an easy target for its conservative opponents.

The tug-of-war between the CDS/PSD on the one side and the PCP on the other for the Socialist hand in a political marriage heated up in the fall. At one point, the notion that the Socialists might be willing to continue governing with Communist support gained some credence, particularly in the wake of remarks made by Soares in the course of a news conference to the effect that Communist votes had a value equal to any other in the National Assembly. The probability of a formal agreement being reached between the PCP and PS was quite low however. Most probably, Soares wanted to use the prospect of collaboration with the Communists as a weapon in his efforts to rally PSD and/or CDS support on the motion-of-

[305]

confidence vote to which the government committed itself in early November.

That strategy did not work at all with respect to the Social Democrats who nearly split on the question. It worked a bit better with the CDS which, although it did not vote with the Socialists on the motion-of-confidence vote, indicated a willingness to negotiate an agreement looking toward the constitution of a new government. (CDS leaders reasoned that taking up the Socialists' offer would give their party an opportunity to develop a less conservative image and might allow it eventually to become the centrist counterpoint to the Socialist party.

The Communists, for their part, negotiated with the Socialists until just hours before the motion-of-confidence vote in December 1977 but in the end decided that the PS leadership had not gone far enough in its willingness to compromise on such Communist demands as that the recently approved agrarian reform law not be implemented, that there be no devolution of nationalized enterprises, that a 20 rather than 15 percent wage raise be decreed, and that Ministers of Agriculture Barreto and of Labor Gonelha not be part of a new government. That decision was probably a mistake. The Communists, after months of insisting that they wanted to negotiate a broad national platform, forsook what may have been a decisive opportunity to create a favorable dynamic for their quest for an eventual alliance with the PS.

Prospects and Conclusions

The formation of the CDS/PS government (and the signing of the Political Accord, the Economic Stabilization program for 1978, and the Medium Term Development Plan which preceded it) represented quite a gamble on the part of both parties. For the Socialists, joining with a group considered by many to be a reactionary force and hostile to the April 1974 revolution was a dangerous step. It left the party open to an erosion of support on the Left. Similarly, for the CDS, the decision meant giving the PSD (at least that part sympathetic to Sá Carneiro and his harder line) and groups on the extreme Right a clear opportunity to lay claim to the mantle of conservative opposition to the government.

Both parties would obviously have liked to hold the coalition together until 1981 when the term of the incumbent National Assembly expired. But Soares could not without seriously losing face give in to CDS demands for remodeling the government, and the CDS feared that to do otherwise was to risk losing votes to the PSD on the right. As it is, Portugal has a serious and worsening economic situation: in 1978, the country has an inflation rate which hovers around 30 percent (highest among the OECD nations) and unemployment affects nearly 17 percent of the active population. Now conditions laid down by the International Monetary Fund for an emergency $750 million loan have been accepted—the principal demands are for a reduction in the balance-of-payments deficit and in the inflation rate by at least a third in 1978 and for setting a 3 percent limit to economic growth—any government has to worry about implementing the austerity measures which that program requires.

This will undoubtedly exacerbate social tensions in Portugal and benefit not only the Communists, who will consolidate further their influence in the labor movement and among the agricultural workers of the South, but also other groups to the Socialists' left, particularly the recently constituted *União de Esquerda Socialista Democrática*. That group has as its leader former Minister of Agriculture Lopes Cardoso, and recent polls indicate the UESD could receive up to 10 percent of the vote in a national election.

Portuguese Communist opposition to the Socialist-CDS government was selective in its intransigence, and indications are that for the most part the PCP will continue to emphasize the broad front tactics and the relatively moderate policies which it has pursued in the period after November 1975. While the Communists do have an interest in weakening the Socialist party, they have to be careful on this score; they also need the PS to be relatively strong so that it can act as a barrier against polarization. As a result, the Communists are not overly interested at this point either in direct confrontation with Soares and his party or in setting up a narrow Socialist-Communist government. Such a shift to the left, indeed anything resembling a return to the "superior forms of struggle" [31] employed by the party and its allies during 1975, would be dangerously counterproductive. Not only might it split the PS (and drive one part of the Socialists into the PSD), but it would increase the strength of a Right whose star is already on the rise in the military and elsewhere in the country. More interested in forcing the creation of a government based upon an agreement on economic and social policies which would have their approval, the Portuguese Communists are not keen on anticipated legislative elections. The Communists would probably match or improve upon their showing in April 1976 (perhaps even come close to the 18 percent they attained in the December 1976 municipal elections), but the general results would be much more likely to favor the Right and thus improve the chances that the most "progressive" sections of the Portuguese Constitution—those dealing with nationalization and agrarian reform—would be amended after

[308]

1980 when by law the first revisions can be made in that charter and elections are scheduled.

Portuguese Communist leaders have certainly toned down their revolutionary rhetoric in the last two years. Their policies have assumed a markedly defensive orientation, and party leaders have become apostles of moderation. In the international sphere, the PCP is no longer as ostentatiously hardline and pro-Soviet as before (although Cunhal did write an article in *Pravda* entitled "Shoulder to Shoulder with the CPSU Today as Always" on the 60th anniversary of the October 1917 revolution), [32] and the party has tried hard to mend relations with various other parties (the Italian in particular) which had been harshly critical of Portuguese Communist actions in the summer of 1975. Relations with the Spanish party, on the other hand, have not improved visibly, an indication perhaps of the virulence of the dispute between the PCE and Moscow. Indeed, Cunhal and others in the PCP leadership must have viewed the disappointing Spanish Communist performance in the June 1977 election (9.2 percent of the vote) with a good deal of self-satisfaction.

It is still too early to tell what impact a continued adherence to broad front policies and the possible consolidation of a parliamentary democracy in Portugal might have on the PCP. Right now the shift is tactical and derives from the danger presented by resurgent conservative forces. A real change in Portuguese Communist attitudes is unlikely to come while Cunhal and his closest associates retain control of the PCP however. Once they are gone, the situation within the party may change, but, it is fair to say, the Portuguese Communist party has a long and tortuous road to travel before its "Euro-communization" can be said to have begun.

[309]

NOTES

1. For other analyses of the Portuguese revolution, see Kenneth Maxwell, "The Thorns of the Portuguese Revolution," *Foreign Affairs,* January 1976, pp. 250-70; Arnold Hottinger, "The Rise of Portugal's Communists," *Problems of Communism,* XXIV (July-August 1975), pp. 1-17; George Grayson, "Portugal and the Armed Forces Movement," *Orbis,* XIX (Summer 1975), pp. 335-78; and Eusebio Mujal-León, "The PCP and the Portuguese Revolution," *Problems of Communism,* XXVI (January-February 1977), pp. 21-41 which has been republished in David E. Albright, ed., *Communism and Political Systems in Western Europe* (Boulder, Colorado: Westview Press, 1978).

2. In this regard, see the autobiographical account of a party functionary's life in J.A. Silva Marques, *Relatos da Clandestinidade— O PCP Visto por Dentro* (Lisbon: SOJORNAL, 1976).

3. *Diario de Noticias,* October 21, 1974.

4. For a comparative analysis of the PCE and PCP, see my chapter "Portuguese and Spanish Communism in Contemporary Perspective" in Morton A. Kaplan, ed., *The Many Faces of Communism* (Glencoe, Illinois: The Free Press, 1978).

5. Fernando Guerreiro, "Bento Gonçalves o PCP e a Questão das Alianças na Luta Antifascista dos Anos 30 em Portugal," in *Seara Nova* (Lisbon), March 1975, pp. 16-26.

6. Eugénio Rosa, *Problemas Actuais da Economia Portuguêsa* (Lisbon: Seara Nova, 1974), p. 121, and *Avante!,* February 12, 1975.

7. Alvaro Cunhal, *Contribucão para o Estudo da Questão Agraria*

(Lisbon: Editorial Avante, 1976). This two-volume study had been written 10 years before.

8. For an excellent analysis of events leading to the coup, see Avelino Rodrigues, Cesário Borga and Mario Cardoso, *Movimento dos Capitães e o 25 de Abril* (Lisbon: Moraes Editores, 1974).

9. *Diario de Noticias,* September 30, 1974.

10. See his speech in *VII Congresso (Extraordinário) do PCP* (Lisbon: Editorial Avante, 1974), pp. 21-48.

11. *Diario de Noticias,* September 30, 1974.

12. See the Central Committee statement released January 27, 1975 and translated in *Foreign Broadcast Information Service* (Western Europe), January 29, 1975, pp. N1-N6.

13. See the prologue to Alvaro Cunhal, *Pela Revolução Democrática e Nacional* (Lisbon: Editorial Estampa, 1975), published in July 1975.

14. *L'Europeo* (Milan), June 15, 1975.

15. José Gomes Mota in *A Resistência: Subsidios para o Estudo da Crise Político Militar do Verão de 1975* (Lisbon: Edições Jornal Expresso, 1976) suggests that one reason Carvalho broke with Gonçalves was that the COPCON leader, a political neophyte in many ways, saw Melo Antunes as his "papa político" (p. 137).

16. See my chapter on Portugal in David E. Albright, ed., *Communism and Political Systems in Western Europe* (Westview Press, 1978).

17. Maxwell, *op. cit.,* p. 263.

[311]

18. *Avante!*, September 18, 1975.

19. *Diario de Noticias,* October 20, 1975.

20. *Avante!*, December 16, 1975.

21. Bela Belassa, "Industrial and Trade Policy in Portugal" in *Conferencia Internacional sobre Economia Portuguesa* (Lisbon: Fundacao Gulbenkian, 1977), vol. I, p. 240. The two-volume study contains the proceedings of a conference held in Lisbon and sponsored by the German Marshall Fund of the United States and the Gulbenkian Foundation.

22. *Ibid.,* 240.

23. See the report delivered by Cunhal to the Eighth PCP Congress in the name of the Central Committee, *A Revolução Portuguesa: O Passado e O Futuro* (Lisbon: Editorial Avante, 1976).

24. *Informaciones* (Madrid), September 2, 1977.

25. *Le Monde,* May 24-25, 1977.

26. See, for example, the Central Committee statement in *Avante!*, December 16, 1975.

27. Alvaro Cunhal interview in *El País* (Madrid), February 2, 1978.

28. The text of the Cunhal speech and of the resolution approved at the National Conference may be found in *Avante!*, June 7, 1977.

29. *Diario de Noticias,* July 18, 1977 for the first quote and *Avante!*, May 26, 1977 for the second.

30. See the interview Cunhal gave to *Expresso* (Lisbon) 30 July 1977.

31. *Avante!,* July 29, 1976.

32. *Pravda,* November 28, 1977.

[SIX]

The Soviet Union and West European Communism

Robert Legvold

For years we have known almost nothing of the importance assigned West European Communist parties by Soviet policy-makers. In large part our ignorance has been for want of caring. If this sounds odd, it is only because our current preoccupation with the rise of a Communist-influenced Left in Southern Europe has made us forget how little West European communism really mattered to Soviet foreign policy during most of the last twenty years. How little it mattered to Soviet relations with the Federal Republic, Great Britain, or even France, how little it mattered to the challenge of combinations like the Atlantic Alliance or the Common Market. Even how little it actually mattered to the course of relations within the socialist camp. On both critical planes—East-West (after the drama of France and Italy in 1947) and within the Communist world (beyond Togliatti's notion of "polycentrism")—West European communism's role has been marginal.

Our ignorance and our indifference have fed one another. Were the Soviet leaders happy to see the PCF launch a campaign for unity with the French Socialists in early 1956, a "new Popular Front" as the French called the appeal? Did they in fact put the French Communists up to it? No one knew and few cared. Were Soviet feelings any different six years later when another more serious movement toward Socialist-Communist collaboration began, inspired by a Gaullist regime for which the Soviet leaders had considerable hopes? Who even asked?

And so it was for virtually every aspect of Soviet foreign policy touched by West European communism: We had no reason to investigate the precise relationship between the Western Communist parties and the Soviet Union—unless we happened to be interested in one or another of these parties; no reason to explore how much direct control the Soviet Union still exercised over them or, on the contrary, how much it had lost. We had no need to contemplate the place these parties occupied in the Soviet strategy toward Western Europe, or the possibility that the very idea represented a growing unreality; and no need to consider the role they played in the conflicts with Tito and Mao—unless we happened to be interested in the internal politics of "international communism." We did assume that these parties continued to be controlled by Moscow. Therefore we did not feel the need of looking closely.

The whole subject was left to a handful of people who were either devoted to analyzing individual parties or primarily concerned with the Sino-Soviet split. They did their work unaided by the contributions of specialists in Soviet policy toward Western Europe or students of European international relations. Excellent as much of this work has been, however, it does not prepare us to unravel the multidimensional challenge

[315]

that Western European communism now presents to the
Soviet Union. For, one group has tended to deal with each
party in isolation, the other only with the issues at the heart of
the dispute with China. But the challenge of West European
communism is now greater than the evolution of any one
party, and the issues raised go much beyond any single theme
or enmity.

Before West European communism is to be understood as a
problem, object, or hope of Soviet foreign policy, the missing
dimensions have to be restored, their interplay sorted out, and
their different, sometimes competing effects put into perspective. Three of these dimensions are basic: First, the inter-party
dimension, that is, these parties in their relations with Soviet
and East European communism; second, the internal dimension, these parties as the bearers of change within their own
societies; and, third, the international dimension, these parties
as an increasingly important factor in East-West relations. All
these dimensions are interconnected. Slight any one of them
and the result will be a distorted impression of the relevance
these parties have for Soviet foreign policy.

In the first instance, and most obviously, the Soviet Union
responds to West European Communist parties as allies in the
world Communist movement. They began as spin-offs of the
original Bolshevik revolution, as creations fashioned in the
image of Lenin's revolutionary instrument, and they were
partners once in a single cohesive revolutionary alliance institutionalized in the Comintern and revived, in part, in the
Cominform. Indeed, in Soviet eyes, they were, for many
years, elements or sections of a single world party. Their
relations with one another, with ruling Communist parties,
and above all with the Soviet Union are part of the Soviet
Union's greatest preoccupation. The challenge of keeping the
network of Communist parties everywhere a cohesive, harmo-

nious force constitutes the most elemental of the Soviet Union's policy concerns. From the Soviet perspective the challenge turns on its ability to rally their cooperation (1) in reinforcing Soviet prestige among these parties and its leadership over them, (2) in sanctioning or, at least, tolerating the course of events in Eastern Europe, and (3) in prosecuting the dispute with China. These are the compulsions that shape the content of "proletarian internationalism," the Soviet phrase for this dimension, with its built-in exhortation to unity and orthodoxy.

Second, each of these parties aspires to transform its home society, and the way it conceives this transformation stirs the deepest Soviet interest. For the Soviet Union, these parties are not merely surrogates in foreign political milieux—participants who conveniently share its ideological traditions. They are the incarnation of the original revolutionary justification. They represent what is left of the vision of capitalism's demise and the proletarian revolution consummated. Since the Soviet leaders base much of their own system's legitimacy on this vision, they care profoundly how these parties serve it. When these parties develop their own contrasting political strategies and programs, more is at stake than Soviet control over the "Communist movement" in the crude sense of the word; the validity of the Soviet Union's own revolutionary experience, not to mention Eastern Europe's, becomes the issue.

Third, increasingly these parties and their Socialist allies figure in Soviet relations with Western Europe. Increasingly they influence the hopes that the Soviet leaders entertain for the success of their foreign policy in this region. And increasingly they are a factor in the Soviet approach to Europe's evolving international order. This is the level at which the West European Communist parties have mattered least for most of the last two decades. But now both as serious contes-

[317]

tants for power, momentarily complicating the political landscape, and as potential victors, opening interesting though uncertain vistas, the likes of French, Italian and Spanish parties make this dimension once more vital.

These dimensions, taken separately, have no ultimate meaning, for they intersect at every turn: the inter-party with the intra-national (or revolutionary); the intra-national with the international; and the international with the inter-party. The inter-party dimension ("proletarian internationalism") intersects with the intra-party (the "roads to socialism") as soon as the issue is how much to honor the Soviet Union and the Soviet revolution. Since the basic criterion of proletarian internationalism remains one's attitude toward the Soviet Union, this occurs very soon. For fundamentally the phrase "attitude toward the Soviet Union" means attitude toward the Soviet model, and this automatically makes an issue of every other party's strategy and tactics, goals, and revolutionary vision.

On the other hand, the Soviet Union's attitude toward the success of communism in West Europe—that is, its enthusiasm for the *Union de la gauche* in France or the *compromesso storico* in Italy—depends to a great extent on the effect that the Soviet leaders think this is likely to have on their West European policy. The link between the inter-party and the international dimension becomes even clearer when the PCF turns the relationship around and invokes "proletarian internationalism" to chastise the Soviet leadership for its faint-hearted support of a radical change in France.

In the longer run, however, provided the external costs can be managed, governments that come under the influence of West European Communists may benefit Soviet policy by substantially altering their own. This prospect furnishes the Soviet Union with another reason to care about the character and program of these parties—which creates the link between the intra-and the international dimension.

In what follows, each of the three dimensions is looked at more closely and then set in motion, that is, judged in the way they interact. The first part of the essay explores through Soviet eyes the three crucial angles on West European communism: What it is (and should be). What its relationship to the "socialist commonwealth" is (and should be). And what its impact on Europe's international relations is (or could be). In the process I want to consider how the answers to any one of these questions bears on the answer to the others. These intersections are what make Eurocommunism such a subtly complicated phenomenon—such a mixed inspiration to Soviet foreign policy. Because Eurocommunism, whatever the pretension of the term, does signify a turning point in the evolution of West European communism, its implications for the Soviet Union need to be considered apart and as a whole.

THE SETTING

How, an outsider might wonder, is the Soviet Union to manage a coherent (not to mention a uniform) approach to something as diverse as West European communism? For the discrepancies among the different parties are enormous, and greater still is the place they occupy within their national political settings. In this area there are twenty parties—not counting splinter parties—and the range extends from the most unreconstructed Leninist (which by style and strategy has been the case of the Portuguese) to the most liberal reformist (which by choice and trend has become the case of a much larger number of parties led by the Italians and the Swedes).

[319]

In between, on virtually every aspect of theory and practice, a grand array of views prevails: On the *dictatorship of the proletariat,* for example, which the Portuguese defend, the French reject, the Italians ignore, and over which the Norwegians quarrel. On *democratic centralism,* to which the Portuguese desperately cling, the Danes pay their respects, the Austrians give scarcely a second thought, and the Norwegians, in 1974, retained so little loyalty that they plotted their self-liquidation in an ultimately unsuccessful effort to convert an electoral alliance into a broad Marxist party. On *proletarian internationalism,* which the Greeks and Irish embrace loyally, the French use against the Soviet Union, the Spaniards suppress in the name of a Communist gaullism, and the Icelanders dismiss as an absurdity. On the *crisis of capitalism,* which the Portuguese view in classical Marxist-Leninist terms but downplay while hoping nonetheless to profit from it; which the French, too, prefer (unsuccessfully) to view in classical Marxist-Leninist terms but play up, even abet, while fearing nonetheless its consequences; and which the Italians view beyond, even without, Marxism-Leninism and work to moderate while worrying that, as a consequence, power may be forced on them prematurely.[1]

On the more immediate issues of political strategy (including a common front with the Social Democrats), domestic priorities, and foreign policy, the contrasts are every bit as pronounced. Some Communists, such as the Italians and the Swedes, embrace pluralism and the ballot as not only the single acceptable path to power but the essence of their socialism. Others, like the Luxemburgers and probably the French, recognize pluralism and the ballot as essential to their success but not necessarily to their vision of socialism. And one party, the Portuguese Communist party (PCP), grants them—or did not so long ago—no priority over the violent and direct seizure of power, not to mention no legitimacy after the "proletarian revolution." Some, such as the French, stake their political future on a formal alliance with the Socialists; others, such as the Swedes, on an informal and unacknowledged collaboration to save the Socialists in power—to no avail. Still others, such as the Danes and the Norwegians, form electoral partnerships with left Socialists to drive the moderate Socialists from power. And one, the Finnish party, until recently, refused the governing role offered by Socialists already in power. Some, such as the Italians, extend their hand to the Church and the captains of industry; others, such as the Portuguese, wage war on them. Some, like the Norwegians, have built their following by opposing their country's entry into the Common Market; others, such as the Spanish, by supporting it. Some, such as the Portuguese, have praised the stifling of the 1968 Czechoslovak liberal experiment; others, like the Danes and Finns, have lamented but forgotten it; still others, like the Italians, Norwegians, and Swedes, have made their condemnation a permanent and invidious part of their claim to national legitimacy.

And these are not even the most striking instances of variety: The most striking are the contrasts marking the place of Communist parties within their national political settings. When the Soviet Union surveys the status of different Communist parties in their own countries, it confronts an almost irreconcilably mixed picture. Beyond the contrast between legal and illegal parties, West European Communist parties vary dramatically in the vote they command, in the alliances they strike, in the influence they wield over the trade unions, and ultimately in the hope they have of implementing any part of their programs. The difference is enormous between a party like the NKP (the Norwegian Communist party), with 1 percent of the vote and slipping, without allies or a foothold in the labor movement, and plagued by Marxist competitors to

[321]

the right and the left, and one like the SKP (the Finnish Communist party) which through its permanent alliance (the SKDL, or Finnish People's Democratic League) has never dipped much below 17 or 18 percent of the vote, a party which dominates important segments of organized labor, and which, while subject to internal rifts, remains a powerful political force in Finnish political life and, in fact, was for four years (from 1966 to 1970) a member of the governing coalition and is now again. The difference has little to do with the character of the party because both the NKP and the SKP are essentially "reformist" and "nationalistic."

There is also the contrast between a 5 percent party like the one in Sweden, which, thanks to the pre-eminent but vulnerable position of the Social Democrats, has in the past and may, again, in the future influence policy, and a major party like the PCF which is closer by the day to power but losing ground to its Socialist partners every step of the way. The contrast is even greater between a 5 percent party like the Dutch—legal, with representation in parliament, but without any influence—and one like the PCE—for forty years illegal, with no access to power, but the spokesman for a substantial part of the Spanish working class. And between a cipherable entity like the West German Communist party and a crucial actor like the PCI, the contrast in infinite.

It might be argued that the jumble among twenty parties does not really count—that the Soviet attitude is determined by developments within and about the three of four major parties of Southern Europe, the parties of consequence in countries of consequence. If so, however, matters are scarcely simplified. With one exception, the contrasts in the condition of French, Italian, Spanish, and Portuguese communism are just as great. The exception, of course, is the sameness of all four parties' growing importance.

[322]

For the Soviets to build a common approach to West European communism on relations with these four parties requires Brobdingnagian ingenuity. Simply to comprehend the ways in which these parties differ one must have considerable imagination.[2] In Portugal—a frail, retarded postrevolutionary society, feeling its way toward democracy after a half century of dictatorship—the party remains a remnant of the pre-1956 period, Stalinist in its organization, Leninist in its strategy, doctrinaire in its social analysis, and Cominternist in its international relations. In Spain—a society also struggling with the passage from corporatism to pluralism, but considerably more advanced economically and considerably more troubled ethnically—the party has become un-Leninist in its political analysis, and the most nationalistic among Communist parties. In France—a politically polarized, ultra-modern but in many ways traditional society, more intricate in its social and economic divisions than any other—the party is increasingly a bizarre mélange of liberal tactics and conservative instincts, drawing "reformist" conclusions from dogmatic analysis, altering its Leninist image but in a Leninist fashion, and, as if to prove its French character, demanding of its international ties support for its national designs. And, in Italy—a sclerotic, half-modern, half-medieval, policy-poor society, living proof that a permanent crisis does not always bring nearer a revolutionary transformation—the party is comfortably and successfully a part of the system, revisionist in its assessment of trends, relaxed in its organization, and above all cautious and broad-visioned in its strategy. Where one party (the PCP) worries about the stability of a Socialist government that only yesterday it would have happily overthrown and represses its sectarian urges in order to become a part of it, another (the PCE) indulges its liberal urges in order to contest a transitional regime that it finds too timid and contaminated, embracing an

[323]

alliance of the Left that it still hopes to dominate. And where one party (the PCF) seeks power through a Left alliance but worries about Socialist allies that are too strong and likely to grow stronger the more the alliance succeeds, another (the PCI) disdains an alliance of only the Left and worries about succeeding without the support of its traditional bourgeois-democratic opponents.

Difficult as it may be, even quixotic, the Soviet Union does struggle to maintain coherence amidst this disorder. It struggles because it is the Soviet faith that there should be coherence, because the Soviet definition of success depends on it, because Soviet foreign policy benefits from it, and because this is the way things generally have been since 1920.

Locating the coherencs in West European communism is not, of course, precisely the same as imposing a common strategy on it, but, as the Soviets do things, one tends to shade into the other. Given their preferences, the Soviet leaders are inclined to cope with the diversity of West European communism by harking back to the "general laws" of socialism—insisting that these oblige the fraternal parties of Western Europe to keep in mind what they and their revolutions have in common with the rest of the movement and, in particular, with those more experienced in it. To the increasing degree that an increasing number of West European Communist parties resist the common approach and find the experience of the more experienced irrelevant or, worse, harmful, the diversity grows and, along with it, the challenge to Soviet policy.

"The Roads to Socialism" (or, the Intra-National Dimension)

This is where the essential interaction of East with West European communism begins: with their differing conceptions

[324]

of socialism and the path to it. At issue is the way different parties assess the "revolutionary situation," the strategy and tactics they adopt, both on the way to power and after, and their notion of what socialism should be or do. Because of the diversity within West European communism, the Soviet Union is almost everywhere at odds with every party. It would do violence to the facts and, as important, to the Soviet viewpoint, to think or, even more, to construe their differences over socialism and its pursuit as clearcut and comprehensive. Important differences exist, but where they are the most extreme, the party or parties at one end of the spectrum are often as far from the majority of West European Communist parties as this majority is from the Soviet Union. This tends to entangle the controversy and blunt its effect. For the future, of course, the dramatic question is whether this complexity is likely to be lost, whether the great variety of differences may not crystallize into a few essential ones with the bulk of West European Communist parties much further from the Soviet Union than from the extremists among them. For the moment, however, the gap is not so simple or complete.

Assessing Contemporary Capitalism

To a real extent, the Soviet Union and nearly all of the West European Communist parties begin their analysis in roughly the same way. They tend to share the same view of industrialized capitalist societies, the evolution of class structure, systemic weaknesses, and the prospects for radical (or socialist) change. They agree that capitalism is, to quote from their texts, in its "third deepening general crisis," meaning that the structural deficiencies of capitalism, its social antagonisms, cycle of economic recessions, corruption, militarization, and international contradictions are all mounting. The current

[325]

economic plight of the West, they are further agreed, constitutes an integral part of the "general deepening crisis of
capitalism," indeed, according to several of them, a "qualitative
new stage" in the general crisis. While, one or two parties,
notably the Italian, tend to stress additional, independent
factors—such as governmental inefficiency, widespread corruption, clientelism, and so forth—all of them portray the crisis
as political, cultural, and moral as well as economic. Soviet
analysts constantly repeat that it is the convergence of crises—
an energy crisis, an urban crisis, a monetary crisis, an eco-
nomic-policy crisis, an overproduction crisis—"a combination
of crisis processes unique in the history of postwar capitalism"
that make the present important, and no West European party
disagrees.[3]

But the Soviet leadership does not draw from this assessment impetuous or simple-minded revolutionary conclusions,
and neither do the West Europeans. Capitalism, Soviet writers
acknowledge, has not exhausted its "entire potential"; it has
not "reached an impasse and an absolutely hopeless situation." [4] That the crisis of state-monopoly capitalism should be
underscored does not mean, they caution, that one dare "underestimate capitalism's potential for further maneuvering and
further adaptation to the new conditions." [5] As a result there is
no tension between the Soviet leadership and West European
parties inclined to put the struggle for economic stability ahead
of the struggle for structural change or the struggle against
fascism ahead of the struggle for power. (This proposition has
several sides, however, and I shall come back to it later.)

The Communist Party of the Soviet Union (CPSU) is not
basically divided from the West European parties in appraising
capitalism's crisis and neither is it in analysing capitalism's class
structure, the way this structure is changing, or the potential
political alignments these changes imply. True, a party like the

PCI has a much more refined perception of social stratification than do Soviet analysts and as a result fancies a more loosely defined political base. But the differences are not fundamental even in this case, much less between the Soviet and the general West European view.

Like their West European counterparts, Soviet theorists see social structures in Western societies as increasingly complex and diverse. Indeed, to link this point with the last, they treat the "social diversity of the working class and the working masses" as one of the major factors "hampering the formation of objective and subjective sociopolitical preconditions for socialist revolution." [6] When they insist that the working class is steadily growing—not dissolving under the impact of the "scientific-technical revolution" as some "anti-Marxist" theorists propose—they have in mind a relatively subtle process: They are at one with the West Europeans in refocusing the definition of the laboring class on status rather than character— on people's "relations to the means of production and their role in the social organization of labor" (a simpler mind would say, on their common problems as hired labor) rather than on differences in the nature of the job or the person's training (the old difference between workers by hand and workers by mind).[7] This adjustment permits them to absorb into the working class not only the new tradesmen, particularly in the service sector, but government employees, even "medium supervisory personnel," and a large part of the "intellectual professions," lawyers, doctors, teachers, journalists.

Admittedly, Soviet theorists still set this amended working class sharply at odds with the "ruling class"—still insisting on society's polarization—but then so do the vast majority of West European Communist parties. The Italians are the exception in suggesting a "historic compromise" to draw the redeemable among the *patronat* into the process of reconstruct-

[327]

ing society and to attenuate sterile antagonisms among (the Soviets would say, between) social divisions. Yet, even between the Italians and the rest of European communism, East or West, the difference is more in tone than in substance. For, Soviet theorists have come around to an extremely expansive notion of whom the working class can turn to in waging the "general-democratic and anti-monopolistic" struggle. Not just the petty bourgeoisie and alienated intelligentsia, but virtually all of the "middle strata," "democratic movements" (anti-war and civil rights groups), and even "Christian-inspired popular forces," committed to social justice and the affirmation of higher moral values. By the time the Soviet list ends, it is nearly as extensive as the PCF's concept of the "Union of the French People" (anyone victimized by state-monopoly capitalism) and this, in turn, is no great distance from the notions of the PCI.

Strategy and Tactics

Here, however, important differences do arise, not in determining with whom to ally but, rather, under what conditions and with what limitations. And these, it turns out, are attached to the whole of strategy and tactics, even to the nature of the revolution itself. From this single aspect, the proletariat's collaboration with non-proletarian elements, the contrast in view inevitably extends to fundamental assumptions about revolutionary alliances, revolutionary principles, revolutionary stages, and revolutionary objectives: from a simple question of how to proceed to *the* question of the revolution's essence. (Again, diversity within West European communism makes the line dividing East from West sometimes obscure, but one exists nonetheless.)

[328]

Accomplishing the revolution within modern capitalist society, Soviet theorists know, is a complicated and indetermi-
nate business. Maybe even fanciful for now. Thus, Communist parties in the West have more immediate and
limited concerns: such as curbing rather than overthrowing
dominant interests, exploiting rather than destroying bourgeois political institutions, enlarging rather than transforming
the economic and social welfare benefits of the system, altering
rather than replacing policy priorities. This is what Soviet
writers mean by the "general-democratic and anti-monopolistic" phase of the revolution. And they make it the central
issue—more important than the question of power, for it both
precedes and survives the rise to power; more subtle than
traditional expectations, for it is both pre-revolutionary and a
part of the revolution, democratic rather than socialist, distinct
from the classical bourgeois-democratic and the proletarian
revolutions, superseding the first and clouding the second. It is
their concession to West European communism and, simultaneously, a formula keeping the progress of events within
their frame of reference.

The Soviet Union grants, perhaps even wants, this first
phase to be pursued on the broadest possible basis. Proletarians
and non-proletarians, feminists and small businessmen, Christians and Socialists—"large groups of people," one leading
Soviet theorist says, are involved in this "special, anti-monop-
oly phase of the revolution." [8] He grants that this "phase of the
revolution" and those that come after may well be peaceful;
but the more advanced the phase, the more special the meaning of "peaceful." [9] He grants that this first phase may be long
and involved, perhaps with several secondary stages, "such as
the formation of a popular government" (meaning a coalition
with bourgeois parties), a "democratic government" (meaning
a government of the Left), and "so on" (whose meaning is the

[329]

source of the problem).[10] And he grants, as Soviet theorists have for many years, that the most advanced element of the working class, the Communist party, should form a united front with others who claim to speak on behalf of the working class, provided they promise more than "right social reformism" and less than "Maoist rabble-rousing." It is an alliance to ensure that the general struggle for democracy can be *combined* with the historic struggle for socialism. And it is an alliance for tomorrow and today.

But it is a conditional alliance. Soviet theorists would let it live on, beyond the "general-democratic anti-monopolistic" phase, the ascent to power, and the first steps toward socialism, only if these allies, primarily the Socialists, mind their principles and join in the uncompromising reconstruction of society.[11] To guarantee their cooperation (and otherwise their defeat), these theorists stress, the Communist party must guard its dominant position, its "leading role," within the united front. It must guard its "leading role," as well, to guarantee beforehand that the general struggle for democracy will be *subordinated* to the historic struggle for socialism. For, the Soviet Union's ultimate reconciliation with the "general-democratic and anti-monopolistic" phase of the revolution is based on the expectation that it will be informed by the socialist phase.

From this concern for the party's "leading role" within the united Left, Soviet theory passes naturally to a concern over the united Left's willingness and ability to protect itself from those outside the working class who, too, aid in this first general phase of the revolution. Extending your hand to "non-proletarian" elements, in particular, the petty-bourgeoisie and others from the "middle strata" does not mean trusting them. No premise is more a part of Soviet theory than the permanent

[330]

unreliability of these elements during the struggle against monopoly capitalism and their certain betrayal at the first success against it. Counterrevolution is as central to the Soviet perception as revolution itself.

The Nature of the Revolution

Ultimately, however, these apprehensions and solutions—the "leading role" of the party, perforce a strong, disciplined party practicing a pure form of "democratic centralism," and the constant superiority of the revolutionary forces over the "middle strata"—are simply a function of the Soviet conception of revolution. Their whole experience has persuaded the Soviet political elite that revolution is a matter of conquest. It is a matter of properly calculating the balance of forces, seizing the moment, imposing change, and fortifying for the counterattack. Hence the emphasis on what they call the "subjective factor": leadership, in a sense, but, more than that, organization and will as much as ever a Soviet theme and as often as not in analyses of Western Europe's current revolutionary prospects. As Alexander Sobolev, the ideologue quoted earlier, wrote recently, whatever the critical importance of objective revolutionary circumstances,

> its victorious implementation depends above all on the subjective factor, on the level of activity, organization and political orientation of the masses and their readiness to make any self-sacrifices for the sake of victory, on the correctness of the policy of the communist parties who stand at the head of the masses, the flexibility of their tactics, their ability to employ all forms of struggle.[12]

[331]

Between this and the PCI's long-preferred policy of "presence in society," of penetrating rather than conquering society, there is a vast difference.[13] For the Italians, the challenge has always been to sink the party's roots into society, to give it a working role, to prove the party, to earn its legitimacy by contributing. To the subjective, the Italians juxtapose the organic.

When Sobolev's superior, V.V. Zagladin, contemplates the current "struggle for democratic demands" in a country like Italy or France and then the problem of getting from it to the socialist revolution, his natural inclination is to tidy up one's tactics, to manipulate the environment, to assert the party. "The crux of the solution," he tells us, is to "present certain slogans of a democratic nature which [will] be comprehensible and accessible to the masses (including that section of them which still fears socialism . . .)"[14] The point to democratic reform—"worker control at factories and banks," "universal labor conscription," for he is citing Lenin between the February and October revolutions—is to give life to the slogans in order that they will have that much more force. To Italian Communists preoccupied with the emergence of socialism from within, democratic reform for its own sake, and representation rather than manipulation of the masses, Zagladin's are alien predilections.

Both parties defend the peaceful path to European revolution, but here is the root of their difference. To the Italians, the peaceful path means the evolution toward socialism through existing institutions, growing into socialism gradually, eroding rather than crushing opposition. To the Soviets, however, the peaceful path means only the avoidance of civil war, not the forswearing of violence or of imposed change. "Peaceful," as the Italians understand the term, means to the Soviets "parliamentary"; and that they are prepared to sanction only as a tactical choice, one deserving loyalty until the revolution comes under attack, and then no longer. Perhaps for countries like Italy and France, the peaceful path *in its parliamentary form* will make the forcible "seizure of power" unnecessary, but never its forcible defense. There is, as contemporary Soviet theorists regularly remind us, nothing incompatible between the peaceful path and Lenin's original stricture: "If we do not control all means of struggle, we may suffer an enormous—perhaps even decisive—defeat."

The issue is not mere theology. On the contrary, it explains the fundamental contrast in the way the CPSU and the PCI reacted to events in Chile in 1973 and in Portugal in 1975. Both experiences had the identical effect of reinforcing opposite conceptions of the revolution. In the case of Chile, as many have noted, the disaster proved to the Italians the dangers of the parliamentary path when inadequately pursued. To the Soviets it proved the inadequacies of the parliamentary path when pursued too long. Chile reinforced the Italian conception of the organic revolution, the need to convert society to socialism on the way to power, the perils of a narrow (a 51 percent) mandate, and the importance of the "historic compromise." Among Soviet observers, it confirmed the wisdom of Bolshevism, the party ascendant over events. Time and again Soviet authors have drawn its lessons: (1) The first mistake of Chile's revolutionaries was not to demolish the state apparatus as swiftly as possible. Instead, the "popular unity leaders" foolishly counted on all classes and all elements of the state to observe the constitutional norms; they should have destroyed existing institutions rather than be destroyed by their loyalty to them. (2) Their second mistake was to rely on "bourgeois constitutional guarantees" rather than on the mobilized masses. (3) Their third mistake was to invent the delusion that critical elements like the armed forces were neutral and nonpolitical, "above-class" and committed to the constitution however intense the social contradictions might grow. (4) But most of all they blundered in neglecting to establish the Communist party's leading role. As a result, no force existed to overcome disagreements among the six parties of the united front, to develop a consistent political line, and none to see to the execution of political tasks: The revolution lacked "authoritative united leadership" and this contributed much to its defeat. Chile drove home for the Soviets the need always, Western Europe included, to master all forms of struggle; for the Italians, it drove home the legitimacy of only one form of struggle.

So there is Bolshevism to *defend* the revolution. In Portugal, it was to *make* the revolution—and the PCI dissented no less. Portugal, of course, is economically less developed than other West European countries and presumably an illustration of the second of Lenin's and the Comintern's three traditional classifications: the countries of developed capitalism, those of medium capitalist development, and the colonial, semi-colonial, and dependent societies. Like Russia in 1917, Portugal was a country "where the objective conditions for socialism had still not fully matured." Zagladin, who uses these categories, goes on to argue—with November 1917 as his proof—that "under certain specific historical conditions it is possible and necessary first to take power and then, backed by the energy of the revolutionary people, to create the material preconditions for future socialism." [15]

When Zagladin wrote this in early November 1975, however, the issue in Portugal had been largely decided and a revolution on the Soviet model was not to be. Still, this was somewhat apart from Soviet preferences, which, when the way seemed open to the "seizure of power" in August, had seemingly yielded to the temptation. Konstantin Zarodov may have been an extreme spokesman, but his August 1975 appeal for "permanent revolution" did not radically misrepresent the general Soviet estimation or hope.[16] Granted, the Soviet Union had not instigated the Cunhal-Gonçalves strategy, nor had it anything to do with the emergence of a revolutionary opportunity—indeed, until summer 1975 the Soviet leaders seemed skeptical about Portugal's immediate revolutionary prospects—but, when the chance came, Zarodov was given his tribune. The use he made of it, to urge the telescoping of the democratic and socialist stages of revolution, to praise "direct revolutionary actions," to dismiss the significance of "arithmetical" electoral majorities and substitute the concept of a "revolutionary majority," clashed directly with the ideas of the PCI and several other West European Communist parties. But, then, Zarodov made it plain that he did not think terribly much of their approach either, of their "fashionable opportunist conceptions that make out the possession of the levers of power to be merely a final act for the proletariat and its party— the result of some kind of nationwide referendum which is allegedly the only thing that can express the will of the majority." [17]

The Italians drew a different lesson from Chile and advanced a different one for Portugal. Like Italy, neither country, they were convinced, was a candidate for Bolshevism: not to save a revolution, not to make one. Revolution had to come from, not to, the society; it had to lead, not drive, a people into socialism; and it had to be won in the political arena, not on the ramparts or at the wall.

Viewed this way, pluralism, competing parties, democratic freedoms, and an open political system become a defensible— even natural as the Italians maintain—side of the advance to socialism. To live with and perfect democratic institutions, they say, is not a tactical recourse but a recognition of the "specific objective and historical conditions" of their country. Revolution conceived as the Italians do leads to a policy of "presence" and the "historic compromise." Or perhaps it is the other way around, but either way the relationship is integral. These policies (or strategies) in turn presuppose a pluralistic and open political system—to which, moreover, a Communist party must sacrifice a certain part of its discipline and authoritarianism.

"General Law-Governed Patterns"

The Soviet Union's instincts run in basically the opposite direction. Because the revolution has been and remains for them something engineered in struggle, an act of will, they worry about a party that has lost its discipline. For, a party that has lost its discipline is likely to compromise the integrity of its principles, chasing after allies and votes; and a party that compromises its principles is sure to undermine the "leading role" of the revolution's vanguard; and a revolution without leadership will either lose its way or fall to the blows of counterrevolution. The critical point is that control conceded in the early moments of the struggle cannot easily be regained later.

Of course, the deterioration does not have to begin with the loss of party discipline. Maybe a party starts with adjustments in its revolutionary strategy, say, by committing itself to the broadest possible political alliances and, in order to do so, sheds notions like the "leading role" of the party or suppresses references to the "dictatorship of the proletariat." [18] From here the rot will spread in both directions: back, to infect the party with notions of internal liberation and organizational laxness; forward, to erode socialist objectives in the quest for power. "Opportunism," the Soviet leaders call concessions to short-run political success and they warn of its heavy price. Opportunism, Brezhnev said at the 25th Party Congress, "may sometimes yield some temporary advantage, but will ultimately be damaging to the party."

But "opportunism," to the Soviet Union's growing dismay, is already the penchant of too many West European Communist parties. Few of them may have gone as far as the PCI, but that begs the issue: There is a logical internal consistency in the waywardness of the Italian party. Even the most modest revisions in doctrine have as their logical climax far-reaching adjustments in a party's organization, strategy and tactics, and socialist conception. Revisionism, Soviet theorists know, is of a piece. In this sense, the totality of the Italian deviation has a natural integrity: That is, the Italians have completed the circle, from the policy of "presence," with the celebration of bourgeois democratic freedoms, to the "historic compromise" predicated on the pluralism of the present and promising as much under socialism. There is something more unnatural and fragile about timid or half-hearted revisionism, and this is precisely the Soviet apprehension. To a Soviet—and the outsider well might agree—fussing with this or that aspect of the ideology is a risky business. One thing leads to another. Repudiate the phrase the "dictatorship of the proletariat" and the concept itself is threatened; go the next step, repress the concept and the revolution is called into question. What is left for the party other than to subordinate itself to the rules and institutions established of, by, and for the bourgeoisie? You begin with an attractive notion like the *Union de peuple français,* a sensible tactical measure to outflank your Socialist allies, and soon you have turned it into the *compromesso storico.*

Pierre Hassner has said of the French Communist party's dilemma, one cannot pursue meaningful "revolutionary actions" and simultaneously insist on the peaceful path, all the more when there is a "tension between the strategy of alliances or unity of action and the affirmation of the Party's primacy and vanguard role . . ., a tension that leads to another between the primacy of the parliamentary path and that of mass action." [19] Soviet theorists agree completely. But Hassner worries about the implications of these contradictions in one way; Soviet theorists worry about them in another. Both understand the instability of the ground between orthodoxy and "reformism": only, the first senses that it may not be great enough (that the party will preserve its ambivalence even after it comes to power) or that the instability will give way to retreat; and the second senses that it will more likely lead to further concessions.

None of this ignores the often-stated Soviet sensitivity to "national peculiarities" and the need to adapt the revolutionary struggle to "specific-historical conditions": to differences in a nation's level of socio-economic development, to different historical traditions, to distinctive "national features," and to "nonidentical degrees of maturity of the objective and subjective preconditions for the transition to socialism." Each national party, accordingly, must perfect its own methods and approach to revolution. As the Soviets say, "the general law-governed patterns of the world revolutionary process are manifested in the most varied forms."

But the point is that, for the leaders to the CPSU, there are "general law-governed patterns," patterns that they have discovered or, more accurately, validated; and these impose common assumptions on the entire Communist movement. Their essence is modified Bolshevism: the "dictatorship of the proletariat," realized by means of the party's "leading role," a party that is more or less the party of Lenin's *What Is To Be Done?*, a party that has mastered all forms of struggle. But what then is "modified" about this Bolshevism? Well, the formula still leaves room for the peaceful path to socialism (that is, for avoiding the armed seizure of power and the revolutionary civil war); it still leaves room for the broadest possible alliances, especially with "other detachments of the working class," provided the party preserves its autonomy and the purity of its principles; and it still leaves room for tactical flexibility, gradualism, and concessions to the habits and institutions of West European societies, provided these are, indeed, tactical (the Soviet version of the Arpège perfume commercial). In short: "Be like us, follow our lead, any way you want."

There is a slightly different way to put the point, one that goes more directly to the heart of the controversy between the Soviet Union and the West European Communist parties: The Soviet Union grants that the revolution in Western Europe must be different from its own—in the same way that the East European revolutionary experience has been different from the Russian. That is, when Soviet theorists envision a model for Western Europe, it is essentially "People's Democracy," without the Red Army as *deus ex machina*. Many of the West Europeans, however—foremost, the PCI, PCE, and Swedish Communist party—reject People's Democracy as in any way appropriate to their countries. And this is what gives force to their rejection of the "general laws." Those who "hold that there are general laws," Luciano Gruppi has said, produce "a divergence of a profound and ideological and cultural character, because the PCI is against the thesis of laws valid for all." [20]

Farther down the road, a more profound, though ambiguous, version of the problem of general laws arises. It concerns the nature of socialism itself and, in this sense, is a post-revolutionary challenge. Ordinarily, of course, revolution is a political act, the transfer of power to those who will carry society to socialism. But, since in Western Europe the revolutionaries may come to power without the political act, yet also without a free enough hand to begin the conversion to socialism, the expression "post-revolutionary" refers to that later point when those in power can finally launch the transformation. In part, because of the lag, Soviet theorists have begun to distinguish among three periods of "socialist construction": a period of transition, which is pre-socialist, during which the "groundwork for the new system is laid"; the period of building a "developed socialist society"; and a period of developed socialist society.[21]

To the extent that the Soviet Union claims to be the only society ever to have reached the third of these stages, the issue is prejudged. Developed socialism, like all else beforehand, will find its essential expression in the Soviet experience. How that is to be formulated remains, for the moment, somewhat vague.[22] What the essence of developed socialism will *not* be, however, is clear enough. One Soviet author says that "pluralistic socialism" in quotation marks, with its "mechanical blend of private and collective modes of production," will "never assure the spread and victory of socialist principles." [23] Another disparages advocates of "democratizing" socialism (again the quotation marks) who in their day "would like the Party's range of activity and influence to be restricted under the pretext of 'separating the Party from power' or of 'political pluralism' in the name of allegedly extra-class democracy." [24] The more Soviet theorists perfect a "scientific definition" of developed socialism, the more they are bound to fuel their differences with the boldest of the reformist parties in Western Europe.

[340]

"Proletarian Internationalism" (or the Inter-Party Dimension)

Because the Soviet leaders believe in "general law-governed patterns," they are inclined to assign their own experience transcending importance; and because they believe so much in their own experience, they are inclined to insist on "general law-governed patterns" In the developing controversy between the two basic (among many) European communisms, the most salient feature is Soviet egoism—not the vacuous, self-indulgent kind, but the egoism of self-assurance and pride. We, they say in a hundred different ways, have been the first to make the revolution, the first to face the problem of building socialism, the first to complete it, and we have "traveled a longer distance on the road to communism than any other country." Not only have we—and those who follow our example—done this, but only we have done it. Hence, they draw lessons: "History has not recorded a single instance of socialism being built and its victory ensured without the revolutionary party of the working class playing the leading role." [25] And, when they stress the importance of "historical experience" to "revolutionary creativity," it is to recommend their own experience.

Not suprisingly, therefore, Soviet speakers tend to make respect for, even fealty to, the Soviet model a central element of proletarian internationalism. Learning from, defending, nay, celebrating this example is for them a way to bind Communist parties together, a way to give coherence and unity to the international movement. Without this reference point, the Soviet leaders have convinced themselves over the

[341]

years, the world revolutionary process will be diminished and, with it, every national revolution. So, of course, will their own.

This, however, is exactly the element of proletarian internationalism least acceptable to the majority of West European Communist parties. They are done treating the Soviet model as a model for anyone other than the Soviet Union. Revering it is a form of unity they no longer want.

The trouble is, however, that this form of unity cannot be abandoned without detracting from the model itself. The Soviets will have it no other way. The more they insist on making their virtues a premise of proletarian internationalism—and condemn those who, to borrow one of their uglier phrases, "absolutize" distinctive national features—the more these others feel compelled to defend their distinctive national features and reject important aspects of the Soviet model. As a result, increasingly the intra-national dimension of East-West Communist relations intersects the inter-party dimension where the Soviet example is disparaged. Increasingly, the West European Communist parties define themselves by repudiating Soviet communism. And they do it in collaboration, evidently, assuming that the repudiation will have more force at home if it has support elsewhere.

For example, in their November 1975 joint statement, the PCI and PCF did not content themselves with praising the idea of democracy—which would have served to distinguish them from the CPSU—they went on to spell out what they mean by democracy. Their definition incorporated a great deal that the Soviet Union is not, and conversely promised not to be much that it is. Thus, they declared their allegiance not only to "all the freedoms" of the "great bourgeois democratic revolutions"—including the freedom of thought and expression, the press, assembly, and association, the freedom to demonstrate, the free movement of people at home and abroad, religious freedoms, cultural and artistic freedom, and more—but to "the plurality of political parties," the right of opposition parties to exist and compete, and the principle that if voted from office they will leave.[26] They pledged themselves to maintain the "secularity and democratic functioning of the state." To respect the "independence of justice." To guard the "free activity and autonomy of the trade unions." And to extend the "democratic decentralization" of society, giving an "increasingly important role to the regions and local authorities."

This, however, is only half the story. No doubt the Soviet leaders find disturbing the tendency of West European Communist parties to create a part of their identity by denying the Soviet model. From their perspective, the French, the Italians—and they represent only the most notable cases—are not merely violating the spirit of proletarian internationalism; they are jeopardizing its essence. Were this but the extent of their sins.

The West European Communists, however, do not stop at renouncing the Soviet model as one for French or Italian society. They go on to censure the Soviet leaders for what they do within their own, for committing political dissidents like Leonid Plyushch to mental asylums, for harrassing would-be emigrants, for repressing nonconformist artists. Their criticism amounts to an incipient challenge to Soviet communism as such, not merely for other societies but for the Soviet Union itself. Thus, the intersection of the intra-national with the inter-party dimension turns out to be still more fateful. In their struggle to increase their own legitimacy—to prove their independence not only from Soviet directives but from Soviet values—the West European Communist parties are beginning to probe, even threaten, the Soviet Union's legitimacy.

In one sense, of course, this is a grossly over-dramatized

[343]

way to make a point. No West European Communist party openly questions the right of the CPSU to rule as it does; their criticisms are of the excesses of the system, not its existence. But in another sense the issue is this grave: When the Soviet Union and its allies moved their armies into Czechoslovakia in 1968, the majority of West European Communist parties condemned the act. Most were condemning a method, condemning the way the Soviet Union dealt with the problem. The Italians, however, condemned the act because they believed in the legitimacy of the Czechoslovak experiment. They believed, as Luigi Longo told *L'Astrolabio* a few weeks after the occupation, that the Czechoslovaks had the situation under control; more than that, that theirs was a program of genuine "democratic renovation," that they were "returning to socialism all its social, humane, and democratic concomitants." [27] In short, their notions of what constituted legitimate changes in *Eastern Europe* were the direct opposite of those held by the Soviets. Were another "Czechoslovakia" to arise today, there can be scarcely any doubt that the Portuguese, not the Italians, would be the minority. To this extent the legitimacy of the Soviet system is at stake.

But does it matter what West European Communist parties say or think about the nature of things in Eastern Europe? Does the Soviet Union have any particular reason to resent or fear the influence of West European "reformism"? Does it have more reason if any of these parties come to power? The answers to these questions are not necessarily so simple or obvious as they might seem and I shall save their more elaborate side for the discussion of Eurocommunism. One comment, however, is worth making in this context: The reference in a preceding section of this chapter to the criticism leveled by a Soviet commentator against "democratized" socialism viewed his remark as an attack on the revisionism of

West European Communist parties. But, significantly, considering the date (1971), Czechoslovakia and the idea of "socialism with a human face" may have been more on his mind. The telling fact is that in Soviet analyses there is no distinguishing the program of the Italians from the ascribed treason of the Czechoslovaks.[28] Whatever the connection between the two, the mere suspicion that one exists reverses the basic relationship between "proletarian internationalism" and orthodoxy: Where orthodoxy once was both the staff and substance of proletarian internationalism, proletarian internationalism is now increasingly burdened with sustaining orthodoxy. And, to complete the circle, the more it is, the weaker each becomes.

The Sources of Unity

Proletarian internationalism, however, has many sides. To stop with its tribulations would account for but a fragment of its complex effect. Thus, real as the discord is over the content of proletarian internationalism, so is the power of the idea. Between the Soviet Union and even the most free-thinking West European Communist party, a fundamental bond survives. It may be more frail than it once was and more frail than the Soviet Union would like, but it is genuine and basic nonetheless.

Because the self-assertion of West European Communist parties catches our eye more nowadays, we tend to slight the considerations that still draw East and West European communism together—easing rather than complicating the interparty dimension. But these remain significant and, for the Soviet Union, an equally important part of the picture.

The attachment that Western Europe's Communist parties feel to their more conservative Eastern counterparts and to some shared purposes or identity, it seems to me, derives from three sources. For one, there is the force of the past. Not only have all these parties, without exception, lived most of a lifetime subordinated to the discipline of the international Communist movement—a movement whose orientation has been heavily and at times totally determined by the Soviet Union—but the great majority of them were once and for long the most orthodox and sectarian of organizations. No party, even the most transformed, can completely escape its own history. At one level, there is the practical reality of old party militants who believe in the past and resent every retreat from unity with the Soviet Union, and no party, not even historically less sectarian ones like the PCI and PCE, is without them. At another level, there are the normal ambiguities in the evolution away from old habits and patterns of thought. And, at a third level, there is a formidable psychological reluctance to break totally with what one has been or to cast doubt on one's origins.

Second, and more important, the Soviet experience contributes critically to each West European Communist party's sense of identity. Even when they dissent from the character of this experience, the leaders of a party like the PCI depend on the fact of its occurrence to establish their party's uniqueness, to distinguish themselves from social democracy, to prove to themselves and others that there is something to the revolution they promise. In many important respects, their aspirations and those of the Soviet leaders have the same heritage and, while they may criticize the manner in which these aspirations are pursued, feel themselves greater because they have been pursued. Thus, a residual loyalty to the Soviet Union constitutes, at its root, an essential means of preserving their own integrity.[29] Hence the crucial paradox of proletarian internationalism: Where, on the one hand, West European

Communist parties are increasingly compelled to judge the Soviet Union critically in order to enhance their *legitimacy,* they, on the other hand, are equally compelled to guard a basic loyalty to it in order to maintain their *integrity.* In one breath, Luigi Longo condemns the Soviet Union for crushing a better kind of socialism in Czechoslovakia; in the next, he pledges his party to "consolidate and extend the prestige and influence of the Soviet Union." [30] It is up to us to understand that he means both.

Third, the solidarity among Europe's Communist parties reflects a simple but essential consensus on the nature of international politics, imperialism, and the "world revolutionary process." This is not to imply that on all foreign policy issues these parties see eye to eye. (Where they do and do not is a subject for the next section.) Still, they share basic assumptions about the "global contest" and its contestants, about the character of Western foreign policies, and about the momentum of events. And in most parts of the world, on most of the world's problems, they prefer roughly similar outcomes. In short, revolution in the abstract—that is, what is left of the original vision of the international revolution or, more conventionally, conceptions of change in the international order—tends to unify East and West European Communist parties (whereas revolution in the particular—what socialism should be in any given case and the road to it—tends to divide them).

The Soviet Union, however, tries to capitalize on these last two sources of unity to contain the erosion of unity and to rally the West European Communist parties to a tighter unity. In the process, it reinforces the link between the intra-national and inter-party dimensions, again, at the expense of proletarian internationalism.

Thus, in the last case, the Soviet leaders know that the West European Communists, despite notable differences, look

[347]

upon the "world revolutionary process" in basically the same way as they do; that, in addition, the West Europeans value the cohesion of "revolutionary forces" in advancing this process. Seizing on their basic sympathy, the Soviet leadership comes to these parties with two basic propositions: First, that the "world revolutionary process has assumed an indivisible nature," meaning that every individual struggle for socialism forms a part of the larger struggle against "world capitalism." One reinforces the other, Sobolev writes, and, by the same token, any divorce between them weakens both.

> A revolution or class struggle in any coutnry cannot be regarded as an isolated phenomenon. Any attempt at economic or political autarky, and at national self-restriction of any link in the international workers movement, not only weakens the potential of that link but also adversely affects the international democratic forces as a whole.[31]

If this sounds like something also addressed to the Romanians, it only demonstrates, as the blur between attacks on Czechoslovak and Italian revisionism did before, how indistinguishable heresies are for the Soviet Union.

The second proposition is closely related. There are, according to Soviet accounts, three factors essential for the peaceful transition to socialism. The first two are internal: (1) the party's domination over the revolutionary alliance of workers, peasants, intellectuals, and petty bourgeoisie and (2) the ability to "contain and isolate" those "opportunist groups" reluctant to break with the exploiting classes. The third, however, is external: If the revolution is to succeed in places like Italy or Spain, they remind their friends in the PCI and PCE, then the international balance of power must ensure that "the country's bourgeoisie cannot have recourse to international imperialism for help." [32] In other words, what happens in Italy or Spain still depends to an extent on the Soviet ability (and readiness?) to deter the imperialists from exporting counterrevolution.

Neither of the propositions on the "world revolutionary process" is particularly subtle, and neither is likely to convince fully many of the West European leaders. They are with their Soviet counterparts as long as the argument focuses on the evils and dangers of imperialism. They are doubtless convinced along with Soviet analysts that capitalism is "an international phenomenon" and requires the strongest possible coordination among "progressive" forces. [33] They may even go along with the notion that the challenge facing them is now larger because the major capitalist nations now work harder at coordinating their anti-Communist efforts. But they part company the moment the argument shifts to suggest that their revolutions are directly dependent on the "world revolutionary process," or to imply that the process is directly dependent on their political orthodoxy, or to insinuate that their lack of political orthodoxy gives imperialism a propaganda tool for damaging the world revolutionary process.

The Soviet Union also tried to capitalize on the second source of unity—the residual loyalty of West European Communists to the Soviet revolution—to service its conception of proletarian internationalism. For years, of course, no obligation stood higher than the duty of "defending" the Soviet Union. The Comintern was founded on the idea, the famous 6th Congress in 1928 made it a formal principle, and parties lived by it well into the 1960s. Even now no European Communist party cares to take part in efforts to denigrate the Soviet Union or to have its criticism of that country used by "anti-Soviet" forces. But the Soviets, as might be expected, insist on more.

Anti-Sovietism, they preach, is anti-communism and the West European Communist parties are expected to see and deplore it as such.

But the West European parties have refused to identify the two. They will defend the Soviet Union against the ill-willed attacks of its detractors, and they will fight anti-communism within their own society. But they will not accept the notion that to criticize the Soviet Union is to be anti-Communist. Their reasons are obvious: Neither do they want to be forced to assail bourgeois critics for criticism with which they basically agree, nor do they want their criticism to be discredited by ranking it with simple anti-communism. Over this issue, they fought long and hard in the preparatory stages of the 1976 East Berlin Conference of European Communist Parties—and with ultimate success, for the Soviet Union did not get its way. Ultimately the reference to these two things as one was removed from the Conference declaration.[34] In its place, a long paragraph was inserted not only avoiding any simple association of anti-Sovietism with anti-communism but even conceding that not all criticism from non-Communists is anti-Communist.

For years the PCI has proclaimed its solidarity with the Soviet Union—but a "critical solidarity." That is, the Italians declare their allegiance to the ideals and accomplishments of the Soviet Union but not unconditionally, not without reserving the right to criticize Soviet excesses or failings. In a sense, at the Berlin conference, the majority of West European Communist parties established the same "critical solidarity" as the general premise of their relations with the Soviet Union.

[350]

SOVIET POLICY TOWARD WESTERN EUROPE (OR THE INTERNATIONAL DIMENSION)

This is the hardest of the three dimensions to assess, partly because the interaction is more subtle between Europe's international relations and socialism's inter-party relations. It is difficult, furthermore, because the foreign policy implications of West European communism are bound up with the question of governing, and Soviet spokesmen conceal their feeling about the prospect of seeing these parties share power. So there is first the problem of relating developments within East and West European communism to the practical concerns of Soviet foreign policy in Western Europe. Second, there is the chore of dealing with the obscurity of Soviet preferences.

Too often we have oversimplified this international dimension by subsuming it under the other two. That is, we have tended to think about the foreign policy positions of West European Communist parties in terms of inter-party rather than international relations, focusing on those relatively rare instances where a party deviates from an established Soviet position. The PCI's early willingness to accept the Common Market, at a time when the Soviet Union remained thoroughly hostile, has always interested us more than the overall pattern of East and West European Communist foreign policy. Since the PCI was in no position to influence Italian foreign policy on this issue and since, in most other instances, it followed the Soviet lead in foreign policy, these moments of independence were treated as an echo of its revisionism, not as a factor of any intrinsic importance to Europe's international relations. The subordination continues. Thus, at the moment, most analysts

[351]

are more fascinated by the ideological restlessness of the West European Communist parties than by their foreign policy constancy. Our attention is fastened on the challenges to "proletarian internationalism" and orthodox Marxism-Leninism and not on the essential similarity in the way most Communist parties—East or West—approach international affairs.

This, it seems to me, is a serious error in emphasis, not because the ideological differences are unimportant, but because the subordination of the foreign policy dimension distorts the complex significance that West European communism has for the Soviet Union. The implications of trends within each of our three dimensions are not necessarily mutually reinforcing but, in important respects, competing. That is, the disadvantages and frustrations of Soviet relations with West European Communist parties in one dimension may be counterbalanced by the welcome aspects of another. Thus, rather than posing a simple dilemma for the Soviet Union the changing complexion of West European communism represents a mixed challenge.

For example, foreign policy, an area where on most issues the Soviet Union and West European Communist parties share similar views, may confuse the effect of other areas more in dispute. Knowing that the Italian Communist party or the French party agrees with them on Angola or sympathizes with their approach to arms control, the Soviet leaders must approach the duels they now fight over the merits of the "dictatorship of the proletariat" and the meaning of socialist freedoms with complicated emotions. In a sense, they (like the Western analysts trying to understand them) must weigh those aspects of imperialism and the outside world unifying Communists against those of socialism and the world inside dividing them. Or, to borrow a slightly different insight from

[352]

Pierre Hassner: The notion of "international solidarity"—the label for the harmony of foreign policy views featured in the documents of the 1976 Berlin conference—must now substitute for "proletarian internationalism," the traditional formula for coordinating theory and practice. Foreign policy has become the lowest common denominator in lieu of a common ideological perspective. But, then, imperfect though it is, a substitute exists; a common denominator remains.

The outsider struggling to disentangle the effect of one dimension on another must also face puzzlement *within* the third dimension, where problems of timeframe and external costs intrude. Thus, for the moment, most of the evidence suggests that the Soviet leaders are not keen on having the Italians or French—to take the two most likely cases—enter government. Seemingly, they did not wish to see François Mitterrand elected President in May 1974, and they have appeared distinctly unenthusiastic about an early "historic compromise" in Italy. In the French case, Soviet observers evidently considered the moment inopportune. Though the direct evidence is slim, their hesitation apparently arose out of a whole series of considerations: (1) For example, so soon after the Guillaume affair (the exposure of an East German spy in Brandt's entourage), they wanted nothing that risked pushing German politics to the right, Germany occupying the center of their attention. (2) Given France's current economic plight, they sensed that a coalition of the Left would soon collapse or, at a minimum, its policies would be plagued by difficulty and failure. In either case, the way would be reopened for the Right, and France's left option would be foreclosed for the foreseeable future. And (3) they feared the general disruptive effect on East-West relations of such far-reaching change in a country of France's importance.[35] In Italy, too, the intimidating condition of the economy, the apparent anxiety of NATO

[353]

allies, and perhaps the risk of an impetuous American response combined to repress Soviet enthusiasm for a government with major direct Communist participation.

Three points are worth making about Soviet reserve. First, a distinction needs to be drawn between the Soviet attitude toward the Left's considerable electoral success and its complete success. The difference is between these parties in power and these parties as a flourishing opposition imposing constraints on others in power. Thus, while the Soviet leaders may not be particularly eager to see them and their allies form governments—not for the moment at least—they almost certainly are pleased to see them gathering strength. For, a strong Left, properly influenced by the Communist party, limits a government's freedom of maneuver in what, from the Soviet perspective, is a most healthy way. Soviet commentators say so openly: "Wherever the communists and their allies win a large size of the vote in elections, sometimes as much as one-half, the ruling circles of the bourgeoisie have to pursue a foreign policy meeting the demands of the democratic opposition in order to stay in power." [36] Or, in the words of Boris Ponomarev, Communist success in these countries now exerts a "pressure on the bourgeoisie that the ruling circles . . . no longer can ignore in the elaboration and conduct not only of internal but also international politics." [37]

Second, their reluctance to have the PCF or the PCI in power does not seem to have antagonized the West European Communist parties—save for one. The French, from all indications, have been angered by Soviet restraint, which, in their view, conceals a basic commitment to Giscard's government; and from time to time they have publicly rebuked those who put peaceful coexistence above social and political change.[38] On this score, however, the PCF has been equally critical of the Spanish and Italians for treading lightly where "imperialism" is concerned in the interest of "domestic opportunities." [39] Thus, the French have been odd-man out, not the Soviets. In fact, because the PCI leadership has itself hesitated to press for power in the present circumstances, the Soviet Union can portray itself as responsive to the assessments of the PCI—as, indeed, it well may be. And virtually all of Western Europe's other Communist parties, including a chastened Portuguese Communist party, share the PCI's current disinclination to go too far too fast.

Third, and much the more important point, the Soviet Union's momentary hesitations scarcely mean that its leaders are *fundamentally* opposed to Communist-dominated or influenced governments in France, Italy, Spain, or Finland. For the time being they may have reasons not to want the triumph of either the "historic compromise" or the *Union de la gauche.* But these are the product of particular circumstances, like economic recessions, the way the political winds are blowing in West Germany, the prevailing configuration of Western insecurities, and the frame of mind of American secretaries of state. They are largely extrinsic to Soviet judgments about West European Communist parties and their foreign policies. And they do not constitute reasons for opposing in principle the rise to power of the PCI, PCF, or PCE.

Were circumstances to change, were the current hazards of sharing power to diminish, were there a chance that the Western powers would react with equanimity to the entry of Communists into the French, Italian, or Spanish government or be unable to react in any significant fashion, then a whole different perspective would unfold. Then the Soviet leaders would be freer to allow themselves to be influenced by the advantages of the European Left's foreign policy. Since some

[355]

or all of these circumstances are likely to change, we need to make more of an effort to come to terms with this other perspective.

There are two ways to evaluate the foreign policy of West European Communist parties: one according to its substance; the other according to its likely effect. The second implies that a party has some actual share of power (the first does not necessarily). By whichever standard one operates, however, the Soviet leadership has a right to be interested.

Weighing the Substance of Policy

Because our attention is captured by the dissension between East and West European communism—over the strategy and tactics of revolution, over the nature of socialism, and over the premises of "proletarian internationalism"—the tendency is to concentrate on the traces of dissension at the level of foreign policy as well. The French, in scarcely veiled terms, appear to be attacking Soviet priorities in pursuit of détente. The Spanish have been urging Spain's entry into the Common Market even though Soviet opposition is clear. The Italians continue to pledge themselves to fulfill Italy's NATO obligations, implying that the stability of Europe will otherwise be endangered. And the British and Swedish parties criticize the Soviet Union for understating the importance of the CSCE's Basket III and for overstating the agreement among Communists at the Berlin conference.

Dissent like this is interesting and noteworthy, and to the extent that the Soviet leaders judge the utility of the foreign policies of West European Communist parties in terms of their perfect orthodoxy, they are doubtless discontented. But, in the area of foreign policy, orthodoxy probably does not serve as the only or even as the primary basis for judgement. More important is the way the foreign policy of these parties appears when compared with the status quo. Viewed in this light, the foreign policy attitudes of these parties come across far more favorably.

For so long we were accustomed to an absolute subordination of West European Communist foreign policies—indeed, to policies quite literally dictated from Moscow—that we have been understandably fascinated more by the passing of an age than by the implications of what remains in its place. It is a newer and more curious development than the challenge to ideological orthodoxy, which, after all, on a limited scale goes back to the mid-1950s. As a result, however, we are not sensitive enough to the advantages that the Soviet Union sees in the foreign policies of these parties. True, these are the advantages of parallel rather than controlled foreign policies, but this hardly eliminates their appeal.

The fact is that on virtually every issue of concern to the Soviet Union in its policy toward Western Europe, the Communist parties have adopted stances that are likely to be more satisfying to the Soviet leaders than are those of the existing governments. From the question of the future development of the Common Market to the question of arms control, from that of NATO's evolution to that of East-West economic cooperation, issue by issue, policy for policy, the Communist parties and their increasingly nationalistic allies offer more.

It is not just that most of these parties, including the PCI, endorse the Soviet policy of détente, echoing the Soviet Union's constant self-praise, agreeing with the claims made by the Soviet leadership on behalf of détente, and giving legitimacy to the Soviet Union's basic foreign policy course. Nor is it only that the rhetoric is comfortably familiar. Or that on a predictable range of issues, such as expanded trade with the

[357]

socialist countries or the importance of arms control, their enthusiasm is roughly similar to that of the Soviet Union. Or, for that matter, that the specific policies they are likely to urge in order to promote trade or to advance arms control are likely to be more congenial to the Soviet leaders.

It is that their basic approach to Atlantic relations, NATO, and the Common Market pleases the Soviet Union more than the approach of present governments in Rome, Paris, and Madrid. This is true even when the vacillations of the PCF's Socialist allies and the disturbing departures of the PCE itself are taken into account—though the case of the PCE poses a special problem. The Communist parties, starting with the PCI, almost all treat NATO as, at best, an awkward and un-desirable necessity and as, at worse, a repugnant "instrument of American interference in the politics and economics of our country and Western Europe." [40] Accordingly, virtually all of them favor the swiftest possible erosion of political-military blocs in Europe, not, of course, the Western political-military bloc alone, but both military alliance systems. In the mean-time, they are opposed to increased defense efforts on the part of member nations, to schemes for improved military integra-tion; and the PCF, in particular, to France's reassociation with the NATO military organization. And their watchword will surely be the dangers and burdens of American pre-eminence within the alliance.

True, since 1976, the Italians have significantly altered their opposition to NATO and even lent tacit support to key parts of Italy's defense program. True, the French have reversed themselves on the *force de frappe* and promised not to seek their country's immediate exit from the Atlantic Alliance. True, the Spaniards have pledged themselves to accept what-ever the popular verdict may be on Spain's entry into NATO. Obviously these are positions which the Soviet leaders would know how to improve. But it does not follow that they have no understanding for the accommodations being made or, more to the point, that in their distaste for aspects of these accommodations they lose sight of the PCI's and PCF's basic mistrust and aversion to their countries' alliance with the United States.

The same can be said of Communist policy toward the Common Market. True, the Soviet Union has been slower to come to terms with the EEC than most of the West European Communist parties and, presumably, at times has thought the PCI, in particular, too eager to work within its institutions. But its own attitude toward West European economic integration has changed enormously over the last six or seven years, and by and large the Soviet Union is now inclined to accept the Community. Its approach is now to struggle against the EEC's further expansion and its further political-military integration, and for its "democratization," meaning the crusade against "the monopolies." This, in large part, is also the approach of most West European Communist parties. Moreover, while no doubt the Soviet leaders think that some of the West European parties concede too much to the Common Market, the other side of the coin is that what they do not concede to it now appears to be having a salutary effect on Socialist allies who before conceded far more. Since one of the Soviet Union's primary concerns centers on the role of the Social Democratic parties, particularly the SPD, in promoting West European integration, a crack in this front, accentuated by Communist-Socialist collaboration in France, represents an encouraging new development.[41]

We make a mistake, then, when we feature the PCI's pledges to remain within the alliance, to keep up Italy's defense spending, and to accept the continuation of NATO basing. From the Soviet perspective, the PCI's underlying attitude toward "Atlantism" and political-military blocs is at

[359]

least as important. Similarly, we make a mistake when we dwell too much on the PCF's impatience with Soviet policy priorities. The Soviet leaders are likely to respond more to the implications of the way in which the PCF criticizes French policy priorities. They may have been less quick to say aloud what Gaston Plissonier said from the tribunal of the 25th Party Congress: that Giscard and his government were "returning our country to NATO, promoting the hegemonic aspirations of West German imperialism," that they erred in "not taking part in any of the disarmament negotiations, and in expressing a readiness to dissolve our national independence in a political-military bloc of 'Little Europe' trusts." [42] But obviously they have agreed all along, and now Brezhnev has openly said so. During his June 1977 visit to France, he complained to Giscard of what he called "new directions" in French defense policy, accusing his government of drawing France back toward NATO and devising a new doctrine (the so-called doctrine of "forward battle") that could only be directed against the Soviet Union and its allies.[43]

All of this can be reduced to a central idea, one that we should pay more attention to in Soviet analysis, for ultimately it is the idea by which the Soviet leaders come to prefer the foreign policy of the West European Communist parties over others. Theirs are policies, Soviet commentaries always underscore, dedicated to maintaining the "autonomy" and "integrity" of the nation. Applied to Western Europe, "national autonomy" means to Soviet minds "one-way Gaullism": "one-way" in the sense that it has nothing to do with Eastern Europe; "Gaullism" in the sense of "autonomy" from entangling alliances and supranational enterprises. This for them is the essence of West European Communist foreign policy. It is also their own essential aspiration for Western Europe.

Weighing the Effect of Policy

Ultimately what we make of the compatibility between the foreign policies of East and West European communism will depend on our notion of the Soviet Union's objectives in Western Europe. If the Soviet Union is assumed to have a rather simple, straightforward, and far-reaching set of aims—such as the demise of NATO, the reversal of West European integration, and the neutralization or "Finlandization" of this area—the foreign policy preferences of the PCI or the PCF, far from compensating for other disagreements, can only be a further source of alienation. These are not the objectives of a state that can easily live with ambiguity and half-success—not the objectives of a state prepared to tolerate much deviation from its own way of defining problems. But if the Soviet Union is assumed to proceed with less assurance, moved by more involved and less decisive purposes, then the nuanced but essentially anti-imperialist foreign policies of the West European parties take on an altogether different hue.

The point of departure of this study is closer to the second view and derives from three basic assumptions about Soviet policy in Western Europe: First, it seems to me that, while Soviet dreams almost surely wish nothing but decay and paralysis for NATO, the EEC, and West European capitalism, they probably have little to do with the Soviet leadership's actual working images. Rather than dramatic transformations—not to mention ones controlled by their policy—the Soviet leaders have come to expect a chaos of partial, unpredictable, and often countervailing trends in this region.

For example, when in the early years of the decade many

[361]

Soviet analysts convinced themselves of the seriousness of the rifts within the imperialist camp (the special effect of a crumbling postwar economic order), they also were worrying about the accelerated progress of West European integration. Now at the end of the decade their concerns are reversed. In the circumstances, Soviet aspirations become far more complex and conditional. The Soviet Union would doubtless like to see the American military presence in Europe diminished, particularly, if in the process the American-West European partnership is also diminshed—but not if in the process the Germans thrust themselves into the breach or military integration in Western Europe acquires a new impetus. The Soviet leaders should be heartened by the economic instability of Western Europe, maybe even optimistic about the prospects for change in several countries because of it, but instead they seem more preoccupied with the damage the recession has done to East-West economic cooperation, the inflation it has passed on to the East Europeans, the distraction it has created from détente, and the prominence it has given the Federal Republic within Western Europe and the Atlantic community.

The second assumption is that the complexity and indeterminacy of trends in Europe stirs as much ambivalence and uncertainty in the Soviet leadership as in any other national leadership. The implication is not that Soviet policy is adrift, that the leadership has little notion of where it wants events to go and thinks they can be encouraged to go, and least of all that its hopes and fears raise no challenge for the West. But there is a fundamental difference between a simplistically self-possessed foreign policy whose architects are thought to believe they have a clear vision of trends and an ability to control them and a less predetermined one designed to exploit (or contain) what are understood to be unpredictable, sometimes short-lived, often contradictory trends.

[362]

The third assumption follows from the first two: If the Soviet leaders recognize that trends within Western Europe defy easy analysis, let alone, management, and if their objectives are dynamic and loosely coordinated rather than fixed and closely coordinated, then they are less likely to dedicate policy to forcing or stifling change than they are to aiding processes fostering or retarding change. Rather than assume the burden for undermining Atlantic unity or for impeding the advance of the Common Market or for splitting Europe's peripheral states from their Western affiliations, they are more likely to entrust events to the favorable effects of processes like détente and, in their phrase, "imperialistic competition." For détente, they constantly repeat, is the best—indeed, the only practical—framework within which East-West cooperation, social and political change in Western Europe, and the natural tensions among the capitalist states can all flourish.

In this calculation, West European communism occupies a very delicate place: It is both a solution and a problem. A solution in the sense that détente is supposed to facilitate the rise of Europe's "progressive forces," and their advance in turn is supposed to reinforce détente. But a problem in the sense that their advance may in fact hinder or even disrupt détente. A solution in the sense that the change these forces embody is theoretically a major point to détente, change incidentally that reaches across the whole of Mediterranean Europe. But a problem in the sense that the Soviet leaders are not sure they can afford it.

The dilemma is in the effects of the Left's success. For example, on the one hand the entry of the PCI or PCF into government may produce what from the Soviet perspective are rather useful and far-reaching consequences. For one, whatever the reassurances of the PCI leadership, an Italian government with Communist participation will pose severe

[363]

practical problems for NATO and almost certainly lead to a special and reduced status for Italy in the alliance. For another, the opening to the Left in key Southern European countries like Italy, France, or Spain will strain the essential homogeneity—harmony would be too strong a word—of West European foreign policies. Or, for still another, a breakthrough in Italy or France may open the way elsewhere to alternative regimes no longer monopolized by the Center and Center-Right.

But, on the other hand, as the Soviet leadership realizes, the arrival of Communists in power may also generate a less happy set of effects. Some of these have already been mentioned—for they are what momentarily dull the Soviet taste for Communist victories in France or Italy. But, in addition, should one or both of these parties actually come to power, the effect may be to frighten other societies away from the left option or, where that is largely irrelevant, to strengthen the parties of national defense and caution. Or it may be to unnerve other neighboring countries and make them jittery and overcautious partners in détente. Or it may be to drive them into narrower but more intense forms of Atlantic and West European forms of cooperation.

Where are the Soviet Union and we then left? That, it seems to me, can only be assessed in a wider context, where the international, inter-party, and intra-national dimensions intersect, where East-West relations merge with Eurocommunism.

EUROCOMMUNISM

Eurocommunism is not, argues William Griffith, peculiar to Western Europe because East European autonomists like the

Romanians and Yugoslavs also partake. Nor, as George Marchais has pointed out, is it even peculiar to Europe because Communist parties in other advanced industrialized societies like Japan and Australia are saying and doing the same things. If ideological revisionism is its hallmark, then it represents no invention, for the Italians have been revisionists for years, perhaps always, and rarely with greater force than in their defense of Dubček's experimentation ten years ago. If it is to be associated with the rejection of Soviet tutelage or dictate, then the Yugoslavs showed the way three decades ago.

The point is that Eurocommunism is no one of these things but all of them and more. (The debate that we must inevitably endure over whether there is such a thing as Eurocommunism will surely reach the same conclusion.) It is "revisionism" but not so much the development of reformist notions as their spread—not the revisionism of the Italians but the "Italianiza-tion" of the others. It is the erosion of "proletarian interna-tionalism" but not because a challenge to Soviet hegemony has been laid down, rather because united action (the famous "Southern Axis") has made the challenge effective. In the end it is European because only in Europe is it sustained by both communisms, ruling and non-ruling, orthodox and revisionist. And so it is West European because only there are there the numbers to create a collective phenomenon and, in contrast to Eastern Europe, only there are there both revisionism and autonomism. Having said this, we might offer a partial modi-fication of this statement and suggest that the situation in Eastern Europe might become fluid enough to accommodate more than one country (Yugoslavia) which is both revisionist and autonomist.

At the same time, it is less than all of these things. As was stressed at the outset, in all respects West European Commu-nist parties are on a continuum, not of a kind. In each of our

[365]

three dimensions (intra-national, inter-party, and international) they run the gamut. They are at many different stages in their reformism and opposition to Soviet dominance. A few are completely Italianized (notably the Italians); at the other extreme one is untouched (the Portuguese); and in between most are at various levels of organizational and ideological experimentation. Some insist on autonomy from the Soviet model and leadership and want to substitute a "regional (West European) socialism." Others insist on autonomy but cannot abide the idea of a separate and exclusive socialism. Still others need and care for neither. All of which goes to confirm Griffith's point that Eurocommunism is also and above all a *process*—not a specific condition.[44]

Finally, in an important way, Eurocommunism is a phenomenon of the South. It is for others to explain why powerful *and* revisionist parties emerged in Latin Europe; but because they have, it is easy enough to see that they form the core of the process. This is not to say that other parties elsewhere are not going through much the same transformation or that they do not contribute to the process; indeed, they make the process universal. But without the Italians, French and Spanish, Eurocommunism would not be terribly interesting or consequential. For it is their importance (within important societies) as much as their revisionism that gives force to the phenomenon. Thus, the crucial development in the emergence of Eurocommunism has been the rapprochement—tactical and ideological—among the three leading southern parties. And among the three, the PCF's shift has been the most important. (If Yugoslavia made the "Southern Axis" possible—the collusion among the Yugoslavs, Romanians, Italians, and Spanish—appropriately it was the PCF's later adherence that permitted this group to carry the day at the Berlin Conference, for the

French were the deciding vote in the eight-party working group.)

By the same token, it seems that French communism holds the key to the future of Eurocommunism. Should the French retreat from their incipient revisionism, not merely from their tactical alliance with the Socialist party, the "process" of Eurocommunism will be jeopardized. The loss of the PCF will have fractured the core—the French being the piece that turned scattered revisionism into a West European phenomenon. Thus, it matters greatly whether the PCF's attack of "cold feet" in the case of its alliance with the Socialists is the first step in a march back into the past or the last moment of temporizing before substantial change begins to sweep through the party.

Apart from what it would mean in Eastern Europe itself, Eurocommunism can lose its East European membership and survive. Without the Yugoslavs and the Romanians, the West Europeans cannot expect to manage so well in the formal gatherings of European Communist parties, but the forces that are transforming West European communism will persist.

The Soviet Union and Eurocommunism

Were the current passage of West European communism merely several parties casting about for a solution to their domestic isolation, the challenge for the Soviet Union would be much simpler. After all, the Soviet Union has long dealt with different strains of revisionism, and, a quarter of a century later, it has after a fashion mastered life with the Togliattis and Titos (if not the Maos) of the world.

But that is not what is happening. Something more significant and complex is at stake than the waywardness of this or that Communist leadership. As reformism and the will to autonomy spreads among the parties of Western Europe and as they begin to reach out to one another, a phenomenon emerges larger than any single party's heresies. Half of European communism is turning the clock back to 1920, to the interlude before the second Comintern Congress, in effect, purging itself of Bolshevism and banding together to defend itself from predictable Soviet censure. It is less the reformism— which in any case varies from party to party—than its generalization that matters so much.

It matters more, of course, because the most important parties in the West are also edging nearer and nearer to political power. Hence the Soviet Union has on its hands a challenge both of international and ideological importance, a phenomenon, not an episode, and one whose impact is growing within a growing range of settings.

But there is also great complexity in these developments, which obscures and entangles Soviet choices. The complexity has many forms but the key ones seem to me (1) the diversity within Eurocommunism. No two West European parties threaten orthodoxy in the same way or to the same degree. (2) The countervailing impulses *within* each dimension of Soviet relations with West European communism. No set of issues is completely divisive. Even the most contentious areas contain some basic sources of accord. (3) The uncertain implications should these parties come to share power. The prospect obviously bears on East-West relations, but does it on Eurocommunism? Does it accentuate trends toward reformism and autonomism? Does it, independent of the answer to that question, make the influence of Eurocommunism more of a problem in Eastern Europe. And (4) The trade-offs among the three dimensions. Are the potential benefits to Soviet policy in

[368]

Western Europe of a strong Left enough to compensate for the grief of a heretical one?

So communism in Western Europe, after two decades of relative insignificance, has re-emerged as a major Soviet concern. But what distinguishes this revival from the 1930s or the period of coalition governments immediately after World War II is the challenge presented Soviet policy; indeed, that a challenge is presented. In the circumstances, a degree of equivocation and incoherence on the Soviet side is understandable.

Still, it is striking how halting the Soviet approach has been. How many obvious questions remain poorly answered or not at all. Do the Soviet leaders, all things considered, want the PCF or PCI in government or not? Do they have some reasonably clear notion of which transgressions by these parties and others like them matter the most? Do they know where and how far they will go in dealing with these transgressions? Do they have some scheme, some framework, or even only some instinct or feeling by which to sort out the balance among the three basic dimensions (inter-party, intranational, and international)?

With one crucial exception to which we shall come in a moment, the answer to these questions appears to be that they are unsure. They know they do not like the basic evolution of Western Europe's major Communist parties—and the evolution of some, less than of others. They disapprove of the permanent compromises the Italians appear ready to make with their bourgeois adversaries. They are unhappy about the PCF's new eagerness to shed inconvenient ideological concepts. They regret the damage done to the unity of the Communist movement by the ostentatious efforts of these parties to assert their independence from the Soviet Union. They resent the right these parties have assumed to criticize

[369]

their institutions and practices. And they are incensed by suggestions that West European communism should constitute a Third Force, all the more when the Spanish offer this as a way to "democratize" the regimes of Eastern Europe.

But what to do about it? So far the Soviet Union has reacted tentatively, in part indulging old habits, but in other ways groping for partial compromises designed to avoid an open split. The Soviet approach has been a strange mix of blandishment and admonition, of sharp, bitter reflexive attacks, usually against unnamed individuals, or, if named, then against lesser lights. An angry little book released in March 1976 condemns the thoughts of Luciano Gruppi, an ideologist of the PCI.[45] The author, Venyamin Midtsev, an obscure party publicist, has taken it on himself to expose the Italian's "right revisionism," the anti-Sovietism, the sell-out to bourgeois opponents. An equally immaterial source, Yuri Sedov, preoccupies himself with the "anti-Leninist fabrications" of Jean Elleinstein, a historian and member of the French Communist party.[46] It is not Georges Marchais or the leadership of the PCF who are attacked—only one of the party's intellectuals.

The polemic against Santiago Carrillo in the *New Times* of June 1977 breaks this pattern.[47] Previously, Soviet writers and spokesmen had refrained from direct, explicit criticism of party leaderships, preferring to make their point indirectly.[48] But their willingness to take another tack with the Spanish leadership either puts the PCE in a special category or else signals a new and more aggressive phase in the Soviet reaction to the challenge of Eurocommunism.

There has also been a temperate and conciliatory side to Soviet behavior—true, not so much that any central issue has been conceded. Rather than force matters to a head, however, or seek a confrontation or attempt to isolate and crush revisionist parties, the Soviet leaders have affected a willingness to talk out areas of disagreement, to argue not impose their case, to stress concerns uniting, not those dividing, East and West European communism. Partially, of course, they have been without any easy alternative; but, still, given earlier episodes and their rigid intolerance on questions of faith, Soviet restraint should have been more noted than it has been.

This is the more interesting feature of the Soviet approach to the Berlin Conference of Communist parties in June 1976, not the traditional notions of orthodoxy that their people brought to the meeting and hoped to impose on those who had strayed; not the conveniently biased interpretation that Soviet spokesmen have given the conference documents since the meeting; and not the very idea that a grand conference would work to bring recalcitrant West European parties back into line. Resisted from the start by an alliance of East and West European parties determined to use the conference for their own purposes and to deny the Soviet Union its purposes, the Soviet leaders yielded step by step their control over events. They wanted a disciplined conference dominated by their party and the East European loyalists, but, by agreeing to proceed only on the basis of consensus, they very early settled for one open to the others' counterproposals. They wanted a conference to rally all of Europe's Communists to a common view of the challenges facing them, but instead they ended by accepting a document dignifying the others' refusal to search for one. They wanted a conference eager to praise Soviet accomplishments and dedicated to the spirit of "proletarian internationalism," but they reconciled themselves to one offering neither.

There are those who argue that the Berlin Conference represents a major Soviet defeat, a watershed in the decline of Soviet influence over what remains of the international Communist movement. That seems vastly overdrawn, for the

[371]

Soviet Union had its successes at the conference—notably on matters of foreign policy—and the Soviet leaders have apparently judged them as such. They do not pretend that the meeting was a perfect triumph, but they do appear to consider it a useful reminder of the considerations that draw Communists together.

Defining success in these terms, however, means that the Soviet Union has itself consciously or unconsciously redesigned the tolerable limits of diversity. The Soviet Union did not disown a conference that was at best a demi-vindication of its views and, worse, a license to autonomy and experimentation in West European communism. Its representatives tried to impose on the conference a narrow standard of orthodoxy, but, when this failed, they did not repudiate the obstructionists nor threaten excommunication. On the contrary, they became patient, if somewhat aggrieved mentors, persuaded of the folly in the new experimentalism, but willing to talk, confident that experience and common sense would prove them right.

At points the whole situation seemed so outrageous that some could not contain themselves. Suslov, for example, exploded against those (still unnamed) "opponents of Marxism" who, disguised as Marxists, take what they want from Marx, Engels and Lenin, use it the way they please, and, in the process, "slander genuine socialism," "emasculate Marxist-Leninist teaching of its revolutionary essence," and "substitute bourgeois liberalism." [49] Suslov may have been more disgusted than most, but no doubt nearly all his colleagues felt much the same anger and frustration. Brezhnev's attack on "opportunism" at the 25th Party Congress must be a partial reflection of how broad the disaffection was. More recently Vasil Bil'ak, a Soviet favorite in the Czechoslovak leadership, has characterized Eurocommunism as a "mixture of the most diverse elements of petit-bourgeois reformism, of so-called national

communism, democratic socialism, and popular capitalism";
the whole idea, he says, is "just junk." [50]

Yet, the countenance presented to the fraternal parties of
Western Europe generally has been mild and forebearing.
"Without laying claim to being the custodians of the ultimate
truth," someone like Alexander Sobolev writes, "we would
like to set forth our view on these questions." [51] And he
proceeds to make the Soviet case, reviling no one, striking a
pose of open-mindedness, almost inviting counter-argument.
"If there were grounds for assuming that the principles of
internationalism formulated by Marx, Engels, and Lenin no
longer accord with the condition of social progress today, if
new and more effective forms of international solidarity" had
been invented, he says, "no one would object to building
solidarity on new foundations." But where is the evidence,
where is the superior argument suggesting that the "Marxist-
Leninist principles of international solidarity are not consonant
with present-day realities?"

Much of this is in tone, of course, not in substance. Soviet
spokesmen have no desire to launch a real dialogue on these
issues because they are utterly convinced that they are right.
Thus, when Sobolev says how "interesting, useful, and fruitful" discussions among Communists are, he does not really
mean it. Instead he means (and indeed says) that discussions
among Communists are "interesting, useful, and fruitful"
provided they are "conducted with a view to finding new
forms of proletarian solidarity." But tone is important in itself.
The soft voice, the gentle demeanor represent policy choices
and, for that matter, whether willed or not, they also represent
concessions to Eurocommunism.

If so, however, then what is to be made of the shrill public
attack on the general secretary of the Spanish Communist
party? Are the Soviet leaders reversing course? Or, more

[373]

accurately, have they found a course, and is it to wage war on the spreading "revisionism" of West European communism? Have they, therefore, decided against the Left—satisfied that the perils of its success outweigh the rewards?

A single incident, of course, proves nothing conclusively. But the decision to rebuke Carrillo publicly—denouncing his latest book and setting the stage for a formal break—constitutes something of a landmark. From it, the limits of Soviet tolerance are much more easily charted. The Soviet Union has been provoked into drawing the line; and, if that still leaves a host of questions unanswered, it does provide a clearer impression of the order in which the Soviet leaders rank the challenges of Eurocommunism.

Carrillo, according to the *New Times* editorial, commits two unpardonable sins. First, by advocating a "third" road for West European socialism and independence from both the United States and the Soviet Union, he in fact rallies to the imperialist conception of international relations in Europe.[52] By setting the West European countries apart, the editorial contends, he is creating them "as a 'force' opposed primarily to the socialist countries." He is fostering Atlanticism. He is placing the West first. He is splitting the European Communist movement—an idea, his Soviet critics maintain, that is "evidently very dear to Carrillo's heart."

Second, in order to ingratiate himself with potential bourgeois allies, he gives vent to an "escalating anti-Sovietism." He, the editorial claims, speaks of "our country and our party in terms which even the most reactionary writers do not often venture to use." He defiles Soviet political practice, denigrates Soviet accomplishments, and dismisses the Soviet Union as a "superpower" bent on the pursuit of "great-power aims" to which it sacrifices the class struggle and internationalism. He has the nerve to suggest that the Soviet Union is not really a

[374]

fair illustration of Marxism-Leninism, and he dares to recommend to his " 'Soviet comrades' " ways of transforming their country into a genuine workers' democracy. The indignity is enormous and the Soviet rage palpable.

But there is also a bargain implied in this assault. Not a bargain that the Soviet leaders evidently expect to strike with the Spanish or, at least, with Carrillo. But one that bears greatly on the Soviet Union's long-term accommodation with Eurocommunism.

Carrillo has passed beyond the pale, but he has done so not by tampering with Marxism-Leninism but by openly impugning the legitimacy of the Soviet Union. He has done so not by twisting the essence of socialism but by repudiating the Soviet Union's basic conception of a European order. And he has done both in the same book.

For that the Soviet leaders will not forgive him. For the other they apparently will—at least for the moment. Carrillo's work, the *New Times* editorial says, deals with two groups of problems: one relating to the strategy and tactics of the West European Communists. While "there are indeed interesting and serious problems here which it is the communist's direct duty thoroughly to study," they are expressly not the focus of the article. The other relates to the "present international situation, characterization of the socialist countries and their policy, and the unity and cohesion of the communist movement." In short, the decisive dimension turns out to be the second one, the inter-party dimension.

The implicit bargain centers on proletarian internationalism. This much the Soviet leaders seem to be saying: We do not like what you, the West European parties, are doing. We think your revisionism is mistaken and dangerous. And we reject the notion of Eurocommunism; it is an invention of bourgeois analysts designed to prejudice the unity of European

[375]

Communists. But we will live with your delinquency. That is, we will tolerate your reformism, though we intend to exhort and pressure you to rethink much of what you are proposing. We will even overlook your eagerness to fraternize among yourselves—perhaps even your references to Eurocommunism, nonsense though the whole idea is, provided you mean by it the "common features of your strategies within developed capitalist countries" and not "some sort of specific brand of communism." [53]

If, however, your deviations lead you to sling mud at us, to call into question the legitimacy of our system, or to attack the status quo in Eastern Europe, then we want nothing to do with you, then we will cast you off as we have other "renegades" before.[54] How much criticism will we let pass? That depends on the premises underlying it. If these involve the least doubt about the essential value or legitimacy of our political order, then you have already gone too far. You are misguided in disapproving of our treatment of dissidents and, by speaking out, you play the game of the imperialists. But there is a difference between censuring aspects of our behavior and denying our faithfulness to Marx and Lenin.

Carrillo has done that and, unless he retreats, we are prepared to break with him. We do not want to cause a further rift in the camp of progressive forces, but it is he who has brought us to this point. And it is with him alone (or with him and those among the PCE leadership who think like him) that we have our quarrel. We have no intention of making this a general quarrel. And we do not intend to alter our relations with the PCI, the PCF, or other parties should a break with Carrillo come—not unless they adopt a position like his.[55]

Carrillo's other basic misdeed also belongs to the second dimension; that is, it, too, violates a fundamental convention of proletarian internationalism, but in a more complicated way.

When the Spanish leader defends a "third way" between Soveit-style socialism and capitalism, he is advocating a peculiar and, from the Soviet point of view, noxious form of "Gaullo-communism." Unlike the French Communists, who also practice a kind of Gaullism, one closer to the original model of their countrymen to the right, the Spanish Communists seek their identity in the struggle against the Soviet colossus. The distinction is absolutely critical: The Spanish version of "Gaullo-communism" ruins whatever remains of the bargain by wrecking the utility a strong Left has for Soviet foreign policy, the third and offsetting dimension. (The PCF's version, in a sense, personifies the bargain.) [56] Carrillo, the *New Times* says, is a secret proponent of NATO.

But to compound matters and bring us back to the second dimension in what for Soviet observers is the most heinous sin of all, Carillo goes on to justify an independent West European model of socialism as the most powerful means for "democratizing" the regimes in Eastern Europe. Never did the imperialists, with their various notions of "bridge-building" and "little steps," conceive a more hostile and subversive policy toward the socialist camp.

Thus, in Soviet eyes, Carrillo has laid down an exceptional challenge deserving the sharpest retaliation. As they define the situation, attacking the Spanish leader reflects no policy shift on their part but rather a growing impertinence on the PCE's part.[57] While carrying an obvious message for the other parties, it presumably signals no change on the Soviet side. Only if the PCI and PCF, too, make a hibit of disputing Soviet legitimacy, urging the erosion of the Eastern status quo, and betraying the foreign policy consensus, will the Soviet Union turn on them.

But how long can these other parties pursue their reformism and quest for autonomy before they have gradually slipped across the same threshold? How long can the Soviet Union fence with these other parties before it begins to force them toward the Spanish position? These are the questions that will determine the ultimate course of Soviet relations with the Western parties.

In the meantime, the Soviet position on Eurocommunism and the rise of the Southern European Left remains essentially agnostic. The Soviet leaders know their mind only where Eurocommunism *openly* and *explicitly* challenges the legitimacy of their own society and those in Eastern Europe. To the extent that each side averts compelling the other to repudiate it, there is room for accommodation. It is in these circumstances that the convolutions and ambiguities in and between Eurocommunism's three dimensions spare the Soviet Union choices. As long as that moment endures, the ambiguities of trends turn the challenge of Eurocommunism into something less stark, softening the bad and commending the good in governments of the left should that prospect again emerge.

NOTES

1. A more detailed comparison along these lines involving the four Southern European Communist parties is in an unpublished paper by Pierre Hassner.

2. See *ibid.,* and William E. Griffith, "Soviet-American Regional Competition, 1976: 'Eurocommunism,' The Third Great Communist Schism?" Center for International Studies, Massachusetts Institute of Technology (November 8, 1976), 41 pp.

3. The list and the quote happen to be from Boris Ponomarev, "The World Situation and the Revolutionary Process," *World*

Marxist Review, no. 6 (June 1974), p. 6, but they are standard in Soviet commentary.

4. V.V. Zagladin, "Preconditions of Socialism and the Struggle for Socialism," *Voprosy Filosofii,* no. 11 (November 1975), p. 3.

5. *Ibid.*

6. *Ibid.,* p. 6.

7. See, "Theses on the Working Class and Its Allies," *World Marxist Review,* no. 7 (July 1975), p. 69.

8. Alexander Sobolev, "Organizer of Revolutionary Action," *World Marxist Review,* no. 2 (February 1974), p. 25.

9. For a discussion of the distinction between the "peaceful" and the "parliamentary" path to socialism and its not so peaceful implications, see Hassner's unpublished paper.

10. Sobolev, "Organizer of Revolutionary Action," p. 25.

11. For a relevant parable see, K. Gusev, "On the Political Course of the Bolsheviks toward the Petty-bourgeois Parties," *Kommunist,* no. 15 (October 1976), pp. 86-97, especially 89-94.

12. A.I. Sobolev, "The Dialectic of the General and Particular in the Development of the World Revolutionary Process," *Voprosy Istorii,* no. 11 (November 1975), p. 30.

13. In addition to Hassner's unpublished paper, see the excellent work of Donald Blackmer and Peter Lang.

14. Zagladin, "Preconditions of Socialism," p. 12.

15. *Ibid.,* p. 15.

[379]

16.   See his article in *Pravda,* August 6, 1975, pp. 1-2.

17.   *Ibid.,* p. 2.

18.   First thing you know, Communists will be putting the word strategy itself in quotation marks. See Jean Kanapa, "A 'New Policy' of the French Communists?" *Foreign Affairs,* vol. 55, no. 2 (January 1977), p. 282.

19.   Hassner's unpublished paper; for more on the dilemma that follows from the contradictions in party's several "faces" or roles, see Ronald Tiersky, "Alliance Politics and Revolutionary Pretensions," in Donald L.M. Blackmer and Sidney Tarrow, eds., *Communism in France and Italy* (Princeton, N.J.: Princeton University Press, 1975) and his "French Communism in 1976," *Problems of Communism,* vol. 25, no. 1 (January-February 1976), pp. 20-47.

20.   In an interview with Giovanni Russo, *Corriere della Sera,* March 18, 1976, quoted by Kevin Devlin, Radio Free Europe *Research Report,* March 25, 1976, p. 8. Gruppi was responding to a Soviet monograph that is a good, if somewhat extreme, illustration of the points that I have been making. See Venyamin Midtsev, *Revisionism in the Service of Anticommunism* (Moscow: Znanie, 1975).

21.   See "Characteristics of Developed Socialism," *World Marxist Review,* no. 1 (January 1975), pp. 93.

22.   Interestingly, Soviet theorists have only recently begun to work on the problem—doubtless, as much because of the conflict with the Chinese and their own internal need for ideological stimulation as the challenge of West European revisionism—and they confess that the "methodological problems of the theory of developed socialism have yet to be worked out adequately." *Ibid.,* p. 83.

23.   Richard Kosolapov, "The Approach to the Study of Developed Socialism," *World Marxist Review,* no. 9 (September 1974), p. 63.

24. Pyotr Fedoseyev, "Vanguard of the Soviet People," *World Marxist Review* (March 1971), p. 6.

25. *Ibid.,* p. 5.

26. For the Joint PCF-PCI Statement, see *L'Unitá,* November 18, 1975, p. 1.

27. See *L'Astrolabio,* September 8, 1968.

28. For cases in point see A. Sobolev, "Aktualnye problemy borby protiv pravogo revizionizma," *Partiinia Zhizn',* no. 5 (March 1974), pp. 75-9, and Kh. I. Momdzhian, *Marksizm i renegat Garodi* [Marxism and the renegade Garaudy] (Moscow: Institute of Philosophy, 1972), esp. pp. 125-32.

29. In the case of the PCI, Donald Blackmer now contends, this is fast eroding. In an unpublished paper, he has written: "The obvious point is that the party, by virtue of its institutional and political successes over a substantial period of time, has been creating the bases for an identity that depends less and less on the Soviet heritage." Indeed, he continues, the party increasingly derives its identity from a repudiation of large parts of the Soviet experience rather than from loyalty to it. With this I have no quarrel. But it does seem to me that until the party comes to that critical juncture where it turns its back on the Soviet revolution and says aloud that the Soviet Union has failed as a socialist experiment, it will retain a dependency on the Soviet idea and ideal, if for no other reason than that these incarnate the PCI's sense of history and the transcendent revolution larger than any single society. It may be, however, that the Spanish Communist party has already arrived at that juncture. If so, it would be a vitally important development, and for that reason something that I consider more carefully in the last section of this essay.

30. *L'Unità,* September 8, 1968.

31. Sobolev, "The Dialectic of the General and the Particular," p. 25.

32. This happens to be the Hungarian version, but Soviet writers make the same point. See Ferenc Várnai, *Népszabadság*, March 20, 1976, in FBIS, March 1976.

33. For one version of the argument see Yu. Stepanov, "Proletarian Internationalism—the Most Important Principle of Marxism-Leninism," *Mirovaya ekonomika i mezhdunarodnye otnosheniia*, no. 11 (November 1976), p. 25.

34. It would appear that on this issue the Soviet position was supported by only the Greek, Irish, and Danish Communist parties. See "The Common Cause of Europe's Communists," *World Marxist Review*, no. 9 (September 1976), p. 8.

35. Many observers also interpreted the Soviet Ambassador's visit to Giscard d'Estaing between the first and second rounds of the election as a sign of Soviet preference—PCF analysts included.

36. E. Silin, "Alignment of Forces in the Capitalist Countries," *International Affairs* (March 1975), p. 83.

37. Ponomaryov's remarks were in a speech to the meeting sponsored by the journal *Problemy mira i sotsializma*, April 27-29, 1977, in Prague. See Boris Vesnin, "Interesting, Useful Meeting," *New Times*, no. 21 (May 1977), p. 19.

38. See *L'Humanité*, May 14, 1975.

39. *Ibid.*

40. The quote is from *L'Unità*, March 1, 1976, and appears in Guiseppe Are, "Italy's Communists: Foreign and Defense Policies,"

Survival (September/October 1976), p. 210. Are provides some of the analysis that I am arguing is too much missing. For Soviet comments on the PCI's "struggle against NATO and imperialistic aggression," see V.K. Naumov, *Kommunisty Italii* (Moscow: "Mezhdunarodnye otnosheniya izdatelstvo," 1972), pp. 331-50.

41. On this subject, see I.M. Krivoguza, ed., *Kommunisty i sovremennaya sotsial-demokratiya* (Moscow: Izdatelstvo "Mysl," 1975), pp. 114, 125, 127-28.

42. *Pravda*, February 29, 1976, p. 8.

43. *New York Times*, June 22, 1977, p. 3.

44. Griffith, " 'Eurocommunism': The Third Great Communist Schism?" p. 35.

45. Midtsev, *Revisionism in the Service of Anticommunism*.

46. Yuri Sedov, "Falsification Instead of Objective Study," *New Times*, no. 5 (January 1977), pp. 12-15.

47. Editorial, "Contrary to the Interests of Peace and Socialism in Europe: Concerning the book 'Eurocommunism and the State' by Santiago Carrillo, General Secretary of the Communist Party of Spain," *New Times*, no. 26 (June 1977), pp. 9-13.

48. There is, of course, nothing sacrosanct about a party's leadership, as the history of Soviet relations with the regimes of Tito, Mao, and Dubček—to name but a few—demonstrates; but when a leadership is openly assailed, this represents a critical turning point far advanced toward an open break.

49. In a speech to the Academy of Sciences, see *Pravda*, March 18, 1976, p. 2.

50. *New York Times*, June 26, 1977, p. 4.

51. Alexander Sobolev, "International Brotherhood of the Workers, *New Times,* no. 11 (March 1977), p. 19.

52. "Contrary to the Interests of Peace and Socialism in Europe," *New Times,* pp. 10-11. The Spanish, of course, claim that this article thoroughly misrepresents Carrillo's view.

53. *Ibid.,* p. 10.

54. The similarity is almost total between the Soviet reaction to Carrillo and its reaction to Roger Garaudy, the French Communist ousted from the PCF in 1970. See Momdzhian, *Marksizm i renegat Garodi,* esp. pp. 124-68.

55. This restraint is evident in an article that V. Zagladin published a week or two after the *New Times* editorial. See *Pravda.* July 2, 1977, pp. 4-5, for his stress on the foreign-policy partnership between East and West European communism, on the accomplishments of that partnership, and on the importance of avoiding the vice of anti-Sovietism. He, too, however, makes it plain that the Soviet Union will rebuff attacks on it from whatever quarter.

56. This is not to say that the Soviet Union has no problems with the PCF in the foreign-policy area. It deserves to be repeated that the French resent mightily a foreign-policy commitment to détente which, they believe, leads the Soviet Union to support the "social status quo" in their country.

57. Carrillo was scarcely chastened. After the event he reaffirmed his positions and said that the Soviet Union regards itself as the Holy Office of the Catholic Church, for which it deserves to be defied. See his interview in *Le Monde,* June 24, 1977.

[SEVEN]

The Diplomacy of Eurocommunism

William E. Griffith

The first part of this chapter sets forth a series of hypotheses about Eurocommunist diplomacy; the second analyzes recent Eurocommunist diplomatic developments.

SOME HYPOTHESES

Other chapters in this volume analyze at length the policies of the Soviet and Eurocommunist parties. Let me, therefore, only set forth briefly a definition and some hypotheses about them. "Eurocommunism" is primarily domestic in origin, therefore best studied on a nation-state basis, centered in, but in my view not confined to, Western Europe. It is a complex variety of alignments composed of varying mixtures of reformism, regionalism, and autonomism (from the Soviet Union).

The reformist aspect of West European Eurocommunism may be defined as the withering away of Leninism and the transition from it toward an economically and socially radical, pluralistic parliamentary democracy. Geographically, Eurocommunist reformism also characterizes the Japanese and Australian parties, i.e., it now includes most Communist parties in advanced industrial societies. Regionally, West European Eurocommunism is moving toward increasingly coordinated nonaligned Communist policies independent from and eventually equidistant between the Soviet Union and the United States.

Eurocommunist autonomism from Soviet control characterizes not only the major West European Communist parties but also two major ones in Eastern Europe, the (only very partially reformist) Yugoslav and the (anti-reformist) Romanian, as well as the (reformist) Japanese and Australian Communist parties. Indeed, its center is the alliance on this issue between the Yugoslav and Italian Communist parties.

Soviet policy toward Eurocommunism has been carried out within a paradoxical context: a continuing major rise in Soviet military power, globally and in Europe, plus the demonstrated willingness in 1968 to use it to crush Czechoslovak Eurocommunism (for that is, *grosso mode.* what it was), accompanied by the near-collapse of the attractiveness in Western Europe of the Soviet economic, technological, political, and cultural model, and the continued decline in Soviet influence within what one can hardly any longer call "the international Communist and workers movement." The principal stages in this decline were Stalin's break with Tito in 1948, the Sino-Soviet break in 1959, the Romanian deviation in 1964, and more recently Eurocommunism itself. Ironically, this had occurred at a time when Soviet military power in Europe has been rising but when first France and later the German Federal Republic and the United States have pursued regional détene in Europe with the Soviet Union. Communist Western Europe has thus been moving toward confrontation with the Soviet Union while non-Communist Western Europe and North America have been moving away from it.

This is not such a paradox as it may seem. Indeed, East-West détente in Europe was one of the preconditions for and causes of the development of Eurocommunism. Why? First, it dimmed West European Communists' perception of the danger of "imperialism" and therefore made them less inclined to unite with the Soviet Union against it. Second, it gave the Yugoslav and Romanian Communist leaders a greater feeling of security against Soviet pressure or intervention and therefore encouraged them to pursue autonomist policies vis-à-vis the Soviet Union. Third, because it encouraged Soviet-American bilateralism, or at least the perception of it, it created among non-Soviet Communists in Europe, West and East, a certain "Gaullo-communism"—a resentment that European affairs, and their views on them, were being disposed of, or in danger of being disposed of, by the Soviet Union and the United States over their heads and against their interests. (This became particularly apparent, not surprisingly, with respect to the PCF's resentment of Soviet support of de Gaulle, Pompidou, and Giscard d'Estaing.)

The principal diplomatic objectives of the Eurocommunist parties are to maximize their security, autonomy, and electoral appeal. These three interacted as Soviet attractiveness declined and European nationalism and self-assertiveness increased. The more autonomy that a major West European party demonstrated vis-à-vis Moscow, the more votes it could reasonably hope to get. When, as with the PCI, this occurred, a party was all the more encouraged to carve out greater autonomy.

We must now turn to the special nature of alliances among Communist states and parties. The Leninist model of relationships among Communist parties presumed that their exclusive loyalty and alliance relationships would be to the international Communist and workers movement, i.e., they give absolute priority to "proletarian internationalism" over any national loyalties, for, as Marx had said, "the proletariat has no fatherland." In practice under Lenin, and in theory and practice under Stalin, this meant total subordination to the Soviet Communist party, symbolized by Stalin's dictum that the international proletariat has only one fatherland, the Soviet Union. Stalin's purges enforced complete conformity in this respect on other Communist parties.

Yet the basic contradiction between nationalism and internationalism remained and was bound to re-emerge, just as it had before and during World War I. Before 1914 the German Social Democratic party (SPD) had gradually moved, first in practice and then in theory, from revolutionary to reformist policies. The main reason for this transformation was that the SPD realized that it could not come to power through revolution, but that it could increase its influence and later participate in power by a gradualist, reformist strategy. The more it participated in power (as in the south German states), the more reformist it became. The same nationalist and reformist tendencies, which might have been called "Eurosocialism," developed in other West and Central European Social Democratic parties. Conversely, in countries where only a revolutionary strategy seemed possible, such as in police-ruled Imperial Russia, neither reformism nor nationalism but revolution and internationalism characterized socialist strategy.

It was thus not surprising but, rather, inevitable that pre-1914 "Eurosocialism" was reformist and nationalist and that Lenin and his Bolsheviks broke with it, as did the left wings of the other Social Democratic parties. Each tendency formed its own international. Neither of the two long remained international: the Socialist International became a weak roof-organization for nationalist Social Democratic parties, and Stalin brought the Comintern under Soviet control. Thus nationalism everywhere won out over internationalism, which in the Communist world became only a synonym for Soviet domination.

The Soviet Union rapidly transformed the Communist world, as Athens had the Delian League, from an alliance into an empire. After World War II, Stalin took control over the East European states as well. Whether or not he ever intended that "domesticism" [1] in Eastern Europe should long continue—and I doubt it, given the rapidity of complete Communist control in Bulgaria, Romania, and East Germany [2]—he certainly did not after the 1948 Soviet-Yugoslav break.

Stalin broke with Tito because Tito refused to accept near-total Soviet infiltration of his party, intelligence, police, and military apparats. (Tito was prepared to accept general Soviet guidance of his foreign and domestic policies.) A secondary cause of the break was Stalin's refusal to tolerate Tito's regional ambitions—the creation of a Balkan federation, which Tito would dominate, including Yugoslavia, Bulgaria, part of northern Greece, and Albania. In sum, Stalin's Russian imperial nationalism clashed with Tito's Yugoslav nationalism and Balkan ambitions—and Tito won. Only several years after the break did Tito feel compelled to modify his domestic extremism (more extreme in some respects than Soviet domestic policy) in order to get U.S. economic and military aid and to strengthen the base of his popular support. Thus, in Communist Yugoslavia nationalism preceded reformism. Tito's domestic liberalization has always been limited by his determination to maintain his own and his party's power. Within these limits, liberalization has been furthered by rising affluence but hindered by endemic tension among the nationalities, which was much greater than in any other country with which this chapter deals.

One initial result of the Soviet-Yugoslav break was the drastic tightening of Stalin's rule over his East European satellites and a bloody purge in most of them. The West European Communist parties endorsed these Stalinist policies, as they had the condemnation of Yugoslavia, in terms as violent as Moscow's. Ironically, at the first Cominform meeting in 1947 the Yugoslavs, presumably on Soviet "advice," had condemned the French and Italian Communist parties for their alleged lack of revolutionary fervor, as demonstrated by their post-1945 participation in bourgeois governments. Both parties had officially accepted this Soviet-inspired criticism. Togliatti, however, did so only formally; *in petto* he continued to favor the policy which he had adopted upon his 1944 return from Moscow: a broad coalition with Catholic and other progressive forces aiming toward legal, electoral assumption of power. 1947, however, was the year that he (and Thorez) were forced out of government in the context of the developing cold war. Thereafter the PCI and the PCF had to rely upon Soviet support against the increasingly anti-Communist West. Tito in contrast, had to rely on U.S. support to keep his economy going and to deter Soviet invasion.

The cold war ended any possibility for effective diplomacy, within or without the Communist world, by the West European Communist parties and, conversely, for Tito marked its beginning, outside the Communist world. From 1948 to 1955 and again from 1958 to the early 1970s Yugoslavia had no party relations with the CPSU and most other European Communist parties. When in 1974 Moscow and Belgrade resumed full party relations, they did so on Tito's terms.

The next major developments for the Soviet Communist

[390]

alliance system were the 1956 Polish October and the Hungarian Revolution. Both were basically Eurocommunist, i.e., reformist and autonomist, in content. Gomułka successfully limited and then reversed both tendencies in Poland, and the Red Army crushed them in Hungary. The West European parties endorsed the Soviet intervention, but reluctantly and at the cost of some defections and significant, although temporary, loss of popular support.

Moscow crushed the Hungarian Revolution because Imre Nagy's dissolution of the Hungarian Communist party, withdrawal from the Warsaw Pact, and establishment of a multiparty system would have meant the loss of Hungary to the Soviet security system and would have infected the other Soviet satellites in Eastern Europe and eventually the Soviet Union as well with democracy and nationalism. Tito condemned the first Soviet intervention in Hungary but reluctantly endorsed the second. He had used its prelude to revive his regional ambitions in Eastern Europe and to push the Soviets to purge his enemies such as Rákosi, but he feared the contagion of multiparty democracy in Hungary and especially the potential territorial revisionism with respect to the three-quarters of a million Magyars in the northernmost province of Serbia, the Vojvodina. Thus Tito again demonstrated that his version of Eurocommunism had limits with respect to reformism and that his Yugoslav nationalism tempered his willingness to allow the potential nationalism of other Communist states to be fully unfolded, particularly when territorial irredenta in Yugoslavia were possibly involved.

In the summer of 1956 Togliatti had enunciated—only to recant formally under Soviet pressure—his famous doctrine of "polycentrism": advocacy of regional centers of Communist parties not under Soviet control.[3] And he, as well as the other West European Communist leaders, endorsed the Soviet crushing of the Hungarian Revolution. Yet, as we shall see, he only submerged, but did not abandon, his reformist and autonomist views. They were not nearly as extensive as Berlinguer's were by 1977, but the trend away from the Soviet model continued under the surface.

Just as Tito had shown in 1955 his desire to resume party relations with Khrushchev but on his own terms, so in 1958, by his defiant rejection of Khrushchev's pressure to revise the Ljubljana Program of the League of Communists of Yugoslavia (LCY), he showed that he would again rather break off party relations than bow to Moscow. By doing so his potential leverage on Moscow increased.

This was the more effective because of two other developments. The first was the gradual rapproachement between the LCY and the PCI. Togliatti had favored the 1955 Soviet-Yugoslav rapprochement, regretted the renewed break in 1958, and continued his contacts with Belgrade.

The second was the single most important post-1945 development in the Soviet Communist alliance system and one of the preconditions for the development of Eurocommunism: the Sino-Soviet split. As a prominent Italian Communist journalist recently put it:

> . . . The "doctrine" of "limited sovereignty" is not Brezhnev's invention. It is a constant method of Soviet action, from the era of the Third International to the invasion of Czechoslovakia, via the Stalinist attempt to overthrow Tito and the Khrushchevian attempt to strangle China economically. . . .[4]

From the Eurocommunist perspective, the Sino-Soviet split had two new and positive characteristics. China was so large that the Soviets could not, or at least chose not to, bring it to heel, militarily or otherwise. Therefore the split gave those European Communist parties that were not under decisive (i.e., military) Soviet influence the possibility to maneuver between the two and to persuade the Soviets to pay them, however reluctantly, a price for their support: greater Soviet tolerance of autonomy and reformism vis-à-vis Moscow. As we shall see, Eurocommunist support of Moscow's aim of "collective mobilization" to excommunicate Peking declined as the years went on.

Thus there developed an objective coincidence of interests between the Eurocommunists, who were or became autonomists vis-à-vis Moscow, and the anti-Soviet Chinese. Besides, the more that the Eurocommunists profited from maneuvering between the Soviets and the Chinese (as was the case with the Romanians) or, as was the case with all of them, from the concessions they extorted from the Soviets in return for attending international or European Communist conferences (though *not* agreeing with Soviet policies), the less they favored either a complete Sino-Soviet reconciliation, which would end their possibility of profiting from the split, or a total break, which would make the Soviets less concerned about their support and themselves less able to keep their own parties united in the face of Maoist splinter groups. Thus they more and more frustrated Moscow's objectives and achieved their own.

Not until the late 1960s did the Spanish and British parties, or until late 1975 the French party, begin to follow this course. The Italian party, however, had long done so. Far more than any other party, the PCI was the vanguard of Eurocommunist diplomacy. As Professor Donald Blackmer has analyzed the course of PCI diplomacy until 1964 in great detail and perspicacity,[5] only the highlights need be touched on here.

The PCI's objective was what Eurocommunism's objective

became by 1975: a reorganization of the international Communist movement to substitute "unity in diversity and autonomy" for Soviet hegemony. This meant the avoidance of a total Sino-Soviet split, much greater toleration of diversity among Communist parties, a more positive attitude toward non-Communist radical nationalists and national liberation movements in the Third World, a more favorable attitude toward Social Democratic and Catholic left-wing movements, and a regional role and policy for communism in Western Europe—indeed, in all advanced industrial societies.

INTER-PARTY DIPLOMACY AND COMMUNIST CONFERENCES

Eurocommunist diplomacy has been bilateral and multilateral. Its bilateral diplomacy has been characterized by its catholicity. Far more than the Soviets (or the Chinese), from 1956 onward it included relations with the Yugoslav party [6] as well as with such neutralist Communist parties as the Korean, Vietnamese, Cuban, and Japanese. Increasingly, however, it centered in Western Europe. There the PCI was instrumental in organizing a series of West European regional Communist conferences which concentrated on domestic and European rather than on international problems.

Until now the most revealing and important aspect of Eurocommunist diplomacy, and the most difficult to analyze, has been in the area of multi-party Communist conferences. Such conferences have a long historic tradition, going back to the Comintern congresses of the interwar period and the Cominform meetings in 1947 and thereafter. Traditionally they were convened and dominated by the Soviet Communist party. They often proclaimed a major Soviet-inspired change in the general international line of the movement, such as, for example, the Popular Front policy enunciated by the 1935 Comintern congress and the turn to the left of the first Cominform meeting in 1947; and more generally they were major instruments of Soviet hegemony. Both organizations had permanent secretariats and press organs, also Soviet-dominated. (Togliatti was during much of the interwar period one of the Comintern's senior officials.) The Comintern secretariat continued to operate after it was officially dissolved during World War II, and was transformed into the Cominform secretariat when the latter organization was set up in the immediate postwar period.

In 1955 Khrushchev initiated the first Soviet-Yugoslav rapprochement. His motives in doing so included de-Stalinization and the desire to get nonaligned Yugoslavia's assistance in the Third World. Thus both domestic and foreign policy considerations influenced Soviet policy within the international movement. Party relations were restored, at his initiative, between the CPSU and the League of Yugoslav Communists (LCY), without Yugoslavia having to abandon any of its ideological heterodoxies or return to a forml international Communist organization. (The Cominform was dissolved in 1956.)

Moscow, however, was still not prepared to surrender its "leading role." It attempted to maintain it in Eastern Europe through the Warsaw Treaty Organization (WTO) and the Council for Mutual Economic Aid (CMEA or Comecon), and globally through multi-party conferences, including the West European Communist parties.

The CPSU's initial purpose in these conferences, after the 1956 Polish and Hungarian developments, was to reconsolidate Soviet control over Eastern Europe, to maintain the Soviet-Yugoslav rapprochement, and to reinforce at home and abroad its authority and legitimacy as the leading Communist party. As the Sino-Soviet split and the second Soviet-Yugoslav break developed, Moscow added two other objectives: to carry out collective mobilization against the Chinese and to put pressure on the Yugoslavs. In neither, as we shall see, did it succeed.

The strategy of the Eurocommunists—initially of the PCI, then of the PCE, and since late 1975 of the PCF—was quite different. Togliatti wanted neither the reconsolidation of Soviet power in the movement nor a break with Moscow but, rather, the reorganization of the international Communist movement on a looser, more autonomist basis. Togliatti's formula, "unity in diversity," was meant genuinely: he believed that only by devolution from empire to commonwealth could split be avoided.

He had, of course, other reasons for this strategy. He also did not want an irreconcilable Sino-Soviet split because Moscow would thereafter feel freer to put pressure on the PCI and other heterodox parties. Nor did he want the subordination of Peking to Moscow again because this would have the same result. Togliatti wanted to delay and thus to foil the Soviet effort to excommunicate the Chinese without breaking with Moscow in the process. For to move toward diversity while retaining unity required that Moscow be gradually brought to its senses, so to speak: to the realization that it *could not* successfully excommunicate the Chinese and therefore *must* readjust to the new, pluralistic realities of the Communist world.

Multi-party Communist conferences have recently been more important for what has happened during their preparation and what has been left out of their declarations than for any positive achievements. They have been preceded by prolonged inter-party negotiations. These included, first, the question of the participants: Shall the Yugoslavs attend? Shall the Chinese be invited? What of the Vietnamese and Koreans? Second, the agenda: Shall it include the Chinese issue? If so, shall excommunication of the Chinese be discussed? Shall the United States be condemned and if so, how? The German Federal Republic? Social democracy? Third, the rules of procedure: Shall there be drafting committees? Who shall participate in them? Shall they be "balanced" (pro-Soviet vis-à-vis autonomist parties?) And, most important of all, how shall decisions be reached? By a majority vote or unanimously (by "consensus")? Shall they be binding on all parties? May a party sign only part of the declaration? Or make reservations if it signs all or only part of it? Only when these issues, or most of them, were decided could negotiation about the content of the declaration begin.

The 1957 Conference

The multi-party conference held in Moscow in November 1957, on the occasion of the fortieth anniversary of the Bolshevik Revolution, was important in three major aspects: (1) a significant albeit essentially secret Sino-Soviet confrontation, (2) the beginnings of the second Soviet-Yugoslav break, and (3) the autonomist and reformist position taken by the PCI and the PCF's sharp rejection of it.

As a result of Chinese disclosures subsequent to the Sino-Soviet split, we now know that there was a serious bilateral Sino-Soviet confrontation before the conference in which most of the major doctrinal and foreign policy issues that later caused the split were put on the table. The result was a compromise, which soon turned out to be unstable.[7]

The deterioration in Soviet-Yugoslav relations had begun with the Soviet suppression of the Hungarian Revolution. The refusal of the Yugoslavs to sign the 1957 ruling party declaration, because of its emphasis on the primacy of the struggle against revisionism (i.e., against themselves), reflected Soviet priority for reconsolidation of the bloc over rapprochement with Yugoslavia. An Italian Communist leader present has recently written that at the conference Mao showed considerable understanding for the Yugoslav and Polish positions.[8] (Gomułka was anxious to avoid further Soviet pressure for more rapid repression in Poland than he intended and for the recollectivization of agriculture.)

Togliatti's summary of the PCI's autonomist and reformist position at the conference, published only three years later, had been foreshadowed by the PCI's 8th Congress in December 1956, after the Soviet crushing of the Hungarian Revolution; the congress formally ratified and made Togliatti's polycentrist position of June 1956 party policy. There he repeated his endorsement of the Soviet intervention in Hungry but termed it a "hard necessity." He reiterated that true de-Stalinization required an analysis of faults in the socialist system and

> liquidating illegality and the absurd limitations of democratic rights, accepting open debate and confrontation with ideologies different from our own, liberating science and art from harmful shackles . . .

He reaffirmed the full autonomy of each Communist party and rejected

> . . . intervention in the internal affairs of other parties . . . open or concealed support for a factional struggle, the promotion of a rift in the unity of other parties or of our

[398]

whole movement . . . the return to any form whatever of centralized organizations . . .

On the other hand, we do not exclude—indeed, we favor . . . for the examination of particularly important problems, for the confrontation between the different ways of solving them in various situations—the organization of international meetings among representatives of a good many parties, not with the aim of working out decisions binding on all but to clarify reciprocal positions and thus increase the unity of the movement . . .[9]

Thus Togliatti set forth his program for the reorganization of the international Communist movement. It included: (1) total autonomy for each party and the end of any "directing center" (i.e., of Soviet hegemony), (2) a special regional role for the West European Communist parties, (3) the institutionalization of diversity within the movement, including for the PCI the right to have its own domestic reformist program and to criticize the domestic line of the U.S.S.R. and the East European Communist parties, (4) the limitation of international meetings to multilateral dialogue to the exclusion of decisions with binding force and of any splits or factionalism, and (5) a much more positive attitude toward non-Communist left-wing forces in Western Europe. This has remained the program of the PCI until the present. It was gradually taken over by the vast majority of Communist parties in Western Europe as well as by the Japanese and Australian parties. However, in 1957, it was still strongly opposed by the PCF, which only began a détente with the PCI in the mid-1960s and finally swung over completely to PCI positions in late 1975.

How much the PCI was aware at the 1957 Moscow

meeting of Sino-Soviet tension we do not know; probably not very much. Togliatti repeated there his December 1956 position. A French communist representative denounced Togliatti's position as "revisionist," [10] presumably in part because Togliatti, although ostensibly setting forth only the PCI position, implied that it should be adopted by the other West European Communist parties.

1958-1960

These were the decisive years in the development of the Sino-Soviet split, which occurred in the summer and autumn of 1959. Only three points about it need be made here. First, while the PCI rejected the Chinese policy positions, it always opposed a Sino-Soviet split. Second, the PCF generally followed the Soviet line. Indeed, Thorez, although he had shown some sympathies for the Chinese because he shared their distaste for Khrushchev's de-Stalinization, was frequently used by the Soviets for their policy purposes, for example, to try to influence the rebellious Albanians.[11] Third, Soviet-Yugoslav relations: Khrushchev's priority for reconsolidation of the camp and the Yugoslav ideological challenge to it in its 1958 Ljubljana Program made Soviet-Yugoslav party relations continue to deteriorate. However, Khrushchev kept trying to avoid a total break. Chinese-Yugoslav relations deteriorated far more sharply, but in my view, Mao, although more strongly opposed than Khrushchev to Yugoslav revisionism, was primarily using the Yugoslavs as "surrogates" for the Soviets. The PCI unenthusiastically went along with Khrushchev's attacks against the Yugoslavs, the more so because of Chinese factional activity.

[400]

The November 1960 Meeting

The June 1960 Bucharest [12] and the November 1960 Moscow [13] multi-party meetings saw the Sino-Soviet dispute break out, behind closed doors, in its full fury. The PCF played a major role in supporting the Soviet position. The PCI was represented at Moscow by Luigi Longo—Togliatti was presumably too sly a fox to get caught in such a clash. Longo's position there was, and had to be, very *nuancé*. On the one hand, he took strong exception to the Chinese position and violently attacked Hoxha for his anti-Soviet diatribes. On the other, while rejecting factionalism (the key issue at Moscow between the Soviets and the Chinese) as strongly as the Soviets did, he made clear that in two significant respects the PCI's position was different from the Soviets'. He strongly stressed the independence of each party; and he successfully pushed for modifying the condemnation of Yugoslavia by removing the call for "isolation" of the LCY, presumably put in at Chinese insistence, which was contrary to the PCI's intensification of contacts with the league.

1960-1969

The 81-party meeting in November 1960 was the last one in which the Chinese, Albanians, Vietnamese, Koreans, and some other East Asian parties took part.[14] After abortive negotiations, Sino-Soviet party relations collapsed, and rising border tensions culminated in the 1969 border clashes. Moscow continued to try, with little or no success, to mobilize

[401]

support against the Chinese and if possible to excommunicate them.

The West European Communist parties were thus faced with a different diplomatic problem. While before the split the PCI had tried to prevent it and the PCF had helped to bring it about, thereafter they had to react to this Soviet strategy. They had other problems arising from the split. They had to combat Maoist splinter groups, set up with Chinese support; to explain and, insofar as they wished, to justify Soviet policies and attack Chinese policies; and to cope with one major result of the Sino-Soviet split: the disastrous damage it did to the Marxist-Leninist myth of proletarian internationalism.[15] Finally and most importantly, the PCI and other autonomist parties had to prevent their growing autonomy from being limited by Soviet mobilization against the Chinese.

Until the mid-1970s, Eurocommunist policies of the PCI and PCE endangered the PCF's rigidly pro-Soviet position on the Sino-Soviet issue (and also its domestic anti-reformist policies). But to the PCI and PCE the answer was clear and already set forth by Togliatti in 1956: supporting Soviet foreign policies in so far as they favored East-West détente and national liberation movements; pushing Soviet policy toward endorsement of PCI reformist and autonomist positions; and resisting Soviet pressure against them and for the excommunication of the Chinese.

From the PCI's viewpoint, one may usefully divide this period in two, before and after Khrushchev's fall from power in October 1964. Khrushchev's attempt to call a conference to mobilize the various parties against the Chinese generated opposition from the PCI and the British Communist party (CPGB), which now also began taking Eurocommunist positions. In October 1963 [16] the PCI made clear that while it favored criticism of the Chinese position, which it opposed, it also insisted that the criticism not be polemical and avoid, rather than be used for, a complete break, that the PCI's own ideological positions (as set forth above) continue to be expressed. In short, the new formula—communist unity—could only be, and therefore must be, "unity in diversity and autonomy"; therefore this was not the time for a new international conference. The Romanians also opposed a conference. Thereupon Moscow ceased polemics with the Chinese, a tactical retreat which indicated its increasing vulnerability to pressure from European Communist parties. In January 1964 Togliatti, visiting Belgrade, made clear that he and the Yugoslavs both rejected a conference at that time. Thus the basis of Eurocommunist autonomism, a Yugoslav-Italian alliance with Romanian support, became obvious and public. The Chinese continued their polemics against Moscow, which replied largely in secret. A Romanian attempt at mediation failed. Bucharest thereupon in April 1964 issued its own autonomist manifesto, which *inter alia* made explicit its neutrality between Moscow and Peking. That same month the Soviets resumed public polemics against the Chinese with, as usual, full PCF support. The PCI, however, maintained its opposition to a conference, as did the Japanese Communist party.

Then in August, on a visit to Moscow, Togliatti died after having written his "Yalta memorandum," which was intended for Khrushchev only but which the PCI made public. The PCI thus committed itself to a major open challenge to Khrushchev's mobilization against Peking. The memorandum proposed reasoned discussion rather than confrontation, with a view toward renewed unity with Peking and an *aggiornamento* of the whole movement toward the PCI positions: "liberty of intellectual life, free artistic creation and scientific progress," autonomy of all parties, no organizational center, and the PCI's right to criticize the socialist world for its lack of thorough de-Stalinization. The Yugoslavs strongly supported the memorandum; the PCF was reserved; and Soviet-JCP polemics broke out, caused by Moscow's attempt to split the Japanese Communist leadership.[17]

Khrushchev's fall in October 1964 was used by the PCI and the CPGB to cement further their autonomist positions. The Soviet policy of collective mobilization against the Chinese and their excommunication did not fundamentally change after Khrushchev fell from power. Rather, Brezhnev modified this policy tactically, first, by taking a more conciliatory attitude vis-à-vis the Chinese, which Peking rejected, and second, in order to enable a Soviet rapprochement with the "neutralist" Communist parties of Vietnam, North Korea, and Cuba, by no longer demanding that they join in mobilizing against Peking. (However, Soviet relations with the JCP continued to worsen.)

Two other developments in 1965 also improved the Soviet position vis-à-vis the Chinese and the PCI: the beginning of massive American military involvement in the Vietnam war and the outbreak of the Chinese Cultural Revolution. The former provided a convenient possiblity of "uniting against"—always the best cement for any alliance: as the Soviets put it, "unity in support of the Vietnamese Revolution." Moscow wisely made this almost the sole point in its global propaganda, while Peking stubbornly resisted it and indeed slowed down Soviet military aid through China to Hanoi. This and the Cultural Revolution's xenophobia and violence repelled the West European Communist parties.

In 1965 the PCI held inconclusive talks with the Chinese—a further indication of its determination to maintain an autonomist position. The Soviets gradually retreated on the conference issue. Even before that, the March 1965 meeting in Moscow had tacitly accepted the PCI precondition that the meeting be only "consultative," i.e., that no binding decisions be adopted, by majority vote or otherwise. The final communiqué essentially reflected the PCI positions: it did not mention the Chinese, it spoke of "strengthening solidarity" and of anti-imperialist unity of action, and any international conference was de facto postponed. (The Romanians did not even attend the meeting.) [18]

At this point the beginning of massive U.S. military intervention in Vietnam and the Chinese Cultural Revolution were successfully used by the Soviets not only to improve their position against the Chinese in Pyongyang and Hanoi but also to move the JCP from a pro-Chinese to a neutral position and, finally, to bring the PCI and other Eurocommunist parties to participate in the renewed Soviet project for a conference.

That same spring of 1965 had marked the beginning of the rapprochement between the PCI and the PCF. It arose primarily because the PCF found it electorally advantageous to come to terms with Mitterand's rising Federation of the Democratic and Socialist Left (FGDS), which later became the Socialist Party (PS), and therefore had to take a more reformist position. The rapprochement occurred on the PCI's terms. It did not, however, initially involve any change in the PCF's resolutely pro-Soviet position in international affairs, but only a limited domestic reformism and a less hostile attitude toward the EEC. (Not until late 1975 did the PCF decisively change its attitude toward the CPSU.) [19]

Part of the Finnish party, influenced by similar developments in the much smaller Swedish and Norwegian parties, moved toward domestic reformism. The small Dutch party became isolationist vis-à-vis all other parties, including the Soviets. The important Spanish Communist party also began to move toward domestic reformism for the same reason as the PCF (the main Spanish Socialist party, the PSOE, was much larger) and thus also began to approach the PCI position. Eurocommunism, autonomist and reformist, was spreading rapidly.

Regional Communist consciousness began to develop, highlighted by two West European Communist conferences, in Brussels in June 1965 and in Vienna in May 1966, devoted to regional affairs rather than to relations with the Soviets or the Chinese. The PCI played a major role in these meetings, which strengthened the Eurocommunist diplomatic position vis-à-vis the CPSU.

Meanwhile, after the CPSU's attempt to call a conference on unity of action for Vietnam failed, primarily because of Korean and Vietnamese opposition in late 1966, the Soviets used the Cultural Revolution and the Vietnamese war to revive their drive for an international conference.

The first Soviet attempt to do so in a multi-party forum, at the European Communist conference at Karlovy Vary in April 1967, got nowhere, apparently because of PCI opposition. This conference was primarily directed against NATO solidarity and the developing West German *Ostpolitik*. The Yugoslavs and Romanians as well as the Norwegians, Icelanders, and Dutch boycotted the conference, and the Swedes sent only observers. The PCI was also developing its own relations with the West German SPD, while Romania unilaterally (i.e., contrary to the Warsaw Pact line) resumed diplomatic relations with Bonn. The PCF, anti-German because of French nationalism, supported the Soviet positions. The conference showed that the West European as well as the East European parties were becoming divided on issues of policies toward Western Europe, particularly toward West Germany, and that the Soviets were making little progress toward their international conference.[20]

The PCI's preconditions for agreeing to any conference

were set forth by Longo in late 1967, when he declared that Peking's obduracy and excesses had made the PCI abandon its opposition to a conference. These preconditions, which amounted to a transformation of the conference so that it would serve PCI but not Soviet purposes, included: (1) the conference must be consultative, not binding; (2) party autonomy must be strictly respected; (3) if any party chose not to attend, this could not affect its status in the movement; (4) each party could accept, not accept, or accept with reservations any decisions; and (5) the conference should establish "new forms of unity and collaboration," even with non-Communist progressive forces. In short, the Chinese could not be excommunicated, and the Soviets would have to ratify the disappearance of their primacy rather than move toward re-establishing it.[21]

A major Soviet-Romanian confrontation took place at a preparatory meeting in Budapest in February 1968, which the Cubans did not attend. The Romanians used a controversy with Arab Communists on Israel to walk out of the meeting after they had rejected an implicitly centralist speech by Suslov. Preparatory meetings continued, however, with all parties invited, including the Yugoslavs, who refused the invitation. The PCI thereafter made clear its continued organizational differences with the Soviets.

Meanwhile, the early 1968 flood of liberalization in Czechoslovakia evoked great sympathy among the Eurocommunist parties, who saw in it the prospect of liberalization in the socialist world, a development in accord with their policies and helpful to their electoral positions. Their protest against the Soviet invasion of Czechoslovakia was the first public condemnation by almost all the West European parties, including the PCF, of a major Soviet foreign policy move.[22] Romania and Yugoslavia also strongly denounced the invasion, and their relations with Moscow sharply deteriorated. So did the Chinese, who immediately ceased their open polemics against the Yugoslavs. The PCE condemnation of the invasion led the Soviets to finance an unsuccessful bid by General Enrique Líster (of Spanish Civil War fame) to depose Santiago Carrillo. (By 1974 the Soviets had abandoned this and agreed to an uneasy rapprochement with the PCE, essentially on the latter's terms—presumably in part to get Eurocommunist participation in another conference.)

Preparations for the conference resumed in early 1969. The Eurocommunists succceeded in removing from the draft declaration any explicit or implicit condemnation of the Chinese. They continued to criticize the invasion of Czechoslovakia and to reject any affirmation of the Soviet leading role. Hundreds of amendments were proposed, and the draft declaration became a kind of least common denominator.[23]

When the international Communist conference finally convened in Moscow in June 1969, it marked, as Kevin Devlin has put it, the institutionalization of diversity in the international movement. For the first time delegations were allowed to make their views public. Unable to obtain a collective condemnation of the Chinese, the Soviets compromised by having as many pro-Soviet parties as possible assail them verbally during the meeting. But in return, the Eurocommunist parties condemned the invasion of Czechoslovakia. For the first time at any international Communist meeting, the declaration was not signed by some parties: the Cuban, Swedish, British, Norwegian, and Dominican; the Romanian and Spanish signed it with reservations; and only one part of it, the anti-imperialist section, was signed by the Italian and Australian parties. Thus the Leninist myth of unanimity, for which the Soviets had fought so long, was publicly laid to rest. Eurocommunism had won the right to dissent, criticize, and reject Soviet policy even when supported by the majority at an international conference.[24]

1970-1976 [25]

For a few years after the 1969 conference, it seemed that the Soviets had persuaded the Eurocommunist parties to tone down their condemnation of the Soviet invasion of Czechoslovakia.[26] Perhaps emboldened by this, Moscow began again in 1974 to try to convene an international conference, with the same aims: to reinforce Soviet influence, condemn the Chinese, and restrain the growth of autonomism in Europe and elsewhere. The result was even more unfavorable for the Soviets than in 1969, for two primary reasons: the participation of the Yugoslavs, for the first time since 1957, and the switch of the PCF in late 1975 to opposition to the Soviet policy positions.

Brezhnev probably wanted the Yugoslavs to attend as part of his recurrent attempts to increase Soviet influence in Yugoslavia and to get them back into the "movement." It also is likely that the PCI and some other Eurocommunist parties made Yugoslav participation a precondition of their own participation as well. In addition, the Eurocommunist parties rejected the idea of an international conference and were only prepared to discuss a European one.

At the first preparatory meeting, in October 1974 at Warsaw, the Soviets felt compelled to agree to the Yugoslav (and, by extension Eurocommunist) procedural and policy conditions. The more important of the procedural conditions included: (1) the meeting must be public; (2) it must not be a continuation of any previous international meeting (i.e., those of 1957, 1960, and 1969, at which the LCY had either been absent and/or condemned); (3) its agenda must not include the convocation of an international conference; (4) no party must be in any way penalized for not attending (i.e., the Chinese must not be condemned); and—most important—all decisions must be taken by consensus, i.e., unanimously. Thus any draft declaration could only be a least common denominator of all views, and the Eurocommunists would have a blocking veto over Soviet proposals. As to policies, the Yugoslav representative declared that national roads to socialism and differing views among Communist parties were inevitable; that nonalignment was necessary and anti-hegemonist (i.e., against Soviet control) as well as anti-imperialist; that proletarian internationalism (the codeword for Soviet control) meant autonomy of and noninterference in the affairs of any party; and that therefore the conference could neither recognize a center, institutionalize itself, nor adopt binding documents.[27]

These Yugoslav positions were supported by the Romanians and Italians [28] and, surprisingly, accepted by the Soviets. The next two years were taken up by Moscow's attempt to backtrack on its acceptance. The Eurocommunists stubbornly maintained their conditions.

The main ideological (i.e., policy) issues which emerged from the prolonged series of preparatory meetings were three: proletarian internationalism, the general line, and the dictatorship of the proletariat, which reflected Moscow's insistence on Soviet primacy and the rejection of Eurocommunist reformism. During the course of the preliminary meetings the unsuccessful attempt of the Portuguese Communist party, allied with radical officers, to take power in Lisbon further polarized the pro-Soviets from the Eurocommunists.

There followed some eighteen months of further Soviet

[410]

attempts to retract their concessions to the Yugoslavs. These were reflected in prolonged Soviet ideological polemics, which arose ostensibly, and to a considerable part in reality, out of controversies arising from the developments in Chile and Portugal. Both were important for Eurocommunism. Berlinguer's elaboration of the *compromesso storico* was in large part the result of the PCI's analysis of Allende's fall. The controversy over Portuguese Communist policies, which Moscow and the PCF supported and which the PCI and PCE rejected, further highlighted Soviet-Eurocommunist tensions. To what extent there were differences in the Soviet leadership on policy toward Portugal, and therefore in part also toward Eurocommunism, remains unclear. In any case, Moscow gradually, reluctantly, but eventually cut back its immediate objectives though not its strategic goals.[29]

The other major event was the switch in policies by the PCF in late 1975. One reason for it was the continuing gains of the Socialists and the consequent rising electoral pressure on the PCF to move to the right. Another was the PCF's resentment at Brezhnev's lack of hostility toward Giscard d'Estaing. These factors probably caused the PCF to reverse its hitherto strongly pro-Soviet line. Reportedly, personal antagonism also developed between Marchais and Brezhnev. In the preparatory meeting in late 1975 the PCF began voting with the Eurocommunists against the Soviets. It also stressed even more its French nationalist line, including attacks on NATO and Bonn and, implicitly, Soviet compromise with the latter.[30]

The European Communist conference, which met in East Berlin at the end of June 1976, was a Soviet defeat and a Eurocommunist victory. True, the conference was held, and its unanimously accepted declaration endorsed the main lines of Soviet foreign policy. But the declaration was neither signed nor declared to be binding, strongly affirmed the independence of each party, gave no special status to the Soviets, endorsed dialogue with non-Communist progressives and non-alignment, and made no mention of (i.e., refused to accept the Soviet position on) proletarian internationalism, the general line, and the dictatorship of the proletariat. Berlinguer and Carrillo reaffirmed their Eurocommunist positions and declared that they would not take part in another such conference.[31]

EUROCOMMUNIST DIPLOMACY AFTER THE EAST BERLIN CONFERENCE [32]

That Moscow had been the loser at the East Berlin conference was clear to most Western analysts and, through their articles and the more veiled coverage in the Eurocommunist press, to most of the politically active West European Communists. The Soviets did not intend, of course, to give this impression within their own sphere. In East Germany, *Neues Deutschland* had to publish the full text of all the speeches. The Soviet and pro-Soviet East European press, however, censored all indications of organizational or ideological differences at the conference and continued to stress proletarian internationalism and the dictatorship of the proletariat as though they had been endorsed in the declaration—indeed, at times saying that they had. Moscow also indirectly indicated that it had not abandoned its goal of a new international Communist conference,[33] one which the Eurocommunists had declared that they would not attend.

Although Belgrade publicized and condemned these Soviet moves,[34] at first the PCI and the PCF did not mention them and paid less attention than before to Soviet dissident activity.

One wondered, therefore, whether a de-escalation of polemics such as had occurred after the 1969 conference [35] might again be under way.

Any hopes that the Soviets may have had in this respect, however, were soon disappointed. PCI-Czechoslovak polemics broke out in August over the anniversary of the Soviet invasion of Czechoslovakia, and the PCI and the PCF replied in kind to Bulgarian and Hungarian attacks on Eurocommunism.[36] Polemics escalated further as a result of increased Soviet and East European repression of dissident activity, especially the Plyushch and Bukovsky cases in the Soviet Union, the Biermann and Havemann cases in East Germany, and the revival in early 1977 of dissident activity in Prague.[37] There is some evidence that Eurocommunism, and especially the publication of the conference speeches in *Neues Deutschland,* had encouraged and given self-legitimization to Soviet and East European dissidents. So, also, had the Helsinki CSCE Final Act, which has turned out to be a boomerang for the Soviets, and also President Carter's human rights declarations and other expressions of Western non-Communist support.

By the end of 1976 Soviet-Yugoslav relations began to worsen again. Brezhnev's unsuccessful visit to Belgrade in late 1976, where reportedly he asked for a Soviet naval base on the coast of Yugoslavia, overflight rights, and high-level Yugoslav representation in the Warsaw Pact, may well have been the major cause for this development.[38] Subsequently, Soviet publications began to voice the kind of criticism of Yugoslav policies which had not been heard for some years, to which Belgrade replied with sharp press attacks.

What was much more important was that in late February 1977 the head of the LCY international department, Aleksandar Grličkov, published the most authoritative and extensive definition of the Eurocommunist autonomist position which

[413]

has so far appeared, and one which directly if implicitly challenged the Soviet ideological position. He declared that there are "objective" and often "antagonistic" contradictions among socialist nations. These cannot be solved by hegemonic or monolithic internationalism, for

> the internationalist interest does not exist in itself and for itself . . . but proceeds from and rests on concrete historic national interests of the working class [and] thus presupposes . . . national interests in their entirety . . .

Therefore,

> . . . in order to become the leading forces of society, the working class and the communist and workers' parties must necessarily raise themselves to the level of national force . . . as authentic representatives . . . of the national interests in their countries . . .

The proper and only possible combination of national and international interests, he concluded, is a "dialectical unity," "unity in diversity" (the PCI slogan), based on "national, autonomist, and independent communist and workers' parties." In short, national interests have priority over Soviet policy.[39]

In Eastern Europe, tension remained high in Poland after the June 1976 workers' demonstrations. The Biermann and Havemann cases sparked significant intellectual protests in East Germany. The "Declaration of 77" in Prague marked the revival of intellectual protest in Czechoslovakia.

Moscow made clear that it would not make ideological or strategic concessions to Eurocommunism. It would accept Eurocommunist tactics but only if their strategic goal re-

[414]

mained the Leninist model of socialism. A Soviet Central Committee resolution of January 31, 1977, identified Soviet "strength" as the principal cause of détente, declared that "in the present stage of world development there is an intensification of the class struggle in the international arena" (an ominous revival of Stalin's ideological formula for justifying the great purges of the 1930s), and insisted on proletarian internationalism and "real socialism," i.e., the Soviet model.[40]

One final point: East-West détente in Europe is objectively at least as destabilizing as it is stabilizing. For by encouraging more contacts between East and West, it produces ideological and political as well as economic re-engagement—i.e., competition.[41] It may be, as Leopold Labedz has called it, a race in "competitive decadence," but it does encourage intellectual dissidence and the regimes' repression of it in the East, while it makes more difficult the maintenance of defense budgets in the West. And by favoring dissidence in the East, it forces the Eurocommunists, whether they want to or not, to take exception to its repression, thus accentuating Soviet-Eurocommunist tensions and further encouraging and giving self-legitimization to the dissidents.

The process of interaction or, as the Soviets must see it, of contamination, between Eurocommunism and the Soviet Union and, even more, East Europe was thus already under way. How long this escalatory cycle would last, however, and to where it would lead, remained unclear in late 1977. And the Eurocommunist leaders were quite aware of it. As an Italian Communist well put it,

... it is inevitable that the socialist opposition to socialist governments in the East (for example, Havemann in the DDR and Medvedev in the USSR) should link themselves at least ideologically with Eurocommunism. It is

[415]

equally inevitable that the Italian, French, or Spanish "model" should become a political problem for the ruling communist parties of Eastern Europe . . .

Or as Carrillo had said earlier, the U.S.S.R. would of course "view with concern" Western European pluralistic socialism

. . . not dependent upon the USSR itself, and with a political structure different from that of the peoples' democracies. There is no doubt that the latter will look more and more toward West European models of social-ism, if we reach that point.[42]

The Eurocommunists, the Chinese, and the Soviets

One might have thought that given the Eurocommunists' bad relations with Moscow, their relations with Peking, which collapsed in the early 1960s, might have revived. Through 1977 and early 1978, however, they had not, in spite of efforts by the PCI and PCE to lower the tension. In 1971 Carrillo visited Peking and was asked by the PCI to try there to improve its relations with Peking as well.[43] However, Carrillo and the Chinese only agreed to disagree. When Mao Tse-tung died in late 1976, the PCI and PCF paid enthusiastic public tributes to him. Peking did not publish them but did not reject them, as it did the Soviet and East European ones. Thereupon both sides publicly reiterated their continuing desire for better relations.[44]

The Eurocommunists have one fundamental common inter-est with the Chinese: independence from Soviet hegemony. Moreover, just as the Chinese had stopped public attacks on Yugoslavia the day that Moscow invaded Czechoslovakia, so

[416]

THE DIPLOMACY OF EUROCOMMUNISM

their post-Mao references to Yugoslavia, although few, were not unfavorable.[45] One may therefore conclude that Peking was waiting until the PCI, PCE, and the PCF became more overtly anti-Soviet before reciprocating their friendly gestures. It was also putting them under pressure by making more favorable references to West European Maoists than before. And as for their "revisionism," which Peking had so denounced in the 1960s, the Chinese made favorable references to the patriotism (but not the liberalism) of the "Charter 77" group in Prague.[46]

Meanwhile, in February 1977 Moscow resumed polemics against the Chinese, after have suspended them after Mao's death in the vain hope that a Sino-Soviet rapprochement would occur. This apparently reflected the failure of the renewed Sino-Soviet border negotiations.[47] Thus the Soviets were likely again to attempt to line up allies against the Chinese, a policy which in the past had created tensions with the Eurocommunists.

In 1977, also, inter-party tension between Moscow and the Eurocommunists were increasing. Whether they would continue to do so or not was unclear. Indeed, there were some signs that the Soviets and the PCI and the PCF were trying to limit polemics. In early March at the Madrid Eurocommunist summit meeting Soviet pressure reportedly prevented Berlinguer and Marchais from joining Carrillo in open criticism of Moscow.[48] Moscow then cut key passages out of its version of the Madrid communiqué.[49] At Soviet-sponsored multi-party meetings at Sofia [50] and Prague [51] in March and April the Czechoslovak and Bulgarian delegations led the attack on Eurocommunism, Ponomarev took a less extreme position, and the Poles and Hungarians even more moderate ones. Carrillo's book was published in April. In June the Soviet *New Times (Novoe Vremya)* published a slashing attack on it.

It charged that Carrillo "counterposed" West and East European Communist parties on an "anti-Soviet platform," discredited socialism, especially the Soviet Union, and renounced a joint multi-party line in favor of division of Europe and a stronger NATO. "Eurocommunism," the *New Times* went on, weakens and splits communism "for the interests of imperialism," leads to a "split in the international communist movement," and interferes in internal Soviet party affairs because of its "conscious anti-Sovietism" and "renunciation of Marxism-Leninism." Communists must struggle, the Soviet article concluded, against "those who would insert divisive ideas into the communist movement." [52]

The PCE replied to Moscow in at least as violent a tone.[53] The Yugoslavs supported Carrillo the most strongly of the other Communist parties.[54] The Romanians reiterated their autonomist position.[55] The PCI downplayed the dispute [56] but sent a delegation to Moscow which reportedly got the Soviets to agree to suspend polemics against the PCE,[57] and Moscow did for a time execute a partial tactical retreat.[58] The PCF downplayed the issue almost completely. Among Moscow's allies, the Czechoslovaks, Bulgarians, and East Germans joined in the Soviet attack. The Poles [59] and Hungarians [60] were more moderate until Moscow brought them back into line. Even the East Germans took a less hard line than the Soviets, Czechoslovaks, and Bulgarians.[61] Later, Kádár reportedly sponsored another attempt at mediation between Moscow and the Eurocommunists.[62] The Soviets then invited Carrillo to attend the November 1977 Moscow ceremonies for the sixtieth anniversary of the Bolshevik Revolution; [63] but when he arrived, he was not called on to address the gathering and was seated in a back row.[64] Thereupon he left Moscow before schedule for Belgrade,[65] Rome,[66] Madrid—and the United

States, where he lectured at Yale, Johns Hopkins and Harvard.[67] As he said to western correspondents in Moscow:

> . . . There must be some kind of debate. Otherwise, they simply would have told me right from the begining they weren't going to allow me to speak. But as to who is on what side—I do not know the secrets of the Kremlin. . . .[68]

And in Belgrade:

> . . . Eurocommunism is going well: when Kissinger agrees with some of the Soviet comrades in affirming that Eurocommunism does not exist and Lister associates himself with this judgment, this confirms that Eurocommunism exists and is in good health. . . .[69]

Shortly thereafter Suslov and Ponomarov, while disclaiming Soviet hegemonic intentions, reiterated the importance of "proletarian internationalism" and the "common objective laws" of the construction of "real socialism" and communism; i.e., while the West European parties may for tactical reasons come to socialism differently from the way Moscow did, once they do, their socialism must follow the Soviet model, which they must not criticize.[70] By the end of 1977 Moscow was thus continuing to polemicize esoterically with the West European Communists, attempting thereby to assert its primacy *de facto* while denying it in theory.

As to issues that might further exacerbate relations, one of the most likely ones, it seemed in 1977, was the question of whether, and if so to what extent, the Soviet Union is a socialist state. The PCE had begun to raise this question and answer it at least partially in the negative, but so far no other Eurocommunist party has. To the extent that they do so, they are not only rejecting the Leninist model for themselves but questioning the Soviet implementation of it, if not, indeed, the model itself.

The other issue may also be only swept partially under the table at present: Moscow's acceptance of Eurocommunist reformism as a tactical method but its insistence on retaining the Leninist model as the universal ultimate strategic goal. Esoteric polemics on this issue continue between Moscow and the Eurocommunist parties.

Eurocommunism and the JCP and ACP

The Japanese [71] and Australian [72] CPs may be seen as in an advanced stage of Eurocommunist autonomism from the Soviet Union—and from the Chinese as well. (The JCP is important—at least as much as the PCE; the ACP is as weak as the CPGB.) As happened with the PCE, Moscow tried to split both parties. In Japan the splinter group which it financed, the "Shiga group," made little progress; but in Australia the largely trade-union-based pro-Soviet group offers serious competition to the more intellectual and somewhat New Leftist ACP. In both parties the center also beat off challenges by Peking-supported Maoist groups. The JPC and the ACP became reformist for the same basically electoral reasons and in large part under the influence of Eurocommunism. (An essentially Eurocommunist challenge in the Venezuelan CP was beaten off by the pro-Soviet leadership.) [73]

It is not surprising, therefore, that contacts have been stepped up among the Eurocommunist parties, including in 1976 the PCF and the JCP. Many more visits have been exchanged. Common declarations made clear the desire of both sides to cooperate on an essentially common platform that included the main themes of Eurocommunist reformism and autonomism.[74] Moscow is thus confronted by the fact that if it were to break with the West European Eurocommunist parties, they would already have allies in East Asia.

Whether or not the JCP and ACP developments portended similar ones in the West European CPs one could not foresee. They did, however, show that Moscow was prepared to continue to use splitting tactics against autonomist and reformist opponents. In East Asia, however, this Soviet "splittism" was probably a result in part of Sino-Soviet rivalry. Its failure to reacquire control over the JCP and the ACP might make similar Soviet tactics in Western Europe more unlikely.

Eurocommunist Diplomacy in the Non-Communist World

One major aspect of the revival of nationalist traditions and the decline of Soviet influence among the West European Communist parties was, as it had been for Belgrade after the 1948 Soviet-Yugoslav break, their development of their own foreign policies toward the non-Communist world, reflecting their own national traditions. I shall discuss them with respect to Western European Socialist parties, the EEC, NATO and the United States, and the Third World.

The European Socialists

As the West European Communists moved toward reformism, regionalism, and autonomy from Moscow, they naturally

[421]

increased their contacts with the West European Socialist parties, thus diminishing the existing gap. With the more left-wing Socialists in France (the PS) [75] and Spain (the PSOE) the Communists hoped—unsuccessfully as it turned out—to form majority parliamentary coalitions. The PCI preferred a coalition with the Christian Democrats but also wanted to keep on good terms with the PSI. And although the West German Social Democratic Party (SPD) was strongly anti-Communist and the West German Communist party (the DKP) was electorally insignificant, pro-Soviet, and a creature of East Berlin and Moscow, the SPD was important for the Eurocommunists because it had so effectively supported the Portuguese Socialists and contributed to the defeat of the pro-Soviet Communists there. After the election of SPD chairman Willy Brandt as its head, the Socialist International began to be revitalized, and the tension within it between the West German and the French Socialist parties seemed somewhat less. Moreover, should a Eurocommunist party come to power, as the minority or, even more, as the majority in a parliamentary coalition, it would need West German credits to stem the inevitable resultant flight of capital. And as long as the SPD remains in power in Bonn, this means that such a coalition would need the SPD all the more. As for the British Labour party, although London's general foreign policy weakness lowers its influence, its importance within the Socialist International makes the Eurocommunists cultivate it as well.

The EEC

The initial hostility of all European Communist parties, east and west, to the EEC has gradually given way to grudging acceptance of it. However much it still symbolizes capitalism,

American influence, multinational, U.S.-controlled corporations, and anti-communism, the EEC, like its West European
members, has become an economic although not a political
success. Even the Soviet Union, therefore, recently began to
face up to dealing with it.

From the beginning of Eurcommunism, first the PCI and
the PCE, and only recently and very partially the PCF, have
taken a less hostile attitude than the Soviets have toward the
EEC. So have the Yugoslavs and Romanians. These attitudes
reflected majority political sentiment in their countries. Most
Italians, like most Belgians and Dutch, approve of the EEC
because it helps their economies and protects them against
French or German domination. Most Spaniards want to "return to Europe." While most Frenchmen favor the EEC in
general, if only because of the enormous advantages that
French agriculture draws from the Common Agricultural
Policy (CAP), the PCF is primarily working-class, not peas-
ant, in membership and it has long shared Soviet hostility to
the EEC. However, PCI participation in the EEC organs has
had some influence on the PCF. Even so, although during the
last year the PCF has become slightly less hostile to the EEC,
the PCF, unlike the PCI and the PCE, still opposes European
political union.

One other, related point. I have said that Eurocommunism
has elements of West European regionalism. Carrillo has made
clear that he envisages a united, socialist Western Europe
equidistant between Moscow and Washington—nonaligned
Communist parties, so to speak, in a nonaligned Western
Europe.[76] By late 1977 the nationalism and anti-Sovietism of
the PCF—stronger by then than the PCI's—could almost be
called "Gaullocommunism": fearful, like most, of West German domination of Western Europe, still deeply suspicious of
the United States, and now of the Soviet Union as well.

[423]

NATO and the United States

The differing Eurocommunist views on the EEC were paralleled by their differing views on NATO and the United States, which largely reflected the national traditions and post-1945 policies of their countries. The PCI and PCE favor their countries remaining in NATO as long as it and the Warsaw Pact Organization continue to exist. Most Italians have preferred alliance with the United States to deter French or German domination. Most Spaniards also do so, for the same reason, and in addition look upon becoming a part of NATO as a step in their re-entry into the Western community of nations.

In contrast, the great majority of Frenchmen, like the PCF, continue to endorse de Gaulle's withdrawal of France from the NATO integrated military command, which they regard, as does the PCF, as an American- and West German-dominated organization. Like the Gaullists, the PCF opposes any French reintegration into the NATO unified command. Finally, the PCI and the PCE also share the fears of Italians and Spaniards that Moscow may re-acquire control over Yugoslavia after Tito's death. This and electoral considerations explain why during the June 1976 parliamentary election campaign, Berlinguer endorsed Italian membership in NATO as a shield behind which socialism can best be constructed in Italy.[77] Moreover, the PCI and the PCE were anxious to improve their relations with Washington, which had considerable influence in both countries, while the PCF, in a country where U.S. influence was low, remained basically anti-American.

The Third World

If anyone expected the Eurocommunist parties to become less supportive of radical movements in the Third World because of their reformism, regionalism, or autonomism, he has certainly been disappointed. It is not difficult to see why the Eurocommunist parties continued these policies. First, support of radical Third World movements protects them from the threat from their own left-wing factions, for whom guerrilla wars against the imperialists are the *summum bonum*. Second, it protects them against Soviet accusations that they are abandoning the Third World to its fate. And third, since many Eurocommunist parties are Mediterranean parties and therefore concerned, like their countries, about Africa and the Middle East, why should they be, for example, less pro-Arab than Giscard d'Estaing? Thus, continued Eurocommunist support of radical Third World movements protects them, while its abandonment would endanger their interests.

* * *

Eurocommunist diplomacy thus far has been remarkably successful in achieving its own aims. It has steadily enlarged its own field of maneuver vis-à-vis Moscow, increased its domestic electoral appeal, and improved its own image in the non-Communist world—all without breaking with the Soviets or the Soviets breaking with it.

Yet its greatest challenges proabbly lie ahead. It is far from clear that the Soviets will never break with the Eurocommunists. As Eurocommunists come closer to participation in West European governments, their foreign policy problems are bound to become more difficult. Finally, post-Tito

Yugoslavia [78] will be less stable and more tempting to Moscow. Because the LCY is the most powerful autonomist European Communist party, and because renewed Soviet control over Yugoslavia would menace Eurocommunism as well as stability in Europe, this may well be the greatest diplomatic challenge that Eurocommunism will have to face.

NOTES

1. I take the term from Zbigniew Brzezinski, *The Soviet Bloc* (New York: Praeger, 1961).

2. See especially Alexander Fischer, *Sowjetische Deutschlandpolitik im Zweiten Weltkrieg 1941-1945* (Stuttgart: Deutsche Verlags-Anstalt, 1975) for Soviet and KPD wartime preparations for bolshevizing all of Germany or at least the Soviet occupation zone.

3. See the standard work on PCI foreign policy, Donald L.M. Blackmer, *Unity in Diversity* (Cambridge, Mass.: M.I.T. Press, 1968).

4. Alberto Jacoviello, *Le Monde,* September 12-13, 1976.

5. Blackmer, *Unity in Diversity.*

6. A. Ross Johnson, "The Sino-Soviet Relationship and Yugoslavia 1949-1971," RAND P-4591, April 1970.

7. What follows is based primarily on work by Kevin Devlin of Radio Free Europe, Munich, and particularly on his unpublished MS. history of Sino-Soviet relations. For the 1957 meeting, see the chapter, "The Moscow Meetings, II."

8. Ingrao in *Rinascita,* September 17, 1976.

9. *Problemi del movimento operaio internazionale, 1956-1961* (Rome: Riuniti, 1962), pp. 222, 228, 230-31, quoted from Devlin, "The Moscow Meetings, I," p. 31.

10. Ingrao, *op. cit.*

11. *Albania Today* (Tirana), no. 6 (25), November-December 1975.

12. Edward Crankshaw, *The New Cold War* (N.Y.: Penguin, 1963).

13. See William E. Griffith, *Albania and the Sino-Soviet Rift* (Cambridge, Mass.: M.I.T. Press, 1963); *The Sino-Soviet Rift* (Cambridge, Mass.: M.I.T. Press, 1964); and *Sino-Soviet Relations, 1964-1965* (Cambridge, Mass.: M.I.T. Press, 1967).

14. William E. Griffith, "The November 1960 Moscow Meeting: A Preliminary Reconstruction," *The China Quarterly,* July-September 1962, to be supplemented by Devlin, "The Moscow Meetings, IV" and especially the revealing new Albanian documentation in *Albania Today,* November-December 1975.

15. Devlin, "The Moscow Meetings, VI," p. 7.

16. *Ibid.,* pp. 20-22.

17. *Ibid.,* pp. 22-85.

18. *Ibid.,* pp. 85-116; Griffith, *Sino-Soviet Relations, 1964-1965,* pp. 83-91.

19. Devlin, "The Moscow Meetings, VI," pp. 116-36.

20. Wolfgang Berner, "Das Karlsbader Aktionsprogramm," *Europa Archiv,* June 10, 1967.

21. Devlin, "Khrushchev's Peak and Brezhnev's Foothill," *Radio Free Europe Research,* June 4, 1969.

22. Devlin, *op. cit.;* Heinz Brahm, "Das Echo im Weltkommunismus auf die Okkupation der Tschechoslowakei," *Europa Archiv,* Oct. 25, 1968.

23. Devlin, *op. cit.*

24. Devlin, "The Interparty Drama," *Problems of Communism,* July-August 1975; Heinz Timmermann, "Das dritte Moskauer Kommunistenkonzil," *Europa Archiv,* October 10, 1969, and "Mehr Vielfalt als Einheit," *Osteuropa,* December 1969.

25. What follows is largely based on my "Soviet-American Regional Competition, 1976: 'Eurocommunism': The Third Great Communist Schism?" M.I.T./Center for International Studies, mimeo., November 1976, q.v. for full bibliographical citations. A revised version will be published in a collective volume edited by Karl Kaiser and Hans-Peter Schwarz for the Deutsche Gesellschaft für auswärtige Politik.

26. Kevin Devlin, "Interparty Relations: Limits of 'Normalization,'" *Problems of Communism,* July-August 1971; William E. Griffith, ed., *The World and the Great Power Triangles* (Cambridge, Mass.: M.I.T. Press, 1975), p. 5.

27. *Socialist Thought and Practice* (Belgrade), October 1974, pp. 44-54. See Devlin, "The Challenge of Eurocommunism," *Problems of Communism,* January-February 1977.

28. *Scînteia,* October 22, 1976; *L'Unità,* October 17, 1976.

29. Kevin Devlin, "The Challenge of Eurocommunism"; Heinz Timmermann, "Die Konferenz der europäischen Kommunisten in Ost-Berlin," *Europa Archiv,* October 10, 1976; Eusebio Mujal-Leon,

"The Portuguese Communist Party in Context," *Problems of Communism*, January-February 1977; Joan Barth Urban, "Contemporary Soviet Perspectives on Revolution in the West," *Orbis*, Winter 1976, and "Socialist Pluralism in Soviet and Italian Communist Perspective: The Chilean Catalyst," *ibid.*, Summer 1974; Gerhard Wettig, "Entspannungs- und Klassenpolitik. Das sowjetische Verhalten gegenüber Portugal," *Beiträge zur Konfliktforschung*, no. 1, 1976.

30. Kevin Devlin, "The Challenge of Eurocommunism"; Leonard Schapiro, "The International Department of the CPSU: Key to Soviet Policy," *International Journal* (Toronto), Winter 1976-77.

31. The official texts of the conference speeches are in *Konferenz der kommunistischen und Arbeiterparteien Europas, 29 und 30 Juni 1976. Dokumente und Reden* ([East] Berlin: Dietz, 1976.) This includes the otherwise unpublished *Geschäftsordnung*, which provides that the document will not be signed, that "The text of the document submitted to the conference will neither be changed nor added to during the course of the conference" (Art. 9), and that all media will have full access to the proceedings. See also Kevin Devlin, "The Challenge of Eurocommunism"; Heinz Timmermann, "Die Konferenz der europäischen Kommunisten in Ost-Berlin"; and B.A. Osadczuk-Korab, "Brezhnev's Pyrrhic Victory: The Pan-European Conference of Communists in East Berlin," *International Journal* (Toronto), Winter 1976-77.

32. See Devlin, "The Challenge of Eurocommunism," and Timmermann, "Eurokommunismus."

33. See the pro-Soviet South African CP's *The African Communist*, no. 67 (Fourth Quarter 1976), p. 19.

34. Slobodan Stanković, "Party Theoreticians Reject Soviet Supremacy," *Radio Free Europe Research*, September 22, 1976; "Yugoslav Reaction to Tough Soviet Articles," *ibid.*, September 27,

[429]

1976; "Yugoslav-Soviet Relations Following Brezhnev's Visit," *ibid.*, February 28, 1977.

35. Griffith, *The World and the Great Power Triangles*, p. 5.

36. Dezsö Nemes, "Lessons of Class Struggle for Power in Hungary," *World Marxist Review*, September 1976; Jean Kanapa in *France Nouvelle*, October 5, 1976; Todor Zhivkov, "A Year of Peace, a Year of Struggle," *World Marxist Review*, December 1976; A. Rubbi, "Berlino: oltre le polemiche," *Rinascita*, July 30, 1976; Kevin Devlin, "Hungarian-PCF Polemics: Kanapa Counterattacks," *Radio Free Europe Research*, October 6, 1976.

37. Thomas E. Heneghan, "Civil Rights Dissent Spreads in Eastern Europe," *Radio Free Europe Research*, January 28, 1977.

38. *The New York Times*, January 9, 1977.

39. See the critical articles by Zoran Zujović in *Politika* (Belgrade), January 27 and 28, 1977 (summary: FBIS/EE/February 4, 1977/I 10-11) on references to the 1948 Yugoslav expulsion from the Cominform in the 5th edition of Boris Ponomarev, et al., eds., *Istoriya KPSS* (Moscow): 1976); and a criticism by B. Jovanić in *Komunist*, February 1977 (summary: FBIS/EE/February 23, 1977/I 13-14) of an article by B.M. Lebyzon in *Voprosy istorii KPSS*, and Grličkov, "The National and the International," *Socijalizam*, March 1977, also in *Borba*, February 22 through 28, 1977 (FBIS/EE/March 18, 1977/I 6-21); analysis: Slobodan Stanković, "Party Official Defends Primacy of 'National Interests,' " *Radio Free Europe Research*, March 8, 1977.

40. *Pravda*, February 1, 1977. See also P. Fedoseyev, "The 25th CPSU Congress and Questions of Marxist-Leninist Theory," and K. Zarodov, "A Victorious Democratic Revolution," *World Marxist Review*, February 1977; Pierre Hassner, "L'U.R.S.S.,

[430]

l'eurocommunisme et l'Europe occidentale," *Défense nationale,* January 1977.

41. See the seminal article by Pierre Hassner, "L'Europe de la guerre froide à la paix chaude," *Défense nationale,* March 1973.

42. Interview with Lucio Lombardo Radice in *La Stampa,* December 8, 1976, analyzed in Kevin Devlin, "PCI Scholar Wants Deeper Analysis of Regimes," *Radio Free Europe Research,* December 13, 1976; Carrillo in *Il Manifesto,* November 1, 1975, quoted from Kevin Devlin, "The Challenge of Eurocommunism." *L'Unità* then publicly took issue with the article.

43. Eusebio Mujal-Leon, "Spanish Communism in the 1970s," *Problems of Communism,* March-April 1975; Ingrao in *Rinascita,* September 17, 1976.

44. Devlin, "The Challenge of Eurocommunism."

45. E.g., *Peking Review,* January 7, 1977, p. 4.

46. *Ibid.,* February 4, 1977.

47. "Observer," "Anti-Soviet Fabrications," *Pravda,* February 10, 1977; departure of Soviet border negotiator Ilyichev from Peking; "New Tsars Push a National Annexation Policy" and "Exploitation and Oppression of Non-Russian People in Central Asia," *Peking Review,* March 4, 1977.

48. Communiqué: *L'Humanité* and *L'Unità,* March 4, 1977; various accounts in FBIS/WEU/March 4, 1977/N1-5.

49. CD [Christian Duevel], "Moscow Uses Censorship to Dissociate Itself from the Madrid Communiqué," *Radio Liberty Research,* March 4, 1977.

50. Frane Barbieri from Budapest, "L'antivertice di Sofia," *Il Giornale,* April 12, 1977; Manuel Lucbert, "La virulence des attaques contre le P.C.E. embarrasse les Polonais et les Hongrois," *Le Monde,* June 26-27, 1977.

51. Ponomarev speech, *Pravda,* April 28, 1977 (FBIS/SOV/May 2, 1977/D1-4); "An Important Political Meeting of Communists," *Pravda,* May 9, 1977; Kevin Devlin, "Soviet Hopes Dashed at Prague Meeting," *Radio Free Europe Research,* May 3, 1977; "Soviet Interpretation of Prague Meeting Stirs Controversy," *Radio Liberty Research,* May 14, 1977; Frane Barbieri, "Ponomariov al contrattacco," *Il Giornale,* April 30, 1977.

52. "Contrary to the Interests of Peace and Socialism in Europe," *New Times,* no. 24, June 1977.

53. PCE CC communiqué, June 25, 1977, and Carrillo conference, June 27, 1977, and interview in *Le Monde,* June 28, 1977 (FBIS/WEU/June 29, 1977/N1-6); wha. [Walther Haubricht] from Madrid, "Die Führung der spanischen Kommunisten wehrt sich gegen Moskauer Pressionen," *Frankfurter Allgemeine Zeitung,* June 27, 1977 (with text of PCE CC communiqué); Kevin Devlin, "Spanish CP Counterattacks: Moscow Rebuked," *RFE Research,* June 28, 1977 and "Carrillo: 'Others Split Communism,'" *ibid.,* September 2, 1977. For general analysis, see Kevin Devlin, "Interparty Echoes of the Carrillo Case," *Radio Free Europe Research,* July 6, 1977; C.A. "Eurocommunist Stocktaking," *ibid.,* August 4, 1977; Leo Mates, "Why Moscow Must Live with Eurocommunism," *The Observer,* August 14, 1977; Frane Barbieri, "Mosca: pluralismo formula famigerata," *Il Giornale,* June 25, 1977.

54. Milika Sundić, Radio Belgrade, June 24, 1977, 1400 GMT and Radio Zagreb, June 26, 1977, 1800 GMT (FBIS/EEU/June 27, 1977/I1-3); *Kommunist,* June 27, 1977 and *Vjesnik,* June 25, 1977, cited from Slobodan Stanković, "Belgrade Defends Carrillo Against Moscow Attacks," *RFE Research,* June 28, 1977.

55. *Scînteia,* July 5, 1977 (FBIS/EEU/July 7, 1977/H2-7); V. M. [Viktor Meier] in *Frankfurter Allgemeine Zeitung,* August 2, 1977 (on Carrillo visit to Bucharest).

56. "Eurocommunism, *Novoye Vremya,* and Us," *L'Unità,* June 28, 1977 (FBIS/WEU/June 30, 1977/L1-3).

57. "Eurocommunism, *Novoye Vremya,* and Us," *L'Unità,* June 28, 1977 (FBIS/WEU/June 30, 1977/L1-3; CPSU/PCI communiqué: July 3, 1977 (FBIS/WEU/July 7, 1977/E1); *Le Monde,* July 5, 1977; Romano Ledda (PCI CC), "Diversity and Internationalism," *Rinascita,* July 1, 1977 (FBIS/WEU/July 20, 1977/L1-3; *L'Unità,* July 7, 1977 (FBIS/WEU/July 14, 1977/L9-11); Urban, "Moscow and the PCI: Kto Kovo," and especially Frane Barbieri from Belgrade, " 'Tu quoque, Santiago,' " *Il Giornale,* July 1, 1977, from Budapest, "Il Pci ha deluso Carrillo rimasto solo contra Mosca," *ibid.,* July 7, 1977, and from Madrid, "Avallato da Pajetta l'attaco a Carrillo?," *ibid.,* July 8, 1977.

58. "Putting the Record Straight," *New Times,* no. 28, July 1977. For PCE reaction, see the interview with Azcárate (PCE Politburo and Secretariat member responsible for international affairs), " 'Non esiste eurocomunismo che non parte da un guidizio negativo sull'Unione Sovietica,' " *Il Giornale,* July 9, 1977.

59. Bogumil Sujka (Deputy Head, International Department, KC PZPR), "W kwestii solidarności internacjionalistycznej," *Nowe drogi,* August 1977; Kazimierz Zamorski, "Polish Criticism of Carrillo: Support for 'Red Socialism,' " *RFE Research,* September 27, 1977; Jerzy Kraszewski in *Trybuna ludu,* August 3, 1977 (FBIS/EEU/August 7, 1977/G1-7).

60. See Kádár's favorable references to Eurocommunism in press conferences in Austria in December 1976 and in West Germany and Italy in June 1977 *(New York Times,* December 6, 1976; *L'Unità,* June 10, July 1, 1977). For retreat, see János Berecz

(Head, International Dept., CC MSzMP), "Our Debates and Our Unity," *Népszabadság,* July 24, 1977 (FBIS/EEU/July 26, 1977/ F1-4).

61. Heinz Timmermann, "Die Beziehungen Ost-Berlins zu den jugoslawischen and zu den 'Eurokommunisten,'" *Berichte des Bundesinstituts für ostwissenschaftliche und internationale Studien,* no. 41, July 1977, and "Carrillo, Moskau und die SED," *Deutschland Archiv,* no. 8, July 25, 1977.

62. Yankovitch from Belgrade in *Le Monde,* Oct. 6, 1977.

63. See the interview with the CPSU emissary Viktor Afanasyev (editor-in-chief of *Pravda),* in *El País,* Oct. 18, 1977 (FBIS/SOV/ October 26, 1977/E1-4), e.g., *"Novoye Vremya's* criticisms of Santiago Carrillo . . . were not the opinion of an official party organ." See also Acoca from Madrid in the *Washington Post,* October 24, 1977.

64. *Pravda,* November 11, 1977 (TASS, English, November 10, 1977, 1545 GMT, in FBIS/SOV/November 11, 1977/A1-8). See also Suslov in *Pravda,* November 3, 1977 (FBIS/SOV/November 2, 1977/P1-18) and K. Zarodov in *ibid.,* August 26, 1977 (FBIS/ SOV/August 30, 1977/A6-11); Flora Lewis, "Tug-of-War Reported in Moscow on Approach to Eurocommunism," *New York Times,* October 17, 1977. For background on the incident, see "Le P.C.E. conteste la version soviétique," *Le Monde,* November 9, 1977; Afanasyev in TASS, quoted in the *New York Times,* November 7, 1977; and especially Kevin Devlin, "Soviets Block Carrillo's Speech," *Radio Free Europe Research,* November 7, 1977.

65. LCY-PCE communiqué, TANJUG in Serbo-Croat, November 10, 1977, 1049 GMT (FBIS/EEU/November 11, 1977/I1-3) (very cordial).

66. See the Italian press coverage in FBIS/WEU/November 14,

1977/L1-8, and "M. Berlinguer marque ses distances à l'égard de M. Carrillo," *Le Monde*, November 12, 1977.

67. Kevin Devlin, "Eurocommunism and the States: Carrillo's Historic Visit," *Radio Free Europe Research*, November 15, 1977.

68. Whitney from Moscow in the *New York Times*, November 4, 1977.

69. Quoted in Barbieri from Belgrade in *Il Giornale*, November 10, 1977. Lister, who recently returned to Spain, headed a Soviet-supported effort in the early and mid-1970s to depose Carrillo. See "La dernière bataille du général Lister contrel 'euro-opportunisme' de M. Carrillo," *Le Monde*, November 10, 1977. See also Zdenko Antic, "Yugoslavs, the October Revolution and Carrillo," *Radio Free Europe Research*, November 14, 1977, and Kevin Devlin, "Lister 'Against Form and Timing' of Soviet Intervention in CSSR," and "The Return of the Native: Carrillo's pro-Soviet Rule," *ibid.*, both November 10, 1977.

70. In speeches at an international scientific-theoretical conference on "The Great October Revolution and the Contemporary Epoch," *Pravda*, November 11, 1977 (TASS summaries: FBIS/SOV/ November 11, 1977/A1-4). See also L. I. Brezhnev, "A Historic Stage on the Road to Communism," *World Marxist Review*, December 1977; Alexander Sobolev, "Common Heritage of the Revolutionary Forces," *New Times*, no. 44, October 1977; and, for analysis, Frane Barbieri, "Stato guida cercasi," *Il Giornale*, November 11, 1977.

71. See Manfred Pohl, *Die Kommunisitsche Partei Japans* (Hamburg: Mitteilungen des Instituts für Asienkunde, no. 79, 1976); and Robert Scalapino, *The Japanese Communist Movement 1920-1966* (Berkeley and Los Angeles: University of California Press, 1967); Kevin Devlin, "Japanese CP To Drop 'Marxism-Leninism,' " *Radio Free Europe Research*, June 4, 1976; Ch. M. [Christian Müller] from

Tokyo, "Revisionskosmetik der japanischen Kommunisten," *Neue Zürcher Zeitung,* August 4, 1976; and especially Hong N. Kim, "Deradicalization of the Japanese Communist Party under Kenji Miyamoto," *World Politics,* January 1976. See also Joachim Glaubitz, *Japan im Spannungsfeld zwischen China und der Sowjetunion* (Ebenhausen: Stiftung Wissenschaft und Politik, November 1976).

72. T.H. Rigby, "Australasia," *Survey,* January 1965; conversations in Australia, August 1976.

73. Benedict Cross, "Marxism in Venezuela," *Problems of Communism,* November-December 1973.

74. See, e.g., the PCI-JCP communiqué, *L'Unità,* January 20, 1977 (FBIS/WEU/January 27, 1977/L 2-4).

75. Jean-François Bizot, *Au parti des socialistes* (Paris: Grasset, 1975); Jean-Pierre Chevenement (of CERES), *Les socialistes, les communistes, et les autres* (Paris: Aubier-Montaigne, 1977).

76. Interview with Carrillo in *Il Manifesto,* November 1, 1975 (JPRS 66212, November, 25, 1975, pp. 85-94); partial criticism by *L'Unità,* November 1, 1975 (FBIS/WEU/November 7, 1975/ M 5).

77. See Giuseppe Are, "Italy's Communists: Foreign and Defense Policies," *Survival,* September-October 1976; Donald Sassoon, "The Italian Communist Party's European Strategy," *The Political Quarterly,* July-September 1976.

78. Carl Gustaf Ströhm, *Ohne Tito* (Graz: Styria, 1976).

[EIGHT]

Eastern Europe in the 1970s: Détente, Dissent and Eurocommunism

Rudolf L. Tőkés

> So what is détente? An ill-defined ex-
> pression which replaces "normalization"
> between the "capitalist" countries of the
> West and the "socialist" states of Eu-
> rope. Such an expression would not have
> appeared if Europe had not been forcibly
> divided and if in Eastern Europe there
> existed normal, i.e., legally founded
> states.
>
> Milovan Djilas [1]

In 1977 Eastern Europe was in the throes of changes that
will have lasting effects on the peoples and politics of the

German Democratic Republic (G.D.R.), Poland, Czechoslovakia, Hungary, Romania, Bulgaria, Yugoslavia and Albania. Since the crushing of the Czech reform movement by the Soviet Army and other Warsaw Treaty Organization (WTO) forces in August 1968, five developments have helped to bring about the present complex situation. First, with the onset of U.S.-Soviet détente, the cold war came to an end and it has evolved into a new kind of East-West relationship. Second, in the early 1970s a global energy crisis developed that cut across the political and ideological divisions of Europe and deeply influenced the political stability and economic viability of both democratic and Communist states. Third, Eurocommunism, once thought to be a relatively unimportant side-effect of the Sino-Soviet schism, has become a force to be reckoned with by all Eastern and Western powers with a stake in the future of European politics. Fourth, the Final Act of the Helsinki Conference on Security and Cooperation in Europe (CSCE), especially its provisions on human rights ("Basket Three"), and a new American foreign policy drive on behalf of human rights around the world have generated widespread and thus far unfulfilled expectations among the peoples of Eastern Europe. Finally, there has been a revival of democratic and socialist intellectual opposition in the GDR, Poland, Czechoslovakia, and Yugoslavia, with specific emphasis on the U.S.S.R. and its relationship to Communist Eastern Europe.

These events have separately and cumulatively created an unprecedented situation in Eastern Europe that is bound to affect the long-term stability of the area and will have a major influence on the future of East-West relations, most prominently American-Soviet relations. They constitute the background for the task at hand, which is to offer an assessment of the effects of U.S.-Soviet détente and the influence of Eurocommunism on the domestic policies, regional integration, and international conduct of the Communist states of Eastern Europe.

I propose to develop my case by focusing on three related matters. These are: (1) Soviet objectives and accomplishments in Eastern Europe in the postwar era; (2) the dynamics of national and regional stability and the development of democratic and socialist dissent in Eastern Europe; and, (3) the impact of Eurocommunism on the domestic and foreign policies of East European states. The concluding part will summarize these concerns and offer guarded speculation about the likely evolution of the East European political scene in the next five to ten years.

COMMUNIST POWER IN EASTERN EUROPE: THE POSTWAR RECORD

The political, economic, and military relationship that exists between the Soviet Union and the Communist states of Eastern Europe is a direct consequence of the occupation of that part of Europe in 1944-45 by the Soviet Red Army. From the Soviet viewpoint the relationship that evolved from Russian military control of Eastern Europe derives its fundamental legitimacy from Soviet strategic security interests. These interests required the establishment of a buffer zone, ruled by governments friendly to the U.S.S.R., between the Soviet Union and its potential Western European and trans-Atlantic adversaries. The Western Allies recognized in the form of various agreements (Teheran, Yalta, Potsdam), treaties, informal understandings and practices of Allied Control Commissions and even accepted, at least initially, the Soviet case. They agreed at the outset that the Russians were entitled to the restoration and future security of their prewar boundaries. It was, or should have been, understood by all concerned that not only the domestic politics but also the *foreign* policies of the states of liberated Eastern Europe were to come under close Soviet scrutiny. Thus, "limited sovereignty" both in the domestic and in the foreign policy fields had been established long before October 1968 when Brezhnev felt it necessary to spell out the permissible limits of deviation for Russia's East European clients.

Stalin's designs for Eastern Europe, as they may be reconstructed from a perspective of thirty years, had been motivated by Russia's historic quest for security, especially on its vulnerable western flank; by the pressing need to restore the U.S.S.R.'s devastated economy, transportation system, and industrial production through the extraction of reparation and booty in money, equipment, and manpower from Germany and its former East European allies; and by Marxist-Leninist ideological and traditional Russian imperialist ambitions to become not only a leading European power but a global one as well.[2]

The clash of incompatible Western and Soviet postwar aspirations were made inevitable by Soviet violations of the Yalta and Potsdam agreements and climaxed in Eastern Europe with the February 1948 coup in Czechoslovakia. As a result, by late 1947-early 1948 a foreign power had taken possession of the territory, economic assets, and human resources of five Eastern European nations and a part of Germany. Because of irreconcilable ideological differences and of geographic non-contiguity, Yugoslavia and Albania, respectively, have escaped this fate.

The division of Europe was one—albeit a major—aspect of what was to become the cold war or, to use Brzezinski's phrase, the "competitive relationship" between the United States and the Soviet Union over the next thirty years.[3]

In terms of basic foreign policy objectives toward Eastern Europe, the U.S.S.R. has adhered to a remarkably consistent set of priorities over the years. First among these is the maintenance, as a general proposition, of the U.S.S.R.'s hegemony over all decisions affecting the sovereignty of individual Eastern Europe states. This relationship has been not merely unequal, tending to benefit one partner over the others, but also has resulted in Soviet political, cultural, economic, ideological, and military penetration of the lives of six adjacent nations to an unparalleled extent historically. The underlying Soviet motive, namely, the satisfaction of Russia's inherently insatiable security needs, has thus far precluded the transformation of this relationship into a mutually beneficial traditional alliance system. The second objective concerns ideology and the Soviet desire to develop a shared world outlook on developmental priorities, specific legal and institutional arrangements, goals and methods of political education. It seeks, above all, unconditional adherence to the Soviet interpretation of systemic goals. Politically, the U.S.S.R. has endeavored to maintain a stable and, if possible, crisis-free institutional equilibrium within each national unit, including the hegemony of the Communist party, government control of the economy, and the availability of domestic coercive resources to ensure compliant behavior by members of society. The enforcement of common, or at least compatible, foreign policy postures on all issues deemed vital to Soviet national security interests has been an important aspect of this objective. In the realm of economic relations, the U.S.S.R. has sought to maintain and to intensify bilateral and intrabloc economic transactions that were deemed to be conducive to overall economic progress

[441]

and beneficial to the continued development and modernization of the Soviet national economy. In terms of specific
military objectives, since 1947-48 the U.S.S.R. has had the
ability to maintain effective control over military resource-
allocation decisions by all member nations on behalf of Soviet
military and foreign policy interests. Although the distinction
between military and foreign policy goals tended to be blurred
in the early 1970s, the two have, in fact, always been inter-
changeable—with a consistent bias in favor of military considerations. A recent authoritative Soviet textbook, *World
Communist Movement,* is quite unambiguous in this regard:
"The Warsaw Treaty Organization is the main coordinating
center for the fraternal countries' foreign policy activities." [4]

The pursuit of Soviet objectives in Eastern Europe, as
elsewhere in the world, has been influenced by domestic
factors, especially the way in which political institutions (particularly the Communist party) have performed and the manner in which the Soviet population and the managerial, bureaucratic, and intellectual elites have responded to leadership
initiatives. It is axiomatic that effective Soviet leadership of
bloc affairs and influence over the world Communist movement depends, in the final analysis, on the ability of the
U.S.S.R. to govern itself in accordance with its stated goals.
Unlike the imponderables of the linkage between domestic and
foreign policies, there is compelling evidence that with the
exception of notable temporary breakdowns of Soviet influence in Eastern Europe (Hungary and Poland in 1956, Czechoslovakia in 1968-69), Moscow has remained in firm control
over Eastern Europe. Because of this, it is tempting to argue
that the maintenance of Soviet supremacy over Eastern Europe requires no more than modest leadership skills as long as
the Red Army is stationed there. Indeed, the staggering
assymetry of respective Soviet and East European resources

might lead one to overlook the considerable political acumen and risk-taking ability of the CPSU Politburo when confronted with difficult situations in areas, such as East Europe, that Moscow seems determined to defend even at considerable, though perhaps not at *all,* costs.

System-building in Eastern Europe: Accomplishments

Turning to the matter of positive Soviet accomplishments in Eastern Europe, let us begin·by stating the obvious. With the exception of Yugoslavia and Albania, the U.S.S.R. has been successful in maintaining its hegemony in Eastern Europe. Be it 1948 or 1977, the same Communist or "united workers" or "socialist workers" parties still rule Eastern Europe. If not the leaders, then most senior cadres and top members of the Establishment are the very people who have been responsible for every good and bad, successful and unsuccessful, popular and unpopular decision and policy that made Eastern Europe what it is today. Continuity has also been maintained with respect to the structure and functions of state administration, the legal system, and the institutions and policies affecting education, culture and welfare. Some of the East European regimes evolved from Peoples' Democracies into socialist republics and the legislatures have amended their Soviet-type constitutions accordingly, but none of these changes has affected the authoritarian and nondemocratic substance of politics and public affairs in Eastern Europe.[5] To date, this is probably the most important Soviet achievement in Eastern Europe.

Next to the successful maintenance of the political status quo, the regimes' efforts to achieve breakthroughs in economic modernization have produced appreciable results. It is beyond dispute that, with the exception of remote and isolated areas such as eastern Slovakia, southern Poland, northern Romania, southern Yugoslavia and parts of Albania, each of the approximately 130 million inhabitants of Eastern Europe has been directly and variously affected by manifestations of modernization and change brought about by Communist power. By the mid-1970s seven East European economies generated an annual gross national product of over $300 billion; the area's average per capita national income was not far from $3,000; illiteracy has, for all intents and purposes, been wiped out; the ratios of population living in the coutryside and the cities has drastically shifted in favor of the latter; and the private ownership of durable goods (automobiles and household appliances) and access to mass communication has increased dramatically in the last ten years. One could go on, but the point has been made: virtually everywhere communism has brought major changes and significant material improvements.[6]

In the midst of these changes, a new generation of East Europeans came of age who have never lived under any other but the Communist system. From the coalescence of the pre- and postwar generations, new societies are about to be born in each Communist-ruled East European country.

Although we know a great deal about the new generation's economic opportunities, life-styles and cultural preferences, the available information about the political beliefs of young East Europeans is inconclusive. The appearance of apoliticality—be it consumerism or preoccupation with economic advancement and career goals—can be mistaken for youth support of the regime and its ideologies. But the record of student politics between 1968 and 1977 at the universities of Warsaw, Cracow, Prague, Bratislava, Budapest, Belgrade, and Zagreb attests to the young generation's profound discontent with the party gerontarchies of East Europe. And even the

loyalties of the offsprings of top party and government officials—or the "heroes' children," to use Paul Neuburg's apt
phrase—are still divided between attachments to family, peer
groups, religious, ethnic and national values and to the party's
official ideology.[7] Moreover, there is no reliable way of pre-
dicting the young people's reaction to unprecedented (and at
least in their lifetime) stressful conditions such as the sudden
curtailment of state education and welfare services, food short-
ages, unemployment, and the like. With these imponderables
in mind, one is entitled to raise questions about the long-term
stability of East European societies and political systems as
they exist today. The incumbents' record seems impressive:
The regimes have been "in place" for over thirty years, and
they have succeeded in laying the groundwork and creating
the necessary material infrastructure for the establishment of
modern industrial societies. Yet, modernization creates its own
problems, and regime ideologues are still at a loss for answers
to philosophical and policy dilemmas raised by the next generation's quest for a more meaningful and spiritually more
satisfying life under communism.

System-building in Eastern Europe: Countervailing Forces

A balanced assessment of this record might begin by identi-
fying some historical and political trends that have helped
thwart and, in some areas, postpone indefinitely, the realization of Soviet aspirations with regard to the integration of this
part of Europe as a stable component of a Moscow-led alliance
system.

The record shows that Russia's hold on Eastern Europe has
never been as complete as the Soviets hoped and the West
feared. Individual Communist parties possessed, even under

[445]

Stalin, a modicum of autonomy and capacity for policy improvisation.[8] Popular resistance to Communist rule, different national traditions, inadequate leadership skills in implementing programs and policies in the period of forced mobilization, and limited availability of resources for the fulfillment of ambitious economic plans have been additional and decisive constraints on the imposition of Soviet patterns in Eastern Europe.

When Stalin died in 1953, a new phase began in Soviet-East European relations. Once "thaw" in the form of the "New Course" and somewhat liberalized policies in Hungary and Poland began, many hitherto latent "domesticist" tendencies came to the surface. As a price of Soviet rapprochement with Yugoslavia and as an attempt to place Soviet-East European relations on more stable foundations, the doctrine of separate roads to socialism was propounded in 1955-56. With the traumatic experiences of 1956 (and the fact of Western noninterference in Poland and Hungary) behind them, the regimes found themselves compelled to devise new ways to remain in power. From the necessity of self-reliance, each Communist party sought to come to terms with its people in ways that were more consonant with the nation's traditional and (Czechoslovakia excepted) authoritarian political culture.[9]

The East European road to post-totalitarian consolidation from the mid-1950s to the late 1960s was uneven, and its length, direction and eventual terminal point were shaped by many internal and external factors.

Each East European regime sought to cope with the problems of the transition period according to its particular traditions and domestic conditions. However, certain common regime responses to dilemmas of post-totalitarian legitimacy do stand out. Regardless of the label—whether "goulash communism," "national consolidation," or "socialist renaissance"—

that Western observers and spokesmen of certain East European parties chose to characterize the substance of these
innovations, common to them all was the strategy of attempting to restore political equilibrium by securing a new and
higher level of political legitimacy in the eyes of the population. This included stress on national rather than ideological
goals; emphasis on indigenous historical and cultural traditions
at the expense of systemic values of Marxism-Leninism; focusing on economics and the attainment of developmental objectives, including the upgrading of real wages and levels of
personal consumption, rather than on the pursuit of voluntarist
and ideologically motivated political goals; striving for national
consolidation, the stabilization of new patterns of social stratification, and the discarding of techniques of mass mobilization
and quantum leaps of social development; and finally the
promotion of a new ideal type of citizenship—that of a doer
and problem-solver rather than a thinker or a revolutionary.

Strategies of this kind produced a political stability of sorts
in the 1960s. In Czechoslovakia, as Novotny's fall and Dubček's rise were to show, such initiatives by the regime could
not prevent the birth of a democratic socialist reform movement.[10] In Yugoslavia, as the Croatian crisis of 1970 was to
show, superficial liberalization only postponed the day of
reckoning.[11] Still, these measures bought time and contributed
to the political survival of many deeply compromised Stalinists,
most of whom are still in power in East Europe today.

The resolution of these domestic dilemmas was complicated
by several international factors. Following the Cuban missile
crisis, the cold war was gradually transformed into a rou-
tinized, if not normal, relationship between the United States
and the U.S.S.R. The Sino-Soviet conflict, the Vietnam war,
and increasingly assertive polycentric tendencies in the international Communist movement helped, at least for a time,

[447]

distract Soviet attention from East Europe. The Romanians and, in a different sense, the Hungarians took advantage of these opportunities. Ceauşescu set out to assert his nation's independence in regional, East-West, and general international affairs. The Kádár regime embarked on a major economic reform program that, in a somewhat truncated form, is still in progress. The East Germans, behind the shelter of the Berlin Wall since 1961, also got down to the business of creating a new Communist society in their half of Germany. Moreover, the Yugoslav example, both as an alternative model to Soviet methods of modernization and political development and as a way to preserve an East European state's political identity by acquiring a prominent status in the councils of the nonaligned world, introduced a new dimension and new opportunities for foreign policy reorientation for the East European states.[12]

Against this domestic and international background we can identify those countervailing factors that have helped to frustrate Moscow's designs for an early consolidation and eventual integration of the area under Soviet aegis.

With respect to political integration, it is clear from Soviet statements such as Brezhnev's doctrine and from more recent wishful suggestions about the transformation of the socialist commonwealth's international relations into those of a multinational state that an "organic relationship" is not yet on the horizon.[13] As a matter of fact, the East European states' hasty adhesion in recent years to many international organizations and the expansion of their foreign contacts, seems to suggest the opposite trend. A Romanian study on that country's foreign policy and its contributions "to outlining the principles of a better and more just world" optimistically argued that Romania's sovereignty was strengthened by the 3,500 treaties and international agreements that it had contracted with states of the world community since 1944.[14] Undoubtedly, other East European states can produce a similar number of documents as proof of their commitment to a "more just world," which to them seems inconceivable without their continued existence as sovereign entities. The absence of a permanent system-wide consultative and decision-making body is another obstacle to meaningful political integration. Neither the Political Advisory Committee of WTO, nor the annual consultations of East European party chiefs with Brezhnev in his Crimean dacha, nor ad-hoc emergency summit meetings are adequate substitutes for this purpose. As readers of the East European parties' theoretical journals can testify, there is substantial disagreement among economic planners and party ideologues on the synchronization and coordination of economic and political development among bloc members. Moreover, there is no evidence of strenuous effort by any East European Communist party to overcome the present ideological discontinuity between long-term national and systemic goals.

Ideological integration, or the growing acceptance of Marxist-Leninist values and their internalization by all decision-making elites and at least by the educated young people, is still an elusive target. By any standard—be it the time devoted to ideological matters at party congresses, or the actual political power wielded by theoreticians in ruling parties—the erosion of ideology is a fact, as is its replacement by new non-Marxist values of the scientific-technical revolution. Ideology and the regimes' founding myths have become institutionalized and serve as symbolic backdrops to the rise of the real ideologies of bureaucratic, technocratic and managerial power. All this, as a possibly unintended consequence, has led to elite demands for reliable and predictable control mechanisms for political behavior. The birth of a new kind of socialist *Rechtsstaat* in

Eastern Europe in the 1960s has generated a certain amount of public support for the regimes' written constitutions as visible guarantees of the post-totalitarian status quo. Eastern European constitutions, however, are not merely basic inventories of a regime's structural characteristics in politics, society and economy, but are also traditional symbols of *state sovereignty*. Thus, by their very existence, constitutions negate or limit the area-wide applicability of Soviet doctrines of proletarian internationalism and Soviet claims for the right to interfere with another socialist country's internal affairs.

Economic integration, unlike politics and ideology, is subject to overwhelming Soviet influence in Eastern Europe. Upon reaching a plateau of industrial maturity, as the G.D.R., Poland, Czechoslovakia and Hungary did in the early 1970s, modern economies become wholly dependent on the uninterrupted availability, on a sharply increasing scale, of imported raw materials, fuel, and agricultural commodities. Except for grain, the U.S.S.R. has ample supplies of iron ore, natural gas, oil and timber—all of which are indispensable to the survival of East Europe as an ongoing economic entity. Given the fact of Soviet supremacy as the ultimate and, in the case of oil and natural gas, virtually the sole supplier of East Europe's raw material needs, it is remarkable how little has, in fact, been achieved in the area of economic integration under the aegis of CMEA.

The Soviets' dependence on deliveries of finished low- and medium-technology industrial goods for reasonable prices payable in rubles, East European resistance to the feared loss of economic decision-making autonomy, the persistence of autarkic tendencies and inroads made by East-West trade into the hitherto Soviet- and bloc-dominated foreign trade balance of these countries may serve as partial explanation of this matter.[15] In a more basic sense, economic integration is hindered by the absence of agreement on fundamental questions of regional economic development. Presumably everyone supports the idea of scientific-technical revolution, yet there is no consensus on methods of transferring scientific-theoretical breakthroughs to the factory assembly line, on ways of measuring optimal economic performance and managerial excellence, let alone coping with problems of land use, environmental control, and many similar matters.

The question of military integration is probably the most difficult one to assess. We know that the U.S.S.R., as the major supplier of manpower, most of the necessary hardware, and all of the advanced military technology, is in complete control of WTO. One of the functions of this military alliance is to protect Soviet security interests in Europe. What we do not know is whether the WTO forces, when called upon to fulfill this or *another* function (or "internationalist duty"), for example, as a multinational police force to protect the political status quo in Eastern Europe against democratic dissidents, liberal Marxist reformers, enraged factory workers or insurgent patriots, will obey Russian orders in combat situations.[16] Moreover, it is quite uncertain whether Eastern European troops would be willing to fight in Western Europe. We should hope that the ultimate test of loyalty will never come; one has the impression that the Soviet General Staff is not eager to find out either.

Cultural integration was once regarded in Stalin's and Zhdanov's time as a feasible systemic goal. However, just as in the Soviet Union, where universal education and improved cultural standards have created conditions favorable to the rebirth of national and cultural identity and opposition to Russian rule, Eastern Europe in the 1960s was the scene of the revival of cultural nationalism and, with it, growing resistance to Soviet inroads. In Hungary, Poland and Yugoslavia where book publishing, music and the arts are governed to some extent by market-like conditions, popular demand for Soviet cultural exports is virtually nonexistent. The widespread rejection of Soviet culture goes hand in hand with the rejection of Russian life-styles and regime efforts to popularize the collectivist values of Soviet science, education and literature.

In sum: Soviet military and economic superiority and political hegemony over all key political decisions in six out of eight East European countries is a historic fact. The status quo is protected by the international balance of power and by the written and unwritten ground rules of the "competitive relationship" between the United States and the U.S.S.R. But both the ground rules and the *raison d'être* of this relationship have changed significantly and perhaps irreversibly in the last fifteen years, and there is reason to believe that the likely long-term consequences of détente and Helsinki will be inimical to future Soviet hegemony in Eastern Europe.

DÉTENTE AND EASTERN EUROPE

The Final Act of August 1, 1975, of the Helsinki Conference on Security and Cooperation in Europe (CSCE) is generally considered a major turning point in East-West relations and a milestone in the postwar history of Eastern Europe.[17] Although interpretations vary, it can be argued that the conference was, to a considerable extent, the result of a decade-long Soviet drive to achieve three goals. These were: the definition of new parameters for future East-West relations by institutionalizing the political consequences of the new military balance of power created by the Soviet achievement of strategic nuclear parity with the United States in 1968-70; the winning of international recognition for the territorial and political changes in Eastern and Central Europe since the Second World War; and the development of a politically advantageous point of departure for future U.S.-Soviet and Soviet-West European relations.

The Final Act contained three sections: general questions pertaining to the security of Europe and a Declaration of Principles Guiding Relations between Participating States (Basket One); Cooperation in the Field of Economics, of Science and Technology, and of Environment (Basket Two); and Cooperation in Humanitarian and Other Fields (Basket Three).

The implications of détente and those of the Helsinki agreements for Eastern Europe have been subjects of much controversy as well as of an unending stream of writings ranging from learned studies to partisan diatribes.[18] Opponents of détente have argued that the Final Act amounted to a betrayal of East Europe by the West, particularly by the United States.[19] Others have claimed that because the Final Act lacked an enforcement mechanism and other instruments of permanent oversight, this document was little more than a statement of good intentions.[20] A third school of thought, and the one I am inclined to support, maintains that, on balance, the Helsinki agreement has been more beneficial to adherents of liberal democracy and to the peoples of Eastern Europe than to the U.S.S.R. and to Moscow's East European clients.

The "betrayal" thesis may be dispensed with by pointing to the abandonment some time prior to the Hungarian Revolution of 1956 by the United States and its European allies of intentions to act on the cold war slogan concerning the "liberation of Eastern Europe." Successive U.S. administrations have discarded this notion in favor of "building bridges to Eastern Europe" and selectively rewarding individual states, such as Poland, Yugoslavia and Romania, for signs of display-

[453]

ing autonomist tendencies at home and/or carrying on independent or unorthodox policies abroad. More recently, Secretary Kissinger's and Mr. Helmut Sonnenfeldt's statements, however ill-timed and diplomatically counterproductive, helped put the matter in a realistic perspective.[21] They declared that the United States' interest in the future of Eastern Europe was to be contingent on and subordinated to the vastly more important matter of bilateral U.S.-Soviet relations.

Those who view the Final Act as an unenforceable and a perhaps cynical way of sweeping the real problems of European security under the rug seem to have a more persuasive case. By likening this document to other well-intentioned statements and agreements issued in the last two decades by the United Nations General Assembly which were subsequently observed by the Russians more by breach than by compliance, we are reminded of the penetration of Stalin's question about the Pope's divisions. Indeed, this argument would have made excellent sense in Stalin's time when the U.S.S.R. chose to remain isolated from the rest of the world, and the nature of Soviet international contacts was limited to orders issued to its satellites and to exchanges of threats and insults with the Western Allies. However, the Soviet decision in 1956 to pursue policies of peaceful coexistence with the West, the commitment in the 1960s to establish a global presence, and the choice (if that is the word) in the 1970s to engage in intensive trading relationships with the United States, Western Europe and Japan has made the U.S.S.R. and its allies increasingly vulnerable to external influences. And this represents new and unprecedented Western opportunities to generate economic (Basket Two), diplomatic and cultural pressures that could, in certain circumstances, serve as adequate safeguards to agreements such as the Final Act. In any event, given the international circumstances and the resources that the West was prepared to invest to achieve the "normalization" of East-West relations in Europe, the Final Act was about the only way to realize this objective at a reasonable cost.

From the East Europeans' viewpoint, Helsinki was something of a mixed blessing. While the reaffirmation of the postwar territorial status quo might have been regarded by pessimists as the last nail in the coffin of an independent Eastern Europe, realists may discern two distinct opportunities arising from the Final Act. The first opportunity, as it could be surmised from the Romanian and Yugoslav governments' vigorous diplomatic activities in the pre-Helsinki period, was presented by the ten Principles Guiding Relations between Participating States. One-half of these dealt specifically with matters of national sovereignty, nonintervention, and inviolability of existing boundaries. The other half was devoted to similar principles and measures of implementation guaranteeing the same. Indeed, it appeared that in return for Western recognition of Russia's thirty-year supremacy in Eastern Europe, the U.S.S.R. (the Brezhnev Doctrine notwithstanding) was prepared to go on record explicitly affirming the right of its allies to independent statehood.

Sovereignty, in the absolute sense, is the doctrine that places the state's right to survive above all other interests and loyalties. Clearly, this is not what the Russians bargained for when demanding of the West the sanctioning of the geopolitical consequences of the Soviet Army's postwar conquest in Europe. From this it does not follow that the Russians, upon exhausting other means of persuasion, would hesitate to reenact the invasion of Czechoslovakia elsewhere in Eastern Europe. However, what is far less certain is whether military action of this kind could be mounted at all against Yugoslavia,

Albania, and perhaps Romania, or against another Soviet-controlled state with the participation of *other* WTO members in fulfillment of their "internationalist" duties.

The other opportunity provided by the Final Act concerns the way in which individual citizens, under the Guiding Principles and the "Third Basket" provisions could lawfully resist state and Communist party encroachment upon their human rights, freedoms, and other liberties guaranteed to them by the Helsinki agreements. The record of democratic and socialist dissident activities in ths U.S.S.R., the G.D.R., Poland, Czechoslovakia, Romania, and Yugoslavia shows a distinct awareness of these provisions as well as a willingness to use them as political levers against authorities anxious to evade compliance especially with "Third Basket" provisions of the Final Act.

Thus, there are two specific ways in which the governments and the peoples of Eastern Europe can assert their respective claims for state sovereignty and individual autonomy by citing one or more relevant provisions of the Final Act, to which the U.S.S.R. was a signatory. However, to make a realistic assessment of the likely impact of détente on Eastern Europe, we must look beyond short-term opportunities to defy the Russians and/or the local Communist authorities and consider some of the underlying historical conditions that ultimately shape collective East European behavior when confronted with political change. For this purpose, I shall discuss those elements of East European political culture that could come into play in response to potentially destabilizing events and circumstances, such as a sudden deterioration of living standards, the threat of internal strife, regional conflict, or a war, or anything else that might be perceived as threat to "normalcy" in public affairs.

To establish predictable limits of potential instability, I shall first briefly list those conditions that the peoples of Eastern

Europe, on the basis of shared historic experiences, themselves identify with "normalcy" in politics. In my view, the meaning of "normalcy" in Eastern Europe might be inferred from the following aspects of East European history.

The area's geographic location and its lack of natural boundaries have historically tempted aggressors and have made Central Europe a natural buffer zone between the great powers of Europe. People living in battlefields are habitually insecure and view the outside world with fear and trepidation. National sovereignty is a desirable goal, but it is seldom attainable under such conditions. Thus, existential insecurity stemming from a legacy of wars, invasions, and subjugation to foreign powers has been the decisive and most universally shared experience of the peoples of Eastern Europe.

Because of vulnerability to external manipulation of domestic politics, the historic burden of local and regional ethnic, linguistic and religious conflicts, the evolution of modern political institutions took place under crisis conditions. And, when "political normalcy" was available, it often came about under foreign auspices. The partitions of Poland, the Hapsburg rule in Central Europe, and the centuries-long Ottoman domination of the Balkans are cases in point. As the result, democratic institutions and a political culture favorable for their development could not flourish, except in isolated cases such as Czechoslovakia between the two world wars. When Eastern Europe's small states did gain their independence after the World War I, neither the economic conditions nor the international environment was conducive to a peaceful evolution of viable democratic systems. In the 1920s the often clumsy and inefficient political institutions of liberal democracy failed to deliver stability and full employment. From the political bankruptcy of democratic experiments, right-wing authoritarian and semi-fascist regimes were born on the eve of

[457]

World War II. These regimes, unlike their democratic predecessors, did provide stability and full employment albeit at the cost of sacrificing individual freedoms and preparing for the next war. For most East Europeans, save the socialists and small groups of liberal intellectuals in the 1930s, one-party dictatorship seemed to be the logical alternative to political instability and unemployment.

Economic development of Eastern Europe did not favor democracy either. The area's industrial modernization took place under state and foreign auspices. Neither of these aided the growth of a native entrepreneurial class whose political beliefs had played a decisive role in the shaping of liberal values and institutions in the formative years of the Western democracies. The state's role in economics has been crucial in this context. The East European governments, through direct ownership of key branches of industry, public transportation, communications, and a monopoly over the production of certain commodities, legitimated traditions of bureaucratic interference in the private economic sector and in the daily lives of the citizens.

Because of the special characteristics of the political and economic modernization of this part of Europe, its societies—again with the exception of the Czech lands—lacked strong urban middle classes and were dominated by traditional, mainly rural, values and interests. In crisis situations, the politically powerless urban middle class and other potentially moderating elements were invariably swept away by the radicalized masses led by alienated intellectuals. The traditional prominence of revolutionary intellectuals in Eastern Europe might make inspiring history, but it is also symptomatic of one of the most important structural flaws of this area's social development.

Traditional ideologies and political beliefs were congruent

[458]

with East Europe's politics, economics and society. Apart from the noble exceptions of Thomas Masaryk, scores of Central European federalists, and democratic and socialist thinkers who were able to transcend the limitations of their intellectual environment, the dominant political beliefs of East Europe have been nationalism, chauvinism, and religious intolerance. All this adds up to a remarkable and frequently demonstrated disposition, especially under stressful conditions, of many, if not most, East Europeans to "escape from freedom" into the embrace of millennial ideas and totalitarian programs.

The legacy of this unhappy and essentially nondemocratic past left an indelible impression on the East European political psyche and especially on popular perceptions of political stability and instability. Thus, if we argue, as we must, that "normalcy" in Eastern Europe has traditionally consisted of external instability, ambivalence toward liberal democratic political institutions, great influence of the state in the economic realm, and recurrent tendencies of hyperattachment to authority figures, we have described a "subject" political culture. A prevailing political culture of this kind, while not excluding volatile and unpredictable outbursts, produces political dispositions that under normal conditions tend to be supportive of the status quo and inimical to or fearful of the unknown exigencies of political change.[22]

When searching for valid explanations for East European passivity under stressful conditions—which has been the rule rather than the exception in the last thirty years—it is not enough to blame Soviet bayonets and to overlook other equally important facts of recent history in the region. The Soviet ability to manipulate the foreign policies of any of its neighbors without the necessity of resorting to military or economic blackmail is a complex issue. Still, it is often forgotten that the postwar territorial status quo, in the final analysis, is guaran-

[459]

teed by Moscow. If it chose to do so, the U.S.S.R. could revive and threaten to take sides in any of the half-dozen, now dormant territorial and ethnic disputes of Eastern Europe. A relatively recent problem like that of German reunification and an old one like the Macedonian question[23] are but two cases that would readily lend themselves to Soviet diplomatic interference and manipulation of the collective behavior of East European nations.

My case for manifest stability on the regional level is compatible with the history of well-known instances of manifest instability on the national level.[24] Revolutions, riots and major disturbances do not inevitably follow from the perceived illegitimacy of an East European regime. Comparative studies of the Hungarian, Polish, and Czechoslovak events of 1956 and 1968 have yet to produce a persuasive explanation, with the potential to predict the future recurrence of such traumatic confrontations.[25] Common to the background of all three political upheavals were documented instances of intolerable provocation of the people by the authorities and the fortuitous coincidence of several external destabilizing factors that made these crises possible, though not necessarily unavoidable. The question is whether future crises of similar magnitude in an East European country are likely to produce a domino-effect and generate a manifest crisis of systemic proportions. The available evidence is suggestive but far from conclusive. We might surmise that the Polish, Hungarian, and Czechoslovak crises were climactic outcomes of protest movements against Stalinism, which was a shared East European condition in the 1950s and the 1960s. But in the late 1970s Soviet policies of *divide et impera* and dissimilar sequences of political development[26] (hence the odds against the simultaneous surfacing of precipitant causes) make it extremely unlikely that two or more East European countries would, at the same time, rise against their native and Russian rulers.

Stalinism was a pervasive yet diffuse phenomenon that could be experienced in many ways, not all of which were conducive to insurgent behavior. While the possibility of the future reimposition of Stalinism and Stalinist governing methods cannot be precluded as long as the ultimate control of Eastern Europe is in Soviet hands, there is reason to believe that another equally pervasive, yet politically perhaps more explosive, shared condition is about to emerge in the late 1970s. The issue may be simply defined as mass protest against static or drastically lowered living standards due to the burden of higher energy costs and of indebtedness to Western creditors. A corollary to this, of course, is the regimes' attempts to throttle grassroots demands for the eradication of the last vestiges of Stalinism from public life and for procedural and substantive guarantees of civil rights under socialism. However, simple definitions can be misleading as they fail to account for the enormous range of *simultaneously* experienced sources of growing popular dissatisfaction of *all* East Europeans with the regimes' performances. The crux of the matter is the inability of the state to meet expectations in areas as diverse as legal safeguards of individual freedoms, educational policies, housing, consumer goods, public services and, above all, ths quality of life under post-totalitarian communism.[27]

These newly surfacing issues need not, in themselves, produce national revolutions and regional upheavals. The East European regimes are not without resources to head off crises from escalating into major confrontations. Self-criticism by the regime, personnel reshuffles, temporary reallocation of resources into the consumer sector and, if all else fails, massive infusion of Soviet aid are time-tested techniques of crisis prevention in Eastern Europe. Moreover, the newly established and increasingly stratified societies of East Europe are likely to uphold the status quo under all but extreme crisis conditions. Ths massive co-optation of technocrats, scientists, economists, educators and, indeed, most intellectuals (save small groups of overt dissidents of whom more will be said later) into the regimes' power structure in the last fifteen years has produced positive results from the incumbents' viewpoint. These elites are beneficiaries of privileged living standards, life styles, social status, and political access which set them apart from the less-educated lower status groups of the society.

The record of the last thirty years is reasonably clear: Except in cases of impending political turmoil of "Hungarian" (1956) or "Czechoslovak" (1968) proportions, the technocrats and intellectuals, who are the natural leaders of discontented industrial workers and the youth, have a vital stake in the regime's continued survival.[28] To attribute, as some Western observers do, politically suicidal proclivities to members of well-entrenched, modestly affluent, and increasingly bureaucratized East European intellectual elites[29] is just as unrealistic as to expect masses of Western middle-class liberals to give up their secure jobs and suburban homes and to lead the politically or economically underprivileged masses for an all-out assault on the bastions of power. For everyone concerned, the stakes in Eastern Europe will be considerably higher in the 1980s than they had been in the 1950s. The regimes will have a record of almost four decades of continuous existence to protect, and the would-be insurgents might lack an alternative program with sufficient appeal to mobilize more than the marginal and bitterly alienated elements of the population. On the other hand, it would be a mistake to underestimate the lasting appeal of traditional ideologies and the way these beliefs

[462]

may affect and, under some unpredictable future circumstances, mobilize substantial segments of the population.

Human Rights and Dissent in Eastern Europe

East-West détente and the Helsinki Final Act have generated new expectations throughout Eastern Europe. The inauguration in January 1977 of the new U.S. administration's human rights policy four months prior to the Belgrade "review session" of the Helsinki agreements helped accelerate the momentum of East European hopes for improvements, especially in the Basket Three area.

Before attempting to assess the impact of this policy on the peoples of Eastern Europe, it is important to clarify the meaning of "human rights" as it might apply to this part of the world. According to Secretary of State Cyrus R. Vance, the U.S. policy of human rights consists of three overlapping dimensions: First, "the right to be free from governmental violation of the integrity of the person"; second, "the right to the fulfillment of such vital needs as food, shelter, health care and education"; and third, "the right to enjoy civil and political liberties."[30] Obviously, this policy can be viewed either as an "operationalized" version of Basket Three, or as a major American ideological attack on the political legitimacy of the Communist world. The first Communist reactions, as these may be judged from angry rebuttals by Brezhnev, Husák, Zhivkov, Honecker and Tito, have been negative. From the active dissidents' viewpoint in the U.S.S.R. and Czechoslovakia, the new U.S. initiative has thus far proved to be ineffective and perhaps counterproductive.

However, in a more general perspective, we may discern certain issues of East European dissident-regime interaction

[463]

that may be vulnerable to external ideological pressures of the kind that President Carter's case for human rights represents. The cessation of large-scale police terror in the 1960s resulted in a drastically reduced number of political prisoners in Eastern Europe. To be sure, there are still hundreds in Czechoslovakia, the G.D.R., Yugoslvia and Romania, and an unknown, though probably smaller, number of (mostly low social status, hence not "newsworthy") citizens in Poland who have been incarcerated for their political beliefs.[31] Thus, most East European regimes are vulnerable on this score. On the other hand, public reaction to sudden price rises (Poland) and insidious regime discriminatory policies in the area of higher education, employment opportunities, and allocation of scarce housing resources is perhaps less affected by the rhetoric of U.S. human rights policy. Most East Europeans would concede that the performance of Western market economies and specifically the delivery of state benefits in welfare, education, and health services, though superior in many respects, still leave much to be desired and would not regard the Western model as an irresistible alternative to the economic status quo in Communist Eastern Europe. Therefore, it is the question of civil liberties that has the potential to generate new tensions between the peoples and the regimes. For these reasons, the likely impact of the new U.S. human rights policy—and it seems to be more and more toned down in each successive Washington "clarification" of this matter [32]—should be incremental rather than revolutionary as far as East European political and social stability are concerned.

Before briefly discussing the goals, achievements and current position of East European dissidents in the 1970s, three comments are in order. First, the men and women who have chosen to criticize openly the Communist parties and governments of Czechoslovakia, Poland, East Germany, Romania and Yugoslavia are not, as the regimes often allege, counter-revolutionaries. Most of them are democrats or socialists who seek reforms within the system and are opposed to the dismantling of the positive social, cultural and economic achievements of the last thirty years.[33] Thus, right-wing extremists and neo-Stalinists are absent from the ideological spectrum—especially in Czechoslovakia, East Germany and Romania, where individuals with such philosophical persuasion control the party and the government. Moreover, it seems that the democrats (that is, non-Marxist dissidents) are more inclined to make use of the language and spirit of the Helsinki agreements than of the message of Eurocommunism, which is, in any case, a more congenial source of inspiration to those who still have faith in reformist Marxist socialism as an ideological weapon against the incumbent Communist party leadership. Although at times the ideologies and programs of both kinds of dissidents tend to overlap, the democrats draw inspiration from history, international law,[34] and their countries' traditional ties to Western Europe, while the socialists still seem to cling to the hope of reform through Marxist "self-analysis and self-criticism." [35] As *The Times* pointed out in commenting on the publication of *Socialist Opposition in Eastern Europe* by the prominent Czech exile, Jiři Pelikán,

> These two different approaches—pressure from the outside or reform from within—derive from different situation, traditions, and aspirations, but they are neither mutually exclusive nor wholly antagonistic. Indeed they find a good deal in common ground in the pursuit of human rights.[36]

The manifesto of the Charter 77 group, issued in January 1977, takes its point of departure from Law No. 120 of the

[465]

Czechoslovak Collection of Laws promulgating that country's accession in 1968 to the International Covenant on Civil and Political Rights and the International Covenant on Economic, Social and Cultural Rights that were subsequently confirmed by the Helsinki Final Act and became law of the land on March 23, 1976.[37] "Since that date," the manifesto submits, "our citizens have had the right, and the State had the duty, to abide by them." The manifesto's key paragraph disavows any subversive intention and reaffirms the signers' lawful intentions:

> Charter 77 is not intended to be a basis for opposition political activity. Its desire is to serve the common inter-est, as have numerous similar organizations of civic initia-tive East and West. It has no intention of initiating its own programs for political or social reforms or changes, but it wants to lead in the sphere of its activity by means of a constructive dialogue with the political and State authorities—and particularly by drawing attention to vari-ous specific violations of civil and human rights, by preparing their documentation, by suggesting solutions, by submitting various proposals aimed at furthering these rights and their guarantees, by acting as a mediator in the event of conflict situations which might result in wrong-doings, etc.

The regime's response was swift and ruthless: The promi-nent signatories were subjected to police surveillance and incarceration. And in early March, Professor Jan Patočka, one of the leading spokesmen on the Charter 77 group, died of heart attack, following an extended interrogation session with the Prague police.

It is probably idle to speculate whether an unprecedented U.S. State Department public protest in late January aided or hindered the Czech dissidents. The fact remains that while the best-known dissidents are forced one-by-one into exile, the remaining more than 800 signers of the Charter manifesto will have to live with and suffer the harsh consequences of their civic courage.[38]

Unlike the tragic and seemingly hopeless predicament of the Czechoslovak opposition, the Polish dissidents, for the first time in recent years, represent a formidable political force that the Gierek regime has not been able to contain as late as autumn 1977. The coincidence of the end of five years (1970-75) of economic prosperity—made possible by Western credits—with the revival of organized dissent has created a unique situation in Poland, with potentially far-reaching consequences for the rest of East Europe. Since December 1975 there have been movements to protest proposed changes in Poland's constitution; widely circulated petitions and manifestos demanding legal guarantees of freedom of conscience and religion, freedom to work, freedom of expression and information, and freedom of scholarly pursuit and learning; [39] and in the summer of 1976 riots and major workers' strikes that were followed by arrests and dismissals from work of 3,000 participants. These events led to the formation of a Committee for the Defense of the Workers (KOR) in September 1976.[40] What began as an ad-hoc group to collect and distribute funds among victims of government repression, by April 1977 became a major political pressure group with 1,000 collaborators and a record sum of over 2.6 million zlotys distributed among unemployed workers. A remarkable dispatch of Richard Davy of *The Times* helps put these events in a larger perspective:

> In the past the Church, the peasants, the workers, the students and the intellectuals have mostly defended their interests in separate ways at separate times. In 1968, for

instance, student demonstrators received no help from the workers. In 1970, the striking workers received no support from students or intellectuals. The Church has supported the oppressed but has tended to claim sole custody of the nation's heritage.

Now there is convergence from all sides. Intellectuals are bridging old differences and have formed a committee to help workers. Students are doing social work among families or workers who have been imprisoned or lost their jobs as a result of the June strikes. The Church, whose main base was among the dwindling peasantry, has been developing its interest in urban workers and in wider issues of human rights. Formerly radical intellectuals are also changing. Mr. Jacek Kuron, once a dissident revolutionary of the far left, has rethought his attitude towards the Church as an institution and became an evolutionary with a deepening respect for tradition.[41]

In the spring and early summer 1977 the Polish scene became more complex. In March another dissident organization, the Movement for the Defense of Human and Civil Rights (ROPCO) was founded. Its members, unlike those of KOR, appear to be non-Marxists. They are lawyers, journalists, and intellectuals, several with a record of past oppositionist activity. In May, prompted by the still unexplained death of Stanislaw Pyjas, a KOR-supporter student at the University of Cracow, massive student demonstrations erupted in that city. This was followed by a hunger strike by sympathizers which, in turn, generated protest petitions and led to the arrest of several prominent dissidents, among them the literary critic Jan Józef Lipski, the philosopher Jacek Kuron, the historians Adam Michnik, Piotr Naimski and Antonin Macierowicz, and the nuclear physicist Miroslaw Chojecki. Although these individuals were eventually released (the last five in mid-July), there are two major forces that have not yet surfaced as full-fledged participants of the Polish dissident movement. The Catholic Church, though supportive of KOR's welfare programs for families of imprisoned workers, has not, at least offically, thrown its enormous influence behind the anti-regime activists. And the industrial workers of Poland, the bellwethers in the major political crises of 1956, 1970, and 1976, still seem to be taking an attitude of wait-and-see.[42] Another unexpected price rise or a new police atrocity, however, could draw Cardinal Wyszynski into the political arena and trigger an elemental outburst from the industrial workers—and with it, raise the possibility of Gierek's fall, or worse, that of a Soviet invasion.

Expectations aroused by Helsinki and the more recent U.S. human rights drive have also contributed to dissident movements of more modest proportions in Yugoslavia, East Germany, and Romania as well.[43] Issues of constitutional rights, travel, censorship, and heavy-handed police interference with basic individual freedoms have dominated the dialogue between dissidents and regime in these countries. Apart from a statement of support, signed by 36 intellectuals, for the Charter 77 group in January 1977, there is no evidence of organized dissident activity in Hungary. And the phrase "human rights" has yet to find its way into the Albanian intellectuals' political vocabulary.

In sum: since World War II, East Europeans have found that resistance to forced collectivization did not succeed; that spontaneous riots, such as those in East Berlin and Pilsen in 1953, could be dispersed by ruthless police action; that major uprising and revolutions were destined to be crushed by Soviet tanks; that "national communism"—be it Yugoslav or Romanian—did not protect civil liberties; that New Left radicalism

[469]

has had no popular support; and that dissident intellectuals, unless they joined forces with the people, were bound to be suppressed by the authorities.[44] The question is whether the Polish strategy and Czechoslovak Charter 77 approach as techniques of coalition-building and as ways of making lawful demands of the government will find a significant number of followers elsewhere in East Europe. And, if and when they do, will the Communist parties and Moscow have the wisdom to come to terms with dissent in the spirit of conciliation instead of resorting to time-tested methods of repression. Once the regimes shed their proclivity to regard all forms of un-authorized advocacy of interests in the area of human rights as subversive attempts to undermine the socio-economic achieve-ments of socialism, ways can be found to introduce reforms without upsetting the political status quo.[45] Clearly, much will depend on the specific circumstances of each case.

In view of the interest of certain Western European Com-munist parties in East European affairs, it is not inconceivable that at some point in the future the Italian or French Commu-nist party as a *ruling* or government coalition partner might offer to step in to serve as an honest broker seeking to mediate East European dissident-regime conflicts over matters of human rights and individual freedoms. This possibility might have seemed far-fetched ten years ago, but cannot be pre-cluded in the 1980s.

EUROCOMMUNISM, EAST AND WEST: THEORY AND PRACTICE

The "cuckoo's egg of Eurocommunism," as Soviet and Czechoslovak political commentators have characterized the heretic ideas of Santiago Carrillo's *Eurocommunism and the State,* has been a familiar sight in the political aviary of Eastern

Europe. In 1919 it was called "national Bolshevism," in the 1920s "right-wing opportunism," in the 1930s "social fascism," in the 1940s "Titoism," in the 1950s "national communism," in the 1960s "polycentrism" and in the 1970s "autonomism." These labels have served to describe, either from the Soviet or from a dissident foreign Communist party's viewpoint, unauthorized autonomist tendencies or attempts at ideological backsliding toward "social democratism" and other nonviolent strategies of political action. These tendencies have often (though not always, as China's and Albania's policies demonstrate) coalesced into a posture of Eurocommunism and the "Yugoslav way" to socialism. In any event, the history of these disputes is instructive and offers conclusive evidence that every one of the issues that are the foci of contention between Moscow and the Communist parties of Western Europe have been once, and in some cases several times, the subject of clashes between the CPSU and the Communist parties of East Europe.

At first in a non-ruling and, after the war, in a ruling capacity, Communists of East Europe have felt compelled to take issue with their Russian superiors on several important matters of strategy and tactics. These have included divergent judgments about the applicability of the Soviet experience in foreign countries; differing perceptions concerning the organizational and ideological implications of "norms of proletarian internationalism"; the discontinuity between indigenous radical philosophical traditions and political attitudes of members, especially the intellectuals, of East European Communist parties and Moscow's views on the same; and finally, personality clashes between the CPSU leaders and the top officials of the East European parties.[46] These conflicts and clashing perceptions have repeatedly exacerbated the tenuous political links between Moscow and Belgrade, Warsaw, Bucharest, Prague

[471]

and Budapest. Indeed, as far as the East European party elites are concerned there is nothing new about Eurocommunism. Its disadvantage lies in the distant threat it poses to the legitimacy of the regimes, but it also provides new opportunities to strengthen a ruling party's bargaining position vis-à-vis Moscow. In East Europe, political breathing spells are always welcome, and the Russians' apparent preoccupation with Carrillo, Berlinguer, Marchais is no exception.

It is axiomatic that all East European parties, probably even the Czechs and the Bulgarians, are potential revisionists or "latent Eurocommunists." Given a chance, they all would wish to have greater ideological flexibility and operational freedom from Soviet interference. In this connection it seems appropriate to recall that after the war even the arch-Stalinist Georgi Dimitrov was prepared to discuss plans (behind Stalin's back) for a Balkan Federation with Tito; that Mátyás Rákosi and Klement Gottwald were anxious to benefit from the Marshall Plan; and that the Romanian, Polish and even the East German Communists had their own ideas about strategy and tactics of the People's Democratic "transition period." The crucial difference, of course, is that between the ruling and non-ruling position of the Eastern and Western branches of "latent" and open Eurocommunism. It is self-evident that the burden of governing responsibilities, the regimes' legitimacy dilemmas, and binding commitments to Soviet-dominated regional organizations (CMEA and WTO) tend to inhibit free expression of potentially deviant East European views. The dual bond of party- *and* state-level Soviet-East relations is obviously not conducive to the free airing of major political and ideological disagreements.

Another major difference between open and "latent" Eurocommunism concerns the way in which these parties view their ideological and political legitimacy and seek to differentiate themselves from other Communist parties. When

Berlinguer says that he feels "safer" in the West, he implicitly refers to the absence of Soviet tanks and the KGB as preconditions to Communist ascendance to power in Western Europe. When Carrillo argues that "what is essential is the independence of the Communist parties with respect to the Soviet state and the development in theory and practice of an unequivocally democratic way," he affirms the inherent supremacy of "authentic socialism" and casts doubts about the legitimacy of the states of "real socialism," or socialism-in-being as the East Europeans characterize the political status quo. Clearly, the Eurocommunist platform is *not* merely a statement about Western Europe's philosophical traditions for Communist strategy and tactics, but is a negation of the ideological legitimacy of the entire Soviet and East European system-building experience.

Berlinguer's speech at the June 1976 East Berlin conference provides a cogent summary of the particulars of the "Italian way" to socialism:

In Italy, where the working class and our Party have been and are protagonists in the fight to restore, defend and develop democracy, we are fighting for a socialist society that has at its foundation the affirmation of the value of the individual and collective freedoms and their guarantee, the principles of the secular, non-ideological nature of the State and its democratic organization, the plurality of political parties and the possibility of alternation of government majorities, the autonomy of the trade unions, religious freedom, freedom of expression, of culture and the arts and sciences.[47]

Thus, in Italy democracy is something that can be "restored" rather than is "yet to be created," as in the East; that, in the hierarchy of freedoms, individual rights take precedence

[473]

over those of the community; further, that the state is to be a nonideological entity, rather than the instrument of one-party dictatorship; that the government's mandate is subject to the outcome of free elections; and that the citizens have the right to religious freedom, free expression, and the organized promotion of individual economic interests. Obviously, this platform has nothing in common with the Soviet model or with the kind of socialism that the Prague, Bucharest, Warsaw, Budapest and Belgrade ideologues call "real."

Manuel Azcárate, a leading PCE spokesman, made this quite clear in an interview in July 1977: " . . . Eurocommunism has become a great political force on our continent, and even on a world scale. We are living at a time when social democracy is in crisis, and the "Soviet model" had ceased to be a source of hope or an example for the revolutionary process." [48]

Thus, implicit in the Eurocommunist case is the suggestion that the Leninist shortcut of building socialism in a politically authoritarian and economically backward country and bypassing the stage of evolutionary bourgeois democratic development must, of necessity, degenerate into Stalinism, police terror, and the dictatorship of the party-state bureaucracy.[49] From the East Europeans' point of view, the Eurocommunists' insistence on political pluralism and the parliamentary road to power also serves as a painful reminder that with the signal exception of the Yugoslavs' authentic revolution, it was not the ballot box but Soviet bayonets that put East Europe's ersatz revolutionaries into power.[50] Moreover, the Eurocommunists' support of private enterprise within the framework of a mixed, state- and privately-controlled economy stems, as the preceding chapter on the PCI makes clear, from extremely critical perceptions of the achievements of the "real socialist" states' centrally planned, mismanaged, and inefficient economic systems. For these reasons, the Eurocommunist-East European dialogue is necessarily confined to debatable (if not necessarily "negotiable") issues of cultural freedoms, human rights, East-West détente, and general ideological questions of the international Communist movement.

Eurocommunism in Transition: Dialogue and Motivations

Although estimates vary on when direct contacts between Western and Eastern European Communist parties were inaugurated, evidence and unverifiable Yugoslav accounts point to the years of 1956-58 as the beginning of a regular consultative relationship between the PCI and the Yugoslav party.[51] The Italians were anxious to make amends for supporting the Cominform resolution of 1948 on the explusion of Yugoslavia from the Soviet camp, and the Yugoslavs were looking for allies in their continuing dispute with the U.S.S.R.[52] The surfacing of the Sino-Soviet conflict further cemented this working relationship into an informal alliance. As ostensible targets of Soviet and Chinese esoteric communication, both Tito and Togliatti were under pressure to go on record with their respective positions on the issues of the Sino-Soviet schism. Although neither took sides in the Sino-Soviet quarrel, these early contacts, Togliatti's "Yalta Memorandum," and the emergence of pro-Chinese factions in Europe paid dividends in the form of growing Western European resistance to Soviet efforts to convene a world conference for the purpose of formally expelling the Chinese from the international Communist movement.

Whether as a defensive reaction to the baiting of native ultra-leftists or for other reasons, the fact remains that from early 1963 on the PCI chose to involve itself in Soviet bloc

[475]

affairs. The PCI's views on Soviet cultural policies in 1964 were moderate but unambiguous: "We consider it our duty to stimulate those elements which can speed up the movement towards greater democracy in the socialist countries, where we think it is not useful or necessary to keep up certain limitations on certain forms of liberty." [53]

The Soviet invasion of Czechoslovakia violated not only "certain forms" of liberty, as the PCI delicately called the brutal repression of Soviet dissidents in the mid-1960s, but the sum total of the ideological, political, economic and cultural content and the achievements of the Prague Spring as well. Observers agree that August 1968 represents a watershed in the history of European Communist relations, especially between the ruling Communist parties of Eastern Europe and the PCI and the PCE.[54]

Why do Western European parties take an active interest in East European and Soviet politics? "Enlightened self-interest" might be the first explanation. Because the Communist parties of Western Europe had been traditionally perceived by voters as ideological and political allies of the Soviet Union, the crises of 1956, the Sino-Soviet dispute, and the events of 1968 led to electoral defeats and widespread defections—especially by younger members and the intellectuals. Communist losses were Socialist and conservative gains in Western Europe. Therefore, support of liberal and dissident intellectuals in the East was a useful way of appealing to the young and educated voters and neutralizing non-Communist political opponents. Furthermore, involvement in East bloc affairs provided party leaders with considerable free publicity that tended to enhance their stature as statesmen of international caliber. In a more fundamental sense, Berlinguer, Marchais, Carrillo, and their colleagues came to the conclusion in the early 1970s that in the age of East-West détente the Communists' political appeal, hence the likelihood of coming to power through parliamentary means, was irrevocably tied to the success or failure of the Soviet and East European record of political liberalization and economic modernization.

These reasons and considerations have bearing on the "but-are-the-Eurocommunists-sincere?" issue as newly converted champions of human rights and civil liberties in Eastern Europe. Those who are inclined to think that the Western European party spokesman are merely going through the motions of criticizing the Russians, Husák, and Honecker, but are not genuinely committed to reforms in Eastern Europe, seem to have a case. The PCI anf PCF, while supportive of persecuted Czechoslovak Communists, have never printed any public criticism against the incarceration of Djilas and Mihajlo Mihajlov or the persecution of the "Belgrade Eight"—people with impeccable credentials as Marxist or socialist intellectuals.[55] Obviously, for both parties Tito was far more important than the fate of a handful of intellectuals—traditional troublemakers for ruling and non-ruling Communist parties. In any case, with the exception of the Gdansk riots of 1970 and the June 1976 workers' strikes in Poland, cases of imprisoned non-elites (peasants, white-collar workers, clergymen, and alleged nationalists everywhere in Eastern Europe and especially in Czechoslovakia, the G.D.R., Romania, Yugoslavia, and the U.S.S.R.) failed to arouse Western Communist sympathies and prompt campaigns of protest. And, when the PCI protested the Husák regime's treatment of leading dissidents and published posthumously Smrkovský's political testament, it did so on the eve of the crucial June 1976 elections. In a July 1977 interview with *Der Spiegel*, Gian-Carlo Pajetta, a leading PCI spokesman, in response to a question about the impact of Eurocommunism on the civil rights movement in Eastern Europe, cleared up the matter

[477]

with refreshing candor: "First of all, these movements in Eastern Europe do not represent any really relevant political forces. They are symptoms of unrest. We very much hope that the governments and parties in the East will carry out what they have promised." [56]

The PCF's sudden interest in the Plyushch case and criticism of the Soviet treatment of political prisoners might be viewed in conjunction with that party's competition with the Gaullists and Socialists rather than as an altruistic gesture.

Former Secretary of State Kissinger also had some doubts about the genuineness of Eurocommunist ideological independence and opposition to Soviet hegemony in international Communist affairs.

We are entitled to certain skepticism about the sincerity of declarations of independence which coincide so precisely with electoral self-interest. One need not be a cynic to wonder at the decision of the French Communists, traditionally perhaps the most Stalinist party in Western Europe, to renounce the Soviet concept of dictatorship of the proletariat without a single dissenting vote among 1700 delegates, as they did at their Party Congress in February 1976, when all previous Party Congresses had endorsed the same dictatorship of the proletariat by a similar unanimous vote of 1700 to nothing. Why was there not at least one lonely soul willing to adhere to the previous view? Much was made of this change as a gesture of independence. Now it turns out that the new Soviet Constitution, in preparation for years, drops the phrase as well.[57]

Perhaps the French comrades knew something that Mr. Kissinger did not wish to acknowledge: namely, that sincerity, or "the appearance of piety" as Machiavelli had it, are legitimate tools of political warfare to which the PCF—just as any other lawfully constituted radical group or party—is entitled in a liberal democracy. One, of course, need not take declarations of democratic Eurocommunist intentions at face value. What matters in this context is that Berlinguer, Marchais, and the rest are practical politicians and not moral philosophers.

An additional complicating factor in East European-Eurocommunist relations is the way in which these parties go about resolving the conflict of interest inherent in their respective positions as *ruling* politicians (in Eastern Europe) and as occasionally bitter opponents (in Western Europe) of the governments with which the East Europeans maintain, on the state level, correct and sometimes embarrassingly cordial relations. If we assume that the Eurocommunists' goal is to come to power and to act on behalf of their respective nations in all areas, including government-to-government contacts with East European party-states, then we have reason to believe that the PCI's and the PCF's present, presumably ideologically motivated, concern with the quality of life in Eastern Europe, would change substantially upon achievement of this goal. Chances are good that the *raison d'etat* of a Communist-led French government would have little in common with the concerns of an imprisoned dissident in a Communist bloc country. Moreover, it is extremely unlikely that Berlinguer as Prime Minister of Italy would or could help out either politically or economically an East European state, however "autonomist" or "revisionist," at the expense of his country's interests.

End of an Era: East Berlin and the Road to Autonomy

The results of the June 1976 East Berlin All-European Conference of Communist and Workers' Parties are the most

[479]

recent and, to date by far the most significant, achievements of Eurocommunism. According to Kevin Devlin's and William E. Griffith's authoritative accounts, three basic ideological platforms, as defined by central issues and measured by extent of divergence from the Soviet positions, were advanced at the East Berlin meeting: the "autonomist," the "revisionist," and "loyalist" or orthodox positions.[58]

The "autonomist" position was succinctly put by Tito: "We have . . . opposed and will continue to oppose all forms of interference in the internal affairs of other countries. Any external interference, regardless of its form, is directly damaging to peace, security and cooperation among the people of Europe and in the world generally." [59] Tito's message skillfully combined the well-known PCI, PCF, and PCE positions with those of his own party, but in this case the matter of "noninterference" clearly implied state-to-state relations as well. The paraphrasing of the wording of the Helsinki Final Act and the insertion of the key words of "peace, security and cooperation" provides us with the quintessential "autonomist" position in the East European context.

The "revisionist" argument has altogether different implications for a ruling East European party than, for example, for the PCF. Marchais went on record in support of " . . . the freedom of thought and expression, of creation and publication, the freedom to demonstrate, to hold meetings and to assemble, the freedom of movement within the country and abroad, the freedom of religion and the right to strike." [60] And he might have added, "minus the dictatorship of the proletariat" as a reminder of an earlier decision of the PCF to abandon that cherished Leninist concept. Surely, the "autonomist" Romanian party and its Secretary General, the object of the most vigorous personality cult in any Communist party in recent years, can hardly be expected to forego the advantages of total police control of his country in order to conform to the logic of his French colleague's position. Indeed, the leadership of *any* ruling Communist party could derive little comfort from Berlinguer's "autonomist-revisionist" statement: "Each people has the incontestable right to freely choose the forms of its own development and government. For example, we are fighting so that the Italian people, within the framework of the international alliances to which our country belongs, can autonomously decide, without any foreign interference, its own political leadership." [61]

The "loyalist" position was articulated, with some semantic variations, by representatives of East Germany, Poland, Czechoslovakia, Hungary and Bulgaria. The burden of the loyalist case may be summarized by quoting Lenin, as cited in a new Soviet textbook on socialism and foreign policy.

> Proletarian internationalism demands: first, that the interests of ths proletarian struggle in any one country should be subordinated to the interests of that struggle on a world-wide scale, and, second, that a nation which is achieving victory over the bourgeoisie should be able and willing to make the national sacrifices for the overthrow of the international capital.[62]

In fairness to the actual diversity of "loyalist" positions we should recognize the existence of ambiguous postures within that camp. János Kádár's speech at the Berlin conference provides the best expression of the Hungarian compromise formula:

> The universally valid teachings of Marxism-Leninism are being applied by individual communist parties according to their countries' national peculiarities and historic con-

ditions. Today, when the world communist movement has no center or a leading party and when the fraternal parties autonomously determine their strategy and tactics, the preservation of the purity of Marxist-Leninist theory is of particular importance as are the ideological utilization of practical experience and the realization of the principles of proletarian internationalism.[63]

A self-cancelling statement of this kind can buy time for a ruling party, allowing it to change its position when circumstances permit. With some effort, a similar case could be made for the Polish position. This inference was confirmed by subsequent press reports quoting an unnamed member of the Polish Central Committee: "We Polish Communists have an ambition to play an important part in Europe, creating a model of socialism acceptable to everyone, including our comrades in both directions." [64] Although it is not clear whether this statement was made before or after the food riots of the summer of 1976 (and the doubt they cast on the viability of the Polish "model"), there is growing evidence that the precedent of the Romanians' ambiguous stance in the early phases of the Sino-Soviet schism, and the subsequent rewards and benefits from the West that befell that country are not forgotten by the Polish party. Kádár's indirect rebuttal, at a Vienna press conference on December 8, 1976, of the loyalist Zhivkov's condemnation of Eurocommunist heresies and the Hungarian leader's guarded approval of the same suggests that in the post-East Berlin temporary ideological vacuum there is room for more than one or two ruling East European parties to play.[65]

In early March 1977 two important conferences were held on the same days in Madrid and Sofia. The purpose of the

Madrid meeting was to demonstrate the French and Italian parties' moral and political support for the still outlawed PCE and its Secretary General Santiago Carrillo. Because the final communiqué refrained from criticizing the U.S.S.R. and the regimes of East Europe, the Soviet sponsors of the Sofia "counter-summit" were content with issuing a relatively bland statement instead of the expected broadside at Eurocommunism. However, what is of interest in this context is that the Soviets could not, even if they tried, produce a clear consensus, let alone unanimity on this issue among the participants. The "autonomist" Romanians refused in advance to sign an anti-Eurocommunist statement; the Hungarian spokesman was incensed by Bulgarian criticisms of János Kádár's well-publicized conciliatory statements on Eurocommunism; and the Poles were probably reluctant to jeopardize their self-appointed middleman's role in the East-West ideological conflict. Moreover, all participants in the Sofia meeting were undoubtedly constrained from opposing the Spanish and Italian reformist platforms, which explicitly endorsed, among other things, Basket Three of the Helsinki Final Act. The Communist bloc delegates' vulnerability on this score at the forthcoming Belgrade review session thus saved until the summer of 1977 the Eurocommunists from Ponomarev's, Zhivkov's, and Bil'ak's public wrath.[66]

The publication of Carrillo's *Eurocommunism and the State* in April 1977 and its immediate impact on the Western European Left was the latest and to date the most comprehensive revisionist critique of the Soviet Union and the Communist states of East Europe. In a July 1977 interview, Manuel Azcárate, a leading PCE ideologue, speaking in defense of Carrillo's theses on Eurocommunist objectives, went a step beyond the traditional limits of an internecine ideological feud

[483]

between estranged Communist parties and linked up the question of party autonomy with the entire issue of European security:

> ... [the Eurocommunist] parties are fighting to achieve peaceful coexistence, an end to military blocs, the removal of [foreign] military bases wherever they may be, disarmament and the total ban on the use of nuclear weapons; they are against any interference in the internal affairs of others, and uphold the right to self-determination of all peoples.[67]

To judge from the East Europeans' initially sluggish response to Carrillo's challenge and Moscow's second thoughts about the adverse foreign reactions to the notorious *New Times* review of the Carrillo book,[68] it is apparent that on the first anniversary of the East Berlin conference the Russians have lost additional ground to the "revisionist" and "autonomist" Communist parties of Western and Eastern Europe. In fact, the Spanish party, with hesitant Italian support, seems to be heading for a showdown and perhaps an irreparable break with the CPSU. Soviet *ad hominem* attacks on Carrillo are reminiscent of an advanced stage of the Sino-Soviet conflict in the early 1960s when the Russians put an end to the charade of esoteric criticism of Chinese policies and named Mao and his associates as the chief culprits for the inter-party rift. However, it is 1978 and not 1948, 1956, 1961, or 1968; and there is no foreign, ruling or non-ruling Communist party that would willingly accept Soviet interference in the makeup of its leadership—especially when it concerns a party's Secretary General.

[484]

Eurocommunism: Limits of Influence

There are several schools of thought on the likely influence of Eurocommunism on the Communist states of East Europe. In the West there are those who believe that Eurocommunist strategies and ideological innovations might enable the ruling Communist parties to introduce domestic reforms and to move toward more independent foreign policies.[69] The official Washington position is still ambiguous, though spokesmen foresee unspecified benefits for the West from the spread of Eurocommunist ideas to the East.[70] Western European leaders, especially the French and the Italians, are closer to the realities of Eurocommunism and tend to regard it both as an internal threat and as a destabilizing factor for European security. They have sought to undercut their domestic Communist political adversaries on the latter front by engaging in an *Ostpolitik* of their own. Intensive diplomacy, and, in particular, economic agreements between the political incumbents in East and West Europe have benefited both sides at the expense of native dissidents and the Eurocommunists, respectively. The Eurocommunists themselves are divided on the ultimate goals of their critical posture toward the U.S.S.R. and Eastern Europe. Unlike the smaller and politically inconsequential Western European Communist parties that have tended to be rather uninhibited critics of policies of the established Communist states, neither the PCF nor the PCI— the "twenty-two" and the "thirty-four percent" parties, to use Robert Legvold's terminology—is likely, unless compelled to do so by ths CPSU, to follow Carrillo (the head of a "nine percent" party) to an open break with Moscow and the East Europeans.

Thus, conflicting Western policies and intentions constitute the first constraint on the unimpeded flow of Eurocommunist influences to Eastern Europe. The second factor is, of course, the Soviets' concern about the demoralizing influence of Eurocommunism on the stability, military strength, and international stature of U.S.S.R. and Communist Eastern Europe. The *New Times* critique of Carrillo was quite explicit on this point: "As regards Carrillo's recommendation to "Soviet comrades" for transforming the Soviet state, it should be noted, first, that the contradicts himself in urging in effect the weakening of the Soviet Union, the might of which, as he himself has to concede in earlier passages of his book, played so important a role in combating imperialism and in changing the world balance of strength." [71]

If by "transformation" of the U.S.S.R. and Eastern Europe we understand, as Carrillo does, the democratization of the political system, the restoration of civil liberties, and the realization of the rest of the Eurocommunist platform, these prospects are undoubtedly just as unacceptable to a ruling East European Communist party, including the League of Yugoslav Communists (LCY), as to the CPSU. The question is, of course, how much voluntary devolution of power can a ruling, or "ninety-nine percent" Communist party afford without being overthrow by the people? If not drastic reforms of the basic institutions of a Communist state, then what aspects of the perhaps less sensitive economic, social and cultural policies could be changed without endangering the regime's stability?

A recent study by Sharon Wolchik lists four factors that have a bearing on a regime's ability to take an open-minded or positive attitude toward proposed reforms in *these* policy areas. These are "(1) the nature of the changes envisioned, (2) the relationship between proponents of the change and the elites in the country contemplating adopting of such innovations, (3)

[486]

the characteristics and cohesion of domestic elites and their relationship to the populace, and (4) the atmosphere in which change is proposed and carried out." [72] When testing these factors against the *realities* of Eastern Europe, one must conclude, as Wolchik does: "Emulation of many aspects of Eurocommunist domestic and foreign policy would be incompatible with many of the existing institutional arrangements and foreign policy commitments of East European states." [73]

While one must not dismiss the possibility that the ruling elites of an East European Communist party might one day feel compelled to adopt some less heretical Eurocommunist innovations, such as actually broadening the participatory base of low-level decision-making processes in factories, offices and professional associations or increasing the accountability of local officials, more drastic reforms are not in the realm of possibility in the foreseeable future. On the other hand, one could argue that externally proposed reforms might stand a better chance of adoption if these originate with another *ruling* Communist party. Obviously, this would exclude the ideas of the Hungarian October and those of the Prague Spring, but might, under certain circumstances, include the "Yugoslav model" or the structural innovations of the Hungarian New Economic Mechanism.

If by the Yugoslav model we understand the institution of the workers' councils, partial political decentralization and division of authority between the central LCY and the republican Communist parties, and significantly increased public participation in local political decision-making within the framework of the Socialist Alliance and thus of ultimate party control, we might conclude that it represents a low-risk alternative to the present legitimacy crisis of the East European regimes. Facts, however, fail to support this theory; for what is politically feasible in a legitimately founded Communist state like Yugoslavia can lead to anti-regime behavior and instability elsewhere in Eastern Europe. It is a matter of historic record that the Poznan workers' committees in June 1956, the Central Budapest Workers' Council in November 1956, the Czech factory workers' committees in 1968, the strike committee of the Gdansk Shipyards in 1970, and the workers' committees of the Ursus Tractor Factory in Warsaw in June 1976 were *not* partners, but articulate opponents of the regimes; that the existence of a few electoral districts with multiple candidates has *not* changed the unanimity and pro-regime stance of the East European legislatures; and that the attempted (and subsequently frustrated) bifurcation of the Czechoslovak Communist party into separate Czech and Slovak components had *not* and, indeed, could not lead to the devolution of the federal Communist party's hegemony over Czechoslovakia.

Therefore, successful innovations and reforms must begin, as they have in Hungary, from within and with as little external interference as possible.

Opportunities for change depend on the delicate interplay of forces within each Communist state. The "forces" in question are the Communist party, the state bureaucracy, the military, the police, the technical and scientific elites, the Church (as in Poland), the politicized intelligentsia, and the "people," however defined. Which of these groups is the most likely to become an internal pressure group on behalf of the "Eurocommunization" of a regime? The answer, again, depends on the operational meaning of Eurocommunist reforms as these are perceived by the various political forces within each Communist polity. The "people" have not responded to Eurocommunist influences, and probably cannot be expected to. The police, the military, and the state bureaucracy are certain to support the *New Times* thesis and resist external attempts aiming at the "transformation" and the likely enfeeblement of the system. The technocrats, though probably less so than the humanistic intellectuals, would, within limits, support initiatives enhancing the autonomy, social status and political influence of their ranks. With the exception of the dissident community (numerically significant in Poland and Czechoslovakia), the interests of both kinds of intellectuals are compatible with those of the party elite—or at least with its reformist wing. It is, therefore, the party elite and, more specifically, the balance of power between its conservative and reform-oriented members that determines which, if any, Eurocommunist proposals might be implemented in the form of state policy.

Party elite support for some aspects of the Eurocommunist platform has, thus far, not been translated into domestic policies in any East European country. As a recent *Scinteia* editorial pointed out: " . . . Communists . . . must particularly avoid comparing the experience of parties in socialist countries, which acted under different conditions, with the methods proposed for the building of the new system by Communist parties in the capitalist countries." [74] This statement, coming as it does from one of the two staunchest supporters of Eurocommunism among the ruling Communist parties, is indicative of the effective limits of Eurocommunist-inspired policy innovations in the domestic field. However, caveats of this sort do not preclude the pursuit of foreign policies that are at variance with Moscow's wishes, nor the possibility, as an unintended consequence of economic benefits reaped from unorthodox diplomacy and improved relations with the West, of the eventual introduction of domestic reforms as internal legitimacy-building measures in support of maverick foreign policies. When that happens, the Communist parties will have

[489]

to come to terms with those democratic and socialist dissidents who seek to expand the dimensions of regime-sponsored innovations into substantive reforms. All this merely postpones the day of reckoning between the incumbents and the reformers of Eastern Europe. The question then is whether the coincidence of the likely evolution in the next five to ten years of Eurocommunist parties and ideas in the West and that of the conservative-reformist intra-party dialogue in the East will favor or hinder the adoption of liberalized policies by the regimes of Eastern Europe. The answer will depend on several predictable and unpredictable contingencies to be discussed below.

Conclusions

Perhaps the most important finding of this study is that Eastern Europe in the 1970s has come of age and has again become a part of Europe. Having survived the Nazi and Stalinist-dominated periods of their recent history and having built up modern industrial economies and developed stratified and, on the whole stable, societies, the peoples of East Europe are ready to rejoin the community of European nations from which they had been forcibly separated forty years ago. Indeed, the kinds of societal and psychological changes that have generated grass-roots disenchantment with the postwar political order in Western Europe and have given the Eurocommunist parties a chance to bid for power also exist in Eastern Europe. The shared condition of alienation from political demagoguery, from the ever-growing and less and less efficient state bureaucracy, from the depersonalization of daily life has led to a loss of faith in established authority and has given rise to doubts about the destiny of liberal democracy and post-totalitarian communism, respectively, in the two halves of Europe.

Another, and rather unexpected, finding of this study concerns the shared characteristics and perhaps the shared destiny of Eurocommunism and democratic and socialist dissent in Eastern Europe. Both have arisen as protest movements against Stalinist orthodoxy and Soviet domination and have been fueled by a perceived sense of powerlessness in the political environments which they seek to change through nonviolent means. In a sense, both are determined to reshape the political consequences of the last war: the Eurocommunists seek to reshape the liberal democratic political system and, less directly, the American political, cultural and economic influences behind it, and the East European dissidents seek to revitalize the stagnant, morally bankrupt and economically inefficient Communist political system and, perhaps more directly than the Eurocommunists, eliminate or ameliorate Soviet influences behind it. These shared ambitions affirm the common heritage of Europeans against all outside powers and openly challenge the hegemony of the two superpowers.[75] For this reason, both the United States and the Soviet Union have a direct interest in thwarting the development of such autonomist forces in their respective spheres of influence in Europe.

The third finding concerns the way in which external and essentially uncontrollable influences affect the development of both Western and Eastern European left-wing reform movements. Global economic conditions, international energy, commodity and trade and banking transactions, the arms race and the unpredictable whims of the two superpowers can, and have, created situations over which neither the political incumbents in Western and Eastern Europe nor their respective ideological adversaries have any control. In the face of these contingencies the political maturity and ideological sophistication of both Eurocommunists and the East European dissidents have been most impressive indeed.

A shared sense of European identity, opposition to the established national and regional political order, and dependence on external forces are the common characteristics of the western and eastern branches of Eurocommunism. Thus far, there has been only one country, Yugoslavia, which has succeeded in developing a model that incorporates features of Western Communist revisionism and East European autonomism. While "the Yugoslav road to Socialism" probably cannot be duplicated elsewhere, it is the combination of an authentic revolution, bold assertion of national sovereignty, political pragmatism, and the creative ideological eclecticism with which Tito and his colleagues have developed the Yugoslav system that is of significance as a possible bridge between Eurocommunism and East Europe. Despite its many shortcomings from the viewpoint of Western liberal democracy and the uncertainties that the country will face after Tito's death, a suitably modified version of the "Yugoslav way" represents a realistic and politically feasible road to reform and internal revitalization for most, though probably not all, East European regimes. If not necessarily the internal political institutions that have not, in any case, fared well elsewhere in East Europe, then the example of Yugoslav foreign policies could be adopted as a reasonably low-risk approach to the uncertainties of international politics in the 1980s.

The essential ingredients of Yugoslav foreign policies are well-known. They consist of "independence, autonomy, sovereignty and absolute noninterference in the internal affairs of others," the denial of Moscow's leading role in international Communist affairs, and the policy of nonalignment and an active role in Third World affairs. The overall philosophy of

Yugoslav foreign policies is derived from what Aleksandar Grlickov, a top LCY official, calls a "dialectical relationship between the national and the international" commitments of his country. In a recent study Grlickov, in somewhat obscure language, spelled out the specifics of this proposition:

It is understood that the relationship between the national and the international is not a mechanical relationship nor a relationship which would be a simple linear function of class internationalist consciousness and solidarity of the workers' class, but the opposite. What is involved is a relationship between the interests of the workers' classes of several countries, which are not only contradictory but under certain conditions are even antagonistic. This relationship is not overcome simply when the workers' class takes over power, but is possible when there is respect for objectively different interests and the contradictions based on them, including attempts at harmonizing these principles on the well-known principles of equality and independence. In such a relationship, the international interest is not an abstract but a concrete form which proceeds from the national interests of the several countries and their workers' class functioning as the supporter of the class and the national interests at the same time. The theoretical and practical political premise, which not only sets a time limit for the relationship, but also imposes an ultimate and full organic unity on it, is to be found in the Marxist position that "the abolition of nations is an act of abolishing the class too." [76]

When translated into practical foreign policy terms, the Yugoslav position upholds the primacy both of national interests and of survival of the state as an independent entity over the ideologically motivated requirements of "internationalism"—"proletarian" or otherwise. By continuing to pay lip-service to the "objective identity" of working class and Communist party interests under ruling and non-ruling conditions, the Yugoslav position seeks to legitimate the right to national experimentation and at the same time to make use of the increasingly tenuous principle of Communist international solidarity by turning it against all comers—most prominently the U.S.S.R. and the United States.

Another component of the "autonomous but internationalist" foreign policy of Yugoslavia has been the effort since the late 1950s to link up with the bloc of newly independent nonaligned nations of Asia, Africa and Latin America. Unlike the Marxist rhetoric of "working class solidarity," the philosophy of "opting out" of the historic antagonisms between East and West, in which the peoples of Eastern Europe have been caught during the last five centuries, has been a widely shared sentiment among liberals, radicals, federalists, and socialists of East Europe. The collective search for a "third road" between fascism and communism before the war and between East and West since the war (hence the search for allies not committed to either side) has been a significant undercurrent of belief among the intelligentsia in Poland, Czechoslovakia, Hungary and Romania, and in Yugoslavia where his aspiration has been adopted as state policy. The writings of Imre Nagy, Ota Sik, and their philosophical heirs attest to the enduring influence of this idea, and Eurocommunism has given a new impetus to initiatives of this kind.[77]

The pursuit of "third road" or non-aligned foreign policies by a Communist state presupposes either a substantial degree of regime legitimacy (as in Yugoslavia) or political stability (as in Romania and Hungary). In either case, foreign policies seeking to attenuate the regional hegemony of the U.S.S.R.

tend to strengthen national sovereignty, contribute to economic development through increased trade with the West and the Third World, and help develop distance between an Eastern European state and the Soviet Union.

The theory and practice of Yugoslav federalism is the third regionally applicable aspect of the Yugoslav model. To the extent that its adoption might alleviate political tensions over ethnic and national minority participation in national politics, others, most prominently Romania and Czechoslovakia, could benefit from it. Since internal consolidation of all social, political and ethic groups of an East European state is essential both to regime stability and the pursuit of autonomist foreign policies, this feature of the Yugoslav road, if adopted elsewhere, could become a first step toward non-alignment.

The Yugoslavs' role as mediators between Eurocommunism and the Soviet bloc and as self-appointed spokesmen for détente in Eastern Europe offers new opportunities to keep alive the issues of sovereignty and autonomy and to promote these concerns as permanent items for the agenda of *any* U.S.-Soviet agreement on the future of Europe. The Yugoslavs' championship of Eurocommunist ideas, including those of Carrillo, against Soviet, Bulgarian and Czechoslovak critics is, in part, a self-serving policy designed to forestall Soviet "expulsionist" inclinations. Should Moscow decide to excommunicate the French, Italian or Spanish parties, Yugoslavia would become almost as exposed and vulnerable to Soviet pressures as it had been before the Sino-Soviet schism. For this reason, Yugoslavia has a vital interest in proselytizing the Eurocommunist course in Eastern Europe.

In certain respects the Romanians' predicament is similar to that of Yugoslavia. What began in the early 1960s as a neutral position in the Sino-Soviet conflict has developed into a quasi-independent foreign policy by the mid-1970s. Ceauşescu at first sought to dissociate Romania from the Council of Mutual Economic Aid and Assistance and next, by refusing to join the invasion of Czechoslovakia, from the Warsaw Treaty Organization as well. This was followed by an aggressive drive to establish trading relations with the West. Successful efforts to join the nonaligned bloc and, more recently, vigorous support of the Eurocommunist line have put Romania in the forefront of ruling Communist parties seeking to lessen Soviet influence in Europe.

The trend toward more independent Romanian foreign policies slowed down and perhaps came to a standstill at the end of 1976. Because of Ceauşescu's inability to overcome the effects of Western economic recession, high energy costs, and the diminished interest of foreign investors in the profit potentials of the Romanian economy, he had no choice but to drift closer to the U.S.S.R. and the CMEA that the regime had spurned in the early 1960s. Neither summit diplomacy nor declarations of independence at Eurocommunist and non-aligned forums can alter economic realities. Upon reaching the limits of internal capabilities to effect rapid economic breakthroughs, Ceauşescu has no choice but to mortgage the regime's economic legitimacy and foreign policy options on the continued availability of external support. Therefore, unless there is a substantial revival of Western interest in Romania, that country's foreign policies will "revert to type" and converge with the orthodoxy of its domestic policies.

The Hungarian case is rather different from that of Romania. The posture of the last two decades of reformist innovations at home and impeccably orthodox foreign policies abroad has changed since 1975. Although the Hungarian government has made efforts to downplay the importance of its shift toward more independent foreign polices, the record since 1975 is quite unambiguous. Since Helsinki and certainly since the East Berlin conference Kádár has been engaged in a quiet campaign to restore Hungary's relations with the country's traditonal Western European trading partners. In what appears as a new kind of personal diplomacy, Kádár has combined state visits to Italy and West Germany with meetings with Berlinguer and Brandt at the same time when Brezhnev refused to see Marchais on his state visit to France. In June 1977 Kádár was also received by the Pope—an event that the Hungarians view as the first step toward the full normalization of relations with the United States.

It is not clear how far Kádár and the Hungarian party wish to pursue this new opening to the West and the remarkable intensification of Hungary's diplomatic and commercial ties with the nonaligned world. The underlying reasons seem to be both economic and political. With the sharp increase of Soviet oil prices in 1974, the Hungarians were faced with the choice between drastically curtailing policies of the consumer-oriented New Economic Mechanism (NEM), or finding alternative energy sources, export markets, and additional Western credits. The political cost of the first course was prohibitive, while the second appeared economically feasible and politically possible in the post-Helsinki period. This strategy, if it is permitted by the Soviets to mature into a new policy orientation, could produce a Yugoslav-type posture in East-West relations. Whether these recent changes in Hungarian foreign policies will actually amount to a significant reorientation will depend, in part, on three internal contingencies. These are: (1) the ability of János Kádár to institutionalize his leadership style by isolating the Hungarian party's conservative factions in the Central Committee and laying the groundwork for an orderly succession; (2) the astuteness of Hungarian economic planners in coping with the conflicting pressures of the Soviet drive for regional economic integration and popular demands for the continuation of NEM; and (3) the regime's ability to contain widely shared popular demands for the withdrawal of Soviet troops from Hungarian soil and the satisfactory resolution of the status of Hungarian ethnic minorities in Romania. These dilemmas are a formidable challenge to the incumbents' political acumen, and it is by no means certain that they will be successful in meeting it.

The situation in Poland has been deteriorating since 1975. In another East European country a crisis of confidence in the government's ability to shelter the population from the burdens both of higher energy costs and of the rapidly mounting indebtedness to Western creditors might be mitigated by means of judicious state intervention and Soviet aid. In Poland, however, the party and the government must share real political authority with the Church and with the resurgent forces of Polish nationalism. Although Eurocommunist influences have not made appreciable inroads among the party elites, this might happen if no solution is found to the regime's deeply rooted legitimacy problems. Because of Poland's pivotal position in the northern tier of the WTO, the threat of chronic instability might, more readily than elsewhere in East Europe, trigger preventive Soviet military action and the actual occupation of that country.

The German Democratic Republic is economically the most developed and, until the emergence of intellectual dissent in the fall of 1976, had been regarded as a politically stable unit of the Soviets' East European empire. The East German case is unique and differs, perhaps more in political and psychological than in economic terms, from that of Poland and Hungary. In the absence of a widely shared sense of an East German national identity by the people and the elites, the Honecker regime has not and, in the foreseeable future, will not be able to contain the economic "pull" and the ideological "push" of

[498]

the Federal Republic. Because of the overwhelming Soviet military presence and Western strategic interests in fostering the development of multiple contacts between the two Germanies, tensions are likely to remain high in the G.D.R. until a mutual and balanced force reduction agreement is reached by the United States and the Soviet Union. And that may not happen until the mid-1980s—if then.

The Husák regime's unyielding hostility to internal reform movements and bitter denunciation of Eurocommunism are obvious signs of insecurity and inability to come to terms with the new configuration of European politics in the age of détente. In a different sense, Czechoslovakia in 1977 may be regarded as an early test case of future Soviet intentions in Eastern Europe. The Prague Spring was a classic example of an innovative-reformist approach to the crisis of post-totalitarian political legitimacy in an Eastern European country. Although the reform program was not allowed to run its full course, it nevertheless proved in Zdenek Mlynař's words, that the "Soviet model (was) inapplicable to the more developed countries" [78]—especially those with well-entrenched democratic traditions. The ideological kinship between the Czechoslovak reform program and Eurocommunism is self-evident, and so is Soviet opposition to Czechoslovak socialist dissident efforts to renew the brutally interrupted dialogue between the party and the people. These are clear signs of Moscow's likely response to future Hungarian and Polish attempts at internal "Eurocommunization" and political reform.

In sum: East Europe is likely to remain subject to the unpredictable cross-currents of future East-West, and particularly U.S.-Soviet, relations. Neither the ground rules, nor the principal actors, nor their basic motivations and interests can be expected to change in the next ten years. Eurocommunist debating points and the Russians' loss of face at the East

Berlin conference should not be mistaken for Soviet weakness, nor viewed as signs of the erosion of Soviet influence in Eastern Europe. It is not, and in the foreseeable future it will not be, Carrillo and his blueprint for socialism (which "will base itself upon the respect for political and ideological pluralism") but the CPSU Politburo and the Soviet General Staff that will determine the extent to which Eurocommunist tendencies will be allowed to take root in six East European states. East Europe may be the touchstone of détente today, but on the global scale it is only one of the several areas of potential tensions and sources of East-West conflict and cooperation. Therefore, its importance must be seen in terms of its relative value to the main antagonists of world politics. And in this sense, the Russians seem to have the better hand. The East Europeans know it, but seem to be able to cope in the no mans' land. After all, they have been doing so with little Western help for the last five hundred years.

Notes

* I wish to acknowledge my indebtedness to Dr. A.H. Brown of Oxford University, Professor Henry Krisch of the University of Connecticut, and Dr. Vladimir V. Kusin of the University of Glasgow for their helpful comments on an earlier draft of this study.

1. Milovan Djilas, "The Limits of Détente," *The Political Quarterly*, vol. 47, no. 4 (October-December, 1976), p. 447.

2. For a useful discussion of this matter, see Marshall D. Shulman, *Stalin's Foreign Policy Reappraised* (Cambridge, Mass.: Harvard University Press, 1963).

3. Zbigniew Brzezinski, "The Competitive Relationship," in C. Gati, ed., *Caging the Bear* (Indianapolis and New York: Bobbs-Merrill, 1974), pp. 157-99.

4. V.V. Zagladin, *The World Communist Movement* (Moscow: Progress Publishers, 1973), p. 88.

5. Cf. Carl Beck, "Patterns and Problems of Governance," in Carmelo Mesa-Lago and Carl Beck, eds., *Comparative Socialist Systems: Essays on Politics and Economics* (Pittsburgh: University of Pittsburgh Center for International Studies, 1975), pp. 123-46.

6. On this see, Paul S. Shoup, "Indicators of Socio-Politico-Economic Development," in *ibid.*, pp. 3-38.

7. Cf. Paul Neuburg, *The Hero's Children* (New York: William Morrow & Co., 1973).

8. Cf. Zbigniew Brzezinski, *The Soviet Bloc* (Cambridge, Mass.: Harvard University Press, 1960, rev. ed. 1967).

9. The classic study on East Europe's political traditions is R.V. Burks, *The Dynamics of Communism in Eastern Europe* (Princeton, N.J.: Princeton University Press, 1961).

10. H. Gordon Skillings's *Czechoslovakia's Interrupted Revolution* (Princeton, N.J.: Princeton University Press, 1976) is the seminal work on this subject.

11. Dennison Rusinow, *The Yugoslav Political Experiment, 1948-1974* (London: C. Hurst & Co., 1977), chap. 7.

12. Cf. Fritz W. Ermarth, *Internationalism, Security and Legitimacy: The Challenge to the Soviet Interests in East Europe, 1964-1968* (Santa Monica, Calif.: Rand Corporation, 1969), and Roman

Kolkowicz, "The Warsaw Pact: Entangling Alliance," *Survey,* no. 70, 71 (1969), pp. 86-101.

13. Teresa Rakowska-Harmstone, " 'Socialist Internationalism' and Eastern Europe—A New Stage," *Survey,* vol. 22 no. 1 (98) (Winter 1976), pp. 38-54.

14. George Macovescu, "The Contribution of Socialist Romania's Foreign Policy to Outlining the Principles of a Better and More Just World," *The Social Future,* Special issue for the 10th World Congress of the IPSA, in Edinburgh, August 15-21, 1976, pp. 3-10.

15. Andrzej Korbonski, "Détente, East-West Trade, and the Future of Economic Integration in Eastern Europe," *World Politics,* vol. 28, no. 4 (July 1976), pp. 568-89.

16. On this, see "Report on the Conference on Eastern Europe: Stability or Recurrent Crises?" held at Airlie House, Warrentown, Va., November 13-15, 1975, pp. 19-24.
17. For complete text, see "Conference on Security and Co-Operation in Europe. Final Act," Department of State Publication 8826, General Foreign Policy Series 298, August 1975.

18. Perhaps the most thought-provoking collection of dialogues on this subject is G.R. Urban, ed., *Détente* (New York: Universe Books, 1975).

19. For a spirited and sophisticated critique of détente along these lines, see Leopold Labedz, "USA and the World Today: Kissinger and After," *Survey,* vol. 22, no. 1 (98), (Winter 1976), pp. 1-37. For some second thoughts on détente, see "The Future of East-West Relations," *Survey,* vol. 22, no. 3/4 (100/101) (Summer-Autumn 1976), pp. 1-162.

20. Gerald L. Steibel, *Détente: Promises and Pitfalls* (New York: Crane, Russak & Co., 1975).

21. For published excerpts, see *New York Times,* April 6, 7, 1976. For Kissinger's amplification of his earlier views, see "Excerpts from Kissinger's Address to the Institute of Strategic Studies in London," *New York Times,* June 26, 1976.

22. "Dominant political culture" consists of four components: previous political experience, values and fundamental beliefs, foci of identification and loyalty, and political knowledge and expectations. Discussion of these categories has been developed by Archie Brown in a pioneering volume on comparative Communist political culture. See Archie Brown and Jack Gray, eds., *Political Culture and Political Change in Communist States* (London: Macmillan, 1977), pp. 16-18.

23. Cf. Robert R. King, *Minorities under Communism* (Cambridge, Mass.: Harvard University Press, 1973).

24. For a useful discussion of general questions of stability and instability in Eastern Europe, see Zvi Y. Gitelman, "The Lessons of History," Paper prepared for the Conference on "Eastern Europe: Stability or Recurrent Crisis?" Airlie House, Warrentown, Va., November 13-15, 1975.

25. For an original and stimulating theoretical discussion of these matters, see Susan Bridge, "Why Czechoslovakia? And Why 1968?" and comments by Galia Golan, Jaroslav Krejci, Vladimir V. Kusin, Robin Remington, and George S. Wheeler, in *Studies in Comparative Communism,* vol. 8, no. 4 (Winter 1975), pp. 413-44.

26. The remarkable diversity of the Communist world's social, political and economic development is discussed in William A. Walsh's excellent "Towards an Empirical Typology of Socialist Systems," in C. Mesa-Lago and C. Beck, eds., *Comparative Socialist Systems: Essays on Politics and Economics,* pp. 52-91.

27. The most original and provocative critique of the post-totalitarian social equilibrium in Eastern Europe is by Iván Szelényi

[503]

and György Konrád, *Az értelmiség útja az osztályhatalomhoz* (Toward the Class Power of the Intelligentsia). The manuscript (unpublished in Hungary) is scheduled for publication by Harcourt, Brace, and Jovanovich in 1978.

28. As Szelényi and Konrád put it, "the ideologue, the policeman and the technocrat are dependent on one another and legitimate each other's positions." *Ibid.*

29. Cf. Cornelius Castoriadis "The Hungarian Source," and Claude Lefort "The Age of Novelty," *Telos,* no. 29 (Fall, 1976), pp. 2-22 and 23-38.

30. Speech by Cyrus R. Vance, on Law Day, before the University of Georgia Law School, Athens, Georgia. News release by Bureau of Public Affairs, Office of Media Services, Department of State, April 30, 1977.

31. Volumes of the international human rights journal *Index on Censorship* (London) have given, since 1972, the best account of violations of human rights, both in the East and the West. For a more detailed coverage of events of the post-Helsinki period, see The Commission on Security and Cooperation in Europe, "Report to the Congress of the United States on Implementation of the Final Act of the Conference on Security and Cooperation in Europe: Findings and Recommendations Two Years After Helsinki," Washington, D.C., August 1, 1977.

32. The latest is President Carter's speech on U.S.-Soviet relations on July 21, 1977, in Charleston, N.C., ". . . [our commitment to human rights] is addressed not to any particular people, or area of the world, but to all countries equally, including our own." News Release by Bureau of Public Affairs, Office of Media Services, Department of State, July 21, 1977. See also Elizabeth Drew, "Human Rights," *The New Yorker,* July 18, 1977, pp. 36-62.

33. This can be amply documented from the dissidents' own writings. András Hegedüs, Agnes Heller, Mária Márkus, and Mihály Vajda, *The Humanization of Socialism* (London: Allison and Busby, 1976); Jiří Pelikán, *Socialist Opposition in Eastern Europe* (London: Allison and Busby, 1976); Václav Havel, "Letter to Dr. Gustáv Husák, General Secretary of the Czechoslovak Communist Party," *Survey*, vol. 21, no. 3 (96) (Summer, 1975), pp. 166-90.

34. István Bibó, *The Paralysis of International Institutions and the Remedies: A Study of Self-Determination, Concord among the Major Powers, and Political Arbitration* (Hussocks, Sussex: The Hungster Press Ltd, 1976).

35. Cf. Letter from András Hegedüs to the Bertrand Russell Peace Foundation on the twentieth anniversary of Khrushchev's secret speech to the 20th CPSU Congress in 1956, in András Hegedüs, *Socialism and Bureaucracy* (London: Allison and Busby, 1976), p. 190.

36. "Typewriters Against Tanks," *The Times*, October 16, 1976.

37. Text in *New York Times*, January 27, 1977.

38. There are two excellent studies on the Czechoslovak situation after Helsinki: H. Gordon Skilling "Czechoslovakia and Helsinki," *Canadian Slavonic Papers*, vol. 18, no. 3 (September 1976), pp. 245-65; and Jan F. Triska, "Messages from Czechoslovakia," *Problems of Communism*, vol. 14, no. 6 (November-December 1976), pp. 26-42.

39. The Polish League for Independence, "A Programme for Poland," *Survey* vol. 22, no. 2 (99) (Spring 1976), pp. 182-93.

40. Thomas E. Henaghen, "One Year After the Polish Price Protests," Radio Free Europe *Research*, RAD Background Report/132 (June 30, 1977).

41. Richard Davy, "Can Mr. Gierek Stop Poland's Powder Keg from Exploding?" *The Times,* November 26, 1976.

42. "Polish Trade Unions and the Right to Strike" (February, 1977), (Evergreen Park, Ill.: The North American Study Center for Polish Affairs, 1977); *Studium News Abstracts,* vol. 1, nos. 1, 2, 3 (January, March, June, 1977); and "New Action by Polish Students," *Le Soir* (Brussels), July 15, 1977, in Foreign Broadcast Information Service (FBIS) *Daily Report—East Europe* (July 20, 1977) p. G3.

43. Melanie Anderson, "The Trial of Mihajlo Mihajlov," *Index,* vol. 5, no. 1 (Spring, 1976), pp. 3-12; "Yugoslav Philosophers Under Fire," *Index,* vol. 2, no. 2 (Summer, 1973); "East Wind Over Yugoslavia," *Index* vol. 5, no. 4 (Winter, 1976), pp. 55-65; Michael Morley, "Hard Times for Poetry. On the songs and poems of Wolf Bierman," *Index,* vol. 2, no. 2 (Summer, 1973), pp. 22-26; Paul Goma, "The Tanase Problem," *Index,* vol. 5, no. 2 (Summer, 1976), pp. 57-60; and "Telephone Interview with Romanian Dissident Writer Paul Goma," News release by the International League for Human Rights, March 7, 1977.

44. For a useful chronological and documentary summary, see Vojtech Mastny, ed., *East European Dissent,* vol. 1, 1953-64, vol. 2, 1965-70. (New York: Facts-on-File, Inc., 1972).

45. Adam Michnik makes a similar point with admirable clarity: "I do not think that Soviet intervention in Poland is impossible. On the contrary: I think it could become inevitable if on the one hand the governments in Moscow and Warsaw, and on the other hand the Polish people, were to lose their sense of reality and their grasp of good sense. The Polish democratic opposition should admit that transformations in Poland have to be made at least in their first stage, in line with the 'Brezhnev doctrine.' " "The New Evolutionism," *Survey,* vol. 22, no. 3/4 (Summer/Autumn, 1976), p. 274. See also

Leszek Kolakowski, Wlodzimierz Brus, and Adam Michnik, "Statement," at press conference, London, December 9, 1976.

46. Cf. Rudolf L. Tőkés, "Polycentrism—Central European and Hungarian Origins," *Studies in Comparative Communism,* vol. 6, no. 4 (Winter 1973), pp. 414-28.

47. Enrico Berlinguer, "For New Roads towards Socialism in Italy and Europe" (Speech to the Conference of the Communist and Workers' Parties of Europe—Berlin, June 29-30, 1976), *The Italian Communists,* Foreign Bulletin of the PCI, no. 2-3 (April-July, 1976), p. 60.

48. Quoted in Kevin Devlin, "Azcárate Answers Soviet Attacks," Radio Free Europe *Research,* RAD Background Report/147 (July 18, 1977).

49. Jean Kanapa, the PCF spokesman on international Communist affairs, makes this point reasonably clear in his response to the Hungarian conservative Politburo member Dezső Nemes' critical essay on Eurocommunism, ("Lessons of the Class Struggle for Power in Hungary," *World Marxist Review* [September, 1976] pp. 11-14):

> If one considers that in order to install socialism in France it is necessary to have recourse to the dictatorship of the proletariat, as was done in Hungary (and also in the Soviet Union and elsewhere), it is necessary to state that one must ban opposition parties, establish censorship, deprive part of the population of the freedom of expression, association, demonstration, etc., and one must tell the French workers, "This is one of the consequences of what the Communists propose to you," because of the dictatorship of the proletariat, no matter what its form is, exactly (not entirely, but exactly) is this. No doubt such restrictions of freedom were necessary at a given time in certain countries for the establishment and preservation of the socialist regime and its

economic, social and democratic progress, its human progress. But we are convinced that they are not necessary for the construction in France during our era. We do not want them, therefore.

Quoted in Kevin Devlin, "Hungarian-PCF Polemic: Kanapa Counterattacks," Radio Free Europe *Research,* RAD Background Report/ 209 (October 6, 1976).

50. Although Marchais has once listed Bulgaria, Poland, and the G.D.R. as states with a "pluralistic" or multiparty system, it would take a remarkably uninformed PCF member to believe this proposition. In fact, it is puzzling why Marchais chose to omit Yugoslavia with its six republican (Communist) parties and the U.S.S.R. with its 14 Union Republic (Communist) parties.

51. My information on PCI-Yugoslav relations comes from personal discussions with Yugoslav foreign policy experts and from Kevin Devlin's excellent reports on Western European Communist politics in *RFE Research* reports.

52. Giorgo Boffa, "The Beginnings of Eurocommunism," paper read at St. Antony's College, Oxford University, on October 18, 1976.

53. *L'Unità,* September 11, 1964, as quoted in *RFE Research,* February 2, 1965.

54. According to Carrillo, "For us, for the PCE, the culminating point in the conquest of our independence was the occupation of Czechoslovakia in 1968 . . . Czechoslovakia was the last straw that led our parties to say: No! That was the end of 'internationalism' for us—the 'old internationalism,' as we call it, and which, we are convinced, must cease. True internationalism is something else, must be something else." Quoted in Kevin Devlin, " 'Eurocommunism and the State': Carrillo's Challenge to 'Real Socialism,' " Radio Free Europe *Research,* RAD Background Report/133 (June 30, 1977).

55. In November 1976, however, the PCI did launch a vigorous protest against the East German authorities' decision to deprive the dissident singer Wolf Bierman of his citizenship while on a concert tour in West Germany. The salient part of the critique reads as follows: "Our position in the Bierman case is extremely clear. We are supporters of the freedom to express opinions, in newspapers, in books, in political speeches and through works of art—drawing, painting, poetry, and songs. We stand for the freedom to approve and to dissent. We are in favor of the freedom of expression for everyone, including those with whom we do not agree. We believe not only in the right but in the duty to discuss and to have the truth emerge from confrontation of even opposing ideas. We are against consensus imposed through coercion." *L'Unità,* November 20, 1976.

56. Quoted in "Ambiguity of PCI-CPSU Relations," Radio Free Europe, *Research,* RAD Background Report/146 (July 14, 1977).

57. Henry Kissinger, "Communist Parties in Western Europe: Challenge to the West," Remarks before the Conference on Italy and Eurocommunism at the Woodrow Wilson International Center for Scholars, Smithsonian Institution, Washington, D.C., (June 9, 1977), pp. 8-9.

58. Kevin Devlin, "The Challenge of Eurocommunism," *Problems of Communism,* vol. 26, no. 1 (January-February, 1977), pp. 1-20; and William E. Griffith, " 'Eurocommunism': The Third Great Communist Schism? Soviet-U.S. Rivalry in Southern Europe" (Cambridge, Mass.: Center for International Studies, MIT, November, 1976). See also, Heinz Timmerman, "Moskau und der europäische Kommunismus nach der Gipfelkonferenz von Ost-Berlin," *Osteuropa,* vol. 27 (April 1977), pp. 282-302.

59. *New York Times,* July 1, 1976.

60. *Ibid.*

61. *Ibid.*

62. Sh. P. Sanakayev and N.I. Kupchenko, *Socialism: Foreign Policy in Theory and Practice* (Moscow: Progress Books, 1976), p. 77.

63. Quoted in András Gyenes, "Korunk követelménye" (The Imperatives of Our Age), *Népszabadság,* November 6, 1976.

64. *New York Times,* August 10, 1976.

65. *International Herald-Tribune,* December 9, 1976.

66. The final communiqué studiously avoided the subject of Eurocommunism but (not unexpectedly) was critical of "anti-communist campaigns of imperialist circles which are trying to distort the content of the domestic and foreign policy of the socialist countries . . ." FBIS *Daily Report,* Eastern Europe, (March 4, 1977), pp. AA 3-4.

67. Cf. *Morning Star* (London), July 11, 1977.

68. "Contrary to the Interests of Peace and Socialism in Europe. Concerning the Book 'Eurocommunism and the State' by Santiago Carrillo, General Secretary of the Communist Party of Spain," *New Times* (Moscow), no. 26 (June 1977), pp. 9-13.

69. Charles Gati, "The 'Europeanization' of Communism?" *Foreign Affairs,* vol. 55, no. 3 (April, 1977), pp. 539-53.

70. Cf. "Vance Says Red Gain in Western Nations May Trouble Soviet," *New York Times* June 19, 1977.

71. "Contrary to the Interests of Peace and Socialism in Europe—Concerning the book 'Eurocommunism and the State' by Santiago Carrillo, General Secretary of the Communist Party of Spain," p. 12.

72.   Sharon Wolchik, "Communism East and West: Eurocommunism's Implications for Eastern Europe," Paper read at the Conference on the Foreign Policy of Eurocommunism, held at Airlie House, Warrentown, Virginia, May 12-14, 1977, p. 8.

73.   *Ibid.,* p. 10.

74.   "For Strengthening the Solidarity of the European Communist and Workers' Parties in the Struggle for People's Security, Peace and Welfare," *Scînteia,* July 5, 1977, in FBIS *Daily Report,* Eastern Europe, July 7, 1977, p. H4.

75.   According to the exiled Zdeněk Mlynař, a former leader of the Charter 77 movement: ". . . the significance of dissidence is not to maintain the status quo and the absolute hegemony of the two superpowers, but to allow the *peoples of Europe,* including those of Eastern Europe, to achieve their aspirations independently without foreign pressures and interventions" (my emphasis), *L'Unità,* July 17, 1977, in FBIS *Daily Report,* Eastern Europe, July 21, 1977.

76.   Aleksandar Grlickov, "The National and the International," *Borba* February 22-28, 1977, in FBIS *Daily Report,* Eastern Europe, March 18, 1977, p. H12.

77.   Imre Nagy, *On Communism* (New York: Praeger, 1957); and Ota Sik, *The Third Way,* (London: Wildwood House Ltd., 1976).

78.   *L'Unità,* July 17, 1977.

[NINE]

Eurocommunism: Policy Questions for the West

John C. Campbell

What if the Communists come to the seats of government in a Western European country? Can it be prevented, and if not, what is to be done? These are the questions asked again and again, particularly in the United States, as if they were the only matters of concern and the only criteria by which the policy of the West on Eurocommunism should be measured and judged.

They are, indeed, legitimate questions, to which individual European nations, the European Community, NATO, and the United States may have to find some answers—or at least have an idea of what the answers should be even as they seek ways to avoid unwelcome contingencies or to minimize the significance of the questions. But if the foregoing chapters of this book have shown anything, it is that no simple question-and-answer procedure corresponds either to the complexity of the situation or to the basic policy decisions to be made. It therefore makes sense first to consider the present and prospective situation in all its variety—not to dodge the direct questions but to return to them later, in context.

Let us first recapitulate briefly the international background against which the broad political trends in the four countries of southern Europe which have been analyzed in this book, including the role of the Communist parties, are taking place. The word "Eurocommunism" is of recent vintage but the phenomena it represents are not. They have roots in the beginnings of Marxism as a system of thought and action. Any revolutionary doctrine with pretensions to universality is bound to raise questions of adaptation and reinterpretation as it gains adherents in different national environments. Once world communism became an organized international movement with a center which determined the authoritative line of thought and action, and that center was the ruling party of a powerful state, then it was inevitable that differences would develop between the center and the national parties over the nature of the road to socialism or communism. As the Communist parties of Western Europe have shifted course or tactics over the years, the ambiguities of their position have always been there. What has been the balance, at any given time, between a party's role as a revolutionary force and its disposition to participate like any other party within the existing constitutional system? How far have its shifts represented genuine transformation, and how far tactical adjustments determined by local conditions or by directions from outside? How much independence does it have to make decisions on national or international affairs that run counter to the policies of the Soviet Union?

[513]

These ambiguities were present at the time of the Popular Front strategy of the 1930s, and again in the early postwar period when Communist ministers were in the governments of a number of Western European states. The picture seemed much clearer during the period of the cold war, when both the Soviet Union and the Communist parties themselves did a great deal to reinforce the Western conviction that the latter were simply agents of Soviet policy. Yet it was not entirely so, as was evident when certain spectacular events in the East (such as Khrushchev's revelations about Stalin in 1956 and the suppression of the Hungarians later in the same year) led some Western Communists to stake out positions of their own. In Italy, as Norman Kogan's historical survey shows, the line of Italian communism runs consistently from Gramsci to Togliatti to Berlinguer right through the period of the cold war and despite the fact that Togliatti himself had been an official of the Comintern and spent many years in Moscow.

In our contemporary period, which has been called the age of détente, all these questions are raised again and in more acute form. Perhaps, as Pierre Hassner suggests, the term is a misnomer for the years of the 1970s. Détente, limited as it is and perhaps a transient phase in East-West relations, may not be the determinant influence on the European and international politics of this period when seen in historical perspective from some future point of vantage. The inability of Western governments to master the economic crisis of the time, the failure of traditional democratic parties and institutions to prevent their own decay, or a crisis in the U.S.S.R. not very clear to us now may be more significant. But there is little doubt that the accommodation between East and West, in reducing international tension between the two halves of Europe, has also given freer rein to political dynamics in each half. Rudolf Tőkés has described how détente has revealed

[514]

systemic weaknesses on both sides. Neither Western democracy nor Soviet-type socialism is flourishing on its own side of the line, and at the same time neither is in a position to take great advantage of the embarrassment of the other.

The Eurocommunism of today presents the same key questions as in the past, but with a difference in degree and at least the possibility that a point of decision is approaching, or may even have been reached. First, as to the nature of the Communist parties: How far have they come toward acceptance of the constitutional democratic order as determining their access to power, the means of putting their programs for change into effect when they get it, and the relinquishment of it when the votes go the other way? Second, as to their independence: How far have they emancipated themselves from the control or guidance of Moscow? It would be a bold and perhaps foolhardy observer who would say categorically that any of the Communist parties of Western Europe has come all the way in either respect. On the other hand, there may be trends in that direction which it would be difficult if not impossible to reverse.

Unfortunately for those responsible for the policies of Western nations, they must make decisions without the benefit of certainty on these matters or the privilege of waiting to see how they turn out. They have to make the best estimates they can, first on what the aims of the Communist parties are, and second, on what prospects they have for ever realizing them. If the Communists have aims inimical to democratic institutions, to national independence and to Western defense, and have a real chance of attaining power, certain conclusions for policy follow. If they have such aims but have little chance of carrying them out, or if they have a good chance of reaching the seats of government but will not represent any real danger when they get there, then the conclusions are different.

It has been the purpose of this book to explore precisely these questions, looking at the available evidence on the role of the Communist parties in Western Europe. We have largely left out of consideration the parties in Great Britain, the Federal Republic of Germany, Scandinavia, the Benelux countries, and Austria. Their influence is negligible and not likely to be otherwise. The focus has been on four Latin countries of Southern Europe and the Mediterranean, where the political trends in recent years have been toward the left: Portugal, Spain, France and Italy. Four specialized chapters have subjected the politics of those countries and the role of the Communists to searching analysis. One cannot without loss of accuracy reduce the complex situation they describe to a few simply phrased conclusions. Nevertheless, as a perspective for policy, it is useful to attempt a brief summary of the situation in each country from the standpoint of the two questions mentioned above as important for Western policy: What do the Communists represent and what chance do they have of gaining power?

II

Eurocommunism is a useful concept, but no matter how one defines it the tendency is to create an illusion of greater uniformity among Western European Communist parties than exists in fact. The beginning of understanding comes only with an examination, and a comparison, of the individual parties in their local habitats.

The Portuguese party, to judge from its record since the revolution of 1974, does not fit any definition of Eurocommunism other than being a Communist party operating in a European country. Alvaro Cunhal, the PCP's veteran leader, acted in accord with Leninist precepts, maintained a Stalinist-type organization in his party, and kept in close touch with Moscow. The Communists' real bid for power came through their alliance with radical elements of the military, through direct action in the streets and on the farms, and finally through participation in an attempted (and unsuccessful) coup d'état in November 1975. They never got more than 15 percent of the vote in any of the national elections and by the time of the legislative election of April 1976 were already out of the running as a serious contender for power.

That summary statement makes the frustration of the PCP's bid sound easier than it actually was. Communist power was a real threat, in circumstances that were not unfavorable. It was only when non-Communist elements in the population themselves took direct action in the streets, when European Socialist parties came to the aid of their Portuguese colleagues with moral and financial support, and when the radicals in the military were outmaneuvered by their moderate and conservative colleagues, that the Communists found their way blocked. The most important foreign influence was that of the Socialist, not the Communist, "international." The Soviet Union, which supported the PCP with propaganda and doubtless with financial aid and political counsel as well, was not prepared to engage in overt intervention and had to reconcile itself to the outcome.

The main problems for the Portuguese government after that election, which gave Mário Soares and the Socialists a plurality but not a majority, were how to revive the economy, provide work for the thousands returning from Europe and from Africa, consolidate the political order, and get help from abroad. The PCP was a problem only in so far as it could capitalize on the inability of the government to deal with those other difficulties. Soares, although heading a government based on a minority of the voters, insisted on governing alone without broadening its base either to the right or to the left. The logical move, if growing problems created a need for greater public support, appeared to be a coalition including parties in the center and thus enjoying a clear majority in the legislature. But Soares was most reluctant to take that route until he had to; and when he did, in February 1978, he made a strange alliance with the conservatives and later had to give way to a non-party government. Meanwhile the Communists did not cease to urge him to turn to them in order to preserve the gains of the revolution and block the road to reaction. It was a siren song by which Soares, a genuine democrat with plenty of experience with the Communists, could not be easily tempted.

Portugal's future will be determined by the way in which the various political forces, including a strong president, General Eanes, manage and adapt to forthcoming events. The PCP is not without assets. It has discipline. It has a base in the trade union movement and another in the rural areas of the south. It is ready to seize on a situation of growing crisis and ineffective government, either by pushing the tactic of the popular front, offering the idea of a united left to preserve socialism, or alternatively by reverting to the tactic of revolution under the slogan of saving the country from chaos or from the threat of a dictatorship of the right. Without overestimating the ability of Soares or of any coalition of democratic parties to cope with Portugal's formidable economic and social problems, however, one can still conclude that the PCP has no promising future. It has little chance of expanding its voter support, it is isolated among political parties in Portugal, and it is isolated among Communist parties of Western Europe.

The story of the PCP tells us very little about Eurocommunism and how to deal with it. Cunhal himself would not have used the word except to repudiate it, and those Communist leaders who personify it—Carrillo and Berlinguer—made no secret of their sympathy for Soares. If there was, in rudimentary form, a "Eurocommunist international," its influence was thrown into the balance against the PCP. The Portuguese case was in some ways a test. It showed the Portuguese people and the Western Europeans that positive action in defense of democracy against a threatened Communist seizure of power can be effective. But it was no test of issues that may arise in Italy, France, or Spain.

In neighboring Spain the first post-Franco free election provided a measure of the public support behind the Communist party. In terms of votes (9 percent of the total cast) it was not impressive. That figure may underestimate the actual influence on the political scene the PCE can exert through organization, propaganda, political alliances, and control of unions and through the tactical skills of its leader. Carrillo has been the very model of a democratic politician, offering cooperation to the center government of Adolfo Suárez and preaching the need for a broad national coalition and program in a Spanish-style "historic compromise," but without the real backing his Italian comrades have for that strategy.

For the next few years it does not look as if other parties would need the cooperation of the Communists in order to govern, and the latter are not going to get into power on their own. As in Portugal and in France, the key to Communist prospects appears to lie with the larger Socialist party (PSOE). We cannot predict how the parties will sort out their alliances and alignments or how far politics may become polarized in a right-left pattern as parliamentary democracy is gradually established in Spain, but the PSOE thus far has shown no inclination to tie its fate to that of the Communists despite the fact that the PCE, in its declarations anyway, is in the forefront of Western Europe's Communist parties in accepting the norms of democracy.

It is also in the forefront of Eurocommunist criticism of the Soviet Union. The publication in 1977 of Carrillo's book, *Eurocomunismo y Estado*, touched off exchanges of polemics so strongly worded as to make a back-down by either side difficult. True, Brezhnev did not commit his own prestige to the deflation or removal of the leader of the Spanish party, but the tone of the various "book reviews" and the statements that appeared in the Soviet press, including the argument that the fault lay not with the PCE as a party but with its general secretary, left little doubt of the general intent. The PCE rallied round Carrillo, and if he could weather the storm—as he had a previous attempt of the Soviets to replace his with a more docile leadership—both he and the party would win applause and public appreciation in Spain in proportion to the denunciations coming from Moscow.

The Soviet connection, however, has not been the main or the only issue holding back wider support of the Communist party by the Spanish people. As Eusebio Mujal's chapter makes clear, there are other factors in Spain's own past, especially those connected with the Civil War, that explain the limited appeal of the PCE and the unwillingness of the voters to accept it as a leading partner in the effort to establish a working democratic system in Spain.

We have dwelt on Spain and Portugal because they are part of the problem of Europe's South, that problem which in general terms is one of holding within the bounds of common institutions the tensions and sharp divisions between social classes, ideological loyalties and political parties. They are also (Spain in particular) part of the problem of Eurocommunism. Developments in both countries, as they take tentative steps toward a constitutional order which will have room for rightists and for Communists without succumbing to the dictator-ship of either, will have their effects on how these problems are dealt with in the wider European context. But Iberia remains, as it has been throughout the centuries, semi-isolated from the rest of Europe. For a number of obvious reasons—size, loca-tion, postwar history, the formation of the new Europe of the six and then of the nine without them—what happens in Spain and Portugal is peripheral to the main topic before us, the role and destiny of European communism in the age of détente. What happens in France and Italy, by contrast, is central.

III

France, with the legislative elections of March 1978 now history, has not chosen the experiment of a government including the Communists. The *Union de la gauche,* until the dispute which broke out between the PCF and its Socialist and Radical partners in September 1977, appeared to have an excellent chance of winning a majority. But the public specta-cle of their bitter dispute over the revision of their common program reduced their appeal to the voters by a sufficient margin to ensure the victory of the Center and the Right. The French people and the nations of the West, therefore, will get no answers, at least not for some time, to some of the hy-pothetical questions they had been asking for the past few years: what ministries the Communists would have; what their weight in the counsels and decisions of a coalition government would be; how the constitutional order would survive the tension brought on by a total shift in power to the left; and above all, how would the PCF's alliance with the Socialist party stand the test of sharing governmental power?

As it turned out, their respective moves in anticipation of

[521]

that test strained and broke their ability to stay together until the election. The half-hearted agreement to support each other's candidates on the second ballot was little more than a gesture in a cause already lost. There are some continuing factors to be taken into account in explaining what happened, factors that have affected the Socialist-Communist relationship in the past and may be expected to affect it in the future. Their alliance was formed with the prime purpose of winning elections and coming to power. The *programme commun,* adopted in 1972, was not so much a vision of the French society they would work for as it was an electoral manifesto for the rank-and-file of both parties and a symbol of their decision to work together to oust the Center-Right parties from power. But the controversies that subsequently arose over how that program should be changed or extended cast doubt on the ability of the Communists and Socialists to work together on any program.

Differences between Communists and Socialists are not just about how many industries or companies are to be nationalized. They reflect the deep distrust that has existed for over half a century, ever since the Third International parted company with the Second. They reflect differing philosophies of government and of party organization. And they reflect continuing doubt on the Socialist side, expressed publicly by Mitterrand, as to whether the PCF has shed entirely and for good and all its Stalinist character and its loyalty to a foreign power. The PS under the new leadership of Mitterrand rescued itself from a decline comparable to that of the Italian Socialist Party by the new strategy of alliance with the PCF, which worked beyond expectations. The support the PS got from the French electorate rose from 5 percent to close to 30 percent. It was able to present itself as a workers' party instead of a powerless appendage to Right-Center coalitions, and thus stopped and reversed the loss of votes to the PCF while also gaining votes from the center parties. That success led party officials to say again and again that they had no interest at all in breaking the unity of the Left, for that would send them back down the hill to 5 percent of the vote, and more specifically it would end François Mitterrand's chances of becoming prime minister or President of the Republic. But the decision on the maintenance of the unity of the Left was not entirely in Socialist hands.

Both parties were looking beyond tactics, including the tactics that brought them together under the banner of unity and the common program. The PS, with its growing success at the polls, had become the senior partner. Although it had a minority left wing that was close to the PCF line, it was hard to see Mitterrand and the central leadership submitting either to Communist predominance or to Communist obstruction. Even if an agreed common program could be patched up again, differences would arise over how to put it into effect and over what should come next. The Communists, while cultivating the Eurocommunist image, remain very conscious of the elements of political power. As Ronald Tiersky reminds us, the PCF is driven by imperatives inherent in its own character.[1] Its strength lies in its discipline, its organization, its ability to mobilize power not just in elections but in labor unions, factories, public services, apartment houses, and in the streets. This is the reason why extensive nationalization is so important: it would give the Communists a grip on economic levers of power to counterbalance Socialist electoral strength and to compete successfully for leadership once they are in the government.

If it did not so compete by using the instruments at its disposal, the PCF could hardly stem the tide or escape the consequences of further loss of votes. Its leaders were well aware that the party has lost its claim to be the first workers' party of France. When they had stood alone the Communists sometimes got as much as 25 percent of the national vote. Participating in the *Union de la gauche,* they fell to a level closer to 20 percent. As long as they were but the tail of the Socialist kite, their percentage could hardly go up.

What are the PCF's alternatives? It has gradually moved along the lines of Eurocommunism in the wake of the Italian and Spanish comrades. It has done so, we may assume, for reasons of French politics. As a party of revolution, or as a party following orders from a foreign power, it could not hope to make its way with the French voters or to compete with the revitalized Socialist Party. On the other hand, if the PCF becomes nothing more than another social democratic party, why should anyone vote PCF rather than PS? This is the dilemma. If the Communists feel compelled to assert themselves and reach for leadership on their own terms, the Socialists will break with them. If they see their party losing its identity and its support, they will break with the Socialists, as Marchais and his colleagues, in demanding clearly unacceptable changes in the common program in late 1977, appear to have done. These are factors inherent in the Socialist-Communist relationship no matter what may be the course of bargaining over a common program or the specific issues to be faced after an election, whatever its outcome. By the time of the election the PCF had not resolved its dilemma. And it wound up with a disappointing 20.6 percent of the vote.

Amid conditions of national economic crisis and ample evidence of disunity and ineptitude on the right and center of the political spectrum, the late 1970s seemed a time of opportunity for a united Left in a France that had divided almost 50-50 in recent elections, and the public opinion polls confirmed it. Yet the prospect of a victory of the Left, despite the tendency of French voters time and again to vote on traditional lines—right or left—raised questions in their minds and in those of political leaders as well. Fear of the likely immediate economic consequences of a victory of the coalition of the Left such as flight of capital, fall of the franc, loss of business confidence, and a decline in production, played up in lurid terms by prominent writers,[2] surely had some influence on the voters when they made their final choice. It is a question, too, how enthusiastically the leftist parties themselves looked forward to a victory that would mean a conflict splitting the country down the middle, disrupting the economy, and requiring drastic measures of coercion and control. Is that a course which the Socialists, who do not represent a constituency dedicated to "the revolution," want? They would not easily enter on it knowing the dangers not only to their own authority but to democratic freedoms and the fabric of French society. Nor would the Communists, whatever their ultimate goals, welcome responsibility for managing a chaotic situation or be ready to carry through an imposed revolution on their own.

Should Mitterrand (and Marchais, too, perhaps) be presumed to be any less perspicacious than Berlinguer in absorbing the lesson of Allende? These are speculations, of course, but the point is that victory in the elections might have brought more problems and harder decisions for the parties of the Left, especially the PCF, than for their opponents on the Right and for France and the nations of the West. It raises the question whether the PCF leaders really wanted to win. It may be that to them the longer-term future appears more favorable because of the break with the PS on the common program in September 1977. The failure of their renegotiation effort, whether temporary or definitive, was clear evidence of the doubts and misgivings on both sides over the prospects of governing together.

Disunity on the Left, or simply the reluctance of French voters in the final analysis to put Communists into the seats of power in the national government, left the *Union de la gauche* short of a majority in the Assembly elected in March 1978. By that event the critical decisions facing all concerned were at least postponed. The alliance of Socialists and Communists might not survive the defeat, with the former turning to veiled cooperation with the Center and the latter retreating from coalition politics and even from Eurocommunism to positions more compatible with its past and more congenial to its leadership. Giscard d'Estaing's bold prediction in 1976 that the PCF had passed its peak and thereafter would decline might well be proved correct.

IV

If France's problem of coping with the Communists has been exaggerated, Italy's has not. The PCI is the one Communist party in Western Europe that already has a voice in vital governmental decisions. After the election of June 1976, which gave it 34 percent of the vote, only about 4 percent less than the Christian Democrats (DC), it assumed a measure of governmental responsibility by supporting (through abstention from voting) a minority DC government and by working out with the DC a national program of retrenchment and reform to meet the country's political and economic crisis. Thus the historic compromise came into being in fact if not in name. It became firmer in 1977 when the PCI began to vote for the government instead of merely refraining from voting against it. The next logical step, which could be taken at any time but might await another election showing further Communist gains, is the formation of a government with Communists participating alongside the Christian Democrats, Socialists and others, the government of national unity Berlinguer has been calling for. Even before then, the parliamentary votes and public support the Communists have makes it impossible for others to govern the country without their consent.

The PCI, far more than the PCF, has built a record of gradually increasing participation in the existing system, first on the local but later on the regional and national levels. Its success is due to its adaptation to that system and promise to improve and reform it, not overthrow it. The party's own experience in Italian politics, plus the conclusions drawn from what happened in Chile, led to what is now the Berlinguer line: that the Communists should not try to govern Italy, even if they could make an alliance with the Socialists that gave the combined Left over 50 percent of the vote (although on occasion he has hinted at that solution for tactical reasons), against the will of the non-Communist half of the population represented mainly by Christian Democracy and the Catholic Church. That is Berlinguer's rationale; the PCI is in the process of proving its responsibility and its legitimacy as an Italian party.

Italy, therefore, is the place to watch, the real laboratory of Eurocommunism. Spain's Communists may be more outspoken in defending the Eurocommunist idea and in arguing with Moscow. The PCF may have come close to power in the last election. But, as we have seen, the PCE is on the fringe of Spain's politics, and the PCF's chances are wholly dependent on its tie with a stronger Socialist party and on the ability of the two to maintain a united Left under stress.

In Italy the Communists *are* the Left. They are not beholden to the Socialists or dependent on them. As their votes

[527]

have gone up to the neighborhood of 35 percent, those of the Socialist Party have declined to less than 10, and of the Social Democrats to less than 5 percent.

Nothing is inevitable in Italian politics. The PCI has encountered trouble within its own ranks, as union leaders and others on the left wing carped at the party's agreement with the class enemy on a common program they saw as demanding disproportionate sacrifices from the workers. The Communists' image as the clean and efficient administrators of cities and regions to the greater benefit of the people began to be tarnished by evidence of waste, mismanagement, and financial crisis. Possibly the election of 1976 marked the high water mark of the PCI's voting strength. Yet even if that were so, there were few signs that the Christian Democrats could arrest their own party's decline or somehow draw the PSI back into the government and reconstitute a coalition capable of governing the country against the opposition of the Communists. In Italy's conditions of crisis a government of national unity, resting on the historic compromise, seemed to be imposed not by the will of the PCI but by events, although the DC still harbored doubts about the real character of the PCI and was doing its best to avoid the final decision.

If and when the compromise is finally made, the PCI will likely be the strongest single organization in the "grand coalition." The DC may split, losing a faction on the right when the leadership makes its historic decision. In any circumstances the DC would tend to be the lesser partner because of its weaker leadership and discipline, its internal fatigue and decay after 30 years power. Does that mean the PCI would move to seize the commanding heights of the economy and the political system? In the short run, every indication is that it would not. In the longer range, one cannot be sure, especially if the grand coalition could not cope with Italy's deepening crisis and if the right-left split deepened in the country despite the political compromise on the official level. The PCI has not abandoned its ultimate goal of a socialist (communist) society in Italy, not just the shoring up of a mixed public-private economy. But as long as its "Italian road" to that goal is a democratic, constitutional one, democratic parties can hardly object.

Meanwhile the PCI, for the very reason that the Right is not just an enfeebled DC party but a number of continuing and strong (and anti-Communist) social and institutional elements in Italian life (the Church, the military, the business interests), probably will not take the road of force, civil war, and imposed revolution, even if that road seems to open up before it. The party has worked for decades, successfully, to increase its following and its political strength by winning the consent of the voters. It is not neglecting other methods to consolidate and to demonstrate its position of strength, but it is not likely to jeopardize the gains of the past thirty years by a sudden attempt at seizure of power by the classic Leninist formula or by a turn to Stalinism as a model for Italy.

We are likely to have, accordingly, a period in which the PCI will be sharing power, first outside of government and then in it, with the Christian Democrats. The argument can be made—and is made by both Pierre Hassner and Norman Kogan in this volume—that the choice of this role by the PCI and its acceptance by the DC is a necessity for Italy if that nation is to find its way to recovery, reform and progress.[3] If that is so, the United States cannot change the situation by urging the DC to hold out indefinitely against it. The point can be argued. Economic shocks such as the advent of Communists to power would bring to France could also happen in Italy, but the gradual nature of the political change in Italy and the known policies of the PCI would make a difference. It has already been demonstrated that in current conditions of crisis the necessary sacrifices and positive action required of all major segments of the population can only be obtained if there is a national effort for which the political leaders of those segments take responsibility. The period immediately ahead, then, will be one that will test the nature of Eurocommunism, at least in its Italian form and perhaps with wider implications.

V

We might draw certain crude conclusions from the above estimates of where the Communists are in the politics of the four Latin countries of southern Europe. These are (1) that no Communist party will come to power except in coalition with others and without authority to impose policies of its own; (2) that in France and in Spain, where the Communist parties are not the leading actors on the left and lag well behind the Socialists in popular support, the formation of left or left-center coalitions would put considerable strain on their relations with their partners, and that should such coalitions come to power the Communist choice would be to accept a subordinate role or get out; (3) that the PCI is the only Communist party in a position to play a major role in government, and that Europe's "Communist problem" in this sense is for all practical purposes limited to Italy; and (4) that, given the character of the PCI, perhaps there is no problem at all.

These conclusions are indeed too crude and too simple. They dismiss too easily the problems residing in the basic continuing strength of the Left in France. They may underestimate the potential for growth of the PCE if Spain's economy falters and its path to political democracy gets rougher. They take more or less at face value the sincerity of the PCI's conversion to democratic and libertarian values and practices. All of which is to say that we cannot speak with certainty about the future, or even about the past. Nevertheless, those crude conclusions do seem to be supported by more than the assertions of Communist leaders and the naive faith of those who would like to believe them. It is at least enough to raise doubts about Western policies based upon dark forebodings of an inexorable Communist forward march to power in Western Europe, or upon a determination to oppose and sabotage any government in which cabinet posts are given to Communists.

The Italian experience seems to show that a Western Communist party can approach power only when it makes clear its patriotism and its acceptance of a free, democratic—in their own classic and denigrating term, bourgeois—constitutional system. As it gains support, takes governmental responsibility and approaches participation in government at the national level, it deepens its commitment to that system and finds it difficult to change course. Difficult, but not impossible, as there is always a hard-core reluctance, for reasons of ideology or class interest, to accept the evolution that has taken place. Communists are not Social Democrats, at least not yet. There is still some element of deception in their professions. They can shift gears, as they have in the past. But it is at least a plausible general proposition—one put in too simple terms but to which the record of recent years gives some support—that to get power they have to win votes, and to win votes they have to be more and more "Eurocommunist." And that proposition suggests another—this one not so well grounded in fact—that by the time they succeed in coming to power (if they do), they will no longer be a threat to democracy.

Let us make the assumptions, then, that Communists are not going to "take over" any Western European country and destroy its democratic institutions, that if they enter government they will do so constitutionally in coalition with other parties they do not control, and that they will not be able to use Eastern European "salami tactics" to dispose of all rivals.

Yet there are other troubling questions concerning the Communists. These questions have to do with the nature of Eurocommunism and the genuineness of the conversion, and with the ties to Moscow and the so-called international Communist movement. These questions are related to the future of the European Community, the effectiveness of NATO, and the security of the West. They deserve examination to see how Western interests are affected by the Eurocommunist phenomenon and what conclusions for Western policy, if any, emerge.

It may seem a little late in the day, in a book devoted to Eurocommunism, to bring up in the middle of the final chapter the question of definition. It has, in fact, been defined and described by the other authors, generally and in its respective national settings. All we need do here is recall and comment on those aspects which are relevant to policy decisions.

Eurocommunism, as Pierre Hassner points out, is a product of détente. Under conditions of intense cold war, Western Communists could hardly be regarded by their own countrymen, by the Soviets, or by themselves as other than soldiers on the Soviet side. They still won a substantial and apparently irreducible bloc of votes in elections in France and in Italy. Most of those votes were cast on national rather than international issues, but the Communist deputies who sat in the parliaments were not a "loyal opposition" participating in the process of government. Their presence was negative and obstructive, making it more difficult for the other parties to build effective majorities and make the system work. In effect, for international reasons a substantial portion of the voters in

[532]

each country was excluded from real participation in political life.

Détente changed that. By reducing tension and removing, partially, the international issues, it made the Western CPs more respectable at home. Other parties could think about working with them rather than (or as well as) against them, and some (like the PS in France) did so. It may not have been inevitable that détente would loosen the Kremlin's grip on them—the Soviets probably expected quite the opposite, a chance to use them more effectively—but that is what happened. In the effort to gain ground at home their leaders found it necessary both to broaden their appeal on domestic issues and to put distance between themselves and the Russians.

It has been a complex process, obscured by our ignorance of sub-surface communications and interactions between Soviet and Western Communist leaders and also by the likelihood that their future relations may hold as many ambiguities and uncertainties for them as for outsiders. There are various tests. How far will a Western CP leadership recognize the existence of central authority, doctrinal or operational, in Moscow? How far will it reject Soviet guidance and publicly take issue with Soviet decisions and policies? How far will it modify the Leninist character of its own party organization? How far will it criticize the existing system and practices in the U.S.S.R. and Eastern Europe? Does it identify the national interests of its own country with the foreign policies advocated by the U.S.S.R.?

On these points, as preceding chapters have shown, real changes have taken place. The Communist parties of Spain, Italy and France, in differing degrees, have declared their independence. They have repudiated certain doctrines still accepted in Moscow as holy writ. They have declared their acceptance of the Western democratic electoral system, not just as a means of getting to power but as a constitutional absolute that requires giving up power when the vote goes the other way. We may not entirely believe them, but it is significant that the declarations have been made.

Santiago Carrillo has openly criticized the Soviet system and abandoned Leninism in theory as well as in practice, prompting a Soviet campaign against him. His Italian and French comrades have been less outspoken. To put it bluntly, they let him down. Berlinguer and the PCI did not want a confrontation with Moscow and said so.[4] Nevertheless, they have criticized particular acts and policies of the Soviet and East European regimes. The occupation of Czechoslovakia in 1968, which they all decried, was a test case and has continued to be a live issue between them and the Soviets ever since.

Does all this indicate a new great schism, comparable to the splits created in the international communist movement by Tito's assertion of independence in 1948 and the later conflict between Russia and China? William Griffith points out that neither the Soviet Communist party nor those of Western Europe reached the point of making an open break and that both want to avoid it. The Soviets wished to avoid an open rupture, which would be a heavy blow to what remains of their claim to authority over the international Communist movement. Berlinguer has argued that a break would be in the interest neither of the PCI nor of Italy. The Western parties still consider the Soviet and East European parties and states as "socialist." Despite all the ambiguities, however, the schism exists. The Eurocommunist heresy has in common with the earlier ones the denial of authority at the center, the primacy of national over international communism, and it adds the rejection of the totalitarian model for its own national society. The Eurocommunists have no Marx or Lenin to codify their doctrine. Carrillo's *Eurocomunismo y Estado* is the most ambitious effort of that kind, but it is a bit too ambitious for Marchais and perhaps for Berlinguer as well. Yet if there is no charter of Eurocommunism and no organized "international," there is unity on some essential points, such as those agreed between Marchais and Berlinguer in November 1975 and common to the statements of the three leaders when they met in Madrid in March 1977.[5] The British and Belgian parties are on the same wavelength.

The PCF, with its Stalinist traditions, keeps providing evidence that the transition is no easy one. Its hard-liners have not been converted, and Moscow continues to stress immutable Leninist principles and to remind the party of the good old days of Maurice Thorez. The break with the Socialists over the common program in September 1977 showed at the very least a reluctance on the part of the Communist leaders to face the election, whether the prospect was victory or defeat, without first stacking the cards on the leftist side in their favor for the real power struggle to come. Perhaps, as some observers suggested, it was a real reversal, a rejection of the whole trend of Eurocommunism, done with Moscow's approval and possibly at its suggestion. But there is no available evidence that the decision was Moscow's. One can adduce reasons why the Soviets may have wanted to see the united Left strategy succeed in France, and others why they may have wanted to see it fail and the PCF return to more orthodox positions. Whatever Moscow thought, there were good and sufficient reasons in French politics for what happened, and recent events in France should not lead to hasty conclusions about the strategy and influence of the Kremlin.

There are ties which continue, of course, and they are not to be overlooked or minimized. The structure of inter-party relations remains. Though the Soviets may not be able to assemble another conference of European parties, after the

[535]

laborious and acrimonious negotiations that finally produced the meeting and the agreed statement at East Berlin in June 1976, bilateral channels for communication and advice are still available. Financial support of one kind or another, especially that which is generated by East-West commercial contracts involving Communist-controlled enterprises, helps Western CPs to meet their bills and run electoral campaigns. Beyond all these connections there are the ingrained habits of mind and the weight of tradition. Even when it is clear that socialism as practiced in the U.S.S.R. and Eastern Europe has repugnant features that Western Communists do not like and could not adopt, criticism is often suppressed or muted by the old sense of solidarity and fear that only the class enemy would profit from it. All those ties together, however, do not add up to Soviet control. Every Western CP, in its leadership and in its rank and file, has hard-liners who do not feel comfortable with the widening breach with Moscow. But the current is not running their way.

The character of these parties is not fixed for all time as of any date past, present or future. What they have become or will become cannot be known beyond all doubt by outside observers, by party members, or even by the party leaders themselves. What Europe has come to know as Eurocommunism is the result of historical trends brought on not only by conditions in Western European society but also by a long-term centrifugal process in the international Communist movement. It is not a tactic, to be easily discarded or reversed by the Western Communist leaders themselves, nor a passing phenomenon to be dismissed as unreal or inconsequential by their opponents.

Much more could be said about the nature of Eurocommunism, but without any assurance that it would inform the consideration of Western policies. Policy conclusions for the

West do not flow inexorably from the fact that the leaders of these parties remain Communists, or from the fact that they have split with Moscow on important questions and asserted their independence. But both facts should be kept in mind as we try to make the best estimates and judgments possible on individual leaders and parties. Lack of certainty is no reason for not taking account of discernible trends and of their international consequences.

Some of the international aspects, of course, are of special concern within Western Europe itself; for example, the question how Communist electoral successes, on a national basis or in direct elections to the European Parliament, will affect the future of the European Community. We are more concerned here, however, with the larger questions of East-West relations and, above all, with those sets of policies that may be described, in one word each, as détente and defense.

VI

Since the beginning of the 1970s the United States and the countries of Western Europe, with a mixture of enthusiasm and skepticism, have supported détente in relations with the East. It has been partly policy, partly attitude and atmosphere. As policy it included treaty arrangements and normalization of relations between the Federal Republic of Germany and the Communist states to the east; international agreements to stabilize the status of Berlin; serious negotiation on limitation of U.S. and Soviet strategic arms and on reduction of NATO and Warsaw Pact forces in Central Europe; elaboration, in the Conference on Security and Cooperation in Europe and the resulting Final Act of Helsinki, of principles and practices to enhance security, cooperation, and human rights in Europe;

[537]

and a general expansion of trade and of contacts between East and West. As atmosphere, détente has meant high-sounding talk about peace and a reduction of U.S.-Soviet and East-West tension by mutual consent. Although the danger of war was not eliminated, both sides saw benefit in reducing it by acceptance of the political and territorial status quo (if not indefinitely at least for the foreseeable future), by restraint in dealing with issues that could grow into conflict, by continuing negotiations on arms control and such matters even when results were meager, and by seeking ways in which constructive cooperation in economic and other fields could create a more normal relationship conducive to peace.

Détente had its limits. As both sides recognized, it did not in itself change the facts of the balance of power in Europe, the military presence of the two superpowers there, or their continuing competition. The military blocs remained, and the security of Europe continued to depend on their balance and mutual deterrence despite much talk of the need for some new and more stable or less dangerous security system. The momentum of détente, moreover, was not sustained after the agreements of the first few years. SALT I was not followed at an early date by SALT II, not even by the time of the original treaty's expiration in 1977. The Final Act of Helsinki in 1975 added but little to what had already been negotiated and, because of the controversy generated by its clauses on human rights, tended to strain détente instead of strengthening it. Trade and economic cooperation between the United States and the U.S.S.R. did not develop as anticipated owing, among other reasons, to the Jackson Amendment and the Soviet denunciation of the trade treaty concluded at the height of détente in 1972. The buildup of strategic and conventional arms on both sides and the development of new weapons increased both mutual mistrust and the difficulty of finding trade-offs that could be the basis of new and stabilizing agreements. The Soviets stuck to their position that there can be no coexistence in matters of ideology, as they might be expected to do regardless of Western pleas, and the West—more particularly the United States—took the counteroffensive on behalf of the principles of human rights and freedom of information.

Détente, however, in the sense of mutual desire not to increase the risk of armed conflict or to revive the excesses of the cold war, survived. Both sides acquired a more sober sense of its limitations but found it useful even at the existing minimum level. Perhaps they can live with that situation for some years although the continued Soviet military buildup and the absence of any progress in the talks on mutual force reductions in Vienna are calculated to increase the feeling and the actuality of insecurity in Western Europe.

In these circumstances, with little forward movement in limitation of arms or in economic relations, the active area is most likely to be that of political competition, and here what is involved is not just the intentions and the political strategies on both sides as they look across the line, but political developments that may confront governments on either side with undesired and unmanageable situations. The political weaknesses in the West are matched by potential challenges to the established order in the East, with the possibility that sharp changes or outbreaks on either side could increase the dangers of international conflict.

The process of détente, on which the Final Act of Helsinki set a seal of approval, had the effect of emphasizing simultaneously Europe's unity and its division. Thirty-three European (and two North American) nations had negotiated as individual states, not as members of blocs, on a set of propositions to enhance their security and open up channels of communication and cooperation. On the other hand, Helsinki represented a semi-formal Western acceptance of what the Soviets called the inalterable consequences of the Second World War, namely the fact of Soviet control of Eastern Europe and the continuing existence of Communist regimes there. It had already been established, by the way the powers acted in the series of crises that bore the names of Hungary, Berlin and Czechoslovakia, that neither side would send its military forces across the dividing line to support revolt or challenge the military position of the other.

The United States shied away from use of the term "spheres of influence" to describe either what it accepted in Eastern Europe or what it practiced in Western Europe. But a main basis of détente, and of the negotiations on European security that détente made possible, was precisely this understanding that frontiers, above all the frontier between the two alliance systems, would not be directly challenged. That was the message of the so-called Sonnenfeldt doctrine, no less authoritative for being stated in camera and not intended for publication, to the effect that the Soviet security interest in Eastern Europe was a fact of international life and that it was unfortunate and possibly dangerous to peace that it had to rest on naked military power alone rather than on a broader and more organic connection.[6]

The other side of détente was more "togetherness." The barriers of the cold war were to come down; trade and industrial cooperation between East and West were to flourish; persons, publications and ideas were to pass more easily across the borders. The motives of those who encouraged these trends were, of course, quite different. The Soviet Union and the Eastern European regimes wanted the trade, and especially the technology of the West. Some of the Eastern European governments, as well as their peoples, wanted more contact with the West as a means of tempering the harsh reality of their lack of freedom and independence. The neutrals wished to avoid being squeezed between the blocs and to find more scope for their own interests. The Western nations hoped to open up the closed systems of the East to the fresh air of freer thought, to help the cause of individual human rights, and to cultivate the sense of a common European civilization and destiny that had been submerged but not erased by the years of the cold war.

For the Soviet Union and the Eastern European regimes, the benefits of this more relaxed atmosphere had always to be measured against the price to be paid in dangers to ideological conformity and political discipline at home. They accepted some opening of windows to the West but not the "subversive" and "decadent" influences that sometimes came through those windows. They stated again and again that peaceful coexistence of states with different political and social systems did not include ideological coexistence. That "struggle" would continue.

VII

We have to look at the problem of Western interests and policy in several ways. One of them has to do with Western Europe's own strengths and weaknesses. Will it have the capacity to master its economic and political crises and strains, maintain its free institutions, and contribute to the necessary solidarity and strength of the West as a whole? Another aspect concerns Soviet policy. Will the U.S.S.R., in addition to protecting its own empire in Eastern Europe from disruption, be trying by political action to create or exploit opportunities to establish its influence or control in parts of Western

Europe, to weaken or break up the Western alliance, and thus alter the present balance in Europe? A third concerns possibly changing views about foreign policy within the Western European countries in the light of both national and international developments. In all of these related matters the role of the Communist parties of Western Europe and the phenomena of Eurocommunism may be of importance.

The Soviet leaders were willing to accept limited relaxation as part of détente because they were confident of limiting its impact on their own controlled society and on Eastern Europe while taking advantage of the opportunities it offered in the West. What were those opportunities? First, the very existence of détente tended to make people in Western Europe less worried about the Soviet threat, less vigilant in their attention to security and defense, and more willing to look benevolently on Soviet proposals for cooperation. Second, the economic difficulties that plagued Western Europe in the 1970s, especially after OPEC abruptly quadrupled world oil prices at the end of 1973, raised in some Soviet minds the thought that now the capitalist world was in crisis, perhaps its final and supreme crisis before collapse. Third, the parties of the Left were clearly making gains, and coalition governments including Communists were a distinct possibility. All these factors seemed to offer channels for the Soviet Union to make its influence felt in Western Europe's politics and on Western policies.

As Robert Legvold has demonstrated in his chapter, these opportunities were largely illusory. Western Europe was no more accessible to Soviet influence than before, not because the channels were not open but because the message found so little echo. The economic crisis shook but did not bring down the political and economic structure of any Western European country. And while there was a trend to the left in France and in Italy, the Socialists were making the gains in France, and in Italy the Communists were using their gains to seek an alliance with the party which represented par excellence the capitalist establishment. The more the Communist leaders expressed themselves, the less reason the Kremlin had for confidence that their success would serve Soviet purposes.

If Soviet theorists felt the collapse of capitalism and bourgeois democracy was at hand in Western Europe, the Soviet government and the CPSU did not act on that assumption and gave the impression of having no grand strategy at all.[7] They did not appear to be waiting for or working for the coming of a revolutionary situation of which they might take advantage. They did not appear to expect or desire the entry of Communists into governments. On the contrary, their main concern was with the official policies of France, Italy and Spain, as governments, and how they affected Soviet interests. If the trends were favorable, well and good; what the local Communists were saying and doing was less important. What a Gaullist or center government in France, in opposing the United States or in putting the brakes on progress toward greater unity in Western Europe, could do to advance Soviet interests was more tangible than what the PCF, with its 20 percent of the electorate, could do. Soviet support for Giscard d'Estaing against the candidate of the Left in the presidential election of 1974, made manifest publicly in an unmistakable way, was a striking example. The PCF did not hide its chagrin at this and later instances of Soviet *Realpolitik*. But if the Western European CPs were going to insist on independence from Moscow's guiding hand, they should not have been surprised that the conduct of Soviet foreign policy should in turn be independent of their wishes.

Such examples, however, do not lead to the conclusion that there are no ways in which Western Communist parties can serve Soviet ends. Those parties took a strong stand for their own independence during the long inter-party negotiations that finally produced the joint statement issued in East Berlin in June 1976. But in that same East Berlin statement they subscribed to a set of propositions on the international situation and the line to be followed that might have been, and probably was, drafted in Moscow. In a way it was a trade. Having protected their independence as parties, they were willing to go along with the Soviet line on East-West relations. It is in this field of foreign policy and international action that the Western CPs can and do serve Soviet purposes even as they declare their independence and their refusal to accept the idea that the international Communist movement has a guiding center. And this may be all that the Soviets, who show no desire to see or face the consequences of a real social revolution in Western Europe, really want.

The Soviet reasons for détente with the governments of the West remained valid even when those governments were in difficulty at home. The trade, industrial cooperation, and transfer of technology that had become so important to the Soviet economy required a necessary minimum level of stability and prosperity in the capitalist countries of the West, so that they would sell the goods (at not too quickly rising prices), transfer the technology, and extend credit. The Soviet leadership adopted the policy of détente prior to the oil crisis of 1973, at a time when Western Europe was thriving economically. The years since 1973 have provided a test not only of Western Europe's ability to master the crisis but also of Moscow's intention to stick to its original decisions under new conditions.

The Soviets, so far as we can tell, have not changed those decisions. They have reasons of long-term political strategy, as well as of economic interest, in continuing to push the idea of détente. To the Western Europeans they stress peaceful coexistence and the unreality of any threat from the East. To their own followers they stress the idea of "the changing correlation of forces" in favor of the socialist camp. Purposes they have held for decades—weakening the E.E.C. and NATO and drawing Western Europe away from America— are still present in the age of détente. One may call it for purposes of convenience the aim of "Finlandization" (although that term has been over-used and abused), the meaning being that on matters the U.S.S.R. deems vital to its security the other state is required, or agrees, to accept limits on its foreign policy. For this partial loss of independence it is not necessary to put Communists into power. It is simpler if a non-Communist government recognizes the facts of geography and the correlation of forces, and acts accordingly.

The Communist parties of the West have their place in this political strategy, not as revolutionary instruments but as political forces within the Western countries which exert an influence in the desired direction. And they may do so even if they are independent of Moscow—in fact, they are more effective in doing so because they have shown their independence in party relations. It is this role of the Western CPs, conscious or unconscious and whether they come into positions of government or not, that raises questions for the security and defense of the West.

VIII

The French and Italian CPs have nominally accepted the membership of their respective countries in the North Atlantic Alliance, and the PCE, while now in opposition to Spain's joining, favors keeping for the time being the base arrangements and defense ties with the United States. All three say they see the need for maintaining the balance until the time comes when both military blocs can be dissolved. The PCI, should it enter the Italian government, would not be likely to jeopardize its position by setting out to sabotage NATO for the benefit of the Soviet Union. The PCI, in its own interest and that of Italy, would not wish to see any change that would encourage a Soviet move against Yugoslavia and the appearance of Soviet forces on the Italian border. Yet a close study of the writings of the Eurocommunist leaders leads to the conclusion that they are not wholly committed to maintaining the strength and solidarity of the Western alliance. In emancipating themselves from automatic commitment to the U.S.S.R., they glory in their independence. That is a big step to take. But it does not necessarily imply commitment to NATO strategy or to cooperation with the United States. It is apparently enough to say that France or Italy should reject domination and guidance from either of the two superpowers. They do not propose neutralism, but their thinking seems to envisage a gradual progress toward non-alignment, Yugoslav style.

Everything the PCI and the PCF say about the international scene strengthens the impression that this is their real aim, to disengage their countries from the competition of the superpowers. Santiago Carrillo says the same thing in his *Eurocomunismo y Estado*. But they do not look upon the two powers in the same way. They are conditioned by their years of denouncing and campaigning against imperialism, i.e., the American role in NATO and in Western European affairs. They interpret Western economic cooperation, as it has developed since World War II, as nothing more or less than American domination of the weaker European economies. They are driven by the desire to put an end to what they see as continuing American intervention in their countries' affairs. If they could determine policy, they say, they would insist on a redefinition of America's positions and bases and a restructuring of the alliance. They are not for their countries' subjection to Russia, which they see as but a hypothesis anyway, and they are not for subjection to America, which for them is an historical reality.

Thus, Eurocommunism in foreign policy is closer to Titoism, independent national communism beholden to nobody and not tied to either bloc, than to Western-type socialism devoted to the defense of democratic values both at home and abroad. Carrillo and Berlinguer have been particularly close to Tito, personally and in their thinking about Europe. From the standpoint of Western security, however, while nonalignment is fine for Yugoslavia, which for three decades has been a buffer state between the alliance systems, it is not fine for Italy or France or Portugal, which are members of the Western alliance, nor for Spain, which cooperates militarily with the United States and is thus indirectly aligned. At the present juncture—though it may not always be true—their association with NATO, regardless of the contribution on the military side, is a vital part of the overall balance with the Eastern bloc.

So long as they are minority parties in opposition, not listened to by others, perhaps it does not make much difference whether the Communists are indifferent to NATO. It makes more difference, if, like the PCI, they appear to be on the threshold of government or if what they are saying represents a growing view in other parties and in sectors of the public much broader than the Communists. In France, for example, the nationalistic views of the PCF on foreign policy run parallel to those of the Gaullists, and both are suspicious of NATO and in favor of a defense policy à *tous azimuts,* aimed at threats from all directions. The Socialists, who favor cooperation for Western defense, feel the pressure from their allies on the left just as Giscard, having moved France somewhat closer to NATO though not rejoining the organization, feels it from the Gaullists on the right. In Italy, the PCI view of the country's need for a more independent and nationally based defense policy has an appeal to those of the center and the right who look to the Mediterranean as a region for Italian initiative and leadership not subordinated to great-power interests.

Indeed, the idea of a role in the Mediterranean has continuing attraction in all the countries of Southern Europe. France, Italy, and Spain have promoted it at one time or another, looking to the forming of closer ties among themselves and with Yugoslavia, Greece, and the Arab countries of North Africa. Thus far this Mediterranean concept has had no meaning as a security grouping, but it has the potential of raising questions in the Southern European countries about the continuing value to them of NATO and the demands it makes upon them. The more détente flourishes, the more contact and cooperation there is between East and West and the more a general war becomes unthinkable, even in the face of a heavy buildup of Warsaw Pact forces in Europe. The more that is so, the less vital does it seem to keep up a posture of deterrence in the West, and the more the efforts of others to do so are seen as serving interests of America as a superpower rather than those of the Western community as a whole.

The problem is potential rather than actual. It holds the prospect of a situation in which Soviet strategy, the attitudes of the Eurocommunist parties, and certain general trends in Europe, each as an independent factor but interacting with the others, may have the combined effect of fatally weakening the Atlantic alliance. The Western allies will have to devise means of separately influencing these three factors, so that the latter two do not reinforce the first. That may require a series of initiatives and policies that take account of prevailing currents of opinion and offer something new to supplement (and not substitute for) the maintenance of military power.

The heart of the matter is the health of Western Europe's economy and of its democratic institutions. It is not difficult to identify the problems, as Europe's political leaders have done at their periodic summit meetings: stagnation, inflation, unemployment, the high cost of energy, imbalances in trade and payments, governments without stable majorities, public disillusion with political leaders and parties, labor unrest, social malaise, increasing violence from extremes of right and left. It is more difficult, however, to be optimistic about the prospects for success in coping with them because the economic troubles have been so severe and the pressure is so strong to resort to protectionism, which may temporarily relieve domestic strains in individual nations but only at the cost of compounding the general crisis. No European country will have an easy time of it, not even the Federal Republic, but as we have seen, the problems are magnified for those countries where the requirements of economic recovery are matched by those of institutional reconstruction and social reform. In practical terms, how does a government gain acceptance of needed austerity measures while balancing the conflicting demands of social groups and keeping them within the bounds of the democratic political structure; or, in the case of Spain and Portugal, while building that structure after a generation of dictatorial rule?

America is no detached observer of this drama, waiting to see whether Europe succeeds or fails, goes left or goes right or stays center. America is a full-fledged participant, indissolubly linked with the Europeans in the common crisis of the West. Neither the governments nor wise men offering advice to governments have yet produced the answers. But it is well to

[549]

remember that this is the West's own crisis, which its governments and peoples have the opportunity to deal with through their own decisions on the national level, in relations with each other, and in relations with the oil producing states. It is not the creation of Soviet strategy or of the challenge of communism, although there is little doubt that failure to cope with it will redound to the advantage of the Soviet Union and its followers in the West.

In this context the question of Eurocommunism falls into perspective. It is directly related to the strength and resilience of the democratic constitutional order. Europe's voters and democratic political leaders, in the absence of political and social collapse, are not going to give power to a party they have reason to believe will suppress freedom. The PCI, with all its adaptation to free institutions, still has no more than a third of the popular vote and does not share in government without the restraining hand of democratic parties on its collar. The PCF, when it appeared to be playing the game according to the rules, was acceptable to its democratic partners in the *Union de la gauche,* but when it appeared to revert to type by aiming for control of bastions of extra-constitutional power, they had second thoughts.

The importance of the Socialist and Social Democratic parties can hardly be overemphasized. Where there is a demand for reform and a trend to the left, the Socialist parties hold the key to keeping that movement within the democratic system. Whether they oppose the Communists or make electoral alliances with them, it is up to the Socialists to insist on democratic norms and to break with them if the norms are violated. That appears to have been the course taken by the Socialist parties of Portugal and Spain and also—although some had their doubts—by François Mitterrand and the PS in France. Italy is the special case where the Socialists first

[550]

fractured their own unity and then dwindled to the status of a minor party through their own mistakes and the emergence of the PCI as *the* party of the Left. Yet it may be too early to count the PSI out as a force in Italian politics. To the extent that the PCI has outdistanced it by itself becoming more socialist than communist, any reversal of direction by the Communists could bring about a reversal by the voters (unless, as some fear, it would then be too late). The Socialist parties of Northern Europe, particularly the SPD in Germany and the British Labour Party, are well aware of the importance of supporting their fellow Socialists in Southern Europe as the most effective means they have of keeping the Communists in check.

The existence of the European Community is another means whereby the Europeans themselves can deal with their Communist problem. The Europe of the nine is not marching toward unity at the rapid pace many of its partisans hoped for several years ago, and the prospective inclusion of three new members from Southern Europe (Greece, Spain and Portugal) will slow the process further. It is still a *Europe des patries* and not a united Europe. Nevertheless, its members will continue to be drawn into cooperation because in the long-run perspective there is no alternative. The trend toward a community-wide political life will be given a forward thrust by the holding of direct elections to the European Parliament.

The indications are that the various Communist parties will be reaching out across the borders so that they may act more effectively as a force for change in the European Community and in European politics generally. The PCI deputies in the existing European Parliament have already formed working arrangements with their comrades from other countries. They obviously want to play on a bigger stage than Italy provides, and they do not feel confined to ties with fellow Eurocommunists. A PCI leader, in a recent statement, looked forward to the forging of links with other parties of the left such as the PS in France, the PSOE, the left wing of the SPD, and Socialist parties in Scandinavia, for political action on the European scale.[8] Given the differences between the PCI, PCE, and PCF, this kind of broad cooperation on the left seems more plausible than a tight alliance of Eurocommunist parties.

Democratic parties of Europe should welcome rather than fear these developments. The Community institutions are not going to be subverted by the Communists. They provide a means whereby the challenge can be absorbed or contained. In so far as events in Italy, for example, become a matter of European concern and action, the weight of the Communist factor is much less than in Italy alone. If the PCI moves forward with the idea of a broad coalition of European parties of the left, the political dangers from Communist parties would be minimal, except in the unlikely event that the Socialist and other democratic parties allow themselves to become dupes of the Communists. It is more probable that the reality of such a coalition would confirm the fact of basic change in the PCI.

IX

The United States can and must help Europe to meet its major problems, for they are also its own. In so far as meeting those problems eases or solves the issues of Eurocommunism, so much the better. The specific question of how to handle the Communist parties, however, is Europe's rather than America's. It is for European governments, European political parties (especially the Socialists), and the European Community. The United States should not tell Europeans how to vote, and it will have to adapt to how they do vote, as long as they do so in free elections.

The concern shown by Secretary Kissinger over the possibility of the entry of Communists into Western European governments was understandable. Seeing it as certain to bring about a weakening of NATO and Western defense, he sought to lessen the chances of that outcome by statements and policies that would discourage the Communists and encourage their democratic opponents. Hence the warnings about the incongruity of Communist ministers sitting in the NATO Council, Communist officials having access to information on NATO's strategy and military plans, or even non-Communist representatives in NATO councils reporting to home governments having Communists in key positions. This was obviously a problem that would not be easy to deal with. NATO had been able to survive the presence of Communist ministers in the government of Iceland and even in that of Portugal after the revolution of 1974, for those two countries were on the periphery of NATO and neither wished to force the issue. But Communists in the government of a centrally placed country like Italy would be another matter, as they would in France although in a different way because France, while remaining a party to the North Atlantic Treaty, was no longer in NATO.

The Kissinger posture of stern opposition had the virtue of clarity. Where it aroused criticism in the United States was among those who found it too clear to permit needed flexibility and recognition of political realities. His policy extended to denial of visas to prominent European Communists who wished to visit the United States and to refusal of any high-level contacts between Communists and American officials abroad. Why, so the argument ran, give them the prestige of an American connection which they might turn to local advantage at the expense of America's friends? Critics argued that there was nothing to be lost and perhaps something to be gained if American officials or private citizens talked with representatives of parties playing a leading part in the politics of their countries; that writing them off as untouchable might backfire if in fact they did come to power, since it would be important at such a time to know them and what to expect from them, good or bad; that any express or implied threats of a change in American policy toward Europe (such as a withdrawal of troops) if Communists entered the government of a NATO country, besides being unwise as a possible limitation on future decisions, would upset our friends and help only the Communists; that Kissinger saw the PCI and the others only as old-line Communists without even weighing the possible changes represented by the term "Eurocommunism"; and that Europeans of all parties resented Kissinger's statements as interference in their own affairs (a conclusion that was true in some respects but not for the Christian Democratic party of Italy, which was most jealous of its claims to American favor and fearful of any signs that America found it necessary to build bridges to the PCI).

The election of Jimmy Carter and the appearance of new faces in the State Department and the National Security Council presaged a change of policy, or at least of emphasis, if only because some of the new faces belonged to former critics of the Kissinger position. The new administration, however, was not inclined toward any dramatic change. With Secretary of State Vance avoiding any long disquisitions on the subject, the Department's position was put forward in several statements to the effect that the United States was of course concerned about Communist gains but regarded the matter as primarily one for Europeans. Zbigniew Brzezinski, the President's Adviser on National Security, conceded that "one cannot be too sanguine as to how most of these communist parties would behave if in power ... We do not favor the communist parties participating in governments, but we will not engage in public statements designed to prevent this from taking place . . ." Secretary Vance said the United States would not be indifferent to the possibility of Communist participation and that a dominant role on their part could present serious problems.[9]

Henry Kissinger, in a major speech in 1977, let the world know that he had not changed his mind. He forcefully restated his view that whatever the Communists might say they did not act like democrats. Their presence in Western European governments was not to be shrugged off as a mere turn of the political wheel. He stressed the point that it would indeed be a threat to the West, not just because of the awkward situation of having Communists in NATO councils but because of the very nature of their attitude on defense. Whether they were Eurocommunists or not, whether they accepted NATO or not, they were simply not much concerned about the need to defend the West against Communist states in the East, with which they would still have "fraternal" links. Therefore, an Italy with the PCI in the government would not play its necessary part in maintaining NATO forces or in cooperating with NATO allies.[10]

There is merit in this argument, and we may assume that the Carter administration is cognizant of it. Indeed, as the French elections of 1978 approached and the Italian crisis deepened, Washington's pronouncements began to look very much like those of Kissinger. President Carter's visit to France was punctuated with veiled and not so veiled warnings about the danger from the Communists, and a State Department statement on Italy clearly expressed America's preference for a government that kept them out.[11]

Whether these were wise tactics, raising as they did the bogey of American intervention, is a different question from what the effects of Communist participation in government would actually be. It seems clear that Communist leadership in Italy or France, even if fully respectful of political freedoms and wholly independent of Soviet control, would not feel the same urgency as the non-Communist parties about maintaining the military balance; they would still see the United States rather than the U.S.S.R. as the main obstacle to what they want to achieve in their own countries, and in the use of national resources they would give priority to those domestic ends rather than to defense. This is, however, as we have noted before, not just a Communist or Eurocommunist problem but may be a more general problem for Europe and for the West in that other parties, of the left or in some cases even of the right, may take a similar view. It could be accentuated if Germany's place in NATO became correspondingly larger, especially if a CDU/CSU government came to power there as the countries of Southern Europe were swinging to the left. The danger would be that NATO would seem to be in essence a U.S.-German alliance, with others playing only minor parts. Whether such a two-tiered NATO is created deliberately by the United States and others because of the presence of Communists in member governments or comes into being by a process of action and reaction, it would be a most unfortunate outcome damaging to the Western solidarity that is needed to meet both the military danger and the political-economic crisis.

X

At the moment the West has a need to maintain NATO on existing lines and to add to its strength and solidarity, especially in the light of the Soviet buildup in both nuclear and conventional arms and of the failure of the Vienna talks to produce any agreement on mutual reduction of forces or limitation of arms levels. In view of the uncertainties, however, and the fact that the Europe of East-West détente, post-Helsinki and post-Belgrade, may come to differ markedly from the more familiar Europe dominated by the concept of the two blocs, the Western nations would do well to take account of political dynamics as well as the military balance in their search for security in freedom. In conditions of some loosening of the blocs and greater cross-penetration of persons, goods, and ideas across the East-West line, policy must take account of politics, not only to counter any trend that could lead to "Finlandization," improbable as that may be, but also to turn the new conditions to the benefit of the West.

The Soviet Union's allies in the Warsaw Pact, to be sure, are not free actors in international affairs in the way that the Western European nations are, and no one in the West should forget that essential security rests on the maintenance of the military balance until there is some fundamental and presently unforeseeable change. Nevertheless, currents set in motion by détente and by CSCE do in fact signal an opening up of East-West relations to new contacts and reciprocal influences that may have a bearing on the "correlation of forces," to use a favorite Soviet term in a broad sense, within the two blocs and between them. Surely it is in the Western interest to explore all possible ways in which developments outside the military sphere may increase the impact of Western upon Eastern Europe, for we can assume that influence running the other way, other than that cast by the shadow of armed might, will be minimal. It is not a question of changing the basic power position of the U.S.S.R. in Eastern Europe, which has been accepted by the West as a fact of life ever since World War II, but of taking advantage of the West's strengths which are economic (in technological advance and a higher standard of living), cultural (in the age-old ties of Eastern European cultures with the West), and political (in the attraction of freedom). Western Europe must itself be a going concern, of course, if these advantages are to be real.

Is Eurocommunism relevant here? Can it serve to enhance the West's security rather than to undermine it? Some observers have answered with an emphatic affirmative, pointing to the disintegrative influence the Western European CPs have already had on international Communist solidarity and the explosive potential for the closed party structures of Eastern Europe of the open espousal by the Western comrades of the ideas of civic and human freedom. Other observers have dismissed altogether the influence of Eurocommunism on the East, saying that to the extent such a challenge is serious the Soviet and Eastern European regimes are quite capable of suppressing it. Official Soviet reaction on the highest level, in statements by Brezhnev and Suslov, leaves no doubt that with this aspect of Eurocommunism, however they may try uneasily to adapt to the rest of it, there is no room for compromise.[12] The question demands, however, a more differentiated and even speculative answer.

Rudolf Tőkés has shown in his careful study of party relations across the East-West line that Eurocommunism is not a magic formula for the conversion or for the undoing of the Communist regimes of Eastern Europe or for the shaking of Soviet control. In the last analysis those regimes do not have a solid independent base of their own. It is none the less true that what has happened in the CPs of the West has stirred up quite a lot of wind in the East, especially among the intellectuals and party ideologists, that is not likely to die down. The most powerful effect flows from the assertion of independence, the denial of Moscow as the fount of authority. As Carrillo says, the universal church is no more. On this issue the

Eurocommunists of the West have the open support of the ruling Communist parties of Yugoslavia and Romania and the unspoken envy and admiration of those of Poland and Hungary. Only the present regimes in Czechozlovakia and Bulgaria are true-blue on the Soviet line.

This issue of independence, like it or not, cannot be wholly separated from the issue of freedom. Thus even the Yugoslavs and Romanians, as they welcome Berlinguer and Carrillo to their capitals, cannot be immune to what those men are saying and doing in their own countries. If Carrillo is to be defended against Moscow's denunciations because he and his party have a right to independence, then the book for which he is denounced is by inference defended, a book which speaks out for civil liberties and political pluralism and criticizes the form of socialism practiced in the U.S.S.R.—and which, incidentally, is circulating widely in Eastern Europe.

To repeat, Eurocommunism works no instant magic in Eastern Europe. The regimes, even the Yugoslav, can hardly be expected to embrace free speech and free elections. But the intensive discussions on socialism and communism it has provoked on both sides of the line do have implications for the state of affairs on the eastern side, especially in the context of the growing economic and other cooperation. The Soviet Union aside, the Eastern European states have no interest in imposing their own system on Western Europe and no capability of doing so. Nor do the Western European states have any intention of subverting the communist regimes in Eastern Europe (and thus of courting a Soviet military reaction), but without conscious decision their influence is bound to have an impact on the East, on the Communist superstructure as well as the anti-Communist populations. The West should of course look skeptically at any "all-European" institutional arrangements that have behind them a Soviet purpose to weaken (perhaps to "Finlandize") the West. But they should not be deterred by that legitimate fear and caution from seeing the political benefits of economic cooperation, cultural ties or, to go a little further, ideological dialogue between Communist parties.

The United States has many reasons to favor and encourage the growth of greater unity, strength and confidence in Western Europe, and not least among them is the potential effect on Eastern Europe. The European Community will not be expanded to include the Eastern European states, nor should it for one minute entertain the idea of being replaced by shadowy "all-European" institutions or security arrangements, but the Community can help to spin a web of relations with the East that will create new dimensions of political reality in Europe and affect the ways in which Eastern and Western Europeans, and the U.S.S.R. and the U.S.A. as well, look at the security problem. Such new ways of thinking could give impetus to East-West negotiations on mutual force reductions and arms control in Europe, and could conceivably help to bring a new generation of Soviet leaders to the idea that Soviet security interests would be served rather than jeopardized by a reduced military presence in Eastern Europe and even by a greater degree of independence for those states than has hitherto been permitted.

Could the Soviet Union accept Eurocommunism in Eastern Europe? Not as long as its own system remains as it is, for that would be an intolerable challenge.[13] But trends, especially if they move slowly, do not necessarily force black-and-white choices. Over time Eurocommunism could exert a considerable influence in Eastern Europe without providing the Kremlin at any point with a clear opportunity and choice to intervene decisively against it. Should certain Eastern European states be able to move gradually to a status something like that of Yugoslavia, it would put East-West relations in a new pattern and attenuate some of the risks involved in a trend toward nonalignment in certain countries of the West.

Over the long run the concepts of democratic socialism or socialist democracy, as both are cut off from Soviet theory, practice or control, may find some common denominators that bring together European Socialists, Eurocommunists, and liberal, reformist and "national Communist" elements in Eastern Europe. The United States and its Western allies should not and cannot at this juncture adopt a strategy aimed at such a socialist erosion of the division of Europe, but they should at least keep their eyes open to the possibilities.

On the plane of current practical policy for the West, Eurocommunism is not an instrument to be manipulated in a cold war against the East. It would be fatuous to favor putting Communists into office in the West for the sake of the example to their comrades in the East. Eurocommunism is simply a phenomenon that exists. It has its influence already just by what Berlinguer and Marchais and Carrillo say and do and by how their parties act. We in the West do not have to wait and see whether those parties pass the test of democratic conduct at home before benefiting from their impact abroad. If Eurocommunism is all an elaborate deception, Westerners are not the only ones being deceived.

All in all it is a very mixed picture. For the West, Eurocommunism is no clearly identified enemy to be fought at all times and at all costs. It takes different forms in different countries and must be dealt with in accordance with each local situation. There is no need to assume that any party's coming to power or a share in power is inevitable, or that on getting there it will destroy democratic liberties. But there is a need to watch each situation closely and to know how to safeguard those liberties if they are threatened. If it means a crisis for democratic government or for Western security, let the democratic forces take measures of defense appropriate to a crisis. It may not be a bad thing if Eurocommunism is thus put to the test. It could clarify many things about which people have been talking and writing without really knowing the answers. But if it is a problem of adaptation on the part of the Communists, then let Western nations deal with it by adjustment and not blow it up into a crisis.

For America, if a policy is to be defined, it might be described roughly as follows:

—to avoid pronouncements that exaggerate or magnify the problem and do not help the Europeans to deal with it on their own terms;

—to avoid ideological rigidity and have a clear understanding of what is happening in Europe, in order to be able to encourage and assist democratic forces—conservative, center, or socialist—to meet economic and social problems within the framework of free institutions;

—to fulfill, with our allies, the requirements of Western defense, adapting the NATO structure to new political situations as we have in the past;

—to take advantage of what détente has done and can do in opening the East to the ideas of the West.

These propositions, one may note, can be stated without mentioning the words "communism" or "Communist party," but they are all relevant to what has been called the Communist or Eurocommunist problem in Western Europe. The point is that the real problem is the ability of Europe to overcome its economic crisis and to preserve its free institutions. Positive measures to that end provide a sounder approach than a defensive obsession with the danger from the

Communists. There is no need and no room for loudly declared policies on Eurocommunism.

There is also a positive side to the Communist issue. While the "communist" part of our title word is cause for vigilance, the "Euro" part of it is cause for hope. It may turn out to be a snare and a delusion—and policy should take account of that possibility—but because the concept pays its respects to the European tradition of political freedom, it has the potential to do three very important things: (1) to end the virtual self-exclusion of a substantial segment of the population in certain Western European countries from the workings of the democratic political process (although there would still be alienated revolutionary groups even if the Communists become loyal democrats); (2) to push to its logical conclusion the fracturing of what was once a united international Communist movement directed from Moscow; and (3) to expose the rigid Marxist-Leninist structures of Eastern Europe and perhaps eventually of the U.S.S.R. itself to the fresh breezes of a different concept of socialism.

Western observers of the ways of Communists over the years have developed a hardened skepticism as to the possibilities of fundamental change either in their doctrine or in their relations with each other. Many were reluctant to accept the reality of the Yugoslav or the Chinese break with Moscow until long after the event. It could be the same with Eurocommunism. Self-deception is a risk on either side of this question.

NOTES

1. See, in addition to his contribution to this volume, his "Western Policy toward the French Left," *Survival*, September/October 1977, pp. 194-201. Also J-B. Duroselle, "France and the West:

Concerns and Hopes," *The Review of Politics*, October 1977, pp. 451-72.

2. Raymond Aron, *Plaidoyer pour l'Europe décadente* (Paris: Robert Laffont, 1977) and others described this prospect.

3. It is also made by the smaller parties now wedged in between the two big ones, namely the Socialists, Social Democrats, and Republicans. See Ugo La Malfa, "Communism and Democracy in Italy," *Foreign Affairs*, April 1978, pp. 476-88.

4. See Enzo Bettiza, "Die Angst von der Exkommunikation," *Europäische Rundschau*, No. 4 (Autumn 1977), pp. 23-31.

5. *The New York Times*, November 18, 1975, and March 3, 1977. For an extended discussion on this subject see Manfred Steinkühler, "Eurocommunism: Myth and Reality," *Aussenpolitik* (English edition), No. 4, 1977, pp. 375-402.

6. A summary of the talk, which was made in London in December 1975, was released by the Department of State and appeared in *The New York Times*, April 6, 1976.

7. Pierre Hassner, "L'U.R.S.S., l'Eurocommunisme et l'Europe occidentale," *Revue de Défense Nationale*, January 1977, pp. 47-61.

8. Giancarlo Pajetta, interview with Flora Lewis, *The New York Times*, December 1, 1977.

9. Zbigniew Brzezinski, "Post-Bonn Thoughts," *Trialogue*, New York, Fall 1977, pp. 12-13; interview of Secretary of State Vance on ABC's "Issues and Answers," Department of State, Office of Media Services, June 19, 1977, p. 3.

10. *The New York Times*, June 10, 1977.

11. *The New York Times,* January 5, 1978; January 13, 1978.

12. See Brezhnev's speech on the 60th anniversary of the October Revolution *(Pravda,* November 3, 1977); also the speech of M.A. Suslov to an international scientific-theoretical conference on Great October and the Present Era *(Pravda,* November 11, 1977).

13. Charles Gati, "The 'Europeanization' of Communism?" *Foreign Affairs,* April 1977, pp. 539-53.

Index

[567]

De Castro, Ignacio Fernandez, 207
De Gasperi, Alcide, 72
De Gaulle, Charles, 31, 139
Democratic centralism, 12-14; and
French CP, 142-44, 149, 189ff.;
and Italian CP, 120; and Portuguese CP, 320; and Spanish
CP, 255-56
De-Stalinization, 11, 395, 514; French
CP, 60, 158-59, 400; Italian CP,
11, 85, 90, 91, 92; Spanish CP, 208
Détente, 25ff., 514, 537-41, 557;
defined, 32-33, 437; and East Eu-
rope, 438, 452ff., 537-41, 557-58;
and Eurocommunism, 32-35,
109-10, 155, 238-39, 357, 387,
402, 415, 533; and the U.S.S.R.,
537ff.; and West European CPs,
20-21, 25-35, 357, 363, 424
Devlin, Kevin, 408, 480
Dictatorship of the proletariat, 12-
14, 410; and French CP, 163,
174-76, 320; and Italian CP, 13-
14, 93, 120, 121-22, 320; and
Spanish CP, 12-14, 222-23, 320;
Soviet theory, 328ff.
Dimitrov, Georgi, 70, 472
Disarmament, 537-39, 556-57, 560
Dissent in East Europe, 414-15,
438, 444-45, 462, 463-70, 491
Dissent, Soviet, and French CP,
161, 343, 478; and Italian CP,
343, 476; and Spanish CP, 227;
and Western CPs, 415, 476-78
Diz, Juan, 225, 236
Djilas, Milovan, 437, 477
Donini, Ambrogio, 71
Dubček, Alexander, 365, 447
Duclos, Jacques, 156, 258

Dutch Communist party, 322, 405,
516

Eanes, Ramalho, 272, 297, 298, 300,
304, 518
East Berlin Conference of European
Communist parties (1976), 7, 11,
107, 112, 123, 154, 161, 162-63,
165-66, 243, 275, 350, 353, 371-
72, 409-12, 473, 479-82, 536,
544
East Europe, 7-8, 437ff.; and détente, 438, 452ff., 537-41, 557-
58; economic integration, 450-51;
and Helsinki agreements, 452-56;
modernization, 443-44, 458, 491;
prospects of democratization,
462-63, 485ff.; sources of stability, 456-63; and U.S. policy, 8-
9, 438, 452, 453-54, 463-64, 485,
499-500, 540, 560; and the
U.S.S.R., 389ff., 439-52, 540; and
Yugoslav model, 448, 471, 487-
88, 492-95
Eurosocialism, 9, 388-89
East European Communist parties,
7-8, 443; and Eurocommunism,
7-8, 316, 364-67, 386, 413, 415,
417, 438, 470ff., 558-60; liberalization of, 446ff.; and Moscow,
389-91, 395, 445ff., 559; Sofia
Conference (1977), 482-83; and
West European Communist parties, 316, 344, 475-79; see also
East Berlin Conference, International Communist movement
East-West trade, 537-39, 544
Economic crisis, 23, 35, 36-39, 49,
438, 549

INDEX

Warsaw Treaty Organization, 395, 424, 442, 449, 451, 496
West European Communist parties: break with Leninism, 5, 10-14, 20-22, 64-66, 533; Brussels Conference (1965), 406; (1974), 169; cooperation among, 112-13, 162-63, 169-70, 309, 405-06, 483, 519, 534-35, 543-44; diversity in, 319ff., 364-67, 368, 385-86; East Berlin Conference (1976), 7, 11, 107, 112, 123, 154, 161, 162-63, 165-66, 243, 275, 350, 353, 371-72, 409-12, 473, 479-82, 536, 544; and East Europe, 316, 344, 475-79; economic programs, 37-38, 56, 60ff.; and electoral victory, 3-4, 15-16; and European Community, 356ff., 422-23, 551-52; and foreign policy, 34-35, 351ff., 422-24; French-Italian declaration (1975), 163, 167, 342, 483; Italian-Spanish declaration (1975), 163; Madrid summit (1977), 112, 142, 164, 167, 257, 535; and Moscow, 1-3, 21, 112-13, 123, 157, 257-58, 314ff., 387ff., 475-79, 485ff., 513-14, 515, 532-37, 542-45; and NATO, 356ff., 424, 545ff.; in 1944-47, 27-28; 1966 Conference (Vienna), 406; Northern European CPs, 4, 24, 27, 59; and political pluralism, 12-16, 22, 35-42, 45-48, 63-66, 162-63, 342-43, 473-74; and Socialist parties, 9-10, 33-34, 320-22, 421-22, 550-51, 552; and socio-economic change, 19-20, 42-44, 49-51, 60-65; Southern European CPs, 4, 8, 9, 15, 24, 27, 309, 322, 366, 516, 530; Soviet attitude on attaining power, 353-56, 363-64, 368; in Soviet foreign policy, 275, 314-19, 351ff., 387, 411; and the U.S., 545ff.; U.S. attitude on attaining power, 512ff., 552ff.; and violent coups, 14-15, 21, 58-59, 63-64, 333, 519, 531-32; vote for, 3, 15; see also Eurocommunism
Wilson, Harold, 65
Wolchik, Sharon, 486
Working class, 42-43, 49-51, 53ff.
World Peace Council, 233-34
Wyszynski, Cardinal Stefan, 469

Yugoslav Communist party, 386, 390, 392, 395, 400, 410, 426; and Italian CP, 105-06, 392, 475; and Moscow, 106, 392
Yugoslav-Soviet break (1948), 19, 315, 386, 389-90; and Portuguese CP, 275; and Spanish CP, 207
Yugoslavia, 8, 34, 104, 105-06, 423, 438, 448ff., 547, 548; and Eurocommunism, 19, 365, 366, 389ff., 413-14, 426, 448, 471, 475, 480, 492-95, 559; as model for East Europe, 448, 471, 487-88, 492-95; and U.S.S.R., 106, 392, 395-96, 397-98, 400, 409, 413-14, 440, 493

Zagladin, V.V., 332
Zarodov, Konstantin, 334-35
Zhdanov, Andrei, 451
Zhivkov, Todor, 482, 483